CHARISMA DYNAMIC ENCOUNTERS

[Features]

Daily Inspirational Messages

Beginning of Every month

*Biblical Numerology: Numbers 1-12

*Jehovah Titles (12)

*Key Verse(s) for every month

Bible Verses: [NIV, KJV, NKJV, NLT, AMPL, NASB, ESV, NAST]

Copyright © 2019 Eugene Asi

DEDICATION

This book is dedicated to all disciples of Christ who long for a dynamic encounter with God on a daily basis.

[Earnest Seekers of God]

"O God, thou art my God; early will I seek thee: my soul thirsteth for thee, my flesh longeth for thee in a dry and thirsty land, where no water is; 2 To see thy power and thy glory, so as I have seen thee in the sanctuary. 3 Because thy loving-kindness is better than life, my lips shall praise thee. 4 Thus will I bless thee while I live: I will lift up my hands in thy name.8 My soul followeth hard after thee: thy right hand upholdeth me.

[Psalm 63:1-4, 8, KJV]

JANUARY

"In the beginning God created the heaven and the earth."

[Gen.1:1, KJV]

"In the beginning was the Word, and the Word was with God, and the Word was God. The same was in the beginning with God. All things were made by him; and without him was not anything made that was made. In him was life; and the life was the light of men. And the light shineth in darkness, and the darkness comprehended it not."

[John 1:1-5, KJV]

****

Yahweh - [LORD, Jehovah] - Exod.3:14

Jehovah Adoni - [LORD, Master] - Exod.3:15

1= [Unity of God] - John 17:21

January 1

A Pacesetter or a Trend Follower?
Bible Reading: [1 Tim.4:11-16]

"Let no man despise thy youth; but be thou an example of the believers, in word, in conversation, in Charity, in spirit, in faith, in purity." [Vs: 13; KJV]

Dear friend, this year, God wants everyone one of us to be a pacesetter and not a trend follower. One thing that is common with all trend followers is that they are tossed to and fro by any wind of doctrine or change. A trend is a general direction in which something is developing or changing. One question each one of us should ask ourselves every day of the year is that, *"Am I changing towards God's direction or towards the direction of the world? Scriptures admonish us not to conform ourselves to the standards of the world [Rom.12:1-2].*

Make yourself available so that God can use you as a pacesetter. He wants us to live so others can see Christ in us. A pacesetter is a person that is the most progressive or successful and serves as a model to be imitated. Apostle Paul told the Corinthian believers, *"Be ye followers of me, even as I also am of Christ." [1 Cor.11:1; KJV].* As a matter of fact, Christ was his model. He told Timothy, *"but be thou an example of the believers..."* Pacesetters are good examples that others can follow. Remember that as a disciple of Christ, when your life-style conforms to the message you teach, only then can there be power in your teaching. Choose today between a pacesetter and trend follower. One of my colleagues Dr. Emilienne T. often says, "Be a pacesetter and not a trend follower." I admonish you to be a pacesetter so that others might see the light of God and have a clear direction [vision].

PRAYER FOCUS

Dear heavenly Father, in Christ I live, move and have my being. Help me each passing day this year to be a worthy example in faith, purity, charity and conversation in Jesus' name.

January 2

Over ambition leads to Unscrupulous Actions
Bible Reading: [Gal.1:13-15; Acts.9:1-3]

"For ye have heard of my conversation in time past in Jews' religion, how that beyond measure I persecuted the Church of God, and wasted it:" [Gal.1:13; KJV]

While we desire to achieve success and are determined to reach specific goals in life, our ambition must be checked from time to time. To be ambitious is not a sin. However, when ambition becomes excessive, people often act in a dishonest, unfair or immoral way to get what they want. Over ambition is often driven by an excessive desire for power, wealth and prestige/fame. Such an excessive desire often causes people to behave in an unscrupulous manner: lying, cheating, blackmailing, rivaling, defrauding, persecuting and even jealous of others. God wants us to check our hearts today if we are over ambitious.

Over ambition sometimes is a result of the fact that a person becomes exceedingly zealous without knowledge *[Prov.19:2]*. Saul's zeal made him so unscrupulous that when he finally surrendered to the Lordship of Jesus Christ, disciples of Christ in Damascus were not sure that he was truly saved [Acts.9:13-15]. Is your ambition advancing a worthy cause or wasting lives? When our ambitions go unchecked, it can be destructive sometimes because of self-interest.

Have you become over ambitious in order to please men and gain their approval? As for Saul, he sought to advance the traditions of his fathers contrary to God's purpose. It is written, *"There is a way which seemeth right unto a man, but the end thereof is the ways of death." [Prov.14:12, KJV]*

PRAYER FOCUS

Dear heavenly Father, I commune as a friend with You. LORD, grant that my will be lost in thine and my desires be in alignment with Your purpose in Jesus' name.

January 3

You Thought They Had Your Back
Bible Reading: [2 Tim.4:9-18]

"At the first trial no one acted in my defense [as my advocate] or took my part or [even] stood with me, but all forsook me. May it not be charged against them!" [Vs:16;Ampl.]

It's a good feeling to know that someone has your back. However, Scriptures condemn the fact that we put our trust in man [Jer.17:5]. To have someone's back means to be willing and prepared to help or defend him or her. The truth is that many find themselves in the state of resentment or lack of forgiveness because nobody looked out for them when they needed assistance. The great Apostle Paul said, "At my first trial no one acted in my defense, but all forsook me." Because of fear that he will possibly be condemned to death, his associates refused to identify with his cause.

Our strength in life comes when we step out in faith doing what God has assigned us. Paul's attitude towards those who deserted him is what each one of us should have. He was forsaken by all his associates, but he asked God not to lay it to their charge. It is written, "Jesus will always remain faithful when everyone else flees". For whatever reason men have abandoned you, God has your back. Therefore, my dear brothers, stand firm. Let nothing move you. Always give yourself fully to the work of the LORD, because you know that your labor in the LORD is not in vain." [1 Cor.15:58, NIV].May the LORD strengthen you to do His will.

PRAYER FOCUS

Dear heavenly Father, man may forsake me, but I am fully persuaded that You have my back and You will defend me today in Jesus' name.

January 4

Victory Over Sin & The Evil One
Bible Reading: [1 John 5:18]

"We know that whosoever is born of God sinneth not; but he that is begotten of God keepeth himself, and that wicked one toucheth him not." [Vs 18KJV]

Dear friend, are you born of God and alive in Christ? If yes, then there is good news for you today. God wants every true disciple of Christ to keep away from anything that might take His place in his/her heart. Practicing sin has become the way of life to many. Those who live in sin or deliberately commit sin shall not inherit the kingdom of God *[1 Cor.6:9-10]*.

Those who are born of God have chosen to obey the gospel and live after the will of God. They have assurance of salvation *[Rom.8:16]* because of their faith in the grace of God that leads to continual cleansing of sin by the blood of Jesus. Remember that those who are born of God have been crucified with Christ. It is written, *"I am crucified with Christ: nevertheless I live; yet not I, but Christ liveth in me: and the life which I now live in the flesh I live by the faith of the Son of God, who loved me, and gave himself for me." [Gal.2:20;KJV]*.

Victory over sin is the result of the finished work of Christ on the cross *[Col.2:15]*, evident in the believer's life. It's an overflow of a living fellowship with God on a daily basis. It is the result of walking in the light and holiness. Although the whole world lies in wickedness, Scripture says, *"For God, who commanded the light to shine out of darkness, hath shined in our hearts, to give the light of the glory of God in the face of Jesus Christ." [2 Cor.4:6;KJV]*. Those who are born of God can't be touched by the wicked one: "because greater is He that is in them, than he that is in the world." *[1 John 4:4]*. Hallelujah! Live a victorious life in Christ.

PRAYER FOCUS

Dear heavenly Father, thank You for all that Christ accomplished for me on the cross. Today, I proclaim victory over sin and shame in Jesus' name.

January 5

When The Majority Is Wrong
Bible Reading: [Acts 27:1-44]

"But the Centurion was more persuaded by the pilot and the captain of the ship, than by what was being said by Paul. And because the harbor was not suitable for wintering, the majority reached a decision to put out to sea from there..." [Vs: 11-12]

Nowadays our world is so much driven by opinion polls. For the most part, everyone would like to side with the majority. Even when a wrong decision is supported by the majority, very few people will have the courage to act differently. The truth is that wrong will never cease to be wrong because the majority share in it. Are you caught in the middle trying to act otherwise? Don't miss out on what God is about to do through you because of the fear of man. It is written, *"The fear of man bringeth a snare: but whoso putteth his trust in the LORD shall be safe." [Prov.29:25;KJV]*

The Apostle Paul warned the Centurion, the pilot and captain of the ship when he realized what would happen if they went on. However, they were not ready to listen to an imprisoned Jewish teacher with no experience at sea. Only time will test every decision whether it's right or wrong. If you are fully persuaded about God's word or the leading of His Spirit, then there is no reason to be afraid *[Rom.8:14]*. After many failed attempts at sea, the majority had to respect Paul's decision. He gave them assurance that God would take them to their expected destination. *"For this very night an angel of the God to whom I belong and whom I serve stood before saying, 'Do not be afraid, Paul;.." [Vs:24]*. Friend, do you belong to God? Are you serving His purpose? If you fear God and walk in His ways, He will stand by you at every crossroad in life.

PRAYER FOCUS

Dear heavenly Father, help me not to be on the side of the majority in order to please men. Grant that I will possess a strong conviction and courage to stand for the truth or what's right each passing day in Jesus' name.

January 6

Get Involved!
Bible Reading: [1 Sam.12:1-24]

"Moreover as for me, God forbid that I should sin against the LORD in ceasing to pray for you: but I will teach you the good and right way: Only fear the LORD, and serve Him in truth with all your heart: for consider how great things he hath done for you." [Vs:23-24;KJV]

One of the reasons we should get involved in the LORD's business is to maintain connection with Him and our fellow man in order to ensure a thriving [flourishing] soul and society . In life, there is no better way to learn than to get involved. Nowadays many Christians are indifferent concerning the things of the kingdom and are caught up in worldly pleasures. To get involved means to have a part in something: in actions, plans, or development of another person for the glory of God. Christ saved us from our sin so we might serve Him. Have you repented of your sins and surrendered to Jesus? God wants all true disciples of Christ to serve Him in whatever situations He puts them. Scripture says, *"For we are his workmanship, created in Christ Jesus unto good works, which God hath before ordained that we should walk in them." [Eph.2:10, KJV]*

Christian service is one of the most important principles of the Christian faith. Every disciple of Christ is required to serve God's purpose and the Body of Christ with a joyful spirit, with wholehearted devotion and with a willing mind. It is written, *"As every man hath received the gift, even so minister the same one to another, as good stewards of the manifold grace of God." [1 Pet.4:10;KJV]*. Do not receive God's grace in vain [2Cor.6:1]. Do not be a spectator or an eye-servant. Serve the LORD's purpose, in season and out of season: in prayer/fasting, in giving, in evangelism, like a workman who needs not to be ashamed, rightly dividing the WORD of truth.

Get involved, not lacking in zeal but fervent in spirit. Serve Him in truth with all your heart. Consider the great things He has done for you. Get involved TODAY!

PRAYER FOCUS

Dear heavenly Father, have mercy upon me for my nonchalant [lukewarm] attitude. I seek to serve Your purpose with undivided interest and a willing heart. Help me LORD each passing day in Jesus' name.

January 7

Are You a Fair-Weather Disciple?

"Be diligent to come to me quickly; for Demas has forsaken me, having loved this present world, and has departed for Thessalonica..." [2 Tim.4:9]

It's a great disappointment when a faithful brother or sister in Christ backslides. A fair-weather Christian easily breaks fellowship with God for other pursuits especially in times of difficulty. "Having loved this present world he departed." Demas considered Thessalonica a safe haven - Remember, there is no safe haven outside Christ. *Do you not know that friendship with the world is enmity with God? [James.4:4]* "Do not love the world or the things in the world. If anyone loves the world, the love of the Father is not in him. For all that is in the world - the lust of the flesh, the lust of the eyes, and the pride of life- is not of the Father but is of the world." [1 Jn.2:15,16].

Like Demas, many believers have never counted the cost of genuine commitment to Christ. Then Jesus said to His disciples, *"If anyone desires to come after Me, let him deny himself, and take up his cross, and follow Me"* [Matt.16:24]. Jesus said to the people who believed in Him, "You are truly My disciples if you remain faithful to My teachings." [Jn.8:31]

PRAYER FOCUS

Anything that makes me unfruitful and unproductive be destroyed in the name of Jesus Christ *[Matt.13:22]*. May the love of God flood my heart, let my zeal be renewed, my passion be ignited and my life be refreshed by the Spirit of God. I proclaim my liberty and victory in Christ!

January 8

Striving In Prayers For One Another
Bible Reading: [Rom.15:29-33]

"Now I urge you, brethren, by our LORD Jesus Christ and by the love of the Spirit, to strive together with me in your prayers to God for me," [Vs:30;KJV]

There comes a time in everyone's life when the need to request prayers from others is obvious. Beloved, do you have the urge to pray for somebody today? Oftentimes we pray, but the truth is that only few actually strive in prayers for others. Striving requires that we make great efforts to achieve or obtain something as we pray. Remember that *"..The effective fervent prayer of a righteous man availeth much." [Jam.5:16]*. The great Apostle made the following requests for others to strive together with him in prayers to God:

- That God may deliver him from those in Judea who do not believe. Sometimes preaching to those who do not believe might be hostile or risky thing to do *[2 Thes.3:2]*. Do you pray for your pastor, missionaries and other servants God?
- That his service may be acceptable to the saints *[Heb.4:12]*. He saw the need for his ministry trip to be beneficial to the brethren in Jerusalem.
- That his presence will bring great joy to the brethren in Jerusalem *[Rom1:11]*.

Friend, like the Apostle Paul, are you courageous enough to plead with others to strive with you in prayers to God? The act of praying for others or requesting prayers from others is something we must not shy away from as disciples of Christ. Scripture gives us an example of a worthy disciple who stood in the gap for others. It is written, *"Epaphras, who is one of you, a servant of Christ, salutes you, always laboring [striving] fervently for you in prayers, that ye may stand perfect and complete in all the will of God." [Col.4:12;KJV]*. Beloved, you can stand in the gap in prayers for others today that God will give them many opportunities, heal and open doors for them.

PRAYER FOCUS

Dear heavenly Father, Your word urges me to make prayers for all men *[1 Tim.2:1-3]*. LORD, I yield myself to You as an instrument to strive in prayers for others in Jesus name.

January 9

Today's Storm, Tomorrow's Story
Bible Reading: [2 Cor.1:1-11]

"For we would not, brethren, have you ignorant of our trouble which came to us in Asia, that were pressed out of measure, above strength, inasmuch that we despaired even of life: But we had the sentence of death in ourselves, that we should not trust in ourselves, but in God which raised the dead:" [Vs:8-9;KJV]

The storm of life is a common occurrence. However, you can never really understand a storm until you are in one. A natural storm is any disturbed state of the environment.

The storm of life presents itself as a test, trial, hardship, affliction or obstacle. Are you going through one at the moment? Whether natural storm or the storm of life, there is going to be disturbance in some way. One writer says, "If the storm of life gives you a big blow, don't worry, just give it a great smile and pursue to leave distinctive footprints with perseverance." [Author: unknown]. Beloved, God works His purpose in every storm. Start seeing God working His purpose in the storm you are going through. All things work together for good to them that love God, who are called according to His purpose *[Rom.8:28]*.

Today's storm is tomorrow's testimony. You must learn to stand up to it and not panic. Apostle Paul and his traveling companions encountered a storm that was beyond their ability to endure. Their deadly experience thought them not to rely on themselves but on God who raises even the dead to life. Scriptures teaches us how to survive a storm in the parable of the wise and foolish builder. For the wise man who built his house [life] upon a rock [Christ], it is written, *"And the rain descended, and the floods came, and the winds blew, and beat upon that house; and it fell not: for it was founded upon a rock." [Matt.7:27]*. Is your life founded upon Christ and his Word? Scriptures say, *"We are troubled on every side, yet not distressed; we are perplexed, but not in despair; persecuted, but not forsaken; cast down, but not destroyed;" [2 Cor.4:8;KJV]*.Hallelujah!

PRAYER FOCUS

Dear heavenly Father, thank You for the storm. Your grace is sufficient for me and I'm fully persuaded it's working out for my good in Jesus' name.

January 10

The LORD Will Provide
Bible Reading: [Gen. 22:1-18]

"And Abraham called the name of that place The LORD Will Provide, as it is said to this day, "In the mount of the LORD it will be provided." [Vs 14;KJV]

Beloved, are you overwhelmed by your needs? Today, I would like to introduce you to a good Father called Yahweh Yireh (in Hebrew). What is phenomenal or extraordinary about His name is the meaning of it "the LORD will see to it." Each one of us has a need(s). However, it all depends on who we can trust to meet our need. If you choose God to see to it, it means He will certainly make sure something is done. Reasons being that He is not man, that He should lie *[Num. 23:19]*. It is written, *"And God is able to make all grace abound toward you; that ye, always having all sufficiency in all things, may abound to every good work:" [2 Cor. 9:8; KJV]*. God has unlimited resources, and it is in His best interest to make all grace [favor] come to us so that under all circumstances and whatever the need, we should be self-sufficient.

It is important to note that the Israelites brought their best to God as a sacrifice three times a year. They did so, trusting that He would continue to provide for their needs. Considering the case of Abraham, very few will give God the little they have, trusting Him for greater blessings. God's provision according to His riches in glory is fulfilled in Christ *[Phil.4:19]*. Surrendering our entity [All that we have & we are to God], draws heaven's attention. After Abraham's obedience, God said to him, "...now I know that you fear God and all the nations of the earth shall be blessed in your seed because you have obeyed my voice." **It is written, "Riches and honor are with me; yea, durable riches and righteousness."** *[Prov. 8:18; KJV]*. Hallelujah!

PRAYER FOCUS

Dear heavenly Father, You lead in the way of righteousness. Silver and gold are Yours. Father, I'm confident that You will meet my need(s) this season in Jesus' name.

January 11

Power Of The Holy Spirit Promptings
Bible Reading: [Acts.16:6-10]

"And after he had seen the vision, immediately we endeavored to go into Macedonia, assuredly gathering that the LORD had called us for to preach the gospel unto them." [Vs:10;KJV]

Dear friend, are you born of God? One of the blessings the LORD promised His disciples is the Holy Spirit. God speaks to us in many ways at various times: through a vision, circumstances, His Word, godly advice, guidance through prayer, prophecy and an inner conviction by His Spirit. Scriptures says, *"For as many as are led by the Spirit of God, they are the sons of God."* [Rom.8:14;KJV]. The Holy Spirit leads us through promptings. Prompting means: to incite or move to action. From personal observations, many believers are in the state of inaction. They lack action and need to be prompted. Prompting is good when it generates a corresponding [right] action. The Holy Spirit that indwells all true disciples of Christ, teaches them all things and brings all things to their remembrance *[Jn.14:26]*.

It is important for us to know that God wants us to go to the right places and do the right things. When we yield to the Holy Spirit, He plays an important role to guide us to the right places, and also to keep us away from the wrong places. Because the devil also has the ability to incite us like he did to David *[1 Chr.21:11]*, it is necessary for us to check our motives, plans and desires by aligning them with the Word of God. Scripture also advices us to test every spirit *[1 Jn.4:1]*. Apostle Paul and his traveling companions wanted to go to the provinces of Asia, but the Spirit of Jesus did not permit them. However, by a night vision, they had an inner conviction [assurance] that God was leading them to Europe. Beloved, is the Spirit prompting you to take an action for the glory of God? Do and may the peace of God be with you.

PRAYER FOCUS

Dear heavenly Father, thank You for fulfilling the promise of the Holy Spirit. LORD, help me to respond and take appropriate actions whenever I'm prompted by Your Spirit in Jesus' name.

January 12

Salvation In His Name
Bible Reading: [Matt.1:18-25]

"And she shall bring forth a son, and thou shalt call his name JESUS: for He shall save His people from their sins" [Vs 21;KJV].

At any given moment, somebody on planet earth needs salvation. Salvation is a multidimensional theme. Salvation belongs to God and it's a precious gift to sinners who repent of their sins. Salvation means to save, rescue, help in distress, set free, deliverance from peril (danger) and hell. The Bible uses salvation to denote health, well-being, and healing (Baker's E. Dic.).There is salvation in the name of Jesus. It is written, *"Neither is there salvation in any other: for there is none other name under heaven given among men, whereby we must be saved." [Acts.4:12;KJV]*

Beloved, are you saved? Salvation is a complete process with a beginning and an end. God saves from sin and its consequences. Salvation from sin is by grace and not by works *[Eph.2:8-9]*. It is God reaching out to humanity in his tender mercies and loving kindness through Jesus Christ.

Whatever your dangers and fears, God is able to bring salvation. It is written, *"Wherefore he is able also to save them to the uttermost that come unto God by him, seeing he ever liveth to make intercession for them." [Heb.7:25, KJV]*. Noah's faithfulness resulted in the salvation of his family and livestock. Walk in obedience today, and enjoy the salvation of the living God.

PRAYER FOCUS

Dear heavenly Father, today I confess that You are my light and my salvation. I trust in Your power to save me to completion in Jesus' name.

January 13

The Power Of Trustworthiness
Bible Reading: [Prov.20:1-7]

"Many a man proclaims his own loyalty, but who can find a trustworthy man? A righteous man who walks in his integrity - How blessed are his sons after him." [Vs:6-7, NASB]

The world is in short supply of trustworthy men and women. Many people are craving for trustworthy information, leaders, husbands and wives etc. It is written, "..But who can find a trustworthy man?" Beloved, let's be sincere, only trustworthy friends can share your secret *[Ps.25:14]*. You are trustworthy only when you are able to be trusted or to be relied on as honest or truthful. Are you honest? People cannot rely on you, follow you or share secrets with you if you are not trustworthy. True friends are reliable even in difficulties.

God is trustworthy. That is who He is. His character is the same and every Word of his can be trusted. It is written, *"And now, O LORD God, thou art that God, and thy words be true, and thou has promised this goodness unto thy servant." [2 Sam 7:28;1 Sam 15:29]*. It is vital for every believer to emulate God's Character. People who are trustworthy and behave with integrity will definitely leave a heritage of integrity for their children.

PRAYER FOCUS

Dear heavenly Father, You are the same yesterday, today and forever. LORD, help me to focus on my spiritual [character] development and be faithful to You each passing day in Jesus' name.

January 14

Cultivating An Attitude Of Gratitude
Bible Reading: [Col.1:9-14]

"Giving thanks to the Father, Who has qualified and made us fit to share the portion which is the inheritance of the saints (God's holy people) in the Light." [Vs:12]

No matter your present situation, there are numerous reasons to be grateful to God. Knowing that ingratitude is sin, each one of us should cultivate a thankful spirit. Being thankful is a decision one has to make. "Whether you feel content where your life is right now or you wish things were different, you can make the decision to be thankful." [Jayson Bradley]. Gratitude is expressed by a deep appreciation for the kindness received. The right motivation for gratitude is a reflection on God's goodness and tender mercies. Had it not been the LORD! *[Ps.124:2-3]*. When you feel worried that you don't have enough money in your account or enough food to eat, know for sure that some people have been going for days without money, food or shelter.

I would suggest you take a moment today to thank God for one thing He has done. Apostle Paul sincerely prays that his readers will be filled with joy, always thanking the Father. Thanksgiving God who by His rich mercies, has qualified us to share in the inheritance of the saints. Being grateful to God for the good and perfect gift of Salvation given to all who have genuinely repented from their sins. Being thankful to God for trials of various kinds, knowing that the testing of our faith produces steadfastness [perseverance]. You can make a big difference for being thankful today! The decision is yours.

PRAYER FOCUS

Dear heavenly Father, he who sacrifices thank offering honors You *[Ps.50:23]*. LORD, grant that a humble attitude of gratitude to You and my neighbor will be my lifestyle in Jesus' name.

January 15

Financially Affluent But Spiritually Bankrupt?
Bible Reading: [Rev.3:14-21]

"Because thou sayest, I am rich, and increased with goods, and have need of nothing; and knowest not that thou art wretched, and miserable, and poor, and blind, and naked:" [Vs:17;KJV]

There are many people who think that they are rich and doing well; but are spiritually bankrupt. Friend, are you aware of your true spiritual condition? To be affluent means having goods, property and money in abundance. It is true that God created everything thing for our enjoyment *[1 Tim.6:17]*. However, Scripture emphatically states that, *"....for a man's life consisted not in the abundance of the things which he possesseth." [Lk.12:15, KJV].*

How can we put our trust so much in uncertain riches, instead of the living God?

Beloved, what will it profit you if you gain the whole world, and lose your soul? *[Mk.8:36]*. Like many Churches and Christians who are complacent nowadays, the people of Laodicea were ensnared [trapped] by their sources of wealth; banking, production of wool cloth and medicines.

The Church became rich, but ignorant of her true spiritual condition. Beloved, it is time to be awakened to your spiritual condition and get things right with God through genuine repentance. The LORD is still gracious no matter your sin(s) and He seeks entrance to change your state of spiritual dryness.

PRAYER FOCUS

Dear heavenly Father, may my heart be kindled to spiritual reality and grant that the Word of Christ may dwell richly in me, in all wisdom in Jesus' name.

January 16

Fit Out - To Fit In
Bible Reading: [John 15:18-27]

"If ye were of the world, the world would love his own: but because ye are not of the world, but I have chosen you out of the world, therefore the world hated you." [Vs:19;KJV]

Many people are still struggling to fit themselves in places that they are not accepted. The worse thing to do on earth is to seek joy in all the wrong places, relationships or companionships. It's time for you to go where you fit! You can't behave like the world, walk like the world and belong to the world, yet, claim to belong to the Kingdom of God *[Rom.12:1-2]*.

If the world that has been deceived by Satan rejected Jesus, the same world would not accept any genuine disciple of Christ either. Preaching the light of truth to the world often brings one into conflict with the established systems of the world. The people of the world like to maintain their status quo. It is written, *"And this is the condemnation, that light is come into the world, and men loved darkness rather than light, because their deeds were evil" [John.3:19]*.

Friend, it's time to fit out, knowing that friendship with the world is enmity with God *[Jam.4:4]*. Fritz Chery said, "I never really fitted in with others, but the one place I did fit in was in Christ and the body of Christ." True disciples must be like their Master in every aspect, showing love, obedience and suffering persecution for living godly in Christ *[2 Tim.3:12]*

PRAYER FOCUS

Dear LORD, grant me the grace to share the fellowship of Your suffering and be totally separated from worldly passions[lust] in Jesus' name.

January 17

Nurturing A Vital Relationship With God In Prayer
Bible Reading: [Matt.14:22-33]

"And when He had sent the multitudes away, He went up into a mountain apart to pray: and when the evening was come, He was there alone." [Matt.22:23]

No matter the busy schedule, our relationship with God must be given due attention. Spending time alone with God is an important aspect of spiritual growth. Friend, when was the last time you fellowshipped with God in prayer? The Psalmist says, *"My voice shalt thou hear in the morning, O LORD; in the morning will I direct my prayer unto thee, and will look up."[Ps.5:3;KJV].* The reason why many people are not able to face life's challenges and break even, is due to the lack of quiet time with God.

Nurturing involves care, protecting and given attention to something that is growing or developing. All those who made giant strides in the faith, were men and women who spent time alone with God. Jesus often sought solitude in order to pray, especially concerning important events in his life and ministry. Being alone with God requires focused awareness, concentration, thought and reflection. Become more like Jesus today by spending time alone with God.

PRAYER FOCUS

Dear heavenly Father, I put my trust in Your grace and unfailing love. LORD, help me to develop the discipline of spending time alone with You daily in Jesus' name.

January 18

The Power Of Prophetic Action
Bible Reading: [2 Kings 13:14-19; 2 Chr.20:20]

Prophetic actions are potent actions guided by the Holy Spirit through God's chosen vessel to avert or destroy the ploy of the enemy. Towards the end of Elisha's great mission on earth, King Joash became troubled by the challenge he would face in the absence of the prophet. The King came to the prophet and cried out, saying, *"O my father, my father, the chariots of Israel and their horsemen!" [Vs 13:14]*. In other words, " my father, my father, I will not let you go until you bless Israel" One last request!

King Joash by so doing acknowledged that the Lord, through Elisha was the real strength and power of Israel against all her adversaries. It is worth noting that in ancient times, the horse-drawn chariot was the fastest means of transport and the mightiest means of warfare. "Elijah put his hands on the King's hands." symbolized the fact that Joash would exert power against the Syrians that came from the Lord through the prophet. Bringing the ploy of your enemy to an end is inevitable! Key elements of a successful prophetic action:

- A recognition of Divine authority
- Obedience to the voice of the prophet
- Taking action in faith
- Action to completion

And the Man of God was angry with the king, and said, "You should have struck five or six times; then you would have struck Syria till you had destroyed it! But now you will strike Syria only three times." (Vs-19). Victory is certain when a prophetic action is directed by the Holy Spirit and divine instructions followed through. The significance of prophetic actions in the Bible cannot be overemphasized.

PRAYER FOCUS

Today, I declare the arrow of the Lord's deliverance and victory over my enemies in Jesus' name.

January 19

Unbroken Fellowship
Bible Reading: [1 John 2:1-6]

"My little children, these things write I unto you, that ye sin not. And if any man sin, we have an advocate with the Father, Jesus Christ the righteous:" [Vs 1,KJV]

Walking in obedience to Christ is not an option or alternative way of life. It is a clear indication that we know Christ and belong to him. Our belonging to him is not limited to Church membership, but a life totally rooted and grounded in the love of God *[Eph.3:17]*. Truth that sets men free is correct knowledge and a demonstration of the reality of God's love. When we yield our lives to the Lordship of Christ, we enter into a living fellowship [communion] with him. It's written, "...and truly our fellowship is with the Father, and with his Son Jesus Christ. If we say we have fellowship with him, and walk in darkness, we lie, and do not have the truth"*[1 Jn.1:3&6]*.

In times of weakness or difficulty, some brethren do compromise their conviction and sin against God. This gives the devil [accuser of brethren], the legal ground to accuse them before the Father *[Zech.3:1]*. Whatever the case may be, Christ pleads our case before the Father. Beloved, God's grace doesn't give anyone a license to commit sin. It's important to note that a believer in Christ [Born again], does not live in sin. Whenever we allow an act of sin to become a habit of life, then fellowship is broken with God. In order to enjoy an unbroken [continuous] fellowship with God, we must walk in the light as He Himself is in the light *[1 Jn.1:7]*. Remember that God doesn't despise a humble confession and a repentant heart.

PRAYER FOCUS

Dear heavenly Father, thank You for the gift of an Advocate [Jesus] who pleads my case and sanctifies me with His blood. Help me each passing day to walk in the same manner as Christ walked on earth in Jesus' name.

January 20

Grace To Speak Straight & Sound Truth
Bible Reading: [Acts.26:19-32]

> "...Paul, thou art beside thyself; much learning doth make thee mad. But he said, I am not mad, most noble Festus; but speak forth the words of truth and soberness."
> [Vs:24-25;KJV]

Nowadays uttering truth in most societies and governments is like a rare episode. Just everywhere you go people like to be "diplomatic". Truth means presenting the real facts about something. It is right for each one of us to speak with wisdom and utter the things that minister grace to the hearer. However, the only thing that can set men free is straight and sound truth [Jn.8:32]. Half-truths do not make a truth. Bending or twisting the truth means to say something that is not completely true in order to achieve an aim. How can one speak the truth when he is not living the truth? Jesus Christ is the truth and hope of glory [Jn.14:6]. Have you surrendered your life Christ?

Regardless of how men perceive us for saying the truth, let's say the truth without fear or favor. Speak straight and sound truth today; let God use it to achieve His aim and purpose. Governor Festus told Paul, "Much learning is driving you mad." However, Paul was not ashamed of the truth [Jn 17:17]. It is written, "For I am not ashamed of the gospel of Christ: for it is the power of God unto salvation to everyone that believeth; to the Jew first, and also to the Greek."[Rom.1:16, KJV].

It is written, "But if our gospel [truth] be hid, it is hid to them that are lost: In whom the god of this world hath blinded the minds of them which believe not, lest the light of the glorious gospel of Christ, who is the image of God, should shine unto them." [2 Cor.4:3-4;KJV]. The truth is what this generation needs to hear in order to come out of darkness, into the marvelous light of God.

Utter truth today fearlessly and may the God of peace be with you.

PRAYER FOCUS

Dear heavenly Father, You take no delight in half-truth. LORD, grant that whenever I open my mouth, right words [divine utterance] be given me to boldly proclaim the mystery of the gospel in Jesus' name.

January 21

Overcoming My Fears
Bible Reading: [Psalm 34:1-22]

*"I sought the LORD, and He heard me,
And delivered me from all my fears." [Vs: 4;NKJV]*

At one moment in time, each one of us has experienced an unpleasant feeling that something painful or dreadful is happening or might happen. This often occurs when we find ourselves in a situation in which something is not known [uncertainty]. Fears in life are many: fear of failure, persecution, discrimination, financial crisis, harm and evil etc.

Friend, what are your fears? Are you uncertain about what the future holds for you? David being afraid of what might happen to him in Gath, changed his behavior to that of a madman *[1 Sam. 21:12-13]*. Fear discourages, torments and sometimes drives us away from God.

The antidote for fear is perfect love, that comes from a right relationship or standing with God *[1 John 4:18]*. Freedom from fear is a covenant benefit that Christ accomplished for us on the cross. He has not given us the spirit that makes us to be afraid, but of love, power and sound mind *[2 Tim.1:7]*

PRAYER FOCUS

Dear heavenly Father, I put my trust in You. Today, I receive strength and courage from You to overcome my fears in Jesus' name.

January 22

Early and Fervent Seekers
Bible Reading: [Psalm 63:1-11]

"O God, thou art my God; early will I seek thee: my soul thirsteth for thee, my flesh longeth for thee in a dry and thirsty land, where no water is;" [Vs:1;KJV]

In our fast-paced world, daybreak sets everything moving. Often, we allow the affairs of this world to replace our meditation on God. Friend, are you a fervent and early seeker? Do you set aside the best part of your day to have a refreshing encounter with the living God? A seeker is someone who is trying to find or get something. It is written, *"I love them that love me; and those that seek me early shall find me." [Prov.8:17;KJV]*.

We seek after many things *[Lk.12:30]*. Often, when our priorities are not set right, we go after the wrong things. However, it's important to note that the best quality of life is found in a genuine relationship with God. There must be a tangible reason for being an early and fervent seeker. In this portion of Scriptures, king David expresses his longing for God's presence, *"So I have looked upon You in the sanctuary to see Your power and Your glory." [Vs:2;Ampl.]*. In God's presence is a revelation of His power and might. If you long for a friend you can trust, be an early and fervent seeker of God in order to kick-start your day in the right direction.

PRAYER FOCUS

Dear heavenly Father, a genuine relationship with You is the most valuable thing in life. LORD, help me daily to disconnect myself from the affairs of life in order to have a deep devotion with You in Jesus' name.

January 23

Values In The Wrong Place
Bible Reading: [Mark 14:1-11]

"And Judas Iscariot, one of the twelve, went unto the chief priests, to betray him unto them. And when they heard it, they were glad, and promised to give him money. And he sought how he might conveniently betray him." [Vs: 10-11; KJV]

Those who come to the Master are called according to His purpose and grace. The LORD's purposes cannot be realized with the wrong values. In simple terms, values are moral principles or accepted standards. These principles help us to decide what is right and wrong, and how to act in various situations. You can make giant strides in life as a believer in Christ if your values are in the right place. Being at the center of God's will for your life is the key i.e. being at the right place, at right time, for the right reason.

The values of Judas Iscariot were misguided when he allowed Satan to influence his desires. It's written, *"Then entered Satan into Judas....., And he went his way, and communed with the chief priests and captains, how he might betray him unto them." [Lk .22:3-4; KJV]*. He carried out the desires of Satan to betray Jesus. Nowadays Satan has deceived the minds of many people with religious misguided beliefs. Beloved, are your values in the right place? Don't conceive in your mind to carry out the desires of Satan today. Setting your values on course to do the Father's will is the secret of a successful Christian life.

PRAYER FOCUS

Dear heavenly Father, I seek to do Your will. LORD, help me daily to set my values in the right place in Jesus' name.

January 24

Sensing The Still Small Voice
Bible Reading: [1 Kings 19:1-15]

Then God said, Go out, and stand on the mountain before the LORD. "And behold, the LORD passed by, and a great and strong wind tore into the mountains and broke the rocks in pieces before the LORD, but the LORD was not in the wind; and after the wind an earthquake, but the LORD was not in the earthquake; and after the earthquake a fire, but the LORD was not in the fire; and after the fire a still small voice. So it was, when Elijah heard it, that he wrapped his face in his mantle and went out and stood in the entrance of the cave.,.." [Vs:11-13]

It's so fascinating when God speaks. Each one of us would like to hear God's voice. When we think that God reveals Himself only in powerful ways, we will certainly be limited in some ways to hear Him speak. God's voice may come when we least expect it. Beloved, have you ever sensed God's presence or heard his voice? Oftentimes our noisy atmosphere and busy lifestyles keep us from hearing His voice. Sometimes feelings of self-pity and discouragement affect our ability to hear from God. Whatever the condition that might have caused us to stray from God, like Elijah fleeing from the threat of Jezebel, we need to connect again with God.

No circumstance in life ought to hinder us from hearing God's voice. God speaks at various times, in different ways and places *[Gen.28:16]*. All great men that God used for great movements heard God's voice in the desert [unpleasant circumstances]. You might have strayed from God's mission because of emotional stress, sin or other issues of life. God wants to set you again on the right track. Repent and reposition yourself to listen humbly and quietly for His guidance. The still small voice can be sensed in the quietness of a humbled heart today.

PRAYER FOCUS

Dear heavenly Father, I confess that I have strayed from Your mission. LORD, help me to retrace my steps back to the place where I ought to be, and move in the right direction in Jesus' name.

January 25

Desperate People Do Desperate Things
Bible Reading: [Luke 5:17-26]

"And behold, some men were bringing on a stretcher a man who was paralyzed, and they tried to carry him in and lay him before Jesus. But finding no way to bring him in because of the crowd, they went up on the roof and lowered him with his stretcher through the tiles into the midst, in front of Jesus."
[Vs 18-19; KJV]

We all don't approach life's circumstances with the same confidence. However, one thing that is common is that desperate people do desperate things, either foolish or reasonable [wise]. Sometimes in life, we have a great need or desire for something. At times, we are willing to do anything to change a very bad situation, and not caring about danger. Friend, has everything else failed for you? Do you have little hope for success? Are your chances for survival slim? Is your situation extremely bad? Friend, it's time to make some desperate moves. The woman with the issue of blood said within herself, "If I should only touch his garment, I will be made well." [Matt.9:21]. In the face of great danger of Hamman's plot to kill all the Jews, Queen Esther was willing to put her life in jeopardy and referred the success to God, knowing it was for His glory and freedom of the Jewish people *[Est.4:16]*. She asked the Jews to fast, while she meets the King. She said, *"I will go to the king, which is against the law; and if I perish, I perish."*

When the paralytic man was brought in front of Jesus, He started with his greater problem, his spiritual need [repentance from Sin], rather than his physical need. Scriptures say, *"And when He saw [their confidence in Him, springing from their faith, He said, Man, your sins are forgiven you!"* [Vs:20, Ampl.]. Beloved, I can see the LORD working wonders this season as you make some desperate moves in the place of prayer, in your study, digging deep into His word and taking steps of faith. Hallelujah!

PRAYER FOCUS

Dear heavenly Father, I know you can do all things; no purpose of Yours concerning me/my family/church can be thwarted in Jesus' name.

January 26

Renewing Your Resolve
Bible Reading: [Judges 5:15]

"And the princes of Issachar were with Deborah; As Issachar, so was Barak; sent into the valley under his command; among the divisions of Reuben there were great resolves of heart." [Vs 15; NKJV]

Life is full of troubles and challenges. There is a period of chaos and uncertainty: wars and rumors of wars, economic crisis, financial difficulties, failures and pressures from the outside. As a result, one's resolve is tested and sometimes weakened by fear and anxiety. Resolve means to decide firmly on a course of action. Resolve keeps you committed to staying on course to your desired objective. In practical terms, "who and what you are today is a reflection of your resolve in the past. Who and what you are to become will be a manifestation of your resolve today" [Robert Silverston].

Has your resolve been weakened by circumstances? At a crucial moment in the history of Israel, the people suffered under the hand of the Canaanites and their cruel commander, Sisera. Deborah rallied the people against Sierra forces for freedom. As tribes woke up for battle *[1 Cor.14:8]*, Scriptures record that there was great resolves [indecision] of heart in the tribe of Reuben. They were not ready to volunteer in order to fight the LORD's battle. Perhaps, because of lack of effort, besetting sin, fear of the enemy or an evil report. In the days of Moses, the ten spies weakened the people's resolve with an evil report *[Num.14:36-39]*.

Friend, a lack of zeal for God's plan is a sign of disobedience. Wake-up today, make-up your mind, be a force that cannot be reckoned with, remind yourself of God's faithfulness and character, and be determined to fight a good fight of faith or freedom. A song of praise to God will affect your attitude positively *[Ps.118:24]*. With God at the center, you are more than conquerors. Hallelujah!

PRAYER FOCUS

Dear heavenly Father, You are mighty to save, heal and deliver. I put my trust in You and confess that I can do all things through Christ who strengthens me in Jesus' name.

January 27

Hallmark Of Faith & Practice
Bible Reading: [Psalm 1:1-6]

"Blessed is the man that walketh not in the counsel of the ungodly, nor standeth in the way of sinners, nor sitteth in the seat of the scornful. But his delight is in the law of the LORD; and in his law doth he meditate day and night."
[Vs:1-2;KJV]

For the most part, each one of us would like to live a life that is spiritually healthy and fruitful. While the wicked take pleasure in ridiculing those who live right with God, His word assures us that happiness does not come from a sinful life-style. The righteous are honorable because they do not follow the advice, plans and purposes of the ungodly. The ways of the ungodly lead to destruction *[Prov.14:12;KJV]*. The Word of God is the hallmark of faith and practice because it spells out what God considers important in all aspects of life. Therefore, those who delight in God's law shouldn't believe like, behave like, or belong to the realm of ungodly men (Ryrie study). The godly do not live under the influence of sinners. The ungodly are spiritually dead, guilty before God and are like chaff which the wind blows away.

A righteous man makes God's word his delight and meditates on it daily. His faith is nourished as he meditates, listens and puts God's word into practice. Because of his trust in God, he shall be like a tree planted by the water and shall prosper *[Jer.17:7-8]*.

One shouldn't choose God's path solely for the blessings of the moment, but because it determines where he or she will spend eternity. Choose this day between the way of folly that leads to destruction or the ways of God that lead to wisdom and salvation.

PRAYER FOCUS

Dear heavenly Father, You've promised a fruitful life to those who are obedient to Your will. LORD, help me to put Your word into practice and grant that my mind will be focused on godly things in Jesus' name.

January 28

Giving Your Assignment Significance
Bible Reading: [Jer.17:12-18]

"LORD, I have not abandoned my job as a shepherd for your people. I have not urged you to send disaster. You have heard everything I've said." [Vs:16;nlt]

Often when the going gets tough at work place, the feeling of resignation sets in. Some reasons why people hurry away from their jobs are obvious; family circumstances, health, their values no longer align with what their employers stand for, desiring a better career opportunity, feeling undervalue in their roles, feeling their performance or output is low. Whatever the case may be, if God truly assigned you, then give no room to a second thought until you get the next instruction from Him.

There is a right and a wrong way to do any task. Many in both secular world and the Body of Christ have abandoned their assignment because of what men say. If God assigned you, there are many things people [scoffers] will say. Friend, are you at your duty post because of man or because of God? Jeremiah was ridiculed but he did not urge God to send disaster *[Lk 9:51-56]*. He was confident before God in his speech. When we are faithful to God, we can trust him to vindicate us. Trust is the disposition of the heart that results in obedience. Be faithful, don't give up! The LORD will certainly give you the next instruction as you make your request known to him *[Philip.4:6]*. May the joy of the LORD be your strength.

PRAYER FOCUS

Dear heavenly Father, thank You for the task You have entrusted to my care. Grant me wisdom and help me to put up a right heart attitude at my duty post in Jesus' name.

January 29

Acts Of Persuading Men
Bible Reading: [2 Cor.5:10-21]

"Knowing therefore the terror of the LORD, we persuade men; but we are made manifest into God; and I trust also are made manifest in your consciences."
[Vs: 11]

Knowing that God will judge all men through Christ, it is the responsibility of every true disciple to ask men to escape from the wrath to come. The nonchalant attitude prevailing in the Body of Christ today is based on a lack of consciousness that many are on the narrow way to destruction [Matt.7:13]. Even Paul, knowing about the coming judgment of God was frightened with the thought of coming up short. Being conscious of serving God with respect and reverence should be the motive of every disciple to win men over. We must preach the gospel in season, and out of season [2 Tim.4:2], persuading men to submit to God who will judge justly, without respect of persons.

Scripture records that governor Felix and wife Drusilla sent for Paul in order to hear him concerning faith in Christ. "And as he reasoned of righteousness, temperance, and judgement to come, Felix trembled, and answered, 'Go thy way for this time; when I have a convenient season, I will call for thee.'" [Acts 24:25, KJV]. The time is now! The blood of the Jesus that was shed at Calvary is too precious to let the devil snatch men to hell fire. The King's business must be treated with urgency. God doesn't want anyone to perish, but that all should come to repentance [2 Pet.3:9]. Let's persuade men with the Word of God and be innocent of their blood today! [Acts 20:26]

PRAYER FOCUS

Dear heavenly Father, thank You for committing to me the word of reconciliation. LORD, give me wisdom and passion to win lost souls in Jesus' name.

January 30

The Power Of Intimacy
Bible Reading: [Psalm 63:1-11]

"My whole being follows hard after You and clings closely to you;
Your right hand upholds me." [Vs:8;Ampl.].
"My soul followeth hard after thee:
thy right hand upholdeth me." [Vs:8;KJV]

Intimacy with God, spouse or someone is not purchase in a market and does not happens overnight. It is scriptural that: *"No man can come to me [Jesus], except the Father which hath sent me draw him:.." [Jn.6:44;KJV].* Scripture also says, "Draw nigh to God, and he will draw nigh to you, Cleanse your hands, ye sinners; and purify your hearts, ye double minded." *[Jam.4:8;KJV].* It is obvious that couples can live under the same roof but are not intimate.

Friend, there must be effort made by both parties in any intimate relationship. Intimacy means to closely acquaint or be familiar with someone. Friend, are you familiar with God? *[Job.22:21].* Remember that those who are familiar [intimate] with God are known by Him. It is written, *"My sheep hear my voice, and I know them, and they follow me: And I give them eternal life; and they shall never perish, neither shall any man pluck them out of my hand." [Jn.10:27-28, KJV].*

Are you following God or you want Him to have intimacy with you on your terms? God does not bargain intimacy with anyone. The Psalmist says, "My soul followers hard after thee:" Three signs of intimacy are obvious:

Desiring: It is a strong feeling of wanting to have something or wishing for something to happen: *"One thing have I desired of the LORD, that will I seek after;" [Ps.27:4]*

Panting: Means to breathe hard and quickly. This is the air I breathe, Your holy presence living in me. *"As the deer pants for the water brooks, so pants my soul for You, O God." [Ps.42:1].* God's presence is indispensable!

Beholding: It involves seeing or observing a thing or person, especially an impressive one. You can't be intimate with God without seeing Him as awesome *[Exod.33:18].* You can't claim to be intimate with the brethren or your husband/wife without longing to see each other at all *times [1 Thes. 3:10].* A casual relationship with God means you are unconcerned or not regular. You are in and out! Consider your ways!

PRAYER FOCUS

Dear heavenly Father, You don't bargain intimacy with anybody. LORD, have mercy upon me for my lukewarm attitude and help me grow in Your presence daily in Jesus' name.

January 31

Restitution Of All Things
Bible Reading: [Amos 9:11-15]

"I will bring back the captives of My people Israel; They shall build the waste cities and inhabit them; They shall plant vineyards and drink wine from them; They shall also make gardens and eat fruit from them." [Vs:14;NKJV]

Whenever we trust and obey God, we can rest assured that we will eat the good of the land. God desires that each one of us should live off the abundance of the land. It is written, *"If ye be willing and obedient, ye shall eat the good of the land: But if ye refuse and rebel, ye shall be devoured with the sword: for the mouth of the LORD hath spoken it." [Isa.1:19-20;KJV]*. Like the Israelites in the days of Prophet Amos, whenever we reject God's revelation and live according to our own desires, His presence will certainly mean judgement, and not comfort to us. Friend, are you living in disobedience to God? The good news is that regardless of where you've been taken captive, what has been stolen from you because of rebellion or how far you've gone astray, if you return to God, He will restore you.

God is able to restitute or perfect that which concerns us *[Ps.138:8]*. Restitution means the restoration of something lost or stolen to its proper owner. By reason of acts of obedience, God's desire for us today is threefold:

Fertility: Being able to conceive or produce fruit [fruitful]."This is to my Father's glory, that you bear much fruit, showing yourselves to be my disciples *[Jn.15:8]*.

Prosperity: Being able to flourish or thrive in all respects and circumstances: "The righteous shall flourish like the palm tree: he shall grow like a cedar in Lebanon." *[Ps.92:12]*

Security: Being free from danger or threat. *"He that dwelleth in the secret place of the most High shall abide under the shadow of the Almighty." I will say of the LORD, He is my refuge and my fortress: my God; in him will I trust." [Ps 91:1-2]*

PRAYER FOCUS

Dear heavenly Father, Your faithfulness is a great blessing. LORD, I put my trust in Your unfailing love in Jesus' name.

FEBRUARY

"Finally, brethren, whatsoever things are true, whatsoever things are honest, whatsoever things are just, whatsoever things are pure, whatsoever things are lovely, whatsoever things are of good report; if there be any virtue, and if there be any praise, think on these things. Those things, which ye have both learned, and received, and heard, and see in me, do: and the God of peace shall be with you."

[Phil.4:8-9, KJV]

****

Jehovah Jireh - **[The LORD who Sees/Provides]** *- Gen.22:14*

2 = **[Duality of man / Two Witnesses]** *- Deut.19:15*

February 1

Demonstrating Simple Faith In God's Great Purposes
Bible Reading: [Joshua.2:1-24]

"And Joshua the son of Nun sent out of Shittim two men to spy secretly, saying, Go view the land, even Jericho. And they went, and came into a harlot's house, named Rahab, and lodged there. And she said unto the men, I know that the LORD hath given you the land, and that your terror us falling upon us, and that all the inhabitants of the land faint because of your." [Vs:9;KJV]

It's so amazing how sometimes God uses simple faith and chooses foolish things of the world to achieve His great purposes. God is no respecter of persons. He uses whomever, whenever, and wherever He pleases. Scripture records that Rahab was a prostitute. However, the openness of her heart and her willingness to be a part of God's great plan attracted His attention. She didn't allow her background or previous lifestyle to get in the way. She believed that the God of Israel was the true God and mighty in power. She understood the times and knew what to *do [1 Chr.12:32].*

Like Rahab who had very little knowledge of God, how many of us are willing today to risk our lives to advance God's purposes? It's important to note that God honored her little faith, and not her falsehood. The preservation of the spies, and Israel possessing the land was of greater importance than the lie. She demonstrated her faith by saving the spies. God expects each one of us to trust him and do the best we know how.

Faith comes by hearing, and hearing by the word of God *[Rom.10:17].* What Rahab heard about the God of Israel produced faith in her. When we begin a faith walk with God, we can expect that He will achieve great things through us. Her faith in God preserved her life and saved her family. Her faith in God, preserved the spies and helped the Israelites conquered Jericho. Her faith in God placed her in the lineage of Christ *[Matt.1:5].* Regardless of how we have lived our lives before, if we are determined to take little steps of faith, God will achieve his great purposes through us and with us. When we trust that God is on our side, even mighty mountains and great adversaries are of no significance.

PRAYER FOCUS

Dear heavenly Father, I choose to align myself with Your purpose and the people of God. LORD, grant that nothing of the past will rob me of Your great plan for my life *[Job.42:2]* in Jesus' name.

February 2

The Marks Of Genuine Conviction & Commitment
Bible Reading: [Acts 19:11-20]

"Many also of those who had believed kept coming, confessing and disclosing their practices. Many of those who practiced magic brought their books together and began burning them in the sight of all." [Vs:18-19]

Putting one's faith into practice is a proof of genuine conviction and commitment to the truth. However, some have carried guilt and issues of the past into their future relationship with Christ. It is written, *"He that covereth his sins shall not prosper: but whoso confesseth and forsaketh them shall have mercy." [Prov.28:13]*. Scriptures record that many who had believed kept coming, confessing and disclosing their practices.

Beloved, are there practices you are covering or stolen property you are keeping? Some believers have made mockery of Christ for too long. It's time to get rid of anything that keeps one trapped into unholy practices. Regardless of the value, those who had practiced magic brought their books together and began burning them in the sight of all men. This is the hallmark of genuine repentance. The outcome of their action was evident as true disciples. *"The Word of the LORD was growing mightily and prevailing."[Vs:20]*. When men see the conviction of those who are committed to the true, they will be convinced Christianity is true.

PRAYER FOCUS

Dear heavenly Father, You manifest Your power only through those You choose. LORD, I yield my life to You and totally devote myself to Your purposes in Jesus' name.

February 3

Power Of The Breath Of God
Bible Reading: [Job 32:1-9]

"I thought age should speak, and increased years should teach wisdom. But it is the spirit in man, And the breath of the Almighty gives them understanding."
[Vs: 7-8;NASB]

For the most part, one will assume that with age comes wisdom because, becoming wise is an ongoing and lifelong pursuit. However, considering the present world and most especially those at the helm of power, one might be mistaken to think so. Scripture gives the difference between earthly wisdom and heavenly wisdom *[Jam.3:13-17]*. When we don't have all the facts, we are likely to make judgments from a wrong perspective without the greater purpose of God in mind *[Job.1:12]*. Considering the nature of earthly wisdom, King Solomon asked God for wisdom.

Elihu being the youngest among Job's friends realized that the others were not aged with wisdom. It is written, *"Who is a wise man and endued with knowledge among you? Let him show out of a good conversation his works with meekness of wisdom." [Jam.3:13;KJV]*.

Often our conversations are flawed and judgments are wrong because of lack of understanding. Understanding is the ability to know the meaning of something, or to know how a person feels and why the person behaves in a particular way. *"Wisdom is the principal thing; therefore get wisdom: and with all thy getting get understanding." [Prov.4:7;KJV]*. The breath of God gives understanding, life and inspiration [illumination]. Even the best human answers are incomplete for lack of understanding.

PRAYER FOCUS

Dear heavenly Father, my judgments are often flawed for lack of understanding. LORD, may Your Spirit give me understanding and keep me on the right path today in Jesus' name.

February 4

The Power Of Instinct
Bible Reading: [Jer.8:4-13]

"Even the stork in the sky knows her appointed seasons, and the dove, the swift and the thrush observe the time of their migration. But my people do not know the requirements of the LORD" [Vs:7, NIV].

God has given animals and humans instinct. Instinct is something you don't need to learn. It's a natural occurrence, even without you thinking about it. In the simplest terms, instinct is all about how we respond to opportunities in life. It is a fact that we don't respond to the same opportunity in the same way. How golden opportunities bypass so many people daily! If certain birds follow their instinct precisely by being able to navigate the sky from summer nesting places to winter feeding grounds, why can't humans especially God's very Elect do better?

It breaks the Father's heart when disciples of Christ ignore divine revelations and fail to know the requirements of the LORD. Remember that people perish for lack of knowledge and revelation *[Hos.4:6, Prov.29:18]*. When we are transformed by the renewing of the mind, we can be able to test and approve what God's will is. His good, pleasing and perfect will *[Rom.12:2]*. God has our best interest in mind and does not want any disciple of Christ to miss his/her opportunity this year. It is written, *"Now we have received, not the spirit of the world, but the Spirit which is from God; that we might know the things that are freely given to us of God." [1 Cor.2:12,KJV]*. If birds with natural instinct don't miss their season of opportunity, how about you?

PRAYER FOCUS

Dear heavenly Father, through the power of Your Spirit in me, help me to follow my instinct precisely. I decree that no opportunity divinely apportioned for me, will bypass me this year in Jesus' name.

February 5

When God Brings You Into Deep Waters
Bible Reading: [Exod.14:13-31]

"And the LORD said unto Moses, Stretch out thine hand over the sea, that the waters may come again upon the Egyptians, upon their chariots and upon their horsemen. And Moses stretched forth his hand over the sea, and the sea returned to his strength when the morning appeared; and the Egyptians fled against it; and the LORD overthrew the Egyptians in the midst of the sea."[Vs: 26-27]

Beloved, are you giving in to despair because you find yourself in deep waters? It's sometimes uncomfortable how we feel when in such a situation. However, a positive attitude in a given situation will determine how victorious we emerge from it. To be in deep waters means finding yourself in a serious situation especially one that is difficult or is beyond the level of your ability. It also means to be in trouble. For the most part, nobody would like to be in deep waters.

The Psalmist prayed to God when he was in deep waters. He said, *"Deliver me out of the mire, and let me not sink: let me be delivered from them that hate me, and out of the deep waters." [Ps.69:14;KJV]*. Today, I decree and declare that no waterflood will overflow you in Jesus' name *[Isa.43:2]*. Remember, God is an ever-present help in times of trouble *[Ps.46:1]*.

Sometimes God brings us into deep waters in order to drown our enemies, and sometimes in order to help us develop character and faith in Him. Whatever the case may be, all things work together for good to them that love God, to them who are called according to His purpose *[Rom.8:28]*. If you are born of God, stop crying to Him and get moving! The deep waters you see today, you shall never see again.

PRAYER FOCUS

Dear heavenly Father, I'm confident that You can intervene in any situation and do with it as You wish. LORD, help me to see deep waters in life as opportunities to depend You in Jesus' name.

February 6

The Power Of Divine Guidance
Bible Reading: [2 Sam.2:1-7]

"And it came to pass after this, that David inquired of the LORD, saying, Shall I go up into any of the cities of Judah? And the LORD said unto him, Go up. And David said, Whither shall I go up? And he said, Unto Hebron." [Vs: 1;KJV]

The fulfillment of our destiny can't be reached without divine guidance. God does not call a man into a life of trial and error, but according to His purpose and grace. Like David, we all come to a point in time that we need divine direction. It's true that we are living in a fast-paced world, but it's rather unfortunate that even the very Elect of God can't afford time to seek God for direction. I find this quote interesting, *"It is the set of the sails, not the direction of the wind that determines which way we will go."* [Jim Rohn]. If you embark on a journey and the wind has to determine your direction, you are likely going to end up in destruction. Are you led by the wind of opinion poll or by the Holy Spirit? *[Rom.8:14].*

The hallmark of men and women of destiny is the ability to seek God for direction. Friend, when did you last ask God for guidance? We can trust in the promises of God today. Thus saith the LORD, thy Redeemer, the Holy One of Israel; *I am the LORD thy God which teacheth thee to profit, which leadeth thee by the way that thou shouldest go." [Isa.48:17;KJV].* God will lead us like David when we surrender our Will and inquire of Him. Oftentimes we seek God only when we are stuck in life. It's important to note that David acted when God directed, not before! The men of Judah heartily welcomed him and publicly anointed him as their king.

PRAYER FOCUS

Dear heavenly Father, the steps of a good man are ordered by You. LORD, I humble myself before You and ask for guidance today in Jesus' name.

February 7

The Power Of Spiritual Checkups
Bible Reading: [2 Cor.13:1-6]

"Examine yourselves as to whether you are in the faith. Test yourselves. Do you not know yourselves, that Jesus Christ Is in you? - unless indeed you are disqualified." [Vs:5;NKJV]

The good news today is that the LORD is concerned about our wellbeing. In order for our body and soul to keep well and prosper, there things that a disciple of Christ ought do. It's obvious that some people don't like routine physical examination. However, physical examination is a preventive measure that ensures we stay in good health. Physical examination helps us to check a serious condition before it causes problems. Friend, are you concerned about your spiritual wellbeing? The LORD's ultimate goal is that we should attain maturity in the faith and spend eternity in heaven with Him.

Knowing that the stakes are high, it is the responsibility of everyone to determine for themselves if they are servants of Christ or representatives of Satan. It is written, *"And if Christ be in you, then even though your body is subject to death because of sin; but the Spirit is life because of righteousness." [Rom.8:10]*. The greatest deception is to think that one us in the faith when in reality, he is not. Of course some will say, "LORD, did we not prophesy, drive out demons and perform many miracles in Your name?" The LORD will say, "I never knew you: depart from me, ye that work iniquity *[Matt.7:23]*.

Spiritual checkups enable us to be aware of Christ's presence and power in our lives. In other words, the lack of Christ's presence and His word will disprove our genuineness as believers. This is a clear cut issue: if you can't recognize the presence of Jesus in your life *[Rom.8:16]*, you have failed the test of genuine faith. Friend, we are not talking about attending church regularly, sowing seed or singing in the Choir. Are you making serious moves to draw closer to God or you are drawing further away from him? I trust that you will not be disqualified as you embark on active spiritual check-up today.

PRAYER FOCUS

Dear heavenly Father, my ways are before Your eyes. Help me to see myself through the lens of Your Spirit and purpose in Jesus' name.

February 8

Lining up Your Practice With Your Position
Bible Reading: [Eph.2:1-10]

"Even when we were dead in sins, hath quickened us together with Christ, (by grace ye are saved;). And hath raised us up together, and made us sit together in heavenly places in Christ Jesus:" [Vs:5-6;KJV]

A disciple of Christ is one with a genuine relationship with Him. Somebody once said, "Your attitude determines your altitude". A godly attitude will enable you to make a difference in the world around you. It is written, *"Whatever happens, conduct yourselves in a manner worthy of the gospel of Christ...," [Phil.1:27].*

In order for one to reign with Christ in the heavenly places, one must first of all be crucified and buried with Him. This exalted position to reign with Christ comes from a resurrected life. It is written, *"Therefore we are buried with him by baptism into death: that like as Christ was raised up from the dead by the glory of the Father, even so we also should walk in newness of life." [Rom.6:4;KJV].* Beloved, no man can reign with Christ in the heavenly places without newness of life. Our attitude must be in alignment with our position. Reigning with Christ in the heavenly places also implies that we are blessed with every spiritual blessing in the heavenly places *[Eph.1:3].* Hallelujah!

PRAYER FOCUS

Dear heavenly Father, I acknowledge that an exalted position requires a godly conduct. LORD, grant that my conduct will reflect my new position in Christ in Jesus' name.

February 9

Adopting The Mind Of Christ
Bible Reading: [Phil.2:5-11]

"Let this mind be in you which was also in Christ Jesus, who, being in the form of God, did not consider it robbery to be equal with God, but made Himself of no reputation, taking the form of a bondservant, and coming in the likeness of men." [Vs:5-7;NKJV]

Beloved, you can't claim to be a disciple of Christ, but having a different mindset from that of Christ. A mindset is an established set of attitudes. The mindset of Christ is that of a humble attitude in obedience to the Father. Being born of the Spirit of God, implies a disciple has assumed or taken on the attitude of Christ. The carnal attitude was done away by the finished work of Christ on the Cross. It is written, *"I am crucified with Christ: nevertheless I live; yet not I, but Christ liveth in me: and the life which I now live in the flesh I live by faith of the Son of God, who loved me, and gave himself for me." [Gal.2:20;KJV]*. Hallelujah!

Jesus Christ being God, humbled Himself to the position of man in order to fulfill God's plan of Salvation for humanity. True disciples of Christ must follow the attitude of Christ by submitting themselves to one another *[Eph.5:21]*. Exalting oneself above fellow brothers or Sisters in Christ is a carnal attitude. As disciples, we must love others as Christ loved us. This implies that we must act in unison with all members with the understanding that being in Christ is by grace and depends on the function we have in Body. *"For who hath known the mind of the LORD, that He may instruct him? But we have the mind of Christ." [1 Cor.2:16;KJV]*. Because we have the mind of Christ, let's function in the Body and the world with the attitude of Christ.

PRAYER FOCUS

Dear heavenly Father, help me to function in the Body of Christ with humility of mind, to edify others and not to tear them down in order to make myself better in Jesus' name.

February 10

When Jesus Is In The House
Bible Reading: [Luke 19:1-10]

"And when Jesus came to the place, he looked up, and saw him, and said unto him, Zacchaeus, make haste, and come down; for today I must abide at thy house." [Vs:5]

Our expectations in life certainly differ based on who we allow to come in. Personalities differ as well, and even children or siblings raised up in the same family may turn out very differently from each other. Jesus does not change regardless of the situation in the house. However, his power is made manifest based on the need of every house. To allow Jesus in is a matter of choice. The good news is that Jesus knocks at the door of every house. He is always ready to come in, but will never force himself on anyone. It is written, *"Behold, I stand at the door, and knock: if any man hear my voice, and open the door, I will come in to him, and will sup with him, and he with me." [Rev.3:20;KJV].*

Beloved, what are your expectations? The truth is that He comes in every house/heart in order to bring change. Like the case of the Pharisees, Jesus' presence will always result in a struggle within especially to those who enjoy their comfort zone, who hold unto the traditions of the fathers or who like to maintain the status quo. Regardless of what happens, Jesus' presence will always result in a positive change. When Jesus is in the house one can expect the following:

- Salvation: This day has salvation come to this house *[Vs:9;Heb.7:25].*
- Order: Jesus Christ is not the author of confusion. He entered the temple courts and drove out all who were buying and selling there *[Matt.21:12].* Expect the power of mammon [spirit of materialism/money] and any evil company to be broken.
- Healing & restoration: *"And when Jesus was come into Peter's house, he saw his wife's mother laid, and sick of a fever. And he touched her hand, and the fever left her: and she arose, and minister unto them [Matt.8:14-15].*
- Protection: *[Lk. 8:22-24; Ps.27:5].*

We can expect many wonderful things to happen when Jesus is in the house. Beloved, is Jesus enthroned in your house/heart?

PRAYER FOCUS

Dear heavenly Father, Your presence in my house is indispensable. I acknowledge Your headship and declare Your Lordship over all in Jesus' name

February 11

I'm Not What I Used To Be
Bible Reading: [1 Tim.1:12-17]

"Although I was formerly a blasphemer, a persecutor, and an insolent man; but I obtained mercy because I did it ignorantly in unbelief. And the grace of God was exceedingly abundant, with faith and love which are in Christ." [Vs:13-14]

Every genuine conversion to Christ has a beautiful testimony that goes with it. Have you ever taken time to sincerely thank God for what He has done for you? As a matter of fact, the devil would like to steal our peace and joy by reminding us of our disgusting past and put us in a very awkward situation. Beloved, you've got a reason to celebrate what the LORD has done in your life as a disciple of Christ. It is written, *"He has delivered us from the power of darkness and conveyed us into the kingdom of the Son of His love, in whom we have redemption through His blood, the forgiveness of sins." [Col.1:30;NKJV]*. All genuine disciples have been transferred from slavery to freedom, from the dominion of darkness to light, from guilt to forgiveness and from the power of Satan to the power of God [hallelujah!]. What a joy to serve the purpose of a rightful king!

Beloved, there is no reason to be guilty-ridden, condemned or held in bondage again by the power of the evil one if you have genuinely repented of your sins. It's written, *"For you did not receive the spirit of bondage again to fear, but you received the Spirit of adoption by whom we cry out, Abba, Father" [Rom.8:15]*. The man born blind answered the Pharisees, *"Whether He[Jesus] is a sinner or not I do not know. One thing I know: that though I was blind, now I see." [Jn.9:25]*. Every true disciple needs to make such a bold confession today: I'm not what I used to be!

PRAYER FOCUS

Dear heavenly Father, I am confident of this one thing, that He who has begun a good work in me will complete it until the day of the LORD in Jesus' name.

February 12

The Power Of Right Fasting
Bible Reading: [Isaiah 58:1-14]

"Is not this the fast that I have chosen? To loose the bands of wickedness, to undo the heavy burdens, and to let the oppressed go free, and that ye break every yoke? Then shall thy light break forth as the morning, and thine health shall spring forth speedily: and thy righteousness shall go before thee; the glory of the LORD shall be thy rearward." [Vs: 6&8]

Fasting is a spiritual exercise that should be cherished by all genuine disciples of Christ. While some problems can be solved by prayer, others cannot be solved by mere prayer except we combine fasting with prayers *[Matt.17:21]*. Fasting is essentially the giving up of food and/or drink for a period of time in order to focus on God and please Him. The practice of right fasting releases tremendous power, while wrong fasting is such a nuisance to God *[Zech.7:5]*. Fasting is not a mere religious activity by which men perform pious acts, but it involves self-denial, repentance, charity and other righteous acts. Beloved, are you deceived by right rituals that do not please God or destroy relationship with him?

True fasting is beyond the performing of right spiritual rituals for personal edification. It creates awareness of injustice and leads to honor through obedience. Oftentimes we perform the right spiritual ritual but get no response from God because of insincerity. While king David humbled himself with fasting *[Ps 35:13]*, some of us instead practice false humility. The true spirit of fasting that releases tremendous power involves sincere humility, regard for the needy, a life-style of mercy and a righteous attitude. A true response to God's Will, will cause God to respond with His presence. His presence refreshes us physically and spiritually. May your light break forth today as the morning, and your health spring forth speedily.

PRAYER FOCUS

Dear heavenly Father, You desire mercy, and not sacrifice. LORD, as I humble myself with fasting, grant that I will please You by reaching to society with acts of kindness and justice in Jesus' name.

February 13

Renewed Strength For Slack Hands
Bible Reading: [Zep.3:8-20]

"In that day it shall be said to Jerusalem, fear thou not: fear thou not: and to Zion, Let not thine hands be slack. The LORD thy God in the midst of thee is mighty; he will save, he will rejoice over thee with joy; he will rest in his love, he will joy over thee with singing." [Vs: 17;KJV]

God is our source of strength when we allow Him to live in us. Beloved, it is important to note that our hands become slack whenever we break fellowship with God by living in sin or we entertain the threat of our enemy. It is written, *"For they all made us afraid, saying, their hands shall be weakened from the work, that it be not done. Now therefore, O God, strengthen my hands." [Neh.6:9;KJV].*

From generation to generation, self-reliance and pride weakened the resolve of the Israelites. They became fearful and insecure whenever they broke fellowship with God. Like the remnant of Israel in the days of Zephaniah, whenever we realize ourselves and grieved over our inability to be in the assembly of God, we can rest assured that:

He will forgive us and grant deliverance from the bondage of sin because of genuine repentance.

He will grant us restoration from any form of captivity and turn our shame into glory and fame. A renewed covenant relationship with God today will make all the difference. He rejoices over those who offer themselves to Him. Be strong in heart and hands today as you allow His Spirit to fill your life today.

PRAYER FOCUS

Dear heavenly Father, I put my trust in You. I am confident that I can do all things through Christ who strengthens me in Jesus' name.

February 14

The Greatness Of God's Plan
Bible Reading: [Eph.3:1-21]

"For this cause I bow my knees unto the Father of our LORD Jesus Christ, Of whom the whole family in heaven and earth is named." [Vs:14-15]

God's overall plan for humanity is too great that no human mind can fully understand. Those who have been chosen by God perform a unique role that He has called them to play in His plan. God's fullness is expressed only in Christ. Having Christ or making His home in our hearts is the source of spiritual power for life. Our Christian life can't be successful without this experience and personal knowledge of God's grace, love and power by the presence of Christ within us.

It has pleased the Father to reveal the mystery of His kingdom. And Jesus said to His disciples, *"To you has been entrusted the mystery of the kingdom of God [that is, that is the secret counsels of God which are hidden from the ungodly]; but for those outside everything becomes a parable."* [Mk 4:1,Amp.]. About God's great plan, Scripture says, *"Even the mystery which hath been hid from ages and from generations, but now is made manifest to His saints"*[Col.1:26;KJV]. His great plan has been revealed to Gentiles and Jews alike. Considering this amazing salvation that God's grace has brought to undeserving sinners, it's humbling to say like Paul, *"For this reason I kneel before the Father, from whom His whole family in heaven and on earth derives its name."* Hallelujah! Beloved, are you a part of this great family in union with Christ?

PRAYER FOCUS

Dear heavenly Father, Your power and essence are far beyond man's imagination. LORD, with confidence, I come under Your headship and worship Your majesty in Jesus' name.

February 15

The Secrets Of Asking & Receiving
Bible Reading: [Mark 11:20-26]

"For verily I say unto you, that whosoever shall say unto this mountain, Be thou removed, and be thou cast into the sea; and shall not doubt in his heart, but shall believe that those things which he saith shall come to pass; he shall have whatsoever he saith." [Vs:23;KJV]

Scripture tells us that we shall receive what we ask for *[Matt.7:7]*. How true is this in real life? As a matter of fact, every covenant [born again] Child of God has the privilege to access His throne of grace in times of need because of the blood of the Lamb and the finished work on the Cross. Our heavenly Father is committed to give us what we ask for. Every good and perfect gift is from above, coming down from Him *[Jam.1:17]*. Nevertheless, why don't we receive what we ask for every time we approach Him in prayer? Today, I would like us to consider some of the reasons why we don't get what we ask for:

- Lack of forgiveness: The heavens are closed wherever lack of forgiveness reigns. God does not answer prayers that come from an unforgiving heart *[Matt.6:15]*
- Lack of Faith: Without faith, it's impossible to please God *[Heb.11:6]*. We must pray in faith without doubting. Scripture describes he who doubts as the wave of the sea driven and tossed by the wind *[Jam.1:6]*
- Wrong motives: You ask and do not receive because you ask amiss *[Jam.4:3]*. When our motives are selfish and corrupt, we shouldn't expect any good thing from God in prayers.
- Impatience: Not willing to wait for something to happen and becoming irritated or disappointed at delays. Remember that the promises of God are inherited by faith and patience *[Heb.6:12]* Cherishing iniquity in the heart: Unresolved issues of sin in our hearts don't only hinder God from hearing us, but also give the devil a legal right to harm or interrupt our *destiny [Ps 66:18; Isa.59:1]*. Asking in His name: Whenever we asked for something in the name of Jesus, the Father is glorified in the Son *[John 14:13]*. "And whatsoever ye do in word or deed, do all in the name of the LORD Jesus, giving thanks to God and the Father by him." *[Col.1:17]*

Having God's interest in mind and praying for the fruitfulness of His kingdom will make all the difference in our prayer life. It is written, *"And this is the confidence that we have in him, that, if we ask anything according to His will, He heareth us." [1 John 5:14;KJV]*

PRAYER FOCUS

Dear heavenly Father, I come before You with a forgiving heart and put my total trust in You. LORD, I'm confident that if I ask anything according to Your will, You'll answer me. In Jesus' name.

February 16

Your Waiting Season Is Over
Bible Reading: [Psalm 123:1-4]

"Behold, as the eyes of servants look to the hand of their master, As the eyes of a maid to the hand of her mistress, So our eyes look to the LORD our God, Until He is gracious to us." [Vs: 2; NASB]

Beloved, we all wait upon the LORD for something: renewed strength, life partner, job, baby, and so forth. Regardless of what each one of us is waiting for, sometimes it's easy to have feelings of discouragement when things don't go as planned or dreams seem to delay. Every disciple of Christ experiences a season of waiting at one moment in time. Waiting upon the LORD is an active and not a passive exercise. It's not idling or sitting around doing nothing. As a true disciple of Christ, you spend time praying and meditating on God's word and precious promises. Waiting is an exercise of trust and develops character [patience] in anyone who sincerely waits upon the LORD. Waiting doesn't last forever.

Beloved, you have waited long enough. God is gracious to you today. The goodness is that your waiting season is over. It is time to break camps and move on. It is time to testify of the goodness of God in the congregation of the saints. It is time to sing a new song, even praise unto our God. The Psalmist says, *"I waited patiently for the LORD; and he inclined unto me, and heard my cry. He brought me up also out of a horrible pit, out of the miry clay, and set my feet upon a rock, and established my goings." [Ps.40:1-2;KJV]*. Hallelujah!

PRAYER FOCUS

Dear heavenly Father, thank You for having renewed my strength. Today, I leap for joy being confident that no man can reverse what You have done for me, and that no purpose of Yours can be thwarted in Jesus' name.

February 17

Influence Of Evil Associations On Spiritual Well-being
Bible Reading: [Hosea 7:1-10]

"Ephraim has mixed himself among the people; Ephraim is a cake not turned. Strangers have devoured his strength, and he knoweth it not: yea, gray hairs are here and there upon, yet he knoweth not." [Vs: 7-9]

For the most part, each one of us would like to have a partner or colleague in business or at work/school. It's important to note that God does not call out any man to live in isolation. However, for the sake of spiritual wellbeing, every disciple of Christ must consider his or her associations. It is obvious that the closer you get to a godless people, sooner or later, you will pick up their attitudes and start imitating their actions. Are you born again and a disciple of Christ? If yes, God has committed to you the message of reconciliation *[2 Cor.5:17-19]*. The LORD prayed to the Father for all His disciples, *"I do not pray that you should take them out of the world, but that You should keep them from the evil one." [John.17:15;NKJV]*

Beloved, there is no neutral zone in the world. Either you point men to God or men influence you negatively by pointing the world and it's pleasures to you. The devil did that to Our LORD Jesus and said to Him, *"All these things will I give thee if thou wilt fall down and worship me." [Matt.4:9]*. Like the Israelites, many Christians have become powerless, their strength has been sapped by evil associations without them knowing. No doubt, nowadays many churches are dead but having the reputation of being alive *[Rev.3:1]*. Many believers have reached the end of their existence with little or nothing to show off their faith. Beloved, is this your condition? Dissociate from evil destroying your spiritual wellbeing and return to the LORD *[Isa.55:7]*.

PRAYER FOCUS

Dear heavenly Father, I acknowledge the fact that bad company corrupts good character *[1 Cor.15:33]*. Have mercy upon me and help me to disconnect from evil associations in Jesus' name.

February 18

Snare of Following
God's Instructions Halfheartedly
Bible Reading: [2 Kings 13:14-21]

"And Elijah said, take the arrows. And he took them. And he said unto the king of Israel, Smite upon the ground. And he smite thrice, and stayed. And the Man of God was wroth with him, and said, thou shouldest have smitten five or six times; then hadst thou smitten Syria till thou has consumed it: whereas now thou shalt smite Syria but thrice." [Vs:18-19]

Many Christians have cultivated the habit of following God's instructions halfheartedly. The words obedience and consistency are lacking in their vocabularies. A man after God's heart is one who follows God's instructions fully. It is written, *"The instructions of the LORD are perfect, reviving the soul. The decrees of the LORD are trustworthy, making wise the simple."* [Psalm 19:7;nlt]. Our souls are revived when we follow the instructions of God fully. Following divine instructions gives a man new strength or energy. In other words, you faint as a believer if you don't follow. God is committed to strengthen those who follow him *wholeheartedly [2 Chr.16:9]*

The prophet Elisha gave the king a simple instruction. This prophetic action was to give Israel an upper hand or complete victory over Aram. Like the king of Israel, have you stop striking after three shots? Do you wonder why the same problem keeps occurring? The answer is simple; you gave once, but stopped, you fasted once, but stopped, you evangelized once and stopped. You studied hard once, but stopped. Remember how Elijah prayed for rain on mount Camel, bowing low to the ground with his face between his knees. He stopped after the seventh time, when his servant saw a little cloud rising from the sea *[1 Kgs.18:41-45]*.

Beloved, has God asked you to stop? Why are you not consistent? Why don't you follow through to the end? By striking the ground only three times, king Jehoash unknowingly, limited his own success against the Arameans. Final victory came only later in the days of his son *[2 Kgs.14:25-28]*. Friend, don't limit your breakthrough in life because of halfhearted commitment.

PRAYER FOCUS

Dear heavenly Father, it's my desire to be a man after Your heart. I repent of my halfhearted commitment to Your instructions. Grant me the grace to follow You wholeheartedly *[Num.14:24]* in Jesus' name.

February 19

God's Word Come Alive
Bible Reading: [Ps 119:129-136]

*"The entrance of thy Words giveth light;
it giveth understanding unto the simple." [Ps 119:130, KJV]*

The most ignorant and unlearned persons who are willing to learn will certainly come out of darkness. When God's Word comes alive, darkness can't overcome it *[John 1:5]*. We all need instruction from God to enable us discern between right and wrong. Nowadays, the challenge is that many don't find God's Word marvelous. They only go after it when in dire need. The Word does two important things when opened in the life of a person: It gives light and direction.

Do you wonder why many are still in darkness? The answer is simple; the Word has not yet come alive in them and their situation. It is written, *"See, darkness covers the earth and thick darkness is over the peoples but the LORD rises upon you and his glory appears over you." [Isa.60:2;NIV]*. It's so amazing to see God's Word come alive in the hearts of those who hear it.

The Word needs to come alive today, so that the oppressed might be set free. Simon held Samaria captive for a long time through the practice of sorcery [witchcraft]. When the Word came alive through the preaching of Philip, many were delivered, healed, and there was great joy in the city *[Acts 8:4-8]*. Hallelujah!

PRAYER FOCUS

Dear heavenly, in Your presence there is revelation of Your power and might. LORD, may Your Word come alive to me today in Jesus' name.

February 20

Gratitude Creates A Future
Bible Reading: [Job 10:8-12]

"You have granted me life and favor,
And Your care has preserved my spirit." [Vs: 12;NKJV]

No matter the situation, each one of us has so much to be grateful for in this life. We can't return God's care with ingratitude. In the midst of busyness and the pressures of life, pause today and give thanks to God for all that he has done. One thing that ingratitude does is that it destroys a person's ability to celebrate the good things in life. Live with gratitude today. You might be getting less than expected, but don't allow envy, resentment and resignation rob your future. Remember that gratitude makes sense of our past and opens the window of peace for today.

In the midst of Jacob fears to meet his brother whom he cheated *[Gen.27:32]*, he reminded the LORD of his promises and concluded, *"I am unworthy of all the kindness and faithfulness you have shown your servant. I had only my staff when I crossed this Jordan, but now I have become two camps." [Gen.32:10;NIV]*. Just imagine how much favor God gave him when he finally met Esau. It is written, *"Whoso offereth praise glorifieth me: and to him that ordereth his conversation aright will I shew the salvation of God." [Ps 50:23;KJV]*. May God show you his salvation as you celebrate the goodness of life today with a thankful heart.

PRAYER FOCUS

Dear heavenly Father, for all that You have done, going to do, and all that You have carried me through, I say thank You.

February 21

Snare Of Forcing Jesus Into Your Own Mold
Bible Reading: [John 6:15-21]

"When Jesus therefore perceived that they would come and take him by force, to make him a king, he departed again into a mountain himself alone."
[Vs 15, KJV]

In our fast-paced world, many Christians have cultivated the attitude of forcing Jesus into their molds. Oftentimes, this is due to impatience. Forcing Jesus into your mold implies you want Him to take a particular direction or form. You want Him to look like something else or behave in a particular way. You want Him to do things outside His own will. You want him to act in a particular way at a particular time to satisfy your desire or interest. Beloved, are you forcing Jesus into Your own mold? Know for sure that he won't fit. Remember that Jesus is not your servant, but LORD and Master. You are not the owner of your life, but Jesus is the creator. He is the one leading. It is written, *"For as many as are led by the Spirit of God, they are the sons of God." [Rom.8:14]*

After the miracle of feeding five thousand men with five barley loaves and two small fish, the people wanted to force Him into an earthly kingship but He departed again into a mountain. When they ran out of wine at the wedding in Cana, Jesus' mother made a request because she knew her son would do something about it. Nevertheless, Jesus told her, *"My hour has not yet come."[John 2:4]*.

When someone said to Him that His mother and brothers were standing outside, seeking to speak to you, He disclosed his true family *"For whoever does the will of my Father in heaven, is My brother and sister and mother." [Matt.12:50]*. Jesus can't fit into someone's mold. Only His counsel shall stand *[Isa.46:10]*, not yours, not Satan/cohorts or anyone else. Hallelujah!

PRAYER FOCUS

Dear heavenly Father to whom all praise is due, today, I bow my knee before You. LORD, may my will be lost in thine in Jesus' name.

February 22

Restorer Of Wasted Years
Bible Reading: [Joel 2:12-29]

"And I will restore to you the years that the locusts hath eaten, the cankerworm, and the caterpillar, and the palmerworm, my great army which I sent among you." [Vs: 25;KJV]

Somebody is saying today in His or her heart, "I can never make up for all those wasted years." Beloved, for whatever reason that your years became wasted, only God's forgiveness will bring rejoicing and restoration. No matter what you have lost, God promises restoration. God is working behind the scenes to bring complete restoration: the restoration of your spiritual life, your marriage, health, business, and the regular pattern of rainfall in your community.

This is your season of restoration. God is restoring the fortunes of his people and will have compassion upon you. He is the God of double restoration. It is written, *"And the LORD turned the captivity of Job, when he prayed for his friends; also the LORD gave Job twice as much as he had before." [Job.42:10;KJV]* *"For your shame ye shall have double " [Isa.61:7;KJV].* Like David who recovered everything the Amalekites had taken *[1 Sam.30:18]*, may you recover all that you have lost. In Jesus' name.

PRAYER FOCUS

Dear heavenly Father; the course of my life is in Your power. I receive double restoration and recovery today in Jesus' name.

February 23

Snare Of A Proud Attitude
Bible Reading: [Obad.1:1-17]

"Behold, I have made thee small among the heathen: thou art greatly despised. The pride of thine heart hath deceived thee, thou that dwellest in the clefts of the rock, whose habitation is high; that saith in his heart, Who shall bring me down to the ground?" [Vs:2-3;KJV]

Pride goes before destruction and a haughty spirit before a fall. Because of the deceitful nature of the heart, every disciple of Christ has the responsibility to guard his or her heart above all else. The saying goes, "Once you reach the top, take care as the only way left to go is down." [Source: Unknown]. Today, I would like us to look at the two sides of the same coin of pride. Firstly, holding oneself in very high regard because of great attainment or remarkable success.

Secondly, rejoicing in the downfall of others especially those you consider rivals.

Edomites and Israelites were descendants of Esau and Jacob respectively. The Edomites became proud because their city was carved right into the rock. The rocky topography made it impossible for any invading army to invade the city. Thus, the Edomites enjoyed natural protection from all their enemies. Edom became a tourist attraction and the Edomites felt secured. They also rejoiced in the fall of their brother Israel.

Like the Edomites, many people have a false sense of security and fail to depend on God for protection and provision. Beloved, have you arrived? Like the fall of Edom, so will proud people fall. It is written, *"But he giveth more grace. Wherefore he saith, God resisteth the proud, but giveth grace unto the humble." [Jam.4:6;KJV]*. King Nebuchadnezzar was given a beast's heart because of pride *[Dan.4:17]*. Stay humble today and enjoy the grace of God. Hallelujah!

PRAYER FOCUS

Dear heavenly Father, You resist the proud, but give grace to the humble person. LORD, help me to serve Your purpose with great humility in Jesus' name.

February 24

Come Out & Be Separate
Bible Reading: [Ezra 10:1-12]

"Then Ezra the priest stood up and said to them, "You have transgressed and have taken pagan wives, adding to the guilt of Israel. Now therefore, make confession to the LORD God of your fathers, and do His will, separate yourselves from the peoples of the land, and from the pagan wives." [Vs:10-21]

The command to separate oneself from the people of the land is not old fashion. Nowadays, it's difficult to draw a line between a believer in Christ and an unbeliever. Many believers [born again] do just the same things and go to the same places like the people of the world. If you are born again, this is God's word for you: You have not received the spirit of the world, but the Spirit who is from God *[1 Cor.2:12]*. Do not conform to the pattern of this world, but be transformed by the renewing of your mind *[Rom.12:2]*. Come out from among them, and be ye separate, says the LORD *[2 Cor.6:17]*. If you are not born again, repent and receive the live and love of God through Christ our LORD.

Consecration means separation of oneself from things that affect one's relationship with a perfect and holy God. Ezra led the people to a God honoring decision. They were determined to do the right thing and made a covenant to put away pagan wives and any unclean thing. Beloved, what are you determined to put away in order to enjoy sweet communion with God? Your relationship with God can't be forfeited for anything less and you can't settle for anything less than God's best. Come out and be separate while grace abounds.

PRAYER FOCUS

Dear heavenly Father, better is one day in Your presence than a thousand elsewhere. LORD, I acknowledge my unfaithfulness and ask for forgiveness. Today, I make a covenant to put away anything that affects my relationship and walk with You in Jesus' name.

February 25

The Reason For Our Hope
Bible Reading: [1 Cor.15:12-20]

"But if there be no resurrection of the dead, then is Christ not risen: And if Christ not risen, then our preaching vain, your faith also vain. And if Christ be not raised, your faith is vain; he are yet in your sins."
[Vs: 13,14,17]

Have you ever been in a situation where you believed in something that ended up being false? Billions of people on earth are still believing in many things [religion, theories, philosophies etc.], that will be proven untrue in the process of time. If you are still considering the resurrection of Christ to be an illusion, that is, "a thing that is likely to be wrongly perceived", there is good news for you. In our text, Paul was writing to a people who had a culture that did not believe in bodily resurrection after death *[John 5:29]*.

Beloved, the resurrection of Christ is the center of Christianity. Christ's resurrection assures of the future resurrection. His resurrection is a proof that His sacrifice has fully atoned for our sins *[Heb.10:10]*. We are no longer guilty and under God's judgment if we have genuinely repented of our sins *[Rom.5:1;8:1]*. We are no longer under the dominating power of sin and death *[Heb.2:14]*.

After all the persecution and deprivation from the pleasures of the world as a believer, there is so much to hope for: resurrection unto life, to be with the LORD forever [eternal life]. Of the blessings of His resurrection, Paul says, *"That I may know him, and the power of his resurrection, and the fellowship of his sufferings, being made conformable unto his death [Phil.3:10;KJV].* Hallelujah!

PRAYER FOCUS

Dear heavenly Father, I believe that Christ died, resurrected, and ascended into heaven. Father, help me daily to work out my salvation with fear and trembling *[Philip.2:12]* in Jesus' name.

February 26

The WORD Can't Be Chained
Bible Reading: [Acts 23:1-22]

"And the night following the LORD stood by, and said, Be of good cheer, Paul: for as thou hast testified of me in Jerusalem, so must thou bear witness also at Rome." [Vs:11;KJV]

Every true disciple of Christ needs encouragement at one moment or the other. It's important to note that Paul was under fire for his faith and everything was against him. However, the LORD assured him that he would go to Rome. Talking about the persecution believers in Christ go through wouldn't be a comforting experience to many in the world. Against all odds, we must move against the wishful thinking of our enemies and be confident in the power of God who assigns us. As usual, Satan continued working against Paul by raising forty men to kill him *[2 Thes.3:2]*. Beloved, whatever conspiracy made against you, let it backfire in the name of Jesus Christ.

The gospel can't be chained, likewise God's spokesman. It is written, *"Behold, they shall surely gather together, but not by me: whosoever shall gather together against thee shall fall for the sake." [Isa.54:15;KJV]*. God takes pleasure to reveal His greater plan to us in order that no faithful witness of His might miss out on what He is going to do. Your mission is too important to compromise your conviction or bow to the threat of the enemy. The joy of the LORD is your strength.

PRAYER FOCUS

Dear heavenly Father, may You accomplish Your purpose through me to take the gospel to the next community and pass it on to the next generation in Jesus' name.

February 27

Power Of Divine Exodus
Bible Reading: [Psalm 114:1-8]

"Tremble, O earth, at the presence of the LORD, at the presence of the God of Jacob. Who turned the rock into pool, the hard rock into springs of water."
[Vs:7-8;NIV]

Whatever your captivity or stagnation, there is a divine direction and design to put honor on you. Like the Israelites, many are stuck, lacking the ability to move from where they are to where God has planned for their lives. When God has decreed that it is time to move, even nature can't stop him! God totally controls all His creation. He divided the red sea in order to deliver His people from captivity. He divided the Jordan river in order that the Israelites might enter into the promised land. The presence of God is indispensable in our lives *[Exod.33:15]*.

Friend, are you saved? Have you surrendered to Christ as your LORD and Savior? God takes delight to dwell in you. May God's presence cause every mountain before you to quake and let the Angels of the LORD chase your enemies in Jesus' name *[Ps 35:5]*. It is written, *"The wicked flee when no man pursueth: but the righteous are bold as a lion." [Prov.28:1;KJV]*.

And it came to pass, when the ark set forward, that Moses said, Rise up, LORD, and let thine enemies be scattered; and let them that hate thee flee before thee." *[Num.10:35;KJV]*. This is your season of exodus. Hallelujah!

PRAYER FOCUS

Dear heavenly Father, I'm fully persuaded that Your presence is with me to usher me into my promised land in Jesus' name.

February 28

Agonizing Under The Threat Of Opposition
Bible Reading: [Neh.4:1-23]

"And it came to pass, when our enemies heard that it was known unto us, and God had brought their counsel to nought, that we returned all of us to the wall, every one unto his work."[Neh.4:15;KJV]

Whenever the enemy realizes that you are on the right track with God's purpose or project, he will certainly do everything to raise opposition. Sometimes people give up when opposition becomes too intense. God does not want His generals to become discouraged because of pressure and abandon their mission. It is written, *"Lest Satan should get an advantage of us: for we are not ignorant of his devices." [2 Cor.2:11;KJV].*

Whatever the assignment, focusing on the task God has given should be our primary concern. Except one is not truly commissioned by God, opposition is obvious. The goal of the enemy is to lower one's morale for the work. However, every disciple of Christ should learn how to rely on God and do what is needed. Are you born of God? There is good news for you: *"For whatsoever is born of God overcometh the world: and this is the victory that overcometh the world, even our faith." [1 John 5:4].*

Like Nehemiah, for any divine project, we must apply faith and wisdom. We must pray, prepare, plan and be watchful for the work of Satan and associates *[Isa.59:19]*. Set your heart on the work today and be confident that God will fight for you *[Vs:20;Isa.54:17]*. You agonize by putting forth great effort of any kind especially in the place of prayer. God accomplishes great things through the hands of those who are determined to labor for His divine plan.

PRAYER FOCUS

Dear heavenly Father, You are the great and glorious God. I'm confident in Your power to protect me from the attack of the enemy. LORD, I receive strength from You as I position myself to take my assignment/project to the finish line in Jesus' name.

February 29

Power Of Prevailing Prayer
Bible Reading: [James 5:15-20]

"....,The effectual fervent prayer of a righteous man availeth much." [Vs:16;KJV]

There is no denying the fact that prayer is an important aspect of a successful Christian living. Prayer is not learned in a classroom but in the closet [E.M Bounds]. Fervent prayer is the result of a righteous man in a sacred [holy] chamber. D. L. Moody said, "He who kneels the most, stands the best." Beloved, do you kneel down in prayer or you expect others to do praying for you? Prevailing prayer is one that is effective or effectual. If there is a man to pray, certainly, there is God to answer. Let's look at a few reasons why prayers are not effective:

- When sin is a hindering factor: *[Isa.59:1]*
- When we pray with wrong motives *[Jam.4:3]*
- When our prayers don't align with God's will *[Eph.1:11]*.
- Lacking faith and not being persistent *[Mk 11:24; Rom.12:11]*

Although a prophet, Elijah was an ordinary man with faith in God like any believer in Christ. One biblical character that each one of us ought to emulate is the man called Epaphras, a servant of Christ, always laboring fervently for the saints in prayers *[Col.4:12]*. It's important to note that if we ask anything according to God's will, He hears us! Hallelujah!

PRAYER FOCUS

Dear heavenly Father, there is nothing too hard for you. LORD, help me to be sensitive to the voice of Your Spirit and use me as a battle axe *[Jer.51:20-21]* in Jesus' name.

MARCH

"Though the mountains be shaken and the hills be removed, yet my unfailing love for you will not be shaken nor my covenant of peace be removed," says the LORD, who has compassion on you."

[Isaiah 54.10; NIV]

"The LORD hath appeared of old unto me, saying, yea, I have loved thee with an everlasting love: therefore with loving-kindness have I drawn thee."

[Jeremiah 31:3; KJV]

****

Jehovah Shalom - **[The LORD is Peace]** - Judges 6:24

3 = [True Nature Of God / God's Perfect Design]

March 1

Enjoying an Atmosphere Of Peace
Bible Reading: [Acts 9:23-31]

"Then had the Churches rest throughout all Judaea and Galilee and Samaria, and were edified; and walking in the fear of the LORD, and in the comfort of the Holy Ghost, were multiplied."[Vs:31;KJV]

There is no single person who wouldn't like to enjoy an atmosphere of peace, except the devil and associates. The devil comes to steal, kill and destroy. However, Jesus Christ promises us peace in a chaotic world, full of persecution, pain, political crisis, family challenges. You may find yourself in such situations, so was the early church. From Scriptures, it is obvious that Saul was a valuable instrument in the hands of the devil before his conversion to Christianity. After his conversion, the Christian community did not immediately trust him because of his history of persecuting Christians. I decree a supernatural arrest of anything/anyone that troubles or threatens your destiny in Jesus' name.

Peace is far-fetched from many homes, churches and nations. However, Scriptures reveal what it takes to enjoy an atmosphere of peace. The result of the peace was that the Church was built up in the LORD and walked after the will of God. Nowadays there is no fear of God, no abiding in the truth and no living in holiness, yet men hope to have peace. It's written, *"Righteousness exalted a nation: but sin is a reproach to any people." [Prov.14:34;KJV]*. Let's not expect to have peace while living in sin. In hell there is no peace. Where will you spend eternity? The Psalmist says, *"I will hear what God the LORD will speak: for he will speak peace unto his people, and to his saints: but let them not turn again to folly." [Ps 85:8;KJV]*. In an atmosphere of peace, brethren in Christ are edified, the walk in the fear of God and in the comfort of the Holy Ghost. The outcome is increase. Hallelujah!

PRAYER FOCUS

Dear heavenly Father, help me each passing day to walk in holiness and enjoy the comfort of Your Spirit in Jesus' name.

March 2

Making a Declaration of Faith
Bible Reading: [Jer.32:1-25]

"And thou has said unto me, O LORD God, Buy thee the field for money, and take witnesses; for the city is given into the hand of the Chaldeans." [Vs:25;KJV]

For the most part, disciples of Christ get excited about God's precious promises. How does it feel like when God gives you an instruction to carry out when circumstances are unfavorable?

Sometimes faith in God would make a man act foolishly in the eyes of men. Imagine God telling you to go buy baby dresses when it's obvious that you are barren and doctor's report has confirmed it. In the case of Jeremiah, God instructed him to buy a piece of land that was captured by a strong army. Jeremiah was in prison at the time and certainly, many people thought he was making a foolish investment. That may not be your case. However, God may be telling you submit an application for a job offer that nobody from your race/tribe has ever been selected, or to apply for citizenship when everyone knows your situation is a bad case.

Making a declaration of faith is very important. It must be done in accordance with God's word. Remember that God works all things according to the counsel of His own will *[Eph.1:11]*. It is written, *"Thou shall also decree a thing, and it shall be established unto thee: and the light shall shine upon thy ways." [Job.22:28;KJV]*. After Jeremiah acted in obedience to God's command, he turned to Him in prayer to affirm his faith. *"Ah, LORD God! Behold, You have made the heavens and the earth by your great power and outstretched arm. There is nothing too hard for You." [Vs:17]*. Beloved, your case is different if you are born again? Make an investment today for the future that God has promised you in His word.

PRAYER FOCUS

Dear heavenly Father, You show lovingkindness to thousands and there is nothing too hard for You. I decree and declare that my expectations in the land of the living shall not be cut off in Jesus' name.

March 3

Growing Strong in the Season of Rumors
Bible Reading: [Jer.20:10-13]

"I have heard the many rumors about me. They call me "The man who lives in terror." They threaten, if you say anything, we will report it." Even my old friends are watching me, waiting for a fatal slip" [Vs10, NLT]

This is the day the LORD has made; let's rejoice and be glad in it. Beloved, while we trust that God will give us this day our daily bread, there are many waiting to feed on rumors. Rumors are not new developments. Like in the days of Jesus Christ, so are rumors today. The only difference is that the channels of rumor have multiplied [social media: WhatsApp, Facebook, Twitter etc.]. Rumor [hearsay] is a circulating story or report of uncertain or doubtful truth. Whether the stories are true or false, each one of us must grow strong in the season of rumors. Because rumors spread like their job, they hardly state specifically the source of their information.

The Prophet Jeremiah found himself surrounded by rumor spreaders. Friend, are you moved when you hear a rumor about yourself? The best thing to do is to place your complete trust in the LORD. Jeremiah says, *"But The LORD stands beside me like a great warrior. Before him my persecutors will stumble. They cannot defeat me..,"* [Vs:11]. It's important to note that rumors fade when exposed to the light. Choose today to live out the truth and you shall see your persecutors humiliated.

PRAYER FOCUS

Dear heavenly Father, I am confident that You are standing by me like a great warrior. Let every mockery, rumor and conspiracy against me backfire in Jesus' name.

March 4

Keeping Your Motives Right
Bible Reading: [John 12:1-8, KJV]

"The said one of his disciples, Judas Iscariot, Simon's son, which should betray him, why was not this ointment sold for three hundred pence, and [money] given to the poor?" [Vs:4-5]

In this portion of Scripture, we see two characters at the LORD's service. Mary, knowing something was about to happen to the LORD, acted with great respect for Him. Because of her deep devotion and extravagant love for God, she offered a sacrifice by anointing Jesus' feet with a costly perfume, and wiped His feet with her hair. Like King David, she certainly said in her heart, *"I will not sacrifice to the LORD my God offerings that cost me nothing." [2 Sam.24:24]*.

What kind of offering or service do you render to God? What is your motive?

While Mary acted with a pure motive out of reverence for the LORD, Judas Iscariot acted otherwise with a wrong motive, using pious words. *"Why not sell the perfume and money given to the poor?"* As a matter of fact, the love of money had a strong bearing on his *life [1 Tim.6:10]*.

Often we use godly words to hide our true motives. If truly we have nothing to hide, let's match our actions with our words. A thief at heart will certainly become a thief in the open. "Wrong motives are not usually revealed in a day" [James Crumpacker]. Because the heart is deceitful above all things, the LORD searches it, and examines the mind, to reward a man according to what his deeds deserve *[Jer.17:9-10]*

PRAYER FOCUS

Dear heavenly Father, search me and know my heart, try me and know my thoughts. LORD, grant that I will keep a right heart attitude in all that I do in Jesus' name.

March 5

When Resistance to The Holy Spirit Becomes A Norm
Bible Reading: [Acts 7:51-60]

"Ye stiff-necked and uncircumcised in heart and ears, ye do always resist the Holy Ghost: as your father's did, so do ye." [Vs:51;KJV]

The charge that God raised against His people in the wilderness is the same charge He is raising against many Christians today. To you unbeliever [pagan] reading this devotional, you have rejected the gospel and are actively resisting the Holy Spirit. You are heathen at heart and deaf to the truth. Now is the time of God's favor! Resistance means refusal to accept or comply with something [Gospel]. Dear believer in Christ, why do you always resist the Holy Spirit, but profess Jesus as your LORD and Savior? It is written, *"For as many as are led by the Spirit of God, they are the sons of God." [Rom.8:14;KJV].*

A norm is something that is usual. It's a pattern that is considered as typical of something or someone. Many believers have become as stubborn as King Saul. They can hardly be led by the Holy Ghost. They will give every reason and make excuses to justify their actions. When the Holy Spirit prompts their hearts on giving, intercession, evangelism, and other acts of righteousness, they will resist. Are you such a one, obstinately resisting the Holy Spirit and rejecting the truth? The Prophet told King Saul, *"For rebellion is as the sin of witchcraft, and stubbornness is as iniquity and idolatry. Because thou hast rejected the word of the LORD, he hath also rejected thee from being king."[1 Sam.15:23;KJV].* If the word of the LORD has become a reproach to you and you have no delight in it, repent! *[Isa.63:10].* Today is the day of God's favor. Hallelujah!

PRAYER FOCUS

Dear heavenly Father, Your word, he who covers his sins will not prosper, but whoever confesses and forsakes them will have mercy *[Prov.28:13].* LORD, I yield myself to You and the prompting of Your Spirit in Jesus' name.

March 6

Gaining Strength
In The Place Of Active Waiting
Bible Reading: [Isaiah 40:28-31]

"But they that wait upon the LORD shall renew their strength; they shall mount up with wings as eagles; they shall run, and not be weary; and they shall walk, and not faint." [Vs 31, KJV]

It's a terrible thing for somebody to keep moving when he/she does not know the way or what to do. No matter how strong and brave we are, as humans, at times we get tired and can't go another step. After the great exploit and victory on mount Carmel against the prophets of Baal, it is said of Elijah, *"But he himself went a day's journey into the wilderness, and came and sat down under a juniper tree: and he requested for himself that he might die; and said, it is enough; now, O LORD, take away my life; for I am not better than my fathers." [1 Kgs 19:4].* I sense someone feeling like taking a break from marriage, business, ministry and walk with God because of persecution, hardships, or threats from an enemy etc. I declare that in your wilderness condition, you shall find grace *[1 Kgs.19:7]*

Though men may grow weak, God will not fail to give strength to those who wait upon him. God wants each one of us to rise above the challenges and distractions of life. We wait upon the LORD when we can't figure out the way. It is written, *"A man's heart deviseth his way: but the LORD directeth his steps." [Prov.16:9, KJV].* Don't lose sight or focus when you don't know how, where, when. God's promises are sure! Receive His promise of strength and mount up with wings as eagles. His purpose is great than your plans and no purpose of His concerning your life can be thwarted. Hallelujah!

PRAYER FOCUS

Dear heavenly Father, You are not influenced by human limitations. Today, I receive Your blessings of strength in Jesus' name.

March 7

Choose Between the Love of Money & the Good News
Bible Reading: [Acts.3:1-8]

"Then Peter said, Silver and gold have I none; but such as I have given I thee: In the name of Jesus Christ of Nazareth rise up and walk." [Vs 6]

Nowadays there is a feeling of anxiety and discomfort [uneasiness], because of insatiable appetite and the lust of the flesh. Men have become money chasers instead of God chasers. Like the lame man at the gate called beautiful, many have strategically positioned themselves to acquire material possession, instead of receiving the living word.

Beloved, God has something better for you than you could imagine. Oftentimes, what we consider a need may not be our real need from God's viewpoint. While the lame man was expecting to receive something (money), God met his need. Do you know what your real need is? Don't miss out on God because of wrong expectations.

In another portion of Scriptures, a Samaritan woman came to draw water from Jacob's well. She had a wonderful encounter with Jesus. He answered her, *If you knew the gift of God and who it is that asks you for a drink, you would have asked him and he would have given you living water." [John 4:10].* She came to Jacob's well for water, but something much more was there: the fountain of life to offer her living water. A seasoned message (Rhema), is what you need. The Centurion said to Jesus, *"but speak the word only, and my servant shall be healed."* God meets big needs through small acts of obedience. Reposition yourself for God's message this season.

PRAYER FOCUS

Dear heavenly Father, You are the fountain of living water and the bread of life. LORD, I'm fully persuaded You have a message for me today. Speak for Your servant is listening in Jesus name.

March 8

Grasping God's Truth with Your Mind
Bible Reading: [Luke 24:40-48]

"Then he opened their minds so they could understand the Scriptures."
[Vs 45, NIV]

The saying goes, "An idle mind is the devil's workshop or playground". What gets your mind gets you. A mind that is broken is likely unable to hear God's voice and cannot connect to God [John Piper]. The mind is the soulish part of a human being in which thoughts take place and perception and decisions to do good, evil, and the like come to expression [Baker's Evang. Dic.]. As a man thinketh in his heart, so is he *[Prov.23:7]*. When we allow our minds to be distracted by negative thoughts, then we are charting the wrong course for our destiny.

God has given us minds to be able to grasp Scripture, think wisely and glorify Him with our thought life. Scripture states clearly what we should allow to occupy our minds: *"whatsoever things are true, whatsoever things are honest, just, pure, lovely, of good report, — if there be any praise, think on these things." [Philip.4:8]*. In essence, He wants us to be transformed by the renewing of our minds, so that we might be able to prove what is good, acceptable and perfect will of God *[Rom.12:2]*. Jesus opened the minds of his disciples, so that they could understand Scriptures. Beloved, God wants you to grasp Scriptures. To grasp means to seize and hold firmly.

If you are a sinner, repent and receive Scriptures in your heart today. Remember, *"...The testimony of the LORD is sure, making wise the simple." [Ps.19:7]*. Hallelujah!

PRAYER FOCUS

Dear heavenly Father, only Your word has the power to convert the soul and enlighten the eyes. LORD, open my understanding and enlarge my heart to receive more of Your will in Jesus' name.

March 9

Observing the Boundaries of Your Divine Assignment
Bible Reading: [Acts.22:11-21]

"And it came to pass, that, when I was come again to Jerusalem, even while I prayed in the temple, I was in a trance; And saw him saying unto me, Make haste, and get thee quickly out of Jerusalem: for they will not receive thy testimony concerning me." [Vs:17-18]

At the present time, there are two major things that if we don't properly check or prayerfully consider, often causes confusion in the Body of Christ. Firstly, people trying to operate in the grace of others and do what they are not assigned. It is written, *"We have different gifts, according to the grace given to each of us.,"* [Rom.12:6]. Secondly, people wanting to stay or go where they are not assigned. It is written, *"We, however, will not boast beyond proper limits, but will confine our boasting to the field God has assigned to us, a field that reaches even to you."* [2 Cor.10:13;NIV].

God wants us to serve His purpose best with what he has given us and where he has assigned us. While some have one, two, three talents, others have five. While some are sent to a particular city, nation or continent, others are assigned worldwide. Failure to observe God's limits or sphere of influence implies planning to fail with your own strength. God told Paul to quickly leave Jerusalem, for the people will not receive the gospel. A man once told me that as black as he is, he has decided for the devil. With such a person, you don't have to insist, but pray and move on as the Spirit leads. To be effective in Christian service means taking divine instructions to the letter. Are you saved from sin? Are you willing to go? Remember, Paul was at the place of prayer before God spoke to him. Some of us hardly seek God's face through prayer and/or fasting, but expect results. LORD, have mercy!

PRAYER FOCUS

Dear heavenly Father, thank You for the talent/gift bestowed upon my life. LORD, I'm willing to go whenever and wherever You commission me in Jesus' name.

March 10

The Snare Of A Dog Returning To His Vomit
Bible Reading: [2 Pet.2:18-22]

"For if, after they have escaped the pollutions of the world through the knowledge of the LORD and Savior Jesus Christ, they are again entangled in them and overcome, the latter end is worse for them than the beginning [Vs:20]

The dawning of a new month. Beloved, I pray that in all respects you may prosper and be in good health. In this last days, there are two things every true disciple of Christ should be on the lookout: wickedness on the increase and the love of most growing cold *[Matt.24:12]*, time will come when they will not endure sound doctrine *[2 Tim.4:3]*. Friend, by the grace of God, you came out of darkness and once tasted of His goodness. Where did you go wrong that you are again entangled by the same things you renounced and rejected? It is written, *"As a dog returneth to His vomit, so a fool returneth to His folly." [Prov.26:11;KJV].*

Scriptures give us examples of men who loved the world and abandoned the faith. Demas was one of Paul's co-workers but later deserted Paul because he loved world values and *pleasures [2 Tim.4:10]*. Remember that if anyone loves the world, the love of the Father is not in him *[1 Jn.2:15]*. Now the just shall live by faith: but if any man draws back, my soul shall have no pleasure in him." *[Heb.10:38, KJV]*. Consider your ways and return to the LORD, for He will heal your backsliding *[Hos.14:4]*. Hallelujah!

PRAYER FOCUS

Dear heavenly Father, to whom shall I go? You have the words of eternal life. LORD, create in me hatred for wickedness [sin] and love for righteousness in Jesus' name

March 11

Joy Unspeakable - Full Of Glory
Bible Reading: [1 Pet.1:3-12]

"Whom ye have not seen [Jesus Christ], ye love; in whom, though now ye see him not, yet believing, ye rejoice with joy unspeakable and full of glory: Receiving the end of your faith, even the salvation of your souls." [Vs 8-9, KJV]

Are you born again, sanctified by the Spirit and cleansed by the blood of Jesus? If yes, I would like you to know that an inheritance: incorruptible, undefiled, that fades not is kept in heaven for you. But as it is written, *"Eye hath not seen, nor ear heard, neither have entered into the heart of man, the things which God hath prepared for them that love him." [1 Cor.2:9, KJV].* In my Father's house are many mansions: if it were not so, I would have told you. I go to prepare a place for you *[Jn 14:2, KJV].* Hallelujah!

Beloved, no matter the trial you might be going through, it can't outweigh the glorious hope we have in Christ. Trials/temptations only proof the genuineness or determine the sincerity of our faith. It's written, *"But he knoweth the way that I take: when he hath tried me, I shall come forth as goal" [Job.23:10].* Our faith like gold is purified when tested. Faith enables us to trust in God to provide the final reward for a walk of faith. Consider today our final salvation at the glorious appearing of Christ *[1 Jn.3:2],* the inheritance kept for us in heaven, and contend earnestly for the faith that was once delivered unto the saints. Christ in you, the hope of glory!

Are you a sinner? Repent and enjoy this glorious hope!

PRAYER FOCUS

Dear heavenly Father, You knew me and chose me long ago. LORD, I trust that You will keep me by Your power until the end in Jesus' name.

March 12

Be It Unto Me According To Thy Word
Bible Reading: [Luke 1:26-38]

"I am the LORD's servant," Mary answered. "May it be to me as you have said." Then the angel left her. [Vs: 38]

This is your season of visitation. God is working behind the scenes to fulfill His plan for your life. Remember, what man cannot do, God can. God works miraculously to bring to realization that which we can't. Like Mary, our selection by God for a divine visitation is not based on merit.

It's important to note that in her time, there were many young women with the same spiritual qualities and testimony. The grace of God located her. Friend, you are next in line, highly favored and appointed to a specific position in such a time as this.

God works best under humanly impossible circumstances. He does so, far more than we could ever ask or imagine. We may not know exactly what God is bringing our way this season.

However, we must put up the right attitude and reposition ourselves to receive from him. Because God watches over His Word to perform it, like Mary, we must say with a sincere heart, "LORD, I am your servant, be it unto me according to Your word." Don't limit divine opportunities. Believe God's word today.

PRAYER FOCUS

Dear heavenly Father, I come to You as Your servant with an expectant heart.
- LORD, I believe that no good thing will You withhold from them that walk uprightly *[Ps.84:11]* in Jesus' name.

March 13

You Can't Have God's Best Without God's Priorities
Bible Reading: [Isaiah 48:12-19]

"Oh, that you had listened to my commands! Then you would have had peace flowing like a gentle river and righteousness rolling over you like waves in the sea." [Vs:18;nlt]

Our success as Christians is inevitable when we give God's priorities the rightful place in our lives. God's priorities are very clear in the Scriptures. It's written, *"But seek ye first the kingdom of God, and his righteousness; and all these things will be provided for you."* [Matt.6:33, KJV]. It's also written, *"Acquaint now thyself with him, and be at peace: thereby good shall come unto thee."* [Job.22:21]. If evil parents know how to give good gifts to their children, God will certainly do much more!

As a disciple of Christ, do you create time to discover God's priorities from the Scriptures? This is what the LORD says —— your Redeemer, the Holy One of Israel: *"I am the LORD your God, who teaches you what is best for you, who directs you in the way you should go."* [Isa.48:17, NIV].

Beloved, God's principles are not affected by the passage of time or changes in fashion and culture. An abundance of comforting peace and overflowing resources of righteousness will be ours if we willing adhere to God's priorities today.

PRAYER FOCUS

Dear heavenly Father, Your principles are timeless and Your promises are timely. LORD, grant me a teachable spirit to learn them and an obedient heart to follow them as a true seeker after God in Jesus' name.

March 14

Witnessing - A Must For Disciples Of Christ
Bible Reading: [Jude 16-25]

"Keep yourselves in the love of God, looking for the mercy of our LORD Jesus Christ unto eternal life. And on some have compassion, making a distinction; but others save with fear, pulling them out of the fire, hating even the garment defiled by the flesh." [Vs: 20-22;NKJV]

Every true disciple of has the responsibility to keep himself or herself in the love of God by growing in the faith. Oftentimes our identity in Christ is threatened by false doctrines or sins that can be enticing. For this reason, we are encouraged by scripture to earnestly contend for the faith that was once for all delivered to the saints *[Jude 3]*. Wisdom to win a soul is not only to get men saved, but also to avoid the trap of becoming like the very people we are trying to reach with the gospel. The starting point is for us to build ourselves up in the most holy faith, praying and being led by the Spirit. To be effective, we must love righteousness and hate sin.

A wise approach to win souls to Christ is obvious. Three categories of men must be targeted: showing mercy to those whose faith is wavering [victims of false teachers], by encouraging them in the faith, rescuing others by snatching them from the flames of eternal[Hell] fire and showing mercy to others by compassion and kindness, but doing so with great care, hating the sins that contaminate their lives. Beloved in Christ, are you an effective witness? Take responsibility today and be a blessing to someone *[Act.8:26-40]*. It is written, *"So we tell others about Christ, warning everyone and teaching everyone with all the wisdom God has given us. We want to present them to God, perfect in their relationship to Christ." [Col.1:28, NLT]*. Hallelujah!

PRAYER FOCUS

Dear heavenly Father, You do not take pleasure in the death of the wicked [sinners]. LORD, grant that soul winning will be my heartbeat now and always in Jesus' name.

March 15

Unlocking The Heavens With A New Song
Bible Reading: [Acts.16:16-26]

"And at midnight Paul and Silas prayed, and sang praises unto God: and the prisoners heard them."
[Vs 25]

Dearly beloved, I cannot overemphasize on the tremendous power that is being released whenever we sing a new song unto the LORD. Oftentimes, it's difficult for many to sing the LORD's song in the valley of trouble or in captivity. Let's consider the case of the Israelites in captivity. It is written, *"By the rivers of Babylon,....For there they that carried us away captive required of us a song; and they that wasted us required of us mirth, saying, sing us one of the songs of Zion. How shall we sing the LORD's song in a strange land?"* [Ps.137:3-4;KJV].

In a strange land [inner prison], Paul and Silas had a different mindset. Knowing that all things work together for good to them that love God [Rom.8:28]. They had read from Scriptures that God dwells in the praises of his people and that with God's presence, nothing is impossible. As they prayed and sang praises, the heavens were opened and God worked wonders. I sincerely pray that God will put a new song in your mouth. The Psalmist says, *"And he hath put a new song in my mouth, even praise unto our God; many will see and fear and will trust in the LORD."* [Ps.40:3, KJV]. Beloved, not only were prison doors opened, and everyone's bands loosed, the keeper of the prison got saved from sin/shame and was baptized. Hallelujah!

PRAYER FOCUS

Dear heavenly Father, inspire my heart and put a new song in my mouth today in Jesus' name.

March 16

Great Men For Defining Moments
Bible Reading: [Esther 4:1-17]

"For if you remain silent at this time, relief and deliverance for the Jews will arise from another place, but you and your Father's family will perish. And who knows but that you have come to royal position for such a time as this?"
[Esther 4:14;NIV]

History has been made through the actions of men and women, whose choices at certain pivotal moments determined the course of the world [Stephen M. Klugewicz]. Difficult times in life are seen by some as a time of disappointment, but to men and women of courage and virtue, such moments are great opportunities. A defining moment is a point in your life when you are urged to make a major decision that will change your life, and transform society.

God wants each one of us to take action in some way [proactive], that will not only shape and change us, but have huge impact on the lives of many. Think about our LORD Jesus Christ. Scripture says, *"And he went a little farther, and fell on his face, and prayed, saying, O my Father, if it be possible, let this cup pass from me: nevertheless not as I will, but as thou wilt."* [Matt.26:39;KJV]. Beloved, Christ endured the cross for our sake, that we might gain freedom and become the righteousness of God. [Heb.12:2; 2 Cor.5:21].

At the time of Esther, the Jews were threatened with genocide. God needed a man to rise up against the senseless schemes of Haman. It is written, *"Who will rise for me against the evildoers? Or who will stand up for me against workers of iniquity?"* [Ps.94:16;KJV]. If Esther had failed to rise up, God would certainly work another means by which to deliver his people.

Are you willing to rise up today against all odds?

PRAYER FOCUS

Dear heavenly Father, prompt my heart and give me boldness & wisdom to rise up against the works of evil men in my community and nation *[Acts.4:23-31]* in Jesus' name.

March 17

Get On Mission With What Matters Most
Bible Reading: [Gen12:1; 13:1-18]

And the LORD said to Abram, after Lot had separated from him: Lift your eyes now and look from the place where you are……..for all the Land which you see I give to you and your descendants forever." [Vs:14]

There is no place in the world void of distractions. Sometimes we allow ourselves to be distracted by everything around us, and we complain thereafter. We are distracted by social media, the worries of life, peer pressures, by the Satan and cohorts etc. Whenever we fail to define our mission and prioritize our time, the devil will set us up in his business. The devil knows that his time is short *[Rev.12:12]*.

To get on mission means to perform or make progress in a specific way or direction as the LORD leads. Are you making progress? Are you purpose driven? Our concern today is not just about what matters, but what matters most. I have come to understand that one of the reasons we don't progress in a specific and right direction is because we try to please men. While laboring to keep good relations with men, it shouldn't be done to the detriment of one's divine mission.

Think about Abram! Paul writing to the Galatian brethren, said, *"For do I now persuade men, or God? Or do I seek to please men? for if I yet please men, I should not be the servant of Christ." [Gal.1:10;KJV]*. Don't be Martha that was distracted by many things *[Lk.10:40]*. Don't be distracted by unreasonable friendships/relationships *[1 Cor.15:33]*. Don't even let pain or affliction distract you, for the grace of God is sufficient *[2 Cor.12:9]*. Get on with what is beneficial and edifying.

Set your time and priorities right and the God of peace will be with you!

PRAYER FOCUS

Dear heavenly Father, help me each passing day to set my priorities right and make the most of my time. Today, I rebuke the spirit of distraction in Jesus' name.

March 18

You Are Not Alone
Bible Reading: [I Kings 19:1-18]

"..And the word of the LORD came to him: "What are you doing here, Elijah? He replied, "I have been very zealous for the LORD God Almighty. The Israelites have rejected your covenant, broken down your altars, and put your prophets to death with the sword. I am the only one left, and now they are trying to kill me too." [Vs:9-10]

Sometimes we are weighed down by the pressures of life, physically and emotionally exhausted, persecuted, feeling depressed and even deserted by the people we consider dear to us. That may be your experience at the moment. Nevertheless, I have come to announce to you that you are not alone. The Prophet Elijah felt that way too. You may even think that nobody has experienced what you are going through. Remember that no temptation/persecution has overtaken you except such as is common to man; but God is faithful *[1 Cor.10:13]*. The LORD said to the Prophet, *"Yet I reserve seven thousand in Israel - all whose knees have not bowed down to Baal and all whose mouths have not kissed him." [Vs 18].*

Beloved, can you imagine anything more comforting than God telling you personally that He will not abandon you and you shouldn't be dismayed? He will strengthen and help you, He will uphold you with His righteous right hand *[Isa.41:10].* Apostle Paul narrating his experience said, *"At my first defense, no one came to my support, but everyone deserted me. May it not be held against them. But the LORD stood at my side and gave me strength; so that through me, the message might be fully proclaimed and all the Gentiles might hear it. And I was delivered from the lion's mouth." [2 Tim.4:16-17].* Your experience is for a purpose, don't feel left out. Hallelujah!

PRAYER FOCUS

Dear heavenly Father, thank You for assuring me in Your word that through the valley of the shadow of death, through burning fiery furnace, and through the rivers, You are with me. LORD, I'm confident that You are greater in me than he who is in the world. Amen

March 19

Give Up to Go Up
Bible Reading: [Matt.19:16-22]

"Jesus said to him, "If you want to be perfect, go, sell what you have and give to the poor, and you will have treasure in heaven; and come, follow Me. But when the young man heard that saying, he went away sorrowful, for he had great possessions." [Vs:21-22;NKJV]

I know that the LORD has been speaking to many of us to give up somethings in life in exchange for a perfect relationship with Him. Beloved, what are you holding unto that keeps you a thousand miles away from God? Scripture records that when the young man heard the saying of Jesus, he went away sorrowful: for he had great possessions. Indeed, he had possession and position that hindered his total commitment to the LORD. And he said unto them, *take heed, and beware of covetousness: for a man's life consisteth not in the abundance of the things which he possesseth." [Lk.12:15;KJV]*.

Jesus Christ is not interested in more religious laws or good deeds that must be performed in order to earn his acceptance. It is by grace alone that we are saved *[Eph.2:8-9]*. Friend, do you sincerely feel that something is lacking in your life? Like the rich young ruler, you need a new starting point which can only come when you humbly submit to the Lordship of Jesus Christ. Whatever thing you are too attached to that supersede or take the place/position of God in your life is a stumbling block and a trap. And he said to them all, *if any man will come after me, let him deny himself, and take up his cross daily, and follow me." [Lk.9:23;KJV]*. Give up to go up today!

PRAYER FOCUS

Dear heavenly Father, I humbly submit myself to You in obedience to Your word. Good Master, with a childlike attitude, I approach You today, willing to give up all that I'm too attached to the detriment of my love for You in Jesus' name.

March 20

Trading The Gift Of God?
Bible Reading: [Matt.10:1-10]

"And as ye go, preach, saying, The kingdom of heaven is at hand. Heal the sick, cleanse the lepers, raise the dead, cast out devils: freely ye have received, freely give." [Vs:7-8]

Nowadays the trading of God's gift is commonplace. Trading involves buying and selling. For some reasons, some people think that they worked hard to merit God's gift. Others think they bought it and therefore must sell it. Whatever the case may be, the reason God gives us spiritual gifts is not for business. It is written, *"And when Simon saw that through laying on of the apostles' hands the Holy Ghost was given, he offered them money, saying, give me also this power, that on whomever I lay hands, he may receive the Holy Ghost." [Acts.8:18-19]*. Those who think they bought it will certainly sell it or be overtaken by pride for every manifestation of God's power. If you have this mindset, scripture is clear on this matter; *"Thou hast neither part nor lot in this matter: for thy heart is not right in the sight of God." [Acts.8:21;KJV]*. Such preach Christ out of envy and selfish ambition.

The high calling of God entails that we preach Christ sincerely. As a matter of fact, scripture supports the fact that the workman is worthy of his meat *[Matt.10:10;1 Cor.9:11]*. However, God wants every true disciple to avoid greed that will give others especially unbelievers the opportunity to defame His name. God has freely given His grace and we should freely proclaim it to others. Therefore, consider how you feed the flock of God: not by constraint, but willingly. Not for filthy lucre *[1 Pet.5:2]*.

PRAYER FOCUS

Dear heavenly Father, thank You for the gift You've blessed me. LORD, I purpose in my heart to serve You willingly and sincerely in Jesus' name.

March 21

The Righteous Shall Flourish
Bible Reading: [Psalm 92:8-15]

"Those that be planted in the house of house of the LORD shall flourish in the courts of our God." [Vs: 13]

Jesus Christ is the same yesterday, today and forever. He is faithful to His promises. Are you living a righteous life? Remember that in God there is no unrighteousness *[Rom.9:14]*. I'm convinced many of us are familiar with the word CHURCH. But what gain is it if practice church going, filling the pew weekly without being transformed? Flourishing in God's court is the result of a life that abides in Christ. A life that lives out of the overflow of the Holy Spirit.

It's the Father's desire that every disciple should be strong and unmoved by difficult situations. God is committed to stand for the righteous in any circumstance. He wants us to be enduring plants in His courts so that He might be glorified in us. The promises of God are fulfilled in our lives when we place our faith firmly in Him. Those who are planted in God's presence grow in His grace and are living memorials of His faithfulness to His promises. They are full of life because of God's word that dwells richly in them. It is written, *"If ye abide in me, and my words abide in you, ye shall ask what ye will, and it shall be done unto you." [John.15:7]*.

PRAYER FOCUS

Dear heavenly Father, today, I enter Your gates with thanksgiving in my heart and Your courts with praise. I'm fully convinced that I shall flourish like a palm tree this year and grow in spiritual vitality in Jesus' name.

March 22

Great Is Our God, Awesome Beyond Words
Bible Reading: [Ps.48:1-14]

"For this God is our God for ever and ever: he will be our guide even unto death." (Vs:14, KJV)

The greatness of God is unsearchable. Whenever we sincerely reflect on the faithfulness, righteousness, and justice of God's rule, it should prompt us to joyfully celebrate his presence. It's unfortunate that many people have not yet made God, their God for ever and ever. Perhaps they have not yet tasted of his goodness and the beauty of his holiness. Elijah approach all the people and said, *"How long will you waver between two opinions? If the LORD is God, follow him; but if Baal is God, follow him."* But the people said nothing *(1 Kgs.18:21;NIV).* Joshua told the people, *"And if it seem evil unto you to serve the LORD, choose you this day whom ye will serve;.....but as for me and my house, we will serve the LORD (Josh.24:15;KJV).*

Have you made God your God for ever and ever? If not, Choose today to make your life the center of God's presence in the world *(1 Cor.6:19)!* God is merciful and willing to extend grace to all. Only those who have decided to follow God or come under the lordship of Jesus Christ can confidently say, *"He will be our guide even unto death."*

PRAYER FOCUS

Dear heavenly Father, Your greatness is indescribable and Your righteousness is like the mighty mountain. LORD, I renew my commitment to follow You all the days of my life in Jesus' name.

March 23

Prepare Yourself And Arise!
Bible Reading: [Jer.1:1-19]

"Get up and prepare for action. Go and tell them everything I tell you to say. Do not be afraid of them, or I will make you look foolish in front of them."
[Vs: 17;nlt]

Beloved, have you been complacent with the assignment God has given you? It's time to prepare and arise! Every true disciple has been assigned to make disciples of Christ. It's written, *"..God was in Christ reconciling the world to Himself, not imputing their trespasses to them, and has committed to us the Word of reconciliation" [2 Cor.5:19]*. God assigned Jeremiah to deliver a harsh message of doom to Judah for their sin of running after other gods. He was sent to call a backsliding (apostate) nation to repentance. As a matter of fact, God knew the people will hate him and even threaten his life. At the time of the message, Jeremiah felt he was young and inexperienced to be God's oracle to the world. Our assignment may not be like that of the prophet. However, sometimes feelings of inadequacy, fear of insults, fear of being hated and despised, do hinder or keep us from obeying the call of God.

Whatever the task or people God is sending us to i.e. friends, classmates, colleagues, family members, government officials etc., He has assured us with His abiding presence according to the scriptures *"....lo, I am with you always, even unto the end of the world. Amen" (Matt.28:20)*. It is obvious that when God's spokesmen deliver a message that the people do not want to hear, they will fight against the messenger, and not the message. We are living in the last hour. It would be foolish of us to refuse to do as God has commanded. Prepare and arise! It is written, *"They will fight against you, but they shall not prevail against you, For I am with you, says the LORD, to deliver you."* *(Jer.1:19)*. Hallelujah!

PRAYER FOCUS

Dear heavenly Father, You do not desire that anyone should perish, but that all men should come to repentance. Thank You for filling me today with power by the Spirit of the LORD to declare to men their sins without fear or favor in Jesus' name.

March 24

The Power
Of Laying Down One's Life For Others
Bible Reading: [1 John 3:16-23]

"By this we know love, because He laid down His life for us. And we also ought to lay down our lives for the brethren. " [Vs:16;NKJV]

In the past few days, twelve boys and their football coach were trapped in a flooded cave in Thailand. The group was found by British rescue divers after 10 days in the cave, standing on a rock shelf in a small chamber about 4km from the cave mouth. Strategizing on how to get the boys out, one of the rescue team members, Saman lost consciousness on his way out of the flooded cave because of low oxygen level (BBC News). Beloved, freedom is not free because someone has to give his or her life for the freedom of others. I want to believe that it wasn't just a sense of duty that caused Saman to offer his life but real love and sacrifice to see others rescued.

It is written, "Greater love hath no man than this, that a man lay down his life for his friends." (John 15:13). Beloved, have you ever laid down your life for somebody? Jesus laid down his life for us so that we should lay down our lives for others. The greatest act of love is laying down one's self for others. By this we know love. True love involves self-sacrifice. True love is evidence of real faith and new life in Christ.

PRAYER FOCUS

Dear heavenly Father, You demonstrated Your love to me in that, while I was still a sinner, Christ died for me. LORD, Help me to live selflessly and manifest true love in Jesus' name.

March 25

Who Is Your Model?
Bible Reading: [2 Tim.3:10-17]

"But you have carefully followed my doctrine, manner of life, purpose, faith, longsuffering, love, perseverance, persecutions, afflictions, which happened to me at Antioch, at Iconium, at Lystra- what persecutions I endured. And out of them all the LORD delivered me." [Vs:10-11]

Beloved, we are living in perilous times. The events that are unfolding in this last days are disturbing. Many strange things are happening in the secular world and the Christendom. We are seeing the fulfilment of Bible prophecies. One question I would like to ask you today is, "who is your model?" Thinking about the challenges and all the negative influences from the world, peers, false teachers, and false prophets, everything must be taken into consideration.

Some have abandoned the faith or changed their doctrine because of the influence of false teachers and evil men. If you are conscious about serving the LORD in sincerity and integrity, you must choose the right person to follow. Those who are honest in their hearts and long for the truth will certainly go the right way. In our text, Apostle Paul mentions some key qualities a true disciple should consider: manner of life (character), purpose, faith, longsuffering, love, and perseverance etc. He didn't talk about miracles, signs and wonders. These are seemingly important but will not help us choose the right model. Paul in another scripture told Timothy, "Be ye followers of me, even as I also am of Christ."[1 Cor.11:1,KJV]. I pray that God will deliver you from any ungodly influence today in Jesus' name.

PRAYER FOCUS

Dear heavenly Father, I trust that You will bring destiny helpers my way, to help me grow in the faith daily and accomplish my mission in Jesus' name.

March 26

We Are Only God's Instruments
Bible Reading: [1 Cor.3:1-10]

"I have planted, Apollos watered;
but God gave the increase.
So then neither is he that planteth anything,
neither he that watereth;
but God that giveth the increase." [Vs:6-7;KJV]

Dearly beloved, have you been called according to God's purpose and grace? Then this message is for you. When a disciple of Christ comes to terms with the fact that he or she is only an instrument that God is using, such will not allow himself/herself to be worshipped by another man. Nowadays, man worship (cult of personality) is a common phenomenon in the secular world and Christendom. True servants of God are those who seek to communicate the gospel to the world and make disciples. Not those who attract men to themselves but lead men to Christ.

Let Christ be the center of it all. Paul refused to allow men to call themselves after him. Likewise Peter refused to be worshipped by Cornelius. It is written, *"But Peter took him up, saying, Stand up, I myself also am a man."* [Acts.10:26]. We are only instruments. Regardless of how great God uses us, credit for increase in soul winning and spiritual growth of those who are saved must be given to God. Every disciple of Christ should serve according to the measure of grace received and each disciple will be rewarded according to what he or she has done. True disciples are accountable to God for the way they serve Christ. We are all servants and only instruments to minister the manifold grace of God.

PRAYER FOCUS

Dear heavenly Father, You are the author of the gospel message. LORD, help me to use my God-given gift to accomplish Your assignment for my life and prepare men for Your heavenly dwelling in Jesus' name

March 27

Judgment Begins At The House Of God
Bible Reading: [Ezek.8:1-17]

"He said to me, Son of man, have you seen what the elders of the house of Israel are doing in the darkness, each at the shrine of his own idol? They say, the LORD does not see us; the LORD has forsaken the land." [Vs:12;NIV]

Nowadays it's easy for men to justify why they are living in sin or committing sin. Some like in the days of old, live in self-deception that God does not see the evil acts they are committing. Beloved, are you a partaker of any form of abomination in the house of God by perverting the truth? Remember that God is omniscient. There is nothing hidden from his eyes. All disciples of Christ, especially spiritual leaders are accountable to God because they have been entrusted with the responsibility to teach the truth. Failure to do so only leads countless of people away from God and consequently to the lake of fire [hell].

The judgment of God is inside-out. It is written, *"For the time is come that judgement must begin at the house of God: and if it first begin at us, what shall the end be of them that obey not the gospel of God?"* [1 Pet.4:17;KJV]. You might be saying, it doesn't matter or that if spiritual leaders are doing it, I have an excuse. Please consider your ways.

It is a terrible thing for lies to be practice in the house of God or temple of the Holy Spirit instead of truth. It is written, *"Because sentence against an evil work is not executed speedily, therefore the heart of the sons of men is fully set in them to do evil"* [Eccl. 8:11;KJV]. The LORD is not slack concerning his promise, as some men count slackness. He is not willing that any man should perish, but that all should come to repentance *[2 Pet.3:8-10]*

PRAYER FOCUS

Dear heavenly Father, I acknowledge my self-deception and repent for perverting the truth. Have mercy upon me, heal my heart and help me to live and walk in holiness in Jesus' name.

March 28

When The Storm Of Life
Is Beyond Your Ability To Endure
Bible Reading: [Acts 27:1-25;KJV]

"And when neither sun nor stars in many days appeared, and no small tempest lay on us, all hope that we should be saved was then taken away." [Vs:20;KJV]

Sometimes in life, we encounter challenges such that we are despaired of life itself. While some in the midst of such a great danger give up their faith, others give up life. The truth is that at least once in a lifetime, such situations do happen to each of us. It's not in the power of man to determine the storm that comes his way. Apostle writing to the brethren at Corinth made mention of his experience, *"We do not want you to be uninformed, brothers, about the hardships we suffered in the province of Asia. We were under great pressure, far beyond our ability to endure, so that we despaired even of life." [2 Cor.1:8;NIV].*

Beloved in Christ, what would be your reaction if you encounter a situation that you feel even the sentence of death? For many days at sea, Paul and his companions could not see sun or stars, and definitely could not determine where they were. It's important for us to understand that God allows some desperate situations in life so that we may learn not to rely on ourselves but on him. When all hope of surviving the storm is gone, in the midst of it, God is present. It's written, *"God is our refuge and strength, a very present help in trouble." [Psalm 46:1;KJV].* There is light at the end of the tunnel. If God brought you to it, he will bring you through it.

Surrendering your life and desperate situation to him is all you need to do today. Even the storms of life obey him!

PRAYER FOCUS

Dear heavenly Father, You calmed the storm and raised the dead to life. Today, I depend on you, for I am confident in Your mighty power to deliver in Jesus' name.

March 29

The Snare Of The Spirit Of Falsehood
Bible Reading: [Mic.2:1-11]

"If a man walking in the spirit and falsehood do lie, saying, I will prophesy unto thee of wine and of strong drink; he shall even be the prophet of this people." [Vs:11]

Dearly beloved, we are living in perilous [dangerous] times. The time is running out, because our salvation is nearer now than when we first believed. Scripture says, *evil men and seducers shall wax worse and worse, deceiving, and being deceived [2 Tim.3:13]*. Men are being deceived because of their itching ears. Many can't even afford time to search scriptures for themselves.

About the Bereans, Scripture says, *"These were more noble than those in Thessalonica, in that they received the word with all readiness of mind, and searched the scriptures daily, whether those things were so." [Acts. 17:11]*. Friend, if you have been deceived or you are under the influence of the spirit of falsehood, it's not late to seek deliverance.

The spirit of falsehood is a lying spirit that is gaining grounds in the Body of Christ. The goal of the spirit of falsehood is to distort or suppress the truth, in order to deceive men, even the very elect. Beloved, have you read about the old prophet and the young prophet in the scripture? The old prophet deceived the young prophet by suppressing the truth *[1 Kings 13]*. Deception i.e. the action of deceiving someone has become a way of life not only to the people of the world, but also to some in the household of faith. It is written, *"For the time will come when they will not endure sound doctrine; but after their own lusts shall they heap to themselves teachers, having itching ears;" [2 Tim.4:3]*.

Do you desire to know more about God but have itching ears? Be careful how you choose your teacher(s). Paul told Timothy, *"But continue thou in the things which thou hast learned and has been assured of, knowing of whom thou hast learned them;" [2 Tim.3:14]*. If you are truly a disciple of Christ, born again, walking in holiness, abiding in Christ and his word in you, then the anointing you have received is able to teach you all things and is truth *[1 John 2:27]*. The word of God does good to him who walks uprightly.

PRAYER FOCUS

Dear heavenly Father, help me to be wise and discerning in this present age in Jesus' name.

March 30

The Object Of Your Worship
Bible Reading: [Exodus 32:1-10; Acts17:22-23]

Nowadays, many have become very religious and have lost the ability to distinguish between the true God and false god. Idols again! Even though Israel had seen the invisible God in action, they still wanted the familiar gods they could see and shape into whatever image they desired. How much like them we are!

Our great temptation is still to shape God to our liking, to make Him convenient to obey or ignore. God responds in great anger when His mercy is trampled on.

The gods we create blind us to the love that our loving God wants to shower on us.

God cannot work in us when we elevate/place anyone or anything above Him. What false gods in your life are preventing the true God from living in you?

Jesus said to the Samaritan woman, *"You worship what you do not know; we know what we worship, for salvation is of the Jews. God is Spirit, and those who worship Him must worship in spirit and truth."* (John 4:22, 24) Consider the object of your worship TODAY!

PRAYER FOCUS

Dear LORD, I have made You too small in my eyes and have leaned on the wisdom of men instead of Your love and mercy. LORD, forgive me and heal my heart!

March 31

Accessing Grace For Unwavering Faith
Bible Reading: [Rev.2:12-17]

"I know thy works, and where thou dwellest, even where Satan's seat is: and thou holdest fast my name, and hast not denied my faith, even in those days wherein Antipas was my faithful martyr, who was slain among you, where Satan dwelleth." [Vs:13;KJV]

In a hostile political and spiritual environment against the truth, sometimes it's difficult for many believers to stay true to the faith. God wants every disciple of his to remain faithful to the faith regardless of the onslaught of persecution, trials and peer pressures. The church in Pergamos was located in a region where the seat of government authority was and where men worshipped pagan gods. The seat of Satan is where the activity of Satan is performed by those who have given themselves over to the lies[deception] of the devil. Ours may not be the same circumstance. However, when we can't stand firm against the strong pressure or the negative influence of society, we'll certainly compromise our faith and walk with God. Bowing to such pressures of sin, leads to destruction.

Beloved, God's grace is sufficient for each one of his disciples to be faithful to him even unto death. The culture where we live shouldn't affect us, instead as true disciples, we ought to influence the world *[2 Cor.5:17-19]*. Disciples of Christ are the salt of the earth and the light of the world. Are you born again? When you feel like giving up your faith, remember, God who has called you is able to keep you from falling, and to present you faultless before the presence of his glory with exceeding joy *[Jude 24]*. Hallelujah!

PRAYER FOCUS

Dear heavenly Father, I'm confident that You will continue to perfect the good work You've begun in my life until the day of the LORD in Jesus' name.

APRIL

"I am crucified with Christ: nevertheless I live; yet not I, but Christ liveth in me: and the life which I now live in the flesh I live by the faith of the Son of God, who loved me, and gave himself for me. I do not frustrate the grace of God: for if righteousness come by the law, then Christ is dead in vain."

[Gal.2:20-21, KJV]

"But if the Spirit of him that raised up Jesus from the dead dwell in you, he that raised up Christ from the dead shall also quicken your mortal bodies by his Spirit that dwelleth in you." ***[Rom.8:11; KJV]***

****

*Jehovah Rapha - **[The LORD That Heals]** - Exod.15:26*

*4 = **[Creative Work of God / Completeness in Form or Function]***

April 1

God Is Enough
Bible Reading: [Psalm 34:1-22]

"O magnify the LORD with me, and let us exalt his name together. I sought the LORD, and he heard me, and delivered me from all my fears." [Vs 3-4;KJV]

Dearly beloved, do you feel like needing something more in this life or depending on someone other than God? When faced with the harsh realities of our daily lives, we must be confident and focus on the wise judgements of God. It is written, *"Wherefore he is able also to save them to the uttermost that come unto God by him, seeing he ever liveth to make intercession for them."[Heb.7:25;KJV]*.

David was confident that God would meet his deepest needs. Like David whose life was spared by God from his enemies, especially king Saul's *[1 Sam.22]*, I decree and declare that the plans and schemes of the mighty will not prevail against you in Jesus' name.

Whatever your need or greatest concern at the moment, you can rest assured that God will not bypass those who earnestly seek him *[Heb.11:6]*. Take advantage of this hour, let's magnify the LORD and exalt his name together. He dwells in the praises of his people. His presence is all you need. God is enough!

PRAYER FOCUS

Dear heavenly Father, You presence is indispensable! LORD, I embrace Your totality [fullness] and magnify Your holy name today in Jesus name.

April 2

Begone, Satan & Associates!
Bible Reading: [Matt.4:1-11]

"Then saith Jesus unto him, Get thee hence, Satan: for it is written, Thou shalt worship the LORD thy God, and him only shalt thou serve." [Vs 10 & Deut.6:13]

The tempter comes to each one of us at various times, in many different ways. It is written, *"And he saith unto Jesus, All these things will I give thee, if thou wilt fall down and worship me." [Vs: 10]*. Nowadays, my heart bleeds because many Christians can't afford time to fellowship with God or serve His purposes with their lives. They have chosen to accept the devil's offers. He uses subtle ways especially with job offers to get many worship him. Satan always seeks to interrupt our worship of God because he desires to be worshipped. If all the time your job or anything else is preventing you from worshipping God, then you are bowing down to the devil.

Beloved, If truly you are a worshipper of the only wise God, then you ought to give him priority or preeminence in all your choices. While the people of the world accept offers from Mammon *[Matt.6:24]* and the spirit of materialism *[24hrs/7]*, Children of the kingdom ought not to conform to the standards of the world *[Rom.12:1-2]*. It is written,*".., And truly our fellowship is with the Father, and with his Son Jesus Christ." [1 Jn.1:3, KJV]*. Scripture says, *submit yourselves therefore to God. Resist the devil, and he will flee from you [Jam.4:7]. The grace of God that brings salvation teaches us to say "No" to ungodliness and worldly passions and to live godly lives in this present age [Titus 2:12].*

PRAYER FOCUS

Dear heavenly Father, only You shall I worship in spirit and in truth. LORD, I surrender to Your Lordship and command Satan and associates to be gone! in Jesus' name.

April 3

Establishing Godly Customs
Bible Reading: [Dan.6:10-23]

"Now when Daniel knew that the writing was signed, he went home. And in his upper room, with his windows open toward Jerusalem, he knelt down on his knees three times that day, and prayed and gave thanks before his God, as was his custom since early days." [Vs:10;NKJV]

Scripture says that for as many as are led by the Spirit of God, they are the sons of God *[Rom.814]*. Simply because we are led by the Holy Spirit, does not prevent us from establishing godly customs. These customs are not just another set of laws, but principles that will help guide us throughout life in all circumstances.

A custom is a way of behaving or something you usually do. Daniel made prayer his lifeline to God. What spiritual discipline have you developed that no matter threats, pressure of schedules or peer pressure, you have kept doing over time? It's worth mentioning that even in a foreign land [exile], Daniel did not stop his godly customs. When he knew that the writing was signed, he went home, and in his upper room, with his windows opened toward Jerusalem, he prayed three times that day as usual. The Psalmist mentions a similar custom, *"But as for me, I will come into thy house in the multitude of thy mercy: and thy fear will I worship toward thy holy temple." [Ps 5:7]*

Successful individuals, businessmen, academics, families, ministries/churches have developed customs. What custom have you put in place regarding studies, business, evangelism, fellowship and family life? Any custom or practice that has its origin in Jesus' culture will stand the test of time. Lydia's conversion in Philippi was at the riverside. It is written, *"And on the Sabbath day we went out of the city to the riverside, where prayer was customarily made; and we sat down and spoke to the women who met there." [Acts.16:13;NKJV]*. Establishing a godly custom today will make all the difference!

PRAYER FOCUS

Dear heavenly Father, You desire that I should prosper in all things. LORD, enable me each passing day to adopt or promote customs that will glorify You. in Jesus' name.

April 4

The Snare Of Asking Amiss
Bible Reading: [James 4:1-6]

"Ye ask, and receive not, because ye ask amiss, that ye may consume it upon your lusts." [Vs: 3]

Each and every one of us would like to ask God for something, but the question is, how many of us do make request to the LORD with the right motive? It is obvious that those who are materialistic would ask for riches in order to consume upon their own lusts. Beloved, God is willing to give when we ask, but our motives will determine what we get from him. It's important to note that God provides us with all things for our enjoyment *[1 Tim.6:17]*.

What is your motive for asking God for something today? It is written, *"Ask, and it shall be given you; seek, and ye shall find; knock, and it shall be opened unto you" [Matt.7:7;KJV]*. Asking anything from God in order to use it for that which will keep you from him or hinder your relationship with him is sinful. Disciples of Christ shouldn't be overwhelmed by the pleasures of the world *[1 John 2:16]*. Satan said to Jesus, *"All these things will I give thee, if thou wilt fall down and worship me." [Matt.4:9;KJV]*.

The right approach to God is to ask according to His will. Ask to meet needs, and not wants, ask for resources to reach out to lost souls with the message of salvation, ask with regard for the poor, orphans, widows and to make substantial contributions to uplift the plight of humanity as God puts a burden on our hearts. *"And this is the confidence that we have in Him, that, if we ask anything according to His will, He heareth us" [1 John 5:14.]*

PRAYER FOCUS

Dear heavenly Father, I repent for having asked amiss. Teach me Your truth and let Your Will override my desires *[Ps.37:4;KJV]* in Jesus' name.

April 5

Inspiration Gives Understanding
Bible Reading: [Job 32:1-9]

"But there is a spirit in man: and the inspiration of the Almighty giveth them understanding."[Vs:8;KJV]

It's often said that with age comes wisdom. However, no matter how intelligent a person may be, it's only the breath of the Almighty that gives him understanding. Each one of us needs special understanding into every matter of life. Divine inspiration fills us with the ability to do something creative for the glory of God. I pray that the LORD will bless you with an understanding heart in Jesus' name. It is written, *"For the LORD gives wisdom; from His mouth come knowledge and understanding;" [Prov.2:6;NKJV]*

The spirit in man is a vital force. It's the channel through which God illuminates our understanding, bringing light to our inward parts by the Holy Ghost. *"The spirit of man is the candle of the LORD, Searching all the inward parts of the belly." [Prov.20:27;KJV]*. Getting understanding is not an optional in life. Let God inspire your heart today!

PRAYER FOCUS

Dear heavenly Father, grant that the eyes of my understanding be enlightened to know the hope of my calling and the riches of the glory of Your inheritance in the saints in Jesus' name.

April 6

Strength In The Inner Man
Bible Reading: [Eph.3:14-21]

"That he would grant you, according to the riches of his glory, to be strengthened with might by his Spirit in the inner man;" [Vs:16;KJV]

Sometimes on our pilgrim journey, the many challenges we encounter on the way cause us to run short of strength. Though outwardly we are wasting away, yet our inner self is being renewed day by day as we abide in Christ and His word in us. The hidden man of the heart is that part of our being which is very precious in the sight of the LORD. It is the immaterial part of man: soul and spirit. As the seat of spiritual influences, it is the sphere in which the Holy Spirit does His renewing and saving work (D.W. Pratt).

One thing every disciple of Christ needs today is strength in the inner man. We gain the power for life and ministry only when we allow Christ to make his home in our hearts *[Rev.3:20]*. Beloved, I pray that God will empower your inner man with strength through his Spirit.

Remember that as a disciple of Christ, you can do all things only through Christ who gives strength.

PRAYER FOCUS

Dear heavenly Father, I acknowledge that my life is made complete only through the fullness of Your grace and presence of Christ in me. LORD, strength my heart with grace today in Jesus' name.

April 7

Fanning The Flames Of Revival
Bible Reading: [Acts 8:4-8]

"Therefore they that were scattered abroad went everywhere preaching the word. And there was great joy in that city." [Acts.8:4,8;KJV]

Dearly beloved, each one of us at a given moment in time needs revival. At times our love and passion for the things of God grow cold *[Matt.24:12]*. The Psalmist made an earnest request to God concerning revival; *"Wilt thou not revive us again: that thy people may rejoice in thee?" [Ps.85:6;KJV]*.Revival means to stir into flame the gift of the Spirit which we have already received of God (W.L.Walker). Are you a true disciple of Christ, born of the Spirit of God? You need to stir the gift of the Spirit in you. Apostle Paul reminded Timothy, his beloved son in the faith to stir up the gift of God in him *[2 Tim.1:6]*.

Beloved, our towns, cities and nations need spiritual awakening and revival. That can only happen when true believers begin to fan into flames the Spiritual gift of God in their lives. Only a living believer or church can cause live in a city. Apostle John writing to the Church in Sardis said; *"You have a reputation of being alive, but you are dead. Wake up and strengthen what remains, which is about to die;.." [Rev.3:1-2]*. Scriptures record that the disciples were scattered abroad and went everywhere preaching the gospel. And there was great joy in Samaria because the people got saved and were healed. Hallelujah!

PRAYER FOCUS

Dear heavenly Father, I yield my life to You. Work in me to will and act according to Your good pleasure, as I trust You to pour Your Spirit afresh on me in Jesus' name.

April 8

Nothing Takes God By Surprise
Bible Reading: [Jer.11:18-23]

"But I was like a lamb or an ox that is brought to the slaughter; and I knew not that they had devised devices against me, saying, Let us cut him off from the land of the living, that his name may be no more remembered. " [Vs: 19;KJV]

Sometimes in life, some things happen to us when we least expect or prepare for. I can imagine how it feels like when temptation shows up or the scheme of the enemy is made manifest. For the most part, as humans, we will tremble. Whatever the case, nothing takes God by surprise. It is written, *"Declaring the end from the beginning, and from ancient times the things that are not yet done, saying, My counsel shall stand, and I will do all my pleasure:" [Isa.46:10;KJV]*. Only the omniscient God knows the future and the plans he has for us.

The prophet Jeremiah found himself in a difficult situation he had no idea of, seeing himself as a lamb be led to the slaughter. Moreover, the plot to kill him in his hometown of Anathoth caught him by surprise because it came from his own relatives. Their goal was to silence Jeremiah's message because they were not ready for the truth. Friend, whatever conspiracy against your life because of the truth, I declare it aborted in Jesus' name. The counsel of the LORD for your life shall stand and you shall taste of the goodness of God in the land of the living. Just like the LORD gave Jeremiah knowledge of what his adversaries where planning to do, may God make known to you the secret schemes of the enemy to destroy you. *"The secret of the LORD is with them that fear him, and he will shew them his covenant." [Ps.25:14;KJV]*.

PRAYER FOCUS

Dear heavenly Father, You know the end from the beginning. I'm fully persuaded that no plan of Yours for my life can be thwarted in Jesus' name.

April 9

LORD —Teach Me To Number Our Days
Bible Reading: [Isa.38:1-5; 2 Chr.32:24-33]

Dearly beloved, when we come to the realization that life is like a vapor that appears for a little time then vanishes away, we'll sincerely ask God to teach us how to apply our hearts unto wisdom *[Ps 90:12]*. Wisdom is the principal thing in life and the fear of God is the beginning of wisdom. Wisdom is the ability to make good judgement especially in practical matters. It's important to note that the fear of God leads to wisdom, and not weakness as some may think. Therefore, the right human response to the LORD is godly fear.

Let's consider the case of king Hezekiah who was informed by prophet Isaiah according to the word of the LORD that his illness will lead to death *[Isa.38]*. He prayed to God and because of his integrity and faithfulness, God added fifteen more years to him. Shortly afterwards, he messed up when envoys came from Babylon. It is written, *"But Hezekiah rendered not again according to the benefit done unto him; for his heart was lifted up; therefore there was wrath upon him and upon Judah and Jerusalem." [2 Chr.32:25]*. Beloved, life is not measured by how long we live, but by what we do with the years God gives us. Purpose living is necessary and realizing that life is short helps us use our years more wisely, for the glory of God. Hallelujah!

PRAYER FOCUS

Dear heavenly Father, teach me to follow the path of wisdom and guide me in Your truth in Jesus' name.

April 10

Don't Let Your Circumstances Dictate Who You Are
Bible Reading: [Mark 10:46-52]

"And Jesus answered and said unto him, What wilt thou that I should do unto thee? The blind man said unto him, LORD, that I might receive my sight. And Jesus said unto him, Go thy way; thy faith hath made thee whole. And immediately he received his sight, and followed Jesus in the way." [Vs:51-52]

Dearly beloved, with God there is no condition under the sun that is permanent. If your circumstance has a beginning, there is obviously an end to it. Some have accepted their condition the way it is, and are comfortable with it. For Bartimaeus, his condition was attached to his name (blind Bartimaeus). Nevertheless, he was determined to receive his breakthrough.

Although many warned Bartimaeus to be quiet, he cried the more a great deal. He recognized who Jesus was and made a specific request when he approached Him, *"LORD, that I might receive my sight."* Many people are still bound because of the fear of man. It is written, *"The fear of man bringeth a snare: but whoso putteth his trust in the LORD shall be safe." [Prov.29:25].*

Like most beggars do, he might simply have asked the LORD for alms. However, he knew what he wanted. An understanding of what Christ's death accomplished for us on the cross is the truth that sets men free. Reach out to Jesus in faith today, and embrace His fullness *[Jn.1:16].He is a rewarder to those who go all the way [Heb.11:6]*

PRAYER FOCUS

Dear LORD, I believe You are the Messiah. Let Your power be made manifest in my life today in Jesus' name.

April 11

You've Got What It Takes To Celebrate Victory Over Your Enemies
Bible Reading: [Judges 16:1-16]

"And Samson said, with the jawbone of an ass, heaps upon heaps, with the jaw of an ass have I slain a thousand men." [Vs:16]

Like the Philistines in the days of Samson, many people are being intimidated daily by the enemy (Satan & associates). How long will a man be under such an oppression when authority is available to all who call upon the name of the LORD in sincerity and truth? [Lk 10:19]. At such a defining moment, Samson received strength from the LORD and found a weapon. Remember the case of Moses; *"Then the LORD said unto him, What is that in thine hand? And he said, A rod." And he said, cast it on the ground. And he cast it on the ground, and it became a serpent;."* [Exod.4:2-3;KJV]

Beloved, you've got what it takes to celebrate victory over your enemies if you have pledged your allegiance to the Lamb who seats upon the throne. It is written, *"Ye are of God, little children, and have overcome them: because greater is he that is in you, than he that is in the world."* [1 John 4:4;KJV]

It's easy to be frightened when evil men surround you and even tremble by the challenges you face. However, one thing is certain, when the enemy shall come in like a flood, the Spirit of the LORD shall lift up a standard against him [Isa.59:19]. Like the Psalmist, be confident in the word of God today, *"A thousand shall fall at thy side, and ten thousand at thy right hand; but it shall not come nigh thee." [Ps.91:7;KJV]*. Knowing that God lives in you, and that He loves you, should cast away all fears from your life. Be still and know that He is the LORD!

PRAYER FOCUS

Dear heavenly Father, I'm fully persuaded that You are greater in me and nothing can snatch me out of Your hands. Today, put my trust in the power of Your name and proclaim victory over my foes in Jesus' name.

April 12

Focusing On The Miracle Or The Message?
Bible Reading: [John 5:1-9, KJV]

"When Jesus saw him lie, and knew that he had been now a long time in that case, he saith unto him, wilt though be made whole? The impotent man answered him, Sir, I have no man, when the water is troubled, to put me into the pool:."

Nowadays, miracles seem to take precedence (priority) over the message. While miracles are seemingly important, without the true message, there can be no salvation and total transformation. Of course, God takes in the prosperity of our health as human beings *[3 Jn.1:2]*.

The impotent man hadn't walk for 38 years. Year after year, he watched as people receive their healing. It's likely that those who focus so much on miracles instead of the message, become vulnerable to the exited minds of misguided people who have no knowledge of the Bible.

Oftentimes, they are led astray from the word of God to follow after the trickery of men. We can know the difference between a true and fake miracles only when our minds are focused on the message. The message is simple and clear, *"But we preach Christ crucified, the power of God, and the wisdom of God." [1 Cor.1:23-24;paraphrased]*

When the message [Jesus] appeared, the man's mind was focused on the miraculous pool. Jesus said to him, "Wilt thou be made whole?" Trying to give reasons for being in that condition for 38 years, the Master had compassion on Him and released the message. The Centurion also told Jesus, *"...speak the word only, and my servant shall be healed."[Matt.8:8]*. Whatever your condition, I command you to rise and walk in Jesus' name.

PRAYER FOCUS

Dear heavenly Father, thank You for the power of Your word. Today, I receive wholeness [spirit, soul & body] in Jesus' name.

April 13

Resistance Leads The To Revelation Of God's Incomparable Power
Bible Reading: [Exod.7:1-14]

"And the Egyptians shall know that I am the LORD, when I stretch forth mine hand upon Egypt, and bring out the children of Israel from among them." [Vs:5;KJV]

Whenever the word resistance is mentioned, what comes to mind is opposition. Resistance is the attempt to prevent or hinder something especially by action. Oftentimes, the devil brings resistance to prevent us from moving forward. It is written, *"Wherefore we would have come unto you, even I Paul, once and again; but Satan hindered us."* [1 Thes.2:18;KJV]. Resistance manifests in various forms. One thing is certain for those who have experienced resistance in life, it wasn't a pleasant experience. As a disciple of Christ, there is something more to resistance: it leads to revelation. Sometimes, God would allow great resistance, so we might have a revelation of his power and might. The greater the resistance, the greater the grace to overcome.

Because of pride and arrogance, Pharaoh hardened his heart against the will of God. Nevertheless, his magicians were not as powerful as God, and could not reverse the plagues upon the Egyptians. Realizing their inability to challenge God's authority, the magicians said to Pharaoh, *"This is the finger of God:.."* [Exod.8:19]. Beloved, whatever the resistance or opposition from the enemy's camp, let the finger of God be revealed today in your circumstance. Not by might, nor by power, but by the Spirit of God, let every obstacle or mountain before you collapse. From this day forward, I decree and declare your advancement in Jesus' name.

PRAYER FOCUS

Dear heavenly Father, none can compare to Your matchless worth. You are mighty and wondrous in design. To You all praises due in Jesus' name.

April 14

Situations Reveal God's Sufficiency
Bible Reading: [Jer.12:1-6]

"If you have run with the footmen and they have wearied you, then how can you contend with horses? And if in the land of peace, in which you trusted they wearied you, then how will you do in the floodplain of the Jordan?" [Vs: 5]

Sometimes in life, as a disciple of Christ, one wonders why a righteous person suffers in the presence of a good and kind God. In the midst of his challenges, prophet Jeremiah cried to God. Life was extremely difficult for him despite his love and obedience to preach to a generation of people that had totally forsaken the word of God. If his own people [family & Friends] dealt with him treacherously, what about his enemies? As a believer in Christ, when the going gets tough and your prayer doesn't bring immediate results, remember that the grace of God is sufficient.

Beloved in Christ, your situation, whatever it is, will reveal the sufficient of God. Apostle Paul, because of a thorn in his flesh, prayed for its removal. However, the cases of Jeremiah and Paul help us understand that answer to prayers don't always come as expected. God told Paul, *"My grace is sufficient for thee: for my strength is made perfect in weakness."** And Paul concluded, *"Most gladly therefore will I rather glory in my infirmity, that the power of Christ may rest upon me." [2 Cor.12:9;KJV].* Hallelujah! No matter the toughness of your situation, let God's sufficiency be revealed today in Jesus' name.

PRAYER FOCUS

Dear heavenly Father, I'm confident in the power of Your name and I'm fully persuaded that Your grace is sufficient for me in Jesus' name.

April 15

Yes LORD To Your Will & Your Way
Bible Reading: [Psalm 86:1-17]

*"Teach me thy way, O LORD; I will walk in thy truth:
unite my heart to fear thy name."[Vs:11]*

Dearly beloved, one request every believer should make to the LORD is that He will teach us His way. It's unfortunate that in this last days, many seek after miracles, instead of the way of God. Every true disciple must know the way and ways of God. It is written, *"He made known His ways unto Moses, His acts unto the children of Israel." [Ps. 103:7, KJV].* Of course, it's important for us to know the acts or works of God. However, if any man must walk and live in God's truth, he ought to know the ways (character) and way (path) of God.

One important blessing God gives us when we enter into a faith walk with Him is the Holy Spirit. It is written, *"But the Comforter, which is the Holy Ghost, whom the Father will send in my name, he shall teach you all things,..." [John 14:26].* Another portion of Scripture says, "But the anointing which ye have received of Him abideth in you, and ye need not that any man teach you: but as the same anointing teacheth you of all things, and is truth, and is no lie, and even as it hath taught you, ye shall abide in Him." *[1 John 2:27;KJV].*

The essence of the Holy Spirit teaching and leading us is that we should abide in Christ. Nowadays many don't abide in Christ because they are not taught. Some have only cultivated the attitude of moving from one church to the next or from one prophet to the other in search of miracles. A man after God's heart is one ready to be taught and live in God's way. It is written, *"..., I have found David the son of Jesse, a man after mine own heart, which shall fulfill all my will." [Acts 13:22;KJV]*

PRAYER FOCUS

Dear heavenly Father, today I make a commitment to walk and live in Your truth. LORD, grant me a teachable spirit and unite my heart to fear Your name. Amen.

April 16

The Priceless Gift Of God
Bible Reading: [John 17:1-5]

"And this is life eternal, that they might know thee the only true God, and Jesus Christ, whom thou hast sent." [Vs:3]

Dearly beloved, do you have eternal life? The only priceless gift in human history that is free is eternal life. It is so precious that its value cannot be determined. It is within the reach of all flesh. Eternal life means knowing God as the only true God, and Jesus Christ whom He has sent. Knowing God is more than an intellectual knowledge. Remember that even the devil believes that there is one God and trembles *[Jam.2:19]*. One can only know God through response to who He is, and what He accomplished on the cross as a result of His grace.

Knowing God means love for God and obedience to Jesus. Many religions in the world have created a god after their own imaginations because they do not know Jesus through the Holy Scriptures. It is written, *"…..for there is none other name under heaven given among men, whereby we must be saved."* [Acts.4:12;KJV]. Jesus is the only one who has the authority to give salvation. When we genuinely repent of our sin and enter into a personal relationship with God, He bestows Christ's love in us by the Holy Spirit. Choose today between eternal life in heaven and eternal punishment in Hell.

PRAYER FOCUS

Dear heavenly Father, it is not Your desire that anyone should perish, but that all should come to repentance and have abundant life in Christ. LORD, I surrender my whole life to You and embrace Your totality in Jesus' name.

April 17

God Values Right Heart Attitude Than Outward Appearance
Bible Reading: [Matt.23:1-33]

"Woe unto you, scribes and Pharisees, hypocrites! for ye are like unto whited sepulchres, which indeed appear beautiful outward, but are within full of dead men's bones, and of all uncleanness. Even so ye also outwardly appear righteous unto men, but within ye are full of hypocrisy and iniquity." [Vs:27-28;KJV]

Dearly beloved, someone once said, "Your attitude, not your aptitude, will determine your altitude." Like the Pharisees, many people make effort to obey rules rather than expressing true love for God. Our loyalty to God demands right attitude than outward appearance. Outward appearance only makes a man look holy, but being holy is a lifestyle that is born out of an intimate relationship with God.

The Pharisees enjoyed the praises of men. They had lost the perspective of inward beauty of the heart and were more concerned about outward or ceremonial cleansing. God has not called us to live as disciples merely as a show for others. He doesn't want us to misplace our priority regarding true love for Him. It is important to note that only our internal purity will result in outward righteousness. A right heart attitude will change you and transform the world around you. The Psalmist made this requests to God, *"Create in me a clean heart, O God; and renew a right spirit within me." [Ps.51:10;KJV]*

PRAYER FOCUS

Dear heavenly Father, You desire right heart attitude. Search me and know my heart: try me, and know my thoughts: and see if there is any wicked way in me, and lead me in the way everlasting in Jesus' name.

April 18

When Heaven Becomes More Real Than This World
Bible Reading: [2 Cor.4:13-18]

"While we look not at the things which are seen, but at the things which are not seen: for the things which are seen are temporal; but the things which are not seen are eternal." [Vs 18, KJV]

Dear friend, my sincere prayer to God for you is that Heaven will become more real to your heart. While multitudes are caught up with the pleasures and glamour of this world, the glimpse of heaven's beauty should be what an earnest disciple of Christ beholds. Ponder over the Psalmist's desire today, *"One thing have I desired of the LORD, that will I seek after; that I may dwell in the house of the LORD all the days of my life, to behold the beauty of the LORD, and to inquire in his temple." [Ps 27:4;KJV]*

Beloved, what are you concerned about in this life? There is no denying the fact that there are lots of competing interests in the world today. Remember that the grace of God has appeared, bringing salvation to all men. It instructs us to say no to ungodliness and worldly passions and to live godly lives in this present age. If truly we are disciples of Christ, then we have not received the spirit of the world, but the Spirit which is from God, so that we may understand what God has freely given us. Eye has not seen, nor ear heard, neither has entered into the heart of man, what God has prepared for them that love him *[1 Cor.2:9]*. No man can ever be satisfied with earthly pleasures and pursuits. Choose heaven and eternal values TODAY!

PRAYER FOCUS

Dear heavenly Father, You created me in Your image and put eternity in my heart. Help me to abide in Your word, and earnestly desire heaven's treasures each passing day in Jesus' name.

April 19

Your Sacrifice Matters To God
Bible Reading: [2 Cor.8:1-7]

"And now, brothers, we want you to know about the grace that God has given the Macedonian churches. Out of the most severe trial, their overflowing joy and extreme poverty welled up in rich generosity. For I testify that they gave as much as that they gave as much as they were able, and even beyond their ability. Entirely on their own." [Vs:1-3, NIV]

Dearly beloved, what kind of sacrifice are you offering to God today? It's important to note that God cares more about the sacrifice you are making than the size of your gift. From our text, it's obvious that God was pleased with the sacrificial actions of the Macedonian Churches, in making contributions to needy saints in Jerusalem out of an economic situation of great poverty. For the most part, some of us would have had a valid reason to justify why we shouldn't make contributions.

There are three important lessons that every true disciple of Christ ought to learn about sacrifices: The greatest sacrifice you can make to God is to offer yourself to Him. The Macedonian believers gave themselves first to the LORD. God is well-pleased when we offer ourselves too Him as a living sacrifice *[Rom.12:1.]*

True Sacrifice is what will cost you something: Think about the widow's offering. It is written, *"They all gave out of their wealth; but she, out of her poverty, put in everything —all she had to live on."** [Mark 12:44, NIV]. King David said to Araunah, *"I will not sacrifice to the LORD my God burnt offerings that cost me nothing"* [2 Sam.24:24].

Every true sacrifice comes from a willing and generous heart with the right motive. Your sacrifice matters to God. Make a covenant with Him by sacrifice today!

PRAYER FOCUS

Dear heavenly Father, I'm freely willing. All that I am and all that I have, I lay them down at Your feet in Jesus' name.

April 20

Men Worthy Of Double Honor
Bible Reading: [Phil.2:16-30]

"Yea, and if I be offered upon the sacrifice and service of your faith, I joy, and rejoice with you all" [Vs:17, KJV].

Beloved in the LORD, the world knows how to honor its own. Oftentimes those who have excelled in secular service, those who are powerful and those who are rich, are being honored. Are the children of this world wiser than the sons of light? Scripture admonishes us to give honor to whom it is due *[Rom.13:7]*. It's important to note that faithful service in the LORD's vineyard is a cause for rejoicing. Remember that nothing done for God is in vain *[1 Cor.15:58]*.

The characteristics of men worthy of honor in the body of Christ are obvious: Men who have offered their lives as a sacrifice and serve others in building their faith, men of proven character or worth, men who have risked their lives or come close to death for the sake of spreading the gospel (missionaries) by going where we cannot go ourselves. About them, Paul says, "Receive him in the LORD with all gladness, and hold such men in esteem" *[Vs:29]*. Beloved, choose this day to honor a servant of God worthy of honor and may the peace of God be with you.

PRAYER FOCUS

Dear heavenly Father, I offer myself holy and wholly to You, devoted to what matters to You and the Body of Christ in Jesus' name.

April 21

When A Generation Stands Up For The Truth
Bible Reading: [Dan.3:8-30]

Dearly beloved, from Scriptures, it is obvious that not all generations of Israel stood up for the truth. It's written, *"…..and there arose another generation after them, which knew not the LORD, nor yet the works which he had done for Israel." [Judges.2:10]*. Christian values are being eroded from our schools and communities because a generation is rising that do not know and fear God.

Recently, the Nigerian government negotiated the release of school children that were captured by Boko Haram militants. Only Leah Sharibu was not released. The freed school children then told Leah's parents that she had been held-back because she had refused to renounce her Christian faith and convert to Islam (Vatican news by Paul Samasumo).

How we so easily compromise our conviction about the truth of God's word nowadays! Those who stand up for the truth know whom they have believed. They know that no matter what happens, God's faithfulness is through all generations *[Ps 119:90]*. The three Hebrew men told King Nebuchadnezzar that God is able to deliver them. *"But if not, be it known unto thee, O king, that we will not serve thy gods, nor worship the golden image which thou hast set up." [Dan.3:8-30;KJV]*. Friend, do you know the truth? Are you standing up for the truth?

PRAYER FOCUS

Dear heavenly Father, I believe that only the truth sets men free. LORD, I yield myself to You, and trust in the power of Your name to stand up for the truth at all times in Jesus' name.

April 22

Clinging Unto Jesus
Bible Reading: [John 6:71]

"Then said Jesus unto the twelve, will ye also go away? Then Simon Peter answered him, LORD, to whom shall we go? Thou hast the words of eternal life." [Vs:67-68;KJV]

Beloved in the LORD, what is your motive to cling to something or someone? Clinging means to hold onto someone or something tightly. It also means to overly depend on someone or something. Just like in Jesus' days, we cling to people for various reasons: for opportunities, status/position, business contacts, provision and friendships etc. Oftentimes people are quick to withdraw when they don't get what they came for. As a matter of fact, thousands followed Jesus but had to withdraw because his teachings were difficult. Because of religious pride and arrogance, they were not open to learn new things. Of course, some followed Jesus because of the miraculous provision of food.

Are you the clinging type to Jesus? As a disciple, there must be a genuine reason why you are following Jesus and a strong conviction about faith in him. Why Jesus?

- He has the words of eternal life *[John 17:3]*
- Without Jesus we can do nothing *[John 15:5]*
- In Him we live, move and have our being *[Acts.17:25,28]*
- We are made free and whole only by knowing the truth about Jesus *[John 8:32]*.

When you feel alone, when all else seem to fail, when others are deserting you, only Jesus can make a big difference in your life and world! Overly depend on Him! He is the way, truth and life!

PRAYER FOCUS

Dear heavenly Father, without You, I can do nothing. LORD, I overly depend on You, grant me a teachable spirit and show me each passing day how to apply Your word in Jesus' name.

April 23

The Power Of God's Watchmen
Bible Reading: [Isa.62:1-7]

"I have set watchmen upon thy walls, O Jerusalem, which shall never hold their peace day nor night: ye that make mention of the LORD, keep not silent, and give Him no rest, till he establish, and till he make Jerusalem a praise in the earth." [Vs:6-7, KJV]

Beloved in the LORD, God has called you to be a watchman. A watchman is a person who hears words from God's mouth and gives warning to the people *[Ezek.3:17]*. He perceives the spiritual and social conditions of the people, and then proclaims the message of God. Some are assigned watchmen over continents, nations, regions, communities, campuses and families. Regardless of where God has positioned you, He wants all His watchmen to be effective. God is displeased when watchmen do not perform their duties. One of the reasons why things go wrong in Society today is because some watchmen are blind and ignorant. It is written, *"His watchmen are blind: they are all ignorant, they are all dumb dogs, they cannot bark; sleeping, lying down, loving to slumber" [Isa.56:10;KJV]*. Remember, while men slept, his enemy came and sowed tares among the wheat, and went his way *[Matt.13:25]*

The goal of a watchman is to proclaim the promises of God, and then intercede for the people through prayer that God's promises be fulfilled. When a watchman is passionate about the salvation of God for his people, he will be moved to pray thus, *"Your kingdom come, Your will be done on earth as it is in heaven" [Matt.6:10]*. Persistent prayer is the key: not being silent day and night, giving God no rest, until He establishes His people. It's important to note that you can't be a watchman for God if Jesus Christ is not the LORD and Savior of your life.

PRAYER FOCUS

Dear heavenly Father, I have understood my role as a watchman. Enable me LORD to hear, pray and proclaim Your word in Jesus' name.

April 24

Adapting To Others
Bible Reading: [Eph.5:11-21]

"Wherefore be ye not unwise, but understanding what the will of the LORD is. Submitting yourselves one to another in the fear of God." [Vs:17,21]

One very important lesson in life is learning to adapt to others and to situations. Life will not always be the way you think or want it. We are living in a changing world. Each day brings forth a new thing and every day we meet new people, new faces and new personalities. To adapt means to adjust to different conditions or to change to meet different situations. It's important to note that the only thing that does not change is the Word of God. That is why we must understand what the will of God is and be thankful in everything, because all things work together for good to them that love God *[Rom.8:28]*.

Adapting to others means submitting to others according to the word of God. Paul says, *"To the weak became I as weak, that I might gain the weak: I am made all things to all men, that I might by all means save some." [1 Cor.9:22;KJV]*. Jesus Christ being God, shared our humanity (flesh/blood); that through death he might destroy him that had the power of death." *[Heb.2:14;KJV]*. As a true disciples of Christ, you don't adapt to the sinful lifestyles of men *[Rom.12:2]*. You can only make yourself a servant unto all, in order to relieve or change their condition. Are you adapting to others?

PRAYER FOCUS

Dear heavenly Father, You shared my humanity through Christ in order to save me. LORD, teach and help me each passing day to adapt to others in Jesus' name.

April 25

Making Wrong Right
Bible Reading: [Neh.5:1-13]

"And I was very angry when I heard their cry and these words. Then I consulted with myself, and I rebuked the nobles, and the rulers, and said to them, Ye exact usury, every one of his brother. And I set a great assembly against them." [Vs:6-7;KJV]

Dearly beloved, our high calling as disciples of Christ in this perverse crooked generation is to make wrong right. Nowadays a lot of things are falling apart in Society. As a true disciple of Christ, do you choose to make wrong right or to continue with the hypocrisy of others? Being responsible as a disciple of Christ means making wrong right especially when others resort to compromising lifestyles to earn the applause of men. One of man's greatest problems is fear. That wasn't the case of Nehemiah at a time when others took pleasure in usury. That wasn't the case of Paul at a time when Peter decided to play the hypocrite with other Jews *[Gal.2:11-14]*.

Some ways to make wrong right:

- Imitate Christ: *"Imitate me, just as I also imitate Christ." [1 Cor.11:1;NKJV]* Don't pay anyone evil for evil *[Rom.12:17]*
- Boldness: Speak without fear or favor.
- Rebuke with love: *[Prov.27:5]*.

Compromise is a vital aspect in getting along with others but we should never compromise the truth of God's word. *"For I am not ashamed of the gospel of Christ: for it is the power of God unto salvation for everyone that believeth" [Rom.1:16]*.

PRAYER FOCUS

Dear heavenly Father, You desire that I should walk in the fear of God. LORD, grant me wisdom and boldness to be straight forward about the truth of the gospel in Jesus' name.

April 26

I Don't Know How, But I Know Whom I Have Believed
Bible Reading: [Luke 1:26-38]

"Then said Mary unto the angel, *How* shall this be, seeing I know not a man? [Vs: 34;KJV]

I know some of us find ourselves at crossroads in life today. Oftentimes, our present reality will prompt us to ask the question, "How shall this be?" Our Christian journey is like a train that runs on rails described in Scriptures as the evidence of things not seen *[Heb.11:1]*. As humans, we make life complex whenever we choose to lean on our own understanding. Our flesh or intellect is the rational part of our being that wants us to figure out every step of the way.

The truth is that sometimes, God takes us to a place deeper than our feels. To a place where there is no profit in the flesh, a place where we are helpless. It's important to note that in every situation, even in the valley of dry bones, it is the Spirit that quickens (gives life). Therefore, we must choose to believe the Word — it is the evidence of things not seen. Jesus Christ told His disciples, *"It is the Spirit that quickeneth; the flesh profiteth nothing: the words that I speak unto you, they are spirit, and they are life."* *[John 6:63;KJV]*

I don't know how, but I know whom I have believed: *He is able to make all grace abound toward me [2 Cor.9:8]. He is able to do immeasurably more than I ask or think [Eph.3:20]. He is able to provide all my need [Philipp. 4:19]. He is able to keep me from falling [Jude 24]. He is able to save to the uttermost [Heb.7:25]. He quickens dead situations and calls into existence the things that do not exist [Rom.4:17].* Hallelujah!

PRAYER FOCUS

Dear heavenly Father, I don't know how, but I believe that Your counsel shall stand and Your promises shall come to fruition in my life.

April 27

Maintaining Composure In The Face Of Criticism
Bible Reading: [2 Sam.16:5-14]

"And as David and his men went by the way, Shimei went along on the hill's side over against him, and cursed as he went, and threw stones at him, and cast dust." [Vs:13;KJV]

Dearly beloved, criticism whether justified or unjustified is something we should expect in life, especially those who are called to lead. Sometimes the devil uses criticism as a tool to discourage or distract us. In life, we must understand that there are always critics, no matter how good you are or how best you perform. That's their job, they have decided to be instruments of the devil.

Self-control or composure in the face of criticism or opposition is very important especially for believers in Christ. Some people will intentionally criticize you to test your character quality. Composure is the state or feeling of being calm, confident and in control of oneself.

Do you easily lose composure amid crisis or become emotional? If care is not taken, some of us will replace our righteous garment with an evil garment for a moment in order to defend ourselves. May God help us in Jesus' name. It's true that criticism, especially destructive criticism can be a trying experience. However, every believer should attain a level of maturity in order to ignore it. David had the authority and might men ready to act on his behalf, but he ignored Shimei a loyalist to king Saul. His mighty men knew that the king's business or command requires urgency *[1 Sam.21:8]*, but David held his peace and kept his men under control.

As a matter of fact, David was innocent; he didn't destroy Saul's family. It's important to note that God does not forbid us from rebuke men sometimes if necessary *[Prov.27:5]*. However, He knows how to vindicate the righteous! Let your self-control and gentleness be evident before all men.

PRAYER FOCUS

Dear heavenly Father, help me to exercise tolerance and self-control in the face of opposition or criticism.

April 28

Let Patience Finish Its Work
Bible Reading: [James 1:2-8]

"But let patience have her perfect work, that ye may be perfect and entire, wanting nothing."[Vs:4;KJV]

Patience is a virtue that each one of us would like to possess in increasing measure. It is the capacity to accept or tolerate delay, trouble, or suffering without getting angry or upset. In life, the depth of our character is revealed by how we react when under pressure. As believers in Christ, whenever we fail to endure, we will certainly wander from the truth. King Saul went against the specific instructions of prophet Samuel. In the face of opposition, he offered a sacrifice that only a priest had to offer *[1 Sam.13:8-13]*.

Our faith in Christ must result in growth in Christlikeness in Character. You may ask the question: how long do I need to be patient in my situation? The answer is: until patience has produced its perfect work in your life. It's worth mentioning that in the waiting season, you are not left alone. God is at work in your life and situation. Like Abraham, don't take matters into your own hands because you are under pressure *[Gen.16:2]*. Enjoy the full assurance and development of your hope until the end. Follow the examples of those who through faith and patience inherited the promises of God *[Heb.6:12]*.

PRAYER FOCUS

Dear heavenly Father, I have come to understand the important role patience plays in my walk with You. LORD, renew my strength as I wait upon You.

April 29

How Strong Is Your Foundation?
Bible Reading: [Luke 6:46-49]

*"Whosoever cometh to me, and heareth my sayings, and doeth them,
I will show you to whom he is like:
He is like a man who build an house, and digged deep,
and laid the foundation on a rock:.. " [Vs: 47,48]*

*"If the foundations be destroyed,
what can the righteous do?" [Ps 11:3;KJV].*

Dear friend, have you ever seen a university or government building that has been existing for centuries? From personal observation especially in the United States, a closer look at architectural designs reveals that most residential buildings have shallow foundation. For the most part, these buildings don't last long, and are vulnerable to fire disasters and storms.

The foundation is the base of everything: family, church, business, and nation etc. Is your life built on a hard foundation? Only a strong foundation with Jesus will protect us from the storms of life. The storm of life comes in diverse ways: persecution, afflictions, losing of a loved one or something precious, failing an exams etc. A strong foundation with Jesus who is the Word of life will make all the difference. It is written, *we are hard pressed on every side, but not crushed; perplexed, but not in despair; persecuted, but not abandoned; struck down, but not destroyed."[2 Cor.4:8-9;KJV].*

When circumstances are frightening and foundations in the world (economic, social and political) are crumbling, only faith in God will sustain us and enable us resist fear. Let the Word of God and prayer be the foundation of your life.

PRAYER FOCUS

Dear heavenly Father, I'm fully persuaded that You are greater than all. LORD, teach me day how to lay the godly foundation as an expert builder in Jesus' name.

April 30

Knowing What You Are Dealing With
Bible Reading: [1 Sam.15:14-23]

"And Samuel said, What meaneth then this bleating of the sheep in mine ears, and the lowing of the oxen which I hear? But the people took of the spoil, sheep and oxen, the chief of the things which should have been utterly destroyed, to sacrifice unto the LORD thy God in Gilgal. And Samuel said, hath the LORD as great delight in burnt offerings and sacrifices, as in obeying the voice of the LORD? " [Vs: 14,21-22;KJV]

The things we deal with in life will either make or break us! What we deal with the most gains our attention. Remember what Scripture says, *"For where your treasure is, there will your heart be also." [Matt.6:21;KJV]*. Saul tried it, Balaam and Judas did same, but they all made a desperate failure. You can't serve two masters. It's obvious that a divided heart will lose both.

If you are dealing with money: money is good and answers all things, but the love of money is the root of all evil: some coveted after, and have erred from the faith *[Eccl.10:19;1 Tim.6:10,17]*. If you are dealing with material things in general, remember that the things seen are temporal.

Therefore, set your heart on things above, which are eternal *[Matt.6:21;2 Cor.4:18]*

If you are dealing with time, remember that the hour which has fled by, can't return again.

Therefore, maximize your time and make the most of every opportunity *[Eph.5:16; Rom 13:11]*.

If you are dealing with your Bible, the Word of life, it makes wise the simple.

PRAYER FOCUS

Dear heavenly Father, You richly provide us with everything to enjoy. LORD, teach me each passing day how to deal with everything in order to glorify You.

MAY

"Thus saith the LORD, thy Redeemer, the Holy one of Israel; I am the LORD thy God which teacheth thee to profit, which leadeth thee by the way that thou shouldest go."

[Isaiah 48:17;KJV]

"Trust in the LORD with all thine heart; and lean not unto thine own understanding. In all thy ways acknowledge him, and he shall direct thy paths."

[Proverbs 3:5-6; KJV]

****

*Jehovah Shammah - **[The LORD is There]** - Ezek.48:35*

*5 = **[God's goodness and grace upon humanity]***

May 1

A New Beginning
Bible Reading: [Philipp.1:1-11]

"Always in every prayer of mine for you all making request with joy, for your fellowship in the gospel from the first day until now; Being confident of this very thing, that he which hath begun a good work in you will perform it until the day of Jesus Christ:" [Vs: 4-6;KJV]

Dearly beloved, if there is going to be a new beginning, one must forget about the past. God is speaking to somebody that the past is over, a new thing is about to happen. It is written, *"Remember ye not the former things, neither consider the things of old. Behold, I will do a new thing; "* [Isa.43:18-19;KJV]. When something isn't working, there is need for a new beginning.

Sometimes we spend so much time, energy and resources on things that are taking us nowhere! We invest so much in a relationship, in sinful lifestyles, in a particular business or area of specialty, and in a particular place. The strangest thing that happens in the middle of nowhere is failure to wait, take stock and prayerfully reflect on options. To take stock means that you pray and think carefully in order to make a decision about what to do next.

Sometimes we stay in our comfort zone not willing to dare into new ventures. If one can risk his or her old lifestyle in the hope of profit in Christ, God will gain the glory. When you feel as though you are not making progress, be confident that God's mercies are new every morning. God can be trusted to continue his work of changing people into the likeness of Christ. Yield to Him today!

PRAYER FOCUS

Dear heavenly Father, great is Your faithfulness toward me. I'm confident today to start it over again because You will perfect Your purpose for me in Jesus' name.

May 2

Passionate Seekers Of God
Bible Reading: [Heb.11:1-6]

Are you a passionate seeker of God? Literally to seek means: to search for someone or something. It also means to ask for help, and advice etc. A spiritual seeker is someone who is looking for the truth. Such a person is determined to grow and learn more. It is written, *"And when he had removed him (Saul), He raised up unto them David to be their king; to whom also He gave their testimony, and said, I have found David the son of Jesse, a man after mine own heart, which shall fulfill all my will."* [Acts 13:22, KJV]

PRAYER FOCUS

Dear heavenly Father, You are a rewarder to those who diligently seek you. LORD, My soul earnestly seeks You in Jesus' name.

May 3

Knowing Who You Are Dealing With
Bible Reading: [Mark 9:38-40]

"For he that is not against us is on our part." [Vs:40, KJV]
Can two walk together, except they be agreed ?

Sometimes in life, we relate to God like we do with fellow human beings. As a result, we take God for granted. Sometimes in life, we expect fellow human beings to behave or act like God. As a result, we make wrong judgments when man fails to act accordingly. There are many different kinds of people in the world.

Knowing who you are dealing with is very important because it determines the kind of relationship you want to establish *[1 John.2:19]*. If you are dealing with God: *"O worship the LORD in the beauty of holiness: fear before Him, all the earth." [Ps 96:9;KJV]*.

If you are dealing with the devil, you shouldn't be ignorant of his schemes. *"Lest Satan should get an advantage of us: for we are not ignorant of his devices" [2 Cor.2:11;KJV]*. If you are dealing with a disciple of Christ, the goal is how to connect more deeply: *"We then that are strong ought to bear the infirmities of the weak, and not to please ourselves. Let every one of us please his neighbor for his good to edification" [Rom.15:1-2;KJV]*. If you are dealing with unbelievers: *Let your light so shine before men, that they may see your good works, and glorify your Father who is in heaven" [Matt.5:16;KJV]*.

PRAYER FOCUS

Dear heavenly Father, grant me the ability to relate to others and wisdom to deal with everyone according to Your word in Jesus' name.

May 4

Freedom From The Power of Sin & Fear
Bible Reading: [Gal.2:20-21; Heb.2:14-15]

Fear is an unpleasant emotion that leads one either to flee or unable to think and act normally. It makes a person feels something bad or evil will happen. Only God's love has the power to quiet our fears and give us the boldness to face every situation with confidence. He that fears has not been made perfect in love. Because perfect love casts out fear, each passing day, we can remind ourselves of God's love *[1 John 4:18]*.

Sin is that condition and activity of human beings that is offensive to God, their Creator (J.D.Douglas). One reassuring fact is that the Spirit of life in Christ Jesus has freed us from the law of sin and death *[Rom.8:2]*. Sin is no longer our master because we are not under the law, but under grace *[Rom.6:14]*. Amazing grace!

We are no longer slaves to sin:

"For He hath made Him to be sin, who knew no sin; that we might be made the righteousness of God in Him" [2 Cor.5:21;KJV]

We are no longer slaves to fear

"For God hath not given us the spirit of fear; but of power, and of love, and of a sound mind." [2 Tim.1:7;KJV]

PRAYER FOCUS

Dear heavenly Father, thank You for Your unconditional love and amazing grace.

I decree and declare that I am no longer a slave to sin and fear. I've been redeemed by the blood of Jesus Christ and empowered by the Holy Spirit in Jesus' name.

May 5

Dangers Of Lip Service
Bible Reading: [Isa.29:13-16]

"Wherefore the LORD said, forasmuch as this people draw near me with their mouth, and with their lips do honour me, but have removed their heart far from me, and their fear toward me is taught by the precept of men:" [Vs:13;kjv]

Dear friend, are you in the business of lip service? You claim to be close to God but your heart is far from Him. You use pious sounding language in prayer and talk, but your heart is far from God. Every human being is capable of hypocrisy. Like false prophets and the Pharisees, sometimes we slip into routine patterns but we are not sincere and devoted in our worship of God. Lip service means saying "Yes" with your mouth but saying "No" in your heart and by your actions. It is honouring God with your lips when your heart is far from Him [Ron Graham]. It is to say that you agree with something but do nothing to support it [Cambridge Dic.].

Nobody can create a culture of success with lip service in both the Body of Christ and the secular world. Do you give lip service to your values, vision, and goals? Your intents are not always carried into action? It is time to make serious considerations. Honoring God in words but insulting Him in practice is vain worship. God sees and knows us! Let's give Him our love and devotion today. Let's ascribe to Him the glory due His name.

PRAYER FOCUS

Dear heavenly Father, forgive me for every act of lip service. I commit myself to worship You and serve Your purposes sincerely. In Jesus' name

May 6

When Your Expectations Don't Match Your Experience
Bible Reading: [1 Sam.17:31-50]

"Then Saul clothed David with his armor; he put a bronze helmet on his head and clothed him with a coat of mail. And David girded his sword over his armor. Then he tried to go, but could not, for he was not used to it. And David said to Saul, I cannot go with these, for I am not used to them. And David took them off." [Vs:38-39]

Dearly beloved, you are dreaming about it and counting on it, but your experience says otherwise. In the secular world, work experience is very important for recruitment. Your experience is what you have personally encountered or lived through, while your expectation is the strong belief that something will happen. In reality, David had never worn a military hardware. And David said unto Saul, I cannot go with these, for I am not used to them. And David took them off." [Vs:39]. About Goliath, Saul said to David, *"Thou are not able to go against this Philistine to fight with him: for thou art but a youth, and he a man of war from his youth." [Vs:33;KJV]*. In other words, Goliath had professional experience for battle from his youth, while David had none.

It is worth mentioning that David's courage did not rest in military hardware (armor) and physical stature. His confidence rested in the fact that he looked at the situation from God's point of view and trusted the fact that God was with him. As a matter of fact, it was a critical time and the God of Israel was challenged by Goliath. David knew whom he had believed and the God he served. Those who know their God shall be strong, and do exploit *[Dan.11:32]*. Others saw a giant but David saw a big God on his side. Others bowed to mockery and retreated but David forged ahead and said, *"I come against you Philistine in the name of the LORD of Host."* When your expectations and experience don't match, viewing circumstances from God's point of view will put giant obstacles in perspective.

PRAYER FOCUS

Dear heavenly Father, I cease to lean on my own understanding. LORD, I'm fully persuaded that victory/success is not based on my desire or effort, but on God who shows mercy *[Rom.9:16]* in Jesus' name.

May 7

Power Of Praise In A Strange Place
Bible Reading: [Psalm 137:1-4]

"How shall we sing the LORD's song in a strange land?" [Psalm 137:4]

It's uncommon for men to sing praises in a strange place. A strange place is an unusual, unfamiliar or a place not known or experienced before. Strange places are obvious: night seasons, valley of the shadow of death or valley of trouble, wilderness or barren land, prison, refugee camp, quarantine environment, and when surrounded by an enemy etc. Life becomes so uncomfortable when we find ourselves in such an environment. Our agony can make it difficult to imagine singing praises.

The Jewish captives questioned why they should sing the LORD's song. However, in such places, we can turn the tide by invoking God's presence through high praises. He dwells in the praises of His people. It is written, *"Sing, O barren, thou that didst not bear! Break forth into singing and cry aloud,." [Isa.54:1;Ps.22:3]*

It is written, *"And at midnight Paul and Silas prayed, and sang praises unto God: and the prisoners heard them. And suddenly there was a great earthquake, so that the foundations of the prison where shaken:." [Acts 16:25-26;KJV]*. The power of praise in a strange land will: Open prison doors, Set prisoners free and Cause men to receive the gift of salvation. You may be having a fresh memory on your mind about the terrible ordeal you've been through. May God put joy in your heart to sing in Jesus name.

PRAYER FOCUS

Dear heavenly Father, thank You for loving me. Today, I receive grace and strength to sing of Your power and goodness in a strange place in Jesus' name.

May 8

When God Speaks
- Things Have Got To Change
Bible Reading: [Matt.8:5-13]

"The centurion answered and said, LORD, I am not worthy that thou shouldest come under my roof: but speak the word only, and my servant shall be healed." [Vs: 8;KJV]

Beloved in the LORD, any word that goes out from the mouth of the LORD cannot be hindered because it is living, powerful and sharper than any two-edged sword *[Heb.4:12]*. Nature and situations obey the authority of God's word - for by it were all things created. Do you find yourself today in a situation that seems uncomfortable? There is a seasoned word from Scriptures to meet your need. Like the Centurion, recognize Jesus' authority by the written and spoken word (rhema). It is written, *So shall my word be that goeth forth out of my mouth: it shall not return unto me void, but it shall accomplish that which I please, and it shall prosper in the thing whereto I sent it."* *[Isa.55:11;Ps.107:20;KJV]*. May the Word run swiftly, prosper and prevail today in Jesus' name.

The Centurion believed in the power of Jesus to reach beyond His presence. He did not allow obstacles (position, pride, money) stand between him and the LORD. He was a Gentile meeting a Jew. Your distance, race and language Can't limit God's mercy, power and operation. As you approach God with a sincere heart and faith in His word, wherever you are, let the Word touch and transform your life/situation in Jesus' name. Your obedience and faith matters because you matter to God. And Jesus said unto the Centurion, *"go thy way; and as thou has believed, so be it done unto thee"* [Vs:13]. Hallelujah!

PRAYER FOCUS

Dear heavenly Father, You are omnipresent, omniscient and omnipotent God. LORD, I believe in the power of Your word and receive my breakthrough today in Jesus' name.

May 9

This Is The Way. Walk In It
Bible Reading: [John 14:1-6]

Your ears shall hear a word behind you, saying, "This is the way, walk in it," whenever you turn to the right hand Or whenever you turn to the left. (Isa.30:21)

God expects a lot from us, and many times following Him can be painful; but He always acts out of His love for us. Whenever the people of Jerusalem left God's path, He would correct them. He will do same for us. But when we hear His voice of correction, we must be willing to follow it. God is still in the business of speaking to us. He speaks every day. Can you hear the voice of God? *"God, who at various times and in various ways spoke in time past to the fathers by the prophets, has in these last days spoken to us by His Son,.." (Heb.1:1,2)*

While God takes pleasure speaking to us, some take pleasure hardening their hearts.

This is what the LORD says, "Stand at the crossroads and look; ask for the ancient paths, ask where the good way is, and walk in it, and you will find rest for your souls. But you said, 'We will not walk in it.' " *(Jer.6:16)*. Remember, *"There is a way that seems right to a man, but its end is the way of death." (Prov.14:12)*.

The Lord is ready to guide the wayward. It is time for those who are wayward to gain understanding. *"These also who erred in spirit will come to understanding, and those who complain will learn doctrine." (Isa.29:24)*. You may be going through difficult time, try to appreciate the experience and grow from it, learning what God wants to teach you. God may be showing you His love by patiently walking with you through adversity. Jesus said to them, *"I am the way the truth, and the life. No one comes to the Father except through Me." (John 14:6)*. "For as many as are led by the Spirit of God, these are sons of God." *(Rom 8:14)*.

This is the way; walk in it. As has been said: *"TODAY, if you hear God's voice, do not harden your hearts as you did in the rebellion." (Heb.3:15)*

PRAYER FOCUS

Dear heavenly Father, have mercy upon me for occasions that I have failed to listen to Your voice and chose to walk in disobedience in Jesus' name.

May 10

The Devil Distracts What He Can't Destroy
Bible Reading: [Mark 4:35-41]

"And he arose, and rebuked the wind, and said unto the sea, Peace, be still. And the wind ceased, and there was a great calm." [Vs:39]

Beloved in the LORD, as pilgrims on a journey, each one of us shouldn't be ignorant of the devices of the enemy *[2 Cor.2:11]*. The thief comes only to steal, kill and to destroy *[Jn 10:10]*. Distraction is anything that that prevents someone from giving full attention to something else. The greatest distraction always comes when we get serious about our walk and fellowship with God through His word and prayer. Nowadays distractions are many. Distraction leads to divided attention or competing interest. Think about the devil, the voice of the world and social media/TV as sources of distraction when we don't exercise self-control.

Christ is the captain of our salvation. Whenever we start losing sight of Him, we are trying to lead the way. Oftentimes this leads us to the wrong direction. Be determined not to allow any form of distraction take your focus away from God and His purpose for your life. Set your priorities right today. *"As many as are led by the Spirit of God, they are the Sons of God"[Rom.8:14;KJV]*.

PRAYER FOCUS

Dear heavenly Father, help me to be sensitive to distractions and exercise discipline. Today, I fix my eyes on Jesus and rebuke any spirit of distraction in Jesus' name.

May 11

The Sure And Secure Source Of Greener Pastures
Bible Reading: [John 10:1-10]

"I am the door: by me if any man enter in, he shall be saved, and shall go in and out, and find pasture." [Vs:9]

In the world, there are many people who wouldn't go through the right door in life even if access is free. They desire an indirect way of achieving something, so that people do not know about it and so should not object it. Are you a back door fan? In this portion of Scriptures, Jesus Christ is not presenting Himself as a back door, but as the door and the only way of access to God. It is written, *"Neither is there salvation in any other: for there is none other name under heaven given among men, whereby we must be saved" [Acts 4:12;KJV].* God wants everyone to enter into the kingdom by the proper entry, no matter how narrow. *"For through Him (Christ), we both have access by one Spirit unto the Father" [Eph.2:18;KJV]*

Friend, do you desire greener pastures? Jesus Christ is the source, and not America or Europe. God cherishes your prosperity in all things, especially your health. Christ is the Word of life. In Him, you will go in and out and find pasture. The Psalmist says, *"He maketh me to lie down in green pastures: he leadeth me beside the still waters" ([Ps 23:2;KJV].*

PRAYER FOCUS

LORD Jesus, You are the Way, the Truth, and the Life. I embrace Your totality today and put my trust in Your power to make me lie down in green pastures.

May 12

Prepare To Meet Thy God
Bible Reading: [Amos 4:1-13]

*"Therefore thus will I do unto thee, O Israel:
and because I will do this unto thee,
prepare to meet thy God, O Israel" [Vs:12;KJV]*

The one who created the heavens and the earth, is both the God of mercy and justice. Sometimes He will discipline us like a Father in order to encourage repentance. Some have forfeited so much in life because they failed to respond with repentance to the chastisement of the LORD. God warns us in many ways. No matter how God warned the Israelites, they were bent on doing evil. It is written, *"Because sentence against an evil work is not executed speedily, therefore the heart of the sons of me is fully set in them to do evil." [Eccl.8:11;KJV].* Beloved, you might have succeeded to commit evil time and again without being caught. Remember, everyone will give an account to God for the things they have done *[Rom.4:12]*

Dear friend, are you still ignoring the rebuke of the LORD? He says today, *"Prepare to meet thy God."* They One you have chosen to ignore today, be rest assured that you will meet Him face-to-face on judgement day. He would be just in His actions if you continue to violate His covenant or ignore His voice. Don't be indifferent to God's chastisement. While there is yet time and His grace still abounds, prepare to meet thy God. Where will you spend eternity? Heaven or Hell!

PRAYER FOCUS

Dear heavenly Father, You discipline those You love. LORD, I turn my heart to You in genuine repentance and ask for forgiveness today.

May 13

Walking In The Same Spirit and Same Steps
Bible Reading: [2 Cor.12:14-19]

"I desire Titus, and with him I sent a brother. Did Titus make a gain of you? Walk we not in the same spirit? Walked we not in the same steps?" [Vs:18]

We have been called into a dignified walk with Christ. If truly we are followers of Christ and born of the Spirit of God, then we ought not to take advantage of the brethren in anything. Our goal should be, to build up one another spiritually (edify) and motivate one another unto love and good works *[Heb.10:24]*

Those who are in Christ are born of the same Spirit. True believers have not received the spirit of the World but of God *[1 Cor.2:12]*. Therefore, all born again Christians regardless of denominational preference ought to be like-minded, and be led by the same Spirit *[Philipp.2:2]*.

Every true believer ought to walk in the footsteps of Christ. It is written, *"The steps of a good/righteous man are ordered by the LORD: and he delighteth in his ways."* [Psalms 37:23]. Beloved, God hasn't called us to enrich ourselves like Gehazi and Judas Iscariot because of greed, but unto a holy and dignified walk with Him.

PRAYER FOCUS

Dear heavenly Father, the ways of man are before Your eyes. LORD, help me each passing day to be like-minded with those in the household of faith and not to take advantage of anyone in Jesus' name.

May 14

The Word That Burns Within
Bible Reading: [Luke 24:27-35]

And they said to one another, "Did not our heart burn within us, while he talked with us by the way, and while he opened to us the scriptures?" [Vs:32]

"Is not my word like as a fire? Saith the LORD; and like a hammer that breaketh the rock in pieces?" [Jer.23:29;KJV]

Nowadays people don't tremble at the proclamation of God's word. Hearts have become callous i.e. hardened, indifferent and insensitive to the word. As a matter of fact, the spirit of the world is taking its toll on many and because of increase wickedness, the love of many has grown cold *[Matt.24:12]*. Beloved, does the Word burns within you when it is proclaimed or when you meditate on it? In Paul's letter to the church of the Thessalonians, he says, *"For our gospel came not unto you in word only, but also in power, and in the Holy Ghost, and in much assurance; as ye know what manner of men we were among you for your sake."[1 Thes.1:5;KJV].*

Today, sincerely pray that the word of God like a hammer, will break every hardened heart and accomplish God's desire and purpose for which it is proclaimed.

For the word to burn within the heart of men, the preacher must live a decent and holy life. The word must be anointed, i.e. preached in power and in the Holy Spirit. The witness or preacher must live a prayerful life. The word must bring strong conviction and much assurance in the heart of the hearer. The hearer must mix it with faith *[Heb.4:2;Rom.10:17]*. Jeremiah says, *"...But His word was in mine heart as a burning fire shut up in my bones" [Jer.20:9]*. On the day of Pentecost, the people were cut to the heart when they heard Peter's sermon *[Acts.2:37]*. The Word makes all the difference in our lives when received with great eagerness and a teachable spirit. If you hear God's voice, harden not your heart.

PRAYER FOCUS

Dear heavenly Father, expand my heart to receive more of Your Word. Oh LORD, let Your Word cut to my heart, let it pierce and burn within me each time I hear it in Jesus' name.

May 15

Divine Exchange Calvary
Bible Reading: [2 Cor.5:15-21]

"For he hath made him to be sin for us, who knew no sin; that we might be made the righteousness of God in him."
[Vs:21;KJV]

I know that many of us are familiar with the concept of money or foreign exchange. Foreign exchange is a process of settling accounts or debts between persons residing in different countries (Merriam Webster). The greatest love God has demonstrated to humanity is the exchange of Christ's righteousness for our sins. In Revelation chapter 5, John saw a scroll (book) containing the full account of what God had in store for the world. Following the proclamation of the Angel, nobody in heaven and earth was worthy to open it except Jesus Christ, the Lamb of God.

Christ was worthy to open the scroll by living a perfect life of obedience to God, evident by His death on the cross for the sins of the world. He exchanged his obedience for our disobedience, His righteousness for our sins, His beauty for our ashes, His glory for our shame, His peace for our punishment, His perfect health for our sicknesses, His cure for our curses, His riches for our debts. It's a done deal! God was in Christ reconciling the world unto Himself, not counting people's sins against them. Hallelujah!

PRAYER FOCUS

Dear heavenly Father, Today I join the redeemed to thank You for Your unconditional love. LORD, You deserve the glory!

May 16

The Emmaus Experience
Bible Reading: [Luke 24:13-35]

*"Then he said unto them, O fools, and slow of heart to believe all that the prophets have spoken:
Ought not Christ to have suffered these things, and to enter into glory?" [Vs:25-26]*

There are many powerful lessons we learn through life experiences. It's obvious that some experiences are uncomfortable while others do leave a glorious memory. Whatever the case, the Emmaus experience is one that any true follower of Christ would desire. The two disciples expressed their sadness and frustration of what just happened in Jerusalem, not being able to recognize that they were talking to Jesus. Whenever we allow our disappointments to overwhelm us, we lose sight of what God is about to do. Understanding Scriptures will keep our focus in the right direction.

It was seven miles from Jerusalem to the village of Emmaus. The LORD helped their ignorance by explaining Scriptures about himself beginning with Moses and all the prophets. I'm fully persuaded that the LORD will reveal Himself to you in a dramatic way if you are determined to take a 7-hour or 7-day faith walk in prayer and meditation this season. The resurrected King is resurrecting and perfecting all things. *"But if the Spirit of Him that raised up Jesus from the dead dwell in you, He that raised up Christ from the dead shall also quicken your mortal bodies by His Spirit that dwelleth in you."* [Rom.8:11;KJV]

PRAYER FOCUS

Dear heavenly Father, no purpose of Yours can be thwarted. LORD, grant me an understanding heart and the ability to discern the fulfillment of Bible prophecies in Jesus' name.

May 17

The Value Of Redemption
Bible Reading: [Psalm 49:7-8; Rom.5:6-11]

"No man can redeem the life of another or give to God a ransom for him— the ransom for a life is costly, no payment is ever enough —" [Ps 49:7-8;NIV]

"For when we were yet without strength, in due time Christ died for the ungodly."[Rom.5:6;KJV]

From a CNN report and other news outlets, recently in Libya, two human beings were sold for 1,200 Libyan dinars [$800]. In ancient slave markets, slaves were ransomed in order to get freedom. Redemption means deliverance from sin and freedom from captivity. There is nobody on earth that was born righteousness *[Rom.3:23]*. Thus, everyone needs redemption. The death of Christ on the Cross is quite telling. As slaves to sin, the blood of Christ purchased our freedom. It is important to note that Christ the Lamb of God was slain from the foundation of the world *[Rev.13:8;1 Pet.1:20]*

God demonstrated His love toward us in that, while we were utterly helpless Christ came to our rescue. He paid a debt He did not owe, we owed a debt we could not pay. Christ paid in full by sacrificing His body once for all *[Heb.10:10]*. Those who are in Christ are no longer in bondage to sin. Eternal life is a redemption package (gift) for those who repent and embrace the love of God through Christ. Hallelujah!

PRAYER FOCUS

Dear heavenly Father, Only You can redeem a soul. LORD, thank You for laying down Your life for me. I proclaim my freedom from sin and bondage.

May 18

Understanding The Necessity Of Christ Crucifixion
Bible Reading: [Matt.16:21-28]

Then Peter took him, and began to rebuke him, saying, Be it far from thee, LORD: this shall not be unto thee. But He turned, and said unto Peter, get thee behind me, Satan: thou art an offence unto me:..." [Vs:21-23]

When we lack understanding of the things God, we give the devil an opportunity to manipulate us. It is obvious that those who lack knowledge of God's purposes, make choices as though this life is all they have. At this point in time, Jesus' disciples knew Him as the Messiah *[Vs: 16]*. As a result, He started revealing important aspects of His mission.

The devil as subtle as he is, sometimes uses even the love and concern we have for others to cause them stumble in their mission. Peter couldn't understand why his Master would die such a shameful death. Thus, he rebuked Jesus. Then said He unto His disciples, *"It is impossible but that offences will come: but woe unto him, through whom they come!" [Lk 17:1;KJV]*. Beloved, offences will always come. Jesus did not rebuke Peter, but Satan because He was able to discern him behind the scene. *"Get thee behind me Satan, thou art an offence unto me:"*

No crucifixion, no exaltation or glory! Satan's goal is to tempt every believer to assume royal privileges without going through the Cross *[Heb.12:2; Phil.1:29;KJV]*. Nowadays, easy believism (no commitment to discipleship) has become a trap to many Christians! Make your boast in the Cross of Christ today!

PRAYER FOCUS

Dear heavenly Father, how can I thank You enough for making a new and life-giving way by the death of Jesus on the cross. LORD, help me each passing day to discern the voice of Satan to sway me from my divine mission.

May 19

When God Bypasses What You Want, To Give What You Need
Bible Reading: [Acts 3:1-10]

"Then Peter said, Silver and goal have I none; but such as I have given I thee: In the name of Jesus Christ of Nazareth rise up and walk." [Vs:6;KJV]

Often in life, things don't happen the way we want. As a matter of fact, sometimes we don't even know what we really need. Some reasons being that we are shortsighted and narrow minded. At times we search for solution(s) to solve our immediate problems, not knowing that God has something even better. Sarai was anxious about her situation and wanted a child regardless of the source *[Gen.16:2]*. As a result, Abram made a compromise. In spite of that, God who is plenteous in mercy and faithful to His promises met their need *[Gen.21:1-3]*.

The lame man at the gate called beautiful strategically positioned himself where people could easily see him and offer what he wanted. In reality, his need was not food or money, but healing. When Peter unleashed the healing power of God upon him, he jumped and leaped everywhere giving praises to God. I declare that God will surprise you in an extraordinary way this season to meet your need in Jesus' name.

PRAYER FOCUS

Dear heavenly Father, I trust in the power of Your name to meet me at the point of my need. Help me to see and appreciate life from Your point of view in Jesus' name.

May 20

Responsibility Unlocks Your Reward
Bible Reading: [Gal.6:5-10]

"Make a careful exploration of who you are and the work you have been given, and then sink yourself into that. Don't be impressed with yourself. Don't compare yourself with others. Each of you must take responsibility for doing the creative best you can with your own life." [Vs:4- 5;MSG]

Many have made a habit of shying away from responsibility. Responsibility means to be accountable for something within one's power, control, or management. Whenever we fail to take responsibility, we lose the ability to develop self-respect or even earn the respect of others. We must take responsibility for our actions, behavior and tasks entrusted to our care. Regarding the Christian life, each believer is responsible for himself in his relationship with God. Each of us will give an account of ourselves to God.

Many people in the world are bearing overload because parents and/or government transferred their responsibilities. The greatest joy of taking responsibility is that we reap in due season if we act nobly and do the right thing. Whatever responsibility entrusted to you, be faithful to it. By so doing, you will reap a reward and gain promotion. His lord said unto him, *"well done, good and faithful servant; thou has been faithful over a few things, I will make you ruler over many things: enter thou into the joy of thy lord"* [Matt.25:23;KJV]

PRAYER FOCUS

Dear heavenly Father, thank You for every task You have entrusted to my care. LORD, enable me to act nobly each passing day and do what You require of me in Jesus' name.

May 21

He Touched Me
Bible Reading: [Luke 5:12-16]

*"And He put forth his Hand, and touched him, saying,
I will: be thou clean. And immediately the leprosy departed from him."
[Vs:13;KJV]*

In His earthly ministry, our LORD Jesus Christ was moved by compassion always, but was never terrified by unpleasant situations. I can imagine the situation someone might be facing right now! Like in the days of old, a contagious disease would separate an individual from social contact. In the outbreak of Ebola disease, people and villages were quarantined in Sierra Leone.

Quarantine is a place of isolation in which people exposed to contagious diseases are placed. Somebody at the moment is in a place of isolation: spiritually, physically and emotionally. Beloved, the challenge is not about how full your disease or sin has become, but the attitude you bring to the Master.

- *Recognition:* It means to have a clear idea, discern or to make out somebody. Do you recognize Jesus as the Savior? *[Matt.16:15-16;Heb.7:25]*
- *Humility:* Are you humble and courageous to approach Him? "..He shall save the humble person *[Job.22:29;Ps 51:17;KJV]*
- *Believe:* Do you believe that Jesus is the Unchanging Changer and Healer? King Asa was diseased in his feet, until his disease was exceeding great: yet in his disease he sought not the LORD, but to the physicians. *[2 Chr.16:12;KJV]*
- *Appropriation:* It means to take something for personal use, without the owner's permission. As a believer in Christ, you don't need permission to access divine blessings. Every situation was taken care of at the Cross and Christ has blessed us with all spiritual blessings *[John 1:16;Eph.1:3]*

When unbelievers say, "Lord, if You are willing," believers ought to say, "LORD, thank you for I know whom I have believed. By Your stripes, I am healed, delivered and restored." Hallelujah!

May 22

Manifesting Kingdom Realities
Bible Reading: [Lk 11:14-20]

"But if I with the finger of God cast out devils, no doubt the kingdom of God is come upon you." [Vs:20;KJV]

Dearly beloved, it is one thing to profess kingdom matters, and another thing to live or manifest kingdom realities. Every true believer has been called into a holy and faith walk with Jesus. It is written, "But be doers of the word and not hearers only, deceiving yourselves." *[Jam.1:22;KJV]*. You can't practice the reality of the word of Christ when it doesn't dwell richly in the you in all wisdom *[Col.3:16]*. Living the realities of the kingdom is possible in this crooked and perverse generation because His divine power has given us all things pertaining to life and godliness, through the knowledge of Him who has called us to glory and virtue (excellence) *[Philpp.2:15;2 Pet.1:3]*.

Nobody on earth can manifest His divine power without His divine nature. When we genuinely and totally surrender our lives to Christ, His divine nature is given to us (His character qualities). This is due to His mercy, by the washing of regeneration and renewing by the Holy Spirit *[Titus 3:5-6]*. His divine power (gifts) enables the believer to perform unusual things. It is written, *"And these signs shall follow them that believe; In my name shall they cast out devils; they shall speak with new tongues; they shall take up serpents;..." [Mk 16:16-20;KJV]*. The disciples went forth, and preached everywhere, and the LORD working with them, and confirming the word with signs following. Amen. Creation waits your manifestation as a son or daughter of God TODAY!

PRAYER FOCUS

Dear heavenly Father, thank You for giving me Your divine nature. Today, I decree and declare that I am destined for signs and wonders in Jesus' name.

May 23

When Your Identity Is Consumed By Your Issues
Bible Reading: [Luke 1:26-38]

"And, behold, thy cousin Elisabeth, she hath also conceived a son in her old age: and this is the sixth month with her, who was called barren." [Vs: 36]

Beloved, at one point in time each one of us has some issues to deal with. These issues may be spiritual, physical or emotional. Those with physical issues always have a hard bone to chew. From Scriptures, you can count the number of people whose issues consumed their identity. Some of us are in real identity crisis. We have not been able to confidently and successfully answer the "who am I" question, then comes an issue that consumes our identity:

- *She who was called barren.*
- *The woman with the issue of blood.*
- *The man with leprosy.*
- *Blind Bartimaeus and the list goes on.*

Friend, whatever Identity that man labels you or an issue gives you, your true Identity is found in Christ *[2 Cor.5:17]*. I'm the redeemed of the LORD. I'm God's chosen

I'm an oak of righteousness and the planting of the LORD etc. God is able to do the impossible.

It is written, "For with God nothing shall be impossible." [Vs: 37]. Today I decree a divine turnaround in your life in Jesus name.

PRAYER FOCUS

Dear heavenly Father, thank You for having touched my life and made it whole again in Jesus' name.

May 24

Declaring The Word From The Rooftop: Without Fear Or Favor
Bible Reading: [Matt.10:16-28]

"What I tell you in darkness, that speak ye in light: and what ye hear in the ear, that preach ye upon the housetops." [Vs:27;KJV]

Dearly beloved, like the businessman who is trading gold and other precious metals, true believers have the Word of life to revive the dead and the word of truth to make them free. We have plenty of work to do and the world to reach until the return of Christ. It's written, *"The LORD gave the word: great was the company of those that published it." [Ps 68:11;KJV].* Are you in the number saved by grace? Are you in the number saved, to serve God's purpose for humanity?

Dear friend, the stakes are high! *"And that, knowing the time, that now it is high time to awake out of sleep: for now is our salvation(final deliverance) nearer than when we believed" [Rom.13:11;KJV].* Let's rise to reality and preach the Word. Being instant in season and out of season. God has placed a value on us that we need not to be afraid of any man, threats or difficulties. Then Peter and the other Apostles answered and said, *We ought to obey God rather than men[Acts 5:29;KJV].* Be bold, be strong, for the LORD your God is with you. The promise remains: ..and lo, I am with you always, even unto the end of the world. Amen *[Matt.28:20;KJV]*

PRAYER FOCUS

Dear heavenly Father, thank You for having chosen me as an instrument to proclaim Your name to the world for whom Christ died. LORD, I trust in Your wisdom, the ability to communicate Your word and power to boldly speak publicly in Jesus' name.

May 25

Acceptable Spiritual Sacrifices
Bible Reading: [1 Pet.2:1-5]

"Ye also, as living stones, are built up a spiritual house, an holy priesthood, to offer up a spiritual sacrifices, acceptable to God by Jesus Christ." [Vs:5]

From the holy scriptures, it is clear that not all sacrifices are acceptable to God. In order for something to be acceptable to God, it must be holy and pleasing to Him. Spiritual sacrifice is defined as any self-dedicating act of the inner man: renewed, consecrated spirit to do good and to communicate mercy and the knowledge of God (Dwight M. Pratt). The temple, priesthood and God Himself are spiritual.

Priests under the old covenant ministered by offering sacrifices on behalf of themselves and the people. Once every year, the high priest offered sacrifices on the day of atonement for the sins of the people *[Heb.9:7]*. It's important to note that everyone who belongs to Christ is a priest under the new covenant. He sacrificed for our sins once for all when he offered himself. It is written, *"For he hath made him to be sin for us, who knew no sin; that we might be made the righteousness of God in him"[2 Cor.5:21;Heb.7:27]*.

Beloved, is your sacrifice acceptable to God? Then the LORD said to Cain, "Why are you angry? And why has your countenance fallen? If you do well, will not your countenance be lifted up? And if you do not do well, sin is crouching at the door; and its desire is for you, but you must master it" *[Gen.4:6-7;NASV]*

PRAYER FOCUS

Dear heavenly Father, thank You for having chosen me. LORD, I yield myself to You as a living sacrifice, holy and pleasing to you in Jesus' name.

May 26

Thou Art My People
Bible Reading: [Hosea 2:14-23]

"And I will sow her unto me in the earth; and I will say to them which were not my people, Thou art my people; and they shall say, Thou art my God." [Hosea 2:23;KJV]

Dear friend, the greatest blessing in this life is for God to recognize you as His own. Because God is plenteous in mercy, He desires to have each one of us into a deep and personal relationship. From the valley of Achor, a place where we experience trouble because of our sinful lifestyles/disobedience, God's grace gives us the opportunity for a glorious hope. The repentant who has nothing is privileged to come to the One who offers all things - giving grace and mercy as a gift. It is written, *"He that spared not his Son, but delivered him up for us all, how shall he not with him also freely give us all things?" [Rom.8:32;KJV]*

The LORD says, *"I will have mercy upon her that had not obtained mercy" [Vs:23]*. Intimate relationship with God is not earned: It is not by merit or human efforts, but by God's grace alone who makes us right with Him. When we enter into such a deep commitment with God, He gets committed to plant us for Himself in the land, giving us stability and safety. We become the planting of God and the tree (Oak) of righteousness. We become a chosen generation, a holy nation and peculiar people: that we might show forth the praises of him who hath called us out of darkness into his marvelous light *[1 Pet.2:9]*. Hallelujah!

PRAYER FOCUS

Dear heavenly Father, Thou art my God. LORD, thanks for betrothing(engaging) me into a permanent relationship according to Your rich mercies: in righteousness and faithfulness in Jesus' name.

May 27

Be Still And Know That I Am God
Bible Reading: [Psalm 46:1-11]

"Be still, and know that I am God: I will be exalted among the heathen, I will be exalted in the earth" [Vs:10;KJV]

In our fast-paced world, many are yet to understand what it means to be still, even those in the household of faith. Each passing day as events unfold in the world, many people are threatened. The obvious question is, "What If?" What if nobody shows up?

What would result if? "What if?" is a question that asks someone to imagine what might happen or what might have happened (Merriam Webster). If your life is conditioned by what if? then you are not ready for the Christian race. The just shall live by faith *[Heb.10:38]* What if? is the question the devil and associates will ask you in order to lower your expectations.

What if nobody shows up? Beloved, I'm fully persuaded that God will, provided I'm doing what pleases Him. In the midst of a fierce battle, what if everyone flees? Beloved, God will stand by me. It is written, "And after him was Shammah the son of Agee the Hararite. And the Philistines were gathered together into a troop, where was a piece of ground full of lentils: and the people (Israelites) fled from the Philistines. *But Shammah stood in the midst of the ground, and defended it, and slew the Philistines: and the LORD wrought a great victory." [2 Sam.23:11-12].*

Beloved, those who know their God shall be still (calm) regardless of what happens on the earth. They shall do great exploits *[Dan.11:32]*. Come, behold the works of the LORD! He is the Unchanging Changer. God is committed to be exalted in your life, family, Church and nation today. God is our refuge, our high tower and stronghold, and a very present help in trouble. Be still, and know that I am God.

PRAYER FOCUS

Dear heavenly Father, age to age You are the same by the power of Your name. You are my portion, therefore I put my hope in You in Jesus' name.

May 28

God Is Not Asking Too Much
Bible Reading: [Jonah 1:1-16]

"Arise, go to Nineveh, that great city, and cry against it; for their wickedness is come up before me. But Jonah rose up to flee unto Tarshish from the presence of the LORD, and went down to Joppa; and he found a ship going Tarshish: so he paid the fare thereof, and went down into it, to go with them unto Tarshish from the presence of the LORD." [Vs:2-3;KJV]

Dearly beloved, whenever you make divine instruction an option, you are likely going to be a stumbling-block to others around us. How can a man escape from God who is omnipresent? *[Ps 139:7-10]*. Being at the right place, at the right time means you are at the center of God's will for your life. Many believers in Christ do seek God for His will, but how many are committed to go God's direction when He speaks?

God is not asking too much. You can't give what you don't have. He needs your obedience. He has called us according to His purpose and grace *[2 Tim.1:9]*. If the great commission becomes an omission, then you are not a blessing to your world. Apostle Paul told the Elders of the Church at Ephesus, *"Therefore I testify to you this day, that I am innocent of the blood of all men. For I have not shunned to declare to you the whole counsel of God" [Acts.20:26-27;NKJV]*.

Like Jonah, some do not want unbelievers/pagans to have the opportunity to repent and be saved *[Jon.4:2]*. Fleeing from divine responsibility is running into worse trouble. Not doing it today means future generation will have to pay the price. God is not asking too much of your time, energy, money and other resources. Just a token of your willingness and obedience will move God to do the unusual things.

PRAYER FOCUS

Dear heavenly Father, I choose not to be stubborn, but to fulfill my God-given mission so that men might be saved[Blessed]. Oh LORD, Your presence is indispensable! in Jesus' name.

May 29

Show Us The Father
Bible Reading: [John 14:1-14]

"Philip said unto him, LORD, show us the Father, and it sufficeth us. Jesus saith unto him, have I been so long time with you, and yet hast thou not known me, Philip? He that hath seen me hath seen the Father; and how sayest thou then, show us the Father?" [Vs:8-9]

Beloved in the LORD, just imagine that every day somebody keeps talking about a biological father you have never seen! Like Philip, each one of us will be curious about the whereabouts of him. Philip wanted to see God physically. It is written, *"No man hath seen God at any time. If we love one another, God dwelleth in us, and His love is perfected in us." [1 Jn.4:12;KJV]*. God is a Spirit: and they that worship Him must worship him in spirit and in truth [Jn 4:24;KJV]

Like Moses and others in the days of old, we have been privileged to see only the manifestations of God. Physical eyes can't behold that which is spiritual. If we have seen Christ, we have seen the Father. It is written, *"Who (Christ) being the brightness of his glory, and the express image of His person,.." [Heb.1:3;KJV]*. If we have seen Christ, the perfect imprint and very image of the Father's nature, then we ought to believe His word *[Ps 119:89]*. For in Christ dwelleth all the fullness of the Godhead bodily [Col.2:9;KJV]. It's only by faith that we can behold the Father. Remember, *"But without faith it is impossible to please Him…" [Heb.11:6;KJV]*

PRAYER FOCUS

Dear LORD Jesus, I believe You are the way, and the truth and the life. Father, You have loved me with an everlasting love and drawn me with unfailing kindness. I decree and declare: that nothing shall separate me from the love of Christ in Jesus' name.

May 30

Commanding Light To Shine Out Of Darkness
Bible Reading: [2 Cor.4:1-10]

"For God, who commanded the light to shine out of darkness, hath shined in our hearts, to give the light of the knowledge of the glory of God in the face of Jesus Christ." [Vs:6;KJV]

Beloved in the LORD, we are living in the last days and spiritual darkness is so overwhelming as wickedness increases. There are billions of people whose minds have been blinded by the god of this world. Minds are blinded to the truth when men desire to fulfill the lusts of the flesh, pride of life and lusts of the eyes. However, One reassuring fact from the Scriptures is that, In Him (Christ) was life; and the life was the light of men. And the light shines on in the darkness; and darkness has never overpowered it *[Jn 1:4-5]*

God has given every true believer the inherent ability to command light to shine out of darkness. It is written, *"Thou shalt also decree a thing, and it shall be established unto thee: and the light shall shine upon thy ways" [Job.22:28;KJV]*. Beloved, as long as we live on the face of the earth, darkness will always want to encroach or occupy the space of light. That's why Satan himself masquerades as an angel of light *[2 Cor.11:14]*. It is worth mentioning that God's action to bring people to Himself is a movement from the dominion of darkness to a realm governed by light in God's presence. Scripture says, *"For, behold, the darkness shall cover the earth, and gross darkness the people: but the LORD shall arise upon thee, and his glory shall be seen upon thee" [Isa.60:2;KJV]*.

Have you made Jesus Christ your personal LORD and Savior? About those who have God's presence in them by the indwelling of the Holy Spirit, it is written, *"You are the light of the world...let your light shine" [Matt.5:14-16]*. If you truly believe the scriptures and have the same spirit of faith like the Father *[2 Cor.4:13]*, therefore speak thus, "let there be light" in my family, community, campus and country. In Jesus' name.

PRAYER FOCUS

Dear heavenly Father, thank You for causing Your light to shine in my heart in order to give me the light of the knowledge of the glory of God. TODAY, I command light to the people living in darkness and in the valley of the shadow of death *[Isa.9:1-4;Col.1:13]*.

in Jesus' name.

May 31

An Enemy Or A Friend Of The Cross? Choose!
Bible Reading: [Philip.3:17-21]

"Brethren, be followers of me, and mark them which walk so as ye have us for an example. For many walk, of whom I have told you often, and now tell you even weeping, that they are the enemies of the cross of Christ: Whose end is destruction,.." [Vs:17-19;KJV]

Scripture declares that there are enemies of the Cross. If any man is an enemy of the Cross, he is an enemy of Christ. Are you an enemy of the Cross? True believers in Christ can't do without the Cross. It is written, *"But God forbid that I should glory, save in the Cross of our LORD Jesus Christ, by whom the world is crucified unto me, and I unto the world." [Gal.6:14;KJV]*. Because of the gains of the Cross, every believer must pursue Christlikeness and focus his or her life on being like Christ.

While friends of the Cross set their minds on things above, enemies of the Cross set their minds on earthly things. If any man loves the world, the love of the Father is not in him. All that is in the world, the lust of the flesh, the lust of the eyes, and the pride of life, are not of the Father, but of the world *[1 John 2:15-17]*. Dear friend, you can't say that you are a friend of the Cross and at the same time love the world and conform to it *[Rom.12:1-2]*. Remember, *"And the world passeth away, and the lust thereof: but he that doeth the will of God abideth forever" [1 Jn.2:17]*.

A man is an enemy of the Cross because he has received the spirit of the world. Those who have received the Spirit which is from God are friends of the Cross, and they know the things that are freely given to them by God *[1 Cor.2:12;Eph.2:3]*.Friend, there is no neutral ground. You are either a friend or an enemy of the Cross. Attending Church weekly is good but doesn't balance the equation. Your position must be clear and resolute! If it seems evil to follow the way of the Cross, choose today whom you will serve. *And he said to them all, if any man will come after me, let him deny himself, and take up his Cross daily, and follow me" [Lk 9:23;KJV]*.

PRAYER FOCUS

Dear heavenly Father, thank You for opening a new and life-giving way to heaven by the shed blood of Christ on the Cross. Today, I yield my life to You and trust in the strength of the Holy Spirit to live daily as a follower of Christ.

JUNE

"For this cause I bow my knees unto the Father of our LORD Jesus Christ, Of whom the whole family in heaven and earth is named, That he would grant you, according to the riches of his glory, to be strengthened with might by his Spirit in the inner man, That Christ may dwell in your hearts by faith; that ye, being rooted and grounded in love, May be able to comprehend with all saints what is the breadth, and length, and depth, and height; And to know the love of Christ, which passeth knowledge, that ye might be filled with all fullness of God. Now unto him that is able to do exceeding abundantly above all that we ask or think, according to the power that worketh in us, Unto him be glory in the Church by Christ Jesus throughout all ages, world without end." Amen

[Ephesians 3:14-21; KJV]

****

Jehovah El Shaddai - **[LORD GOD Almighty]** *- Exod.6:3*

6 = **[Fallen Nature Of Humanity / Imperfection]**

June 1

Intimacy Requires Proximity
Bible Reading: [Isaiah 29:13]

"Wherefore the LORD said, forasmuch as this people draw near me with their mouth, and with their lips do honor me, but have removed their heart far from me, and their fear toward me is taught by the precept of men." [Vs: 13]

All true relationships in life are built on the foundation of intimacy and love. God desires intimacy with anyone longing for Him. It is written, *"Draw nigh to God, and He will draw nigh to you "[Jam.4:8;KJV]*. While intimacy is close familiarity or friendship, proximity is nearness in space, time, or relationship.

Nowadays, social media plays a vital role in proximity. Technology has virtually reduced the world to a global village. We can't talk about intimacy with someone we are not committed to in our heart. As humans, we are all capable of hypocrisy. It's hypocrisy when we draw near to God or someone with our lips but our hearts are a thousand miles.

Beloved, how intimate are you with God or your spouse? It's important to note that there are people in life that each one of us ought to draw near in an intimate relationship. We lose so much in life when intimacy and proximity are out of place. Is there somebody God is speaking to you to draw close to? Please don't allow prejudice or pride to rob you. It is written, *"Acquaint now thyself with Him, and be at peace: thereby good shall come unto thee" [Job.22:21;KJV]*. The greatest blessing of intimacy is not just the good that comes but the loving friendship and living fellowship or communion we enjoy. *"Henceforth I call you not servants; for the servant knoweth not what his lord doeth: but I have called you friends; for all things that I have heard from the Father I have made known unto you" [Jn.15:15;KJV]*

PRAYER FOCUS

Dear heavenly Father, thank You for having drawn me with Your lovingkindness. Today, I command anything that hinders my intimacy with You, to be removed in Jesus' name.

June 2

He's Got It Under Control!
Bible Reading: [Isa.41:1-12]

"Fear thou not; for I am thy God: I will strengthen thee; yea, I will help thee; yea, I will uphold thee with the right hand of my righteousness." [Vs: 10]

It's so reassuring when the creator of heaven and earth says, "I Am In Charge". In this life, there are many things people worry about: jobs, paying of bills, education, marriage, what to eat, what to wear, where to live and the future of their children. If you are a true believer in Christ, it is important to note that you are God's treasured possession, redeemed by the blood of Jesus. *[Deut.7:6]*.

Although each generation gets caught up in its own problems, God existed before history began. He is ever-present and unchanging God. His redemption plan took everyone and everything into consideration; past, present and future. No child of God has need to look around himself or herself in terror and be dismayed. Only those who know their God shall be strong and do exploits *[Dan.11:32]*

Are you so concerned about the future and overwhelmed with life's difficulties? It is written, *"For I know the thoughts that I think toward you, saith the LORD, thoughts of peace, and not of evil, to give you an expected end." [Jer.29:11;KJV]*. Beloved, I'm fully convinced that God will strengthen you and harden you to difficulties this year in Jesus' name. Put your trust in God's faithfulness, even when you feel alone and life seems crushing you. God is still at work, He's got it under control, even the hearts of kings and the governments of the world.

PRAYER FOCUS

Dear heavenly Father, thank You for giving me the assurance of Your strength and victory over sin and death. LORD, because You are completely trustworthy, I can rest assured that Your right hand of righteousness sustains me, and all who are enraged and inflamed against me shall be put to shame in Jesus' name.

June 3

Under Fire For The Sake Of The Gospel?
Bible Reading: [Acts 23:1-22]

*And the following night the LORD stood by him,
and said, "Be of good cheer, Paul: for as thou hast testified of me in Jerusalem,
so must thou bear witness also at Rome." [Vs:11]*

Dear friend, as we desire to take the message of God's love and redeeming grace to the lost world, it's obvious that we will encounter all kinds of challenges. What will be your reaction when you come under fire for presenting your testimony about the love of Christ? Paul writing to Timothy, made it clear that although suffering even to the point of being chained like a Criminal, the God's word is not chained. *[2 Tim.2:9]*. As competent ministers of the new covenant, we must never lose sight of the fact that the LORD will vindicate His people and have compassion on His servants *[Ps 135:14]*.

Often, Paul pleaded with the brethren to pray for him and his traveling team; that they may be delivered from wicked and evil people, for not everyone has faith *[2 Thes.3:2]*. Beloved, we shouldn't be ignorant to the fact that not everyone has faith. For this reason, we must be ready to overcome and crush the enemy through the word and the power of the Holy Spirit. Coming under fire simply means that one is exposed or subjected to the attack of the enemy. If you are under fire for the sake of the gospel today, God says, " Be of good cheer." Today I decree and declare: let the ploy of the enemy or any evil conspiracy against you and yours, backfire. In Jesus' name.

PRAYER FOCUS

Dear Heavenly Father, thank You for the opportunity to present my testimony about Christ finished work on the Cross. LORD, grant me utterance, wisdom and enable me to speak boldly, without fear or favor in Jesus' name.

June 4

Commanding With Ultimate Authority
Bible Reading: [Mark 1:21-28]

"And they were all amazed, in so much that they questioned among themselves, saying, What thing is this? What new doctrine is this? For with authority commandeth He even the unclean spirits and they do obey Him." [Vs:27;KJV]

Beloved in the LORD, the ultimate authority of God is placed at our disposal. A command is an order given by one in authority. Your command is without effect (powerless) if you are not a man or woman under authority. The Centurion said to Jesus, *"For I am a man under authority, with soldiers under me; and I say to this man, Go, and he goeth; and to another, Come, and he cometh; and to my servant, Do this, and he doeth it"* [Matt.8:9;KJV]. In a worldly sense (secular world), the Centurion knew how to exercise authority.

Our authority as believers in Christ is not meant for us to command fellow human beings but situations, demons, all satanic influences and abnormalities. A lot is going wrong in our lives, communities, campuses and nations. Until we have a full understanding of the believers authority in Christ, many things will not give way.

He taught as one with authority.

He commanded demons with authority and they obeyed him. He commanded the winds and sea obeyed Him [Matt.8:27].

And Jesus came up and spoke to them, saying, *"All authority has been given to Me in heaven and on earth."* [Matt.28:18;NASV]

"Behold, I have given you authority to tread on serpents and scorpions, and over all the power of the enemy, and nothing will injure you." [Lk 10:19;NASV]

Jesus Christ is the ultimate authority. At the mention of His name, every knee bows and every tongue confesses that Jesus is LORD to the glory of the Father *[Phil.2:9-11].*

PRAYER FOCUS

Dear heavenly Father, thank You for ultimate and delegated authority in Jesus Christ. Amen.

June 5

You Are Valuable in the Kingdom !
Bible Reading: [Matthew 5:13; KJV]

"Ye are the salt of the earth: but if the salt have lost his savor, wherewith shall it be salted? it is thenceforth good for nothing, but to be cast out, and to be trodden under foot of men."[Matthew 5:13;KJV]

True believers in Christ are the salt of the earth. God has deposited a lot of good virtues in believers because of the gospel of our Lord Jesus Christ. Wherever you find yourself, God expects you to make a difference in the lives of people. Salt brings out the true taste and sweetness of food; it is used to preserve food and other substances; it can also be used to heal.

Beloved in the LORD, those who come into contact with you should taste the good virtues in you and give glory to God. Preserve lives today by sharing the gospel with the unsaved so that they can be saved *[Rom.10:14-17;Rom.1:16]*.

Be a healing ambassador of the broken hearted with the gospel. When you are at a place and something is going wrong, don't wait for somebody to fix it. Ask for grace and wisdom from God so that you can help put the place in order. Be a world changer and God will continue to elevate you. May the grace, mercy and peace of God be multiplied to you. In Jesus' name.

June 6

Serving God's Purpose With Integrity
Bible Reading: [2 Cor.7:1-4]

"Receive us; we have wronged no man, we have corrupted no man, we have defrauded no man. I speak not this to condemn you: for I have said before, that ye are in our hearts to die and live with you." [Vs:2-3;KJV]

Beloved in the LORD, from one generation to the next, integrity should be a personal quality we should all aspire to possess in increasing measure. Integrity is the quality of being honest and having strong moral principles (Cambridge Dic.). It means doing the right thing in a reliable way. It's a quality that should be admire at the marketplace, workplace, school, church and government. As a matter of fact, it is a personal choice to hold oneself to a consistent spiritual and moral standards.

Throughout his earthly ministry, Apostle Paul and his traveling companions by the grace of God held integrity to a high degree. He was confident to make such an earnest appeal: received us;

We have wronged no man: to wrong someone means to act unjustly or unfairly.

We have corrupted no man: to corrupt means to manipulate or convince someone to do something wrong or to act illegally for personal gain [Lk 19:8]

We have defrauded no man: it means to trick, cheat someone or use fraud in order to get money [Gen.29:25].

Pleading with the brethren at Corinth to extend love toward him and his team again, he reminded them of the fact that they have not served deceitfully or coveted their money *[Acts.20:33]*. On the other hand, he is not saying that a worker doesn't deserve support from the brethren *[1 Tim.5:18.* Dear friend, can people be confident to receive you in their home, church, office etc.? It is written, *"Having therefore these promises, dearly beloved, let us cleanse ourselves from all filthiness of the flesh and spirit, perfecting holiness in the fear of God." [Vs:1].*

PRAYER FOCUS

Dear heavenly Father, You desire integrity to the highest degree. LORD, grant me the grace to live each passing day as a man/woman of integrity, whatever the circumstances.

June 7

Snare Of Making Ourselves Vulnerable Because Of Pride
Bible Reading: [Isa.39:1-8]

"Then came Isaiah the prophet unto king Hezekiah, and said unto him, what said these men? and from whence came they unto thee? And Hezekiah said, they are come from a far country unto me, even from Babylon. Then said he, what have they seen in thine house? And Hezekiah answered, all that is in mine house have they seen: there is nothing among my treasures that I have not shown them." [Vs: 3-4;KJV]

Every one of us ought to sincerely thank God for His blessings. However, I would like to say that not everyone who draws near, comes with good intentions. Oftentimes we have allowed pride in our riches to cloud our judgment. Individuals, families, churches, businesses and even nations have been ruined by people who came close pretending to have good motives. It is worth mentioning that even Satan transforms himself as an angel of light *[2 Cor.11:14]*. The word of God makes wise the simple *[Ps.19:7]*

King Hezekiah was a good and faithful king. However, his prosperity, achievements and deliverance from sickness only made him proud. A proud man would like everyone, even his enemies to know that he is in a leading or dominant position (on top). Let's not allow pride take hold of us to the extent that we have no privacy. Pride goes before a fall. Don't live a life of regret by being hasty to disclose everything about yourself to those who come close. Learn from King Hezekiah's mistakes. His pride in the riches of Judah eventually became a bait that attracted the Babylonians one hundred years after his death to plunder Judah's gates.

PRAYER FOCUS

Dear heavenly Father, thank You for all that You've blessed my life. LORD, help me to be wise and not vulnerable to the enemy by being hasty to expose my treasures in Jesus' name.

June 8

Somebody's Freedom
Is Riding On Your Obedience
Bible Reading: [Acts 8:26-40]

"And Philip said, If thou believest with all thine heart, thou mayest. And he answered and said, I believe that Jesus Christ is the Son of God. And when they were come up out of the water, the Spirit of the LORD caught away Philip, that the eunuch saw him no more: and he went on his way rejoicing." [Vs:37&39]

Beloved in the LORD, there are many people in the world like the Ethiopian eunuch with zeal for the things of God but lack understanding. It is written, "How then shall they call on him in whom they have not believed? And how shall they believed in him of whom they have not heard? And how shall they hear without a preacher?" *[Rom.10:14;KJV]*. It is worth mentioning that God doesn't assign angels to do the work of evangelism. He will always need a man to communicate His message. Philip acted without questioning, he arose and went at the LORD's command.

God wants a people that will give Him their obedience. When He speaks, let's act accordingly. Sometimes we may not fully understand His plans. However, the outcome will prove that God's direction is right when we walk in obedience. Scriptures record that the eunuch went on his way rejoicing. Regardless of the social class or race of men, we must be effective as believers to bring the good news to them in order that they might be saved.

PRAYER FOCUS

Dear heavenly Father, I choose to obey the Holy Spirit's leading. LORD, help me to seize every opportunity to share the Good news in Jesus' name.

June 9

Saved To Serve
Bible Reading: [Acts 9:1-22]

"For by grace you have been saved through faith, and that not of yourselves; it is the gift of God, not of works, lest anyone should boast. For we are His workmanship, created in Christ Jesus for good works, which God prepared beforehand that we should walk in them" [Eph 2:8-10]

God's call is twofold and is confirmed in two ways. There is a general calling He offers to everyone; anyone who responds to Him is considered the "called" *(Isa.6:8)*. But a second call is more specific. This call is given to individuals who are meant to serve in a particular role *(Acts 9:3-6)*. This calling is confirmed both by an inward witness of the heart and an outward recognition by the body of Christ (John Maxwell).

What is your calling? How is your call recognized by others?

PRAYER FOCUS

Dear heavenly Father, thank you for calling me according to your purpose and grace in Jesus' name.

June 10

Finding Stability In Unstable Times
Bible Reading: [Matt.7:24-29]

"Therefore whosoever heareth these sayings of mine, and doeth them, I will liken him unto a wise man, which built his house upon a rock: And the rain descended, and the floods came, and the winds blew, and beat [Vs:24-25]

Stability is one of the greatest treasures of life. Stability in marriage, economy, politics, finance, health, and career et cetera. All of Satan's work creates instability. A person or thing is stable when it is dependable, consistent, not subject to sudden or extreme change. Whenever we fail to obey God's word, instability is obvious. Sin creates instability in sinners that their lives come crashing down. To hear God's word and fail to obey it is to choose the wide gate and broad way that lead to destruction. Many people are unstable mentality, emotionally and in their relationships. Because of instability in the world, many are anxious of the future. Scriptures tell us not to be anxious about anything *[Phil.4:6-8;NIV]*

We gain a much stronger foundation when we build our lives, homes, schools, societies and nations, directly on the rock. The song writer says, *"my hope is built on nothing less than Jesus Christ, my righteousness."* On Christ the solid rock, I stand. Christ is the only sure foundation. I strongly believe according to God's word that Christ is, and will be the stability of our times *"And He will be the stability of your times, A wealth of salvation, wisdom and knowledge; the fear of the LORD is his treasure." [Isa.33:6;NASB].* Therefore, let's willingly submit to him, and walk the genuine path that leads to blessings. Let's be steadfast and unmovable in the LORD's work *[1 Cor.15:58;KJV]*

PRAYER FOCUS

Dear heavenly Father, I acknowledge that there is no sure foundation, except that which is of Christ. I command stability to my life, marriage, business, church and nation in Jesus' name.

June 11

Mercy Triumph Over Judgment
Bible Reading: [John 8:1-12]

"When Jesus had lifted up Himself, and saw none but the woman, He said unto her, Woman, where are those thine accusers? Hath no man condemned thee? She said, No man, LORD. And Jesus said unto her, Neither do I condemn thee: go, and sin no more." [Vs:10-11]

Beloved in the LORD, all of us whether great or small deserve God's punishment because of sin. Oftentimes, even after we've been save by grace, our attitude toward a brother or sister caught in sin is still poor. Like the Pharisees, many of us are so quick to pass judgment. Jesus views sin and judgement seriously yet he looks graciously and forgivingly on those caught in sin's grip. If we behave like the Pharisees after having known the truth, it means that we are seeking to please ourselves instead of helping the weak. It is written, *"Now we who are strong ought to bear the weaknesses of those without strength and not just please ourselves"* [Rom.15:1;NAB].

And Jesus Christ asked the woman who committed adultery, Woman, where are those thine accusers? *She said, No man, LORD. And Jesus said unto her, Neither do I condemn you: go, and sin no more."*[Vs:11]. It is written, *"For he shall have judgement without mercy, that hath no mercy; mercy rejoiceth against judgement"* [Jam.2:13;KJV]. Only mercy can remove the sting of sin. Those who deserve His wrath are forgiven in spite of their sins. By law, every sin must be punished. Through mercy, the grace of God is made manifest. Because of God's faithfulness, she received forgiveness, for the LORD extended His mercy to her. Praise the LORD!

PRAYER FOCUS

Dear heavenly Father, thank You for having extended great mercy toward me. LORD, I acknowledge that it is Your role to judge. Help me to show forgiveness and demonstrate compassion daily in Jesus' name.

June 12

Hope Never Disappoints
Bible Reading: [Rom.5:1-11]

"And hope maketh not ashamed; because the love of God is shed abroad in our hearts by the Holy Ghost which is given unto us." [Vs:5]

The saying goes, "where there's a will, there's a way." Going by God's word, where there is hope, disappointment only becomes an appointment, for therein is God's love made manifest. Because of His love, when all things seem to fall apart, He turns that situation into a door of hope [Hosea 2:15]. It is written, *"And we know that all things work together for good to them that love God, to them who are the called according to his purpose"* [Rom.8:28].

The love of God shed abroad in our hearts by the Holy Spirit ushers us into a glorious hope. It is written, *"what manner of love the Father hath bestowed upon us, that we should be called the sons of God:."* [1John 3:1;KJV]. If we are sons, then we are certainly heirs of God, and joint-heirs with Christ. Hope means to trust in, wait for, to desire something or someone; or to expect something beneficial in the future [William B.]. Every true believer in Christ hopes in God because He is worthy of trust. Christ in us, is the hope of glory [Col.1:27]

In Scriptures, the prophet Jeremiah gives us a valid reason why we should put our hope in God. *" Are there any among the false gods of the nations who can cause rain? Or can the heavens [of their own will] give showers? Are You [alone] not He, O LORD our God? Therefore we will wait [expectantly] for You, for You have made all these things [the heavens and the rain]."* [Jer.14:22;Ampl.] Whatever your situation, hope in the LORD. Those who wait for Him shall not be disappointed.

PRAYER FOCUS

Dear heavenly Father, You are my hope. I'm confident that You are able to bring about the realization of my expectations in Jesus' name.

June 13

Being About My Father's Business
Bible Reading: [Luke 2:41-52]

"And he said unto them, How is it that ye sought me? Wist ye not that I must be about my Father's business?" [Vs: 49]

Beloved in the LORD, if Christ were to come today, where will he find you? We are living in perilous times and the cares of life, and love for material things are taking a heavy toll on many, even believers in Christ. I have a strong feeling that many have lost touch with the realities of the Christian faith. Many are no longer interested in discussions concerning the Word of God. Giving up meeting together has become a regular phenomenon. Some have the reputation of being alive, but are dead.

At twelve, Jesus was aware that His greatest loyalty belonged to His heavenly Father and His number one priority was to be about His Father's business. My sincere prayer is that the zeal of the Father's house will consume each one of us. As believers, we must be able to make a clear distinction between that which is earthly and that which is heavenly. Only a growing awareness of our unique relationship with the Father will help us to stay connected with God's big plan for humanity.

PRAYER FOCUS

Dear heavenly Father, I acknowledge the fact that Your business requires urgency. LORD, instill in me a strong sense of purpose and passion for gospel outreach in Jesus' name.

June 14

God's Power Is Not Limited By Unfair Play
Bible Reading: [Gen.31:1-13]

Everyone at one moment in time has been a victim of unfair play. Unfair play is a common phenomenon. It happens in society, in government and in the body of Christ. Unfair play is any behavior that contravenes the spirit of a game, work ethics or Biblical standards. We do acknowledge the fact that people make mistakes. However, when it's a regular occurrence, then unfair play is obvious.

What will be your reaction as a believer in Christ when experiencing unfair play especially from a loved one, a trusted member in the Body of Christ or at the job site? The most common attitude I have seen is that a person grumbles, complains and leaves. While it is important to note that God doesn't turn a blind eye to unfair play, wisdom is needed in every situation. Bible records that as the number of disciples was increasing in the early Church, a complaint arose on the part of the Greek-speaking Jews against the native Hebraic Jews. *The twelve apostles appointed seven men of good reputation, full of the Holy Spirit and wisdom to solve the problem [Acts.6:1- 3].*

Are you a child of God and you find yourself in a similar situation like Jacob? It is written, *"For the arms (power) of the wicked shall be broken: but the LORD upholdeth the righteous." [Ps.37:17;KJV].* I strongly believe that if you are diligent in your business or duty, God will make you thrive even though others mistreat you. Do not return evil for evil. Remember that jealous is given a foothold especially by those who don't cherish your success or progress.

Promotion comes from God. Encouragement comes from God. If God is for you, who can be against you? And the Angel of the LORD spoke to Jacob in a dream, saying, *"Lift up now thine eyes, and see, all the rams which leap upon the cattle are ringstraked, speckled, and grisled: for I have seen all that Laban doeth unto thee." [Vs:12]. "The secret of the LORD is with them that fear him; and he will shew them his covenant" [Ps.25:14;KJV].*

PRAYER FOCUS

Dear heavenly Father, I believe You can do all things and no purpose of Yours concerning me can be thwarted.

June 15

The Power Of God's Love
Bible Reading: [1 John 3:1-17]

"Behold, what manner of love the Father hath bestowed upon us, that we should be called the sons of God: therefore the world knoweth us not, because it knew him not." [Vs:1;KJV]

In every heart is the desire to be loved by someone special. While a person may feel alone in thinking that no one loves him or her, the good news is that God is love. One amazing thing about God is that He bestows full measure of love to hearts longing for it. In this portion of Scriptures, Apostle John is amazed at the manner of love by which God has loved us *[John 3:16]*.

The world does not know true love because those who are of the world enjoy that which is of the world. Our obedience to God's word is evidence of our sonship, which is the result of God's unconditional love. We wouldn't have any true Identity as believers in Christ without this love. It is written, *"seeing ye have purified your souls in obeying the truth through the Spirit unto unfeigned love of the brethren, see that ye love one another with a pure heart fervently:" [1 Pet.1:22;KJV]*. I pray that the ground of our hearts will be broken more and more, and that we may rejoice in the fruit it bears: true love!

PRAYER FOCUS

Dear heavenly Father, thank You for Your tender mercies. LORD, grant that I may be able to understand with all the saints what is the length and width, height and depth of Your love in Jesus' name.

June 16

God Doesn't Move By Human Dates
Bible Reading: [John 5:1-9]

"For an angel went down at a certain season into the pool, and troubled the water: whosoever then first after the troubling of the water stepped in was made whole of whatsoever disease he had." [John 5:4;KJV]

The most interesting thing I have seen under the sun is that people set the next date for God to move in an unusual way. Certainly when it doesn't happen, they lose heart. Date in simple words is the day of the month or year as specified by a number. Scripture says this about the coming of the Son of Man, *"the day or hour no one knows, not even the angels in heaven, nor the Son, but only the Father."* [Matt.24:36]*. However, one thing is certain, *"God works all things according to the counsel of His own will" [Eph.1:11]*. Every true believer was chosen in Christ and predestined or marked out beforehand according to God's purpose. Therefore, to everything there is a season, and a time to every purpose under the heaven *[Eccl.3:1;KJV]*

Going by divine timing, with the LORD, one day is as a thousand years, and a thousand years as one day *[2 Pet.3:8]*. Going by ancient Greek timing, there are two words for time: Chronos and kairos. Chronos is calendar time. To some people, as the clock ticks, time is running out and they become impatient. Perhaps they have set a date with great expectations from God. When it fails, they become discouraged.

In principle, we live in Chronos or sequential time but God lives in eternity (lives forever) and operates in kairos (seasons). Kairos is the opportune moment - that is right for something to occur or right for action. Remember, the sons of Issachar were men who understood the times and knew what Israel should do *[1 Chr.12:32]*. Your miracle is found in kairos. It's the season God has designed according to the counsel of His will to move in your life or community. At a certain season the angel went down into the pool and troubled the water for healing purposes. Understand the times and make the most of the moment. God is about to move again!

PRAYER FOCUS

Dear heavenly Father, my times are in Your hands. LORD, enable me to prophetically discern the season we are living in so that I may move according to the leading of Your Spirit in Jesus' name.

June 17

Unexpected People & Places
Bible Reading: [John 1:42-51]

"And Nathaniel said unto him, can there any good thing come out of Nazareth? Philip saith of him, Come and see." [Vs: 46]

Beloved in the LORD, because of the standards of the world, man has become a stereotype by having a fixed image or idea of a particular type of person or thing. People and places have become too easily stereotyped, and oftentimes our judgements are wrong in the light of God's WORD. Whenever the name Silicon Valley is mentioned, the first thing that comes to mind is a home to many start-up and global technology companies like Apple, Google, Facebook et cetera. Whenever Hollywood is mentioned, what comes to mind is the home of entertainment business or industry, not to mention GRA, Victoria Garden City etcetera. All these have influenced man's way of describing social status of people and defining places.

Dear friend, it is not so with God. By human judgement, Nazareth was not considered famous enough to be the hometown for a great leader. Our standards have plunged humanity into unbelief and sometimes caused us to see no value in people and places. It is written, *"And Jacob awaked out of his sleep, and he said, Surely the LORD is in this place; and I knew it not...He said, how dreadful is this place! This is none other but the house of God(Bethel), and this is the gate of heaven." [Gen.28:16-17]*. It is so fascinating how God chooses unlikely places, good-for-nothing and the foolish things of the world to shame the wise *[1 Cor.1:27]*. Don't limit God with human judgements. Jesus said, "I judge only as the Father tells me, so my judgement is right *[John 5:30]*. You can't afford miss God's love and grace because of stereotypes.

PRAYER FOCUS

Dear heavenly Father, my preconceived opinion has caused me sometimes to put You in a box. Have mercy upon me and help me to discern and understand Your purpose in every situation in Jesus' name.

June 18

The Mystery Of Divine Healing - A Done Deal
Bible Reading: [2 Chr.16:7-14]

"And Asa in the thirty and ninth year of his reign was diseased in his feet, until his disease was exceedingly great: yet in his disease he sought not to the LORD, but to the physicians." [2 Chr.16:12;KJV]

Dear friend, the good news for you today is that God takes pleasure in your well-being. Beloved, I wish above all things that thou mayest prosper and be in health, even as thy soul prospereth *[3 John 1:2;KJV]*. Can you imagine how it feels like living on earth daily without sound heath! With God, there is nothing like "curable or incurable" disease because He specializes in impossibilities. It is written, *"Behold, I am the LORD, the God of all flesh: is there anything too hard for me?" [Jer.32:27;KJV]* Your body may be wasting away outwardly, do not lose heart!

In the 90s I encountered God's supernatural touch at a time when no medical or herbal treatment could. And now I know whom I have believed. Beloved, at the heart of Job's predicament, he released a tremendous faith. He says, "for I know my redeemer lives". Faced with a deadly malady, Job was still confident to see God in his body *[Job.19:25-26]*. Today, I decree and declare: you shall not die, but live, and declare the works of the LORD. May God renew you inwardly and outwardly day by day, by the quickening power of the Spirit that raised Christ from the dead in Jesus' name.

The mystery of divine healing was unlocked at the Cross. It's a done deal. *"But he was wounded for our transgressions, he was bruised for our iniquities: the chastisement of our peace was upon him; and with his stripes we are healed." [Isa.53:5;KJV]*. Whatever your condition, and wherever you are, receive the healing power of God from the crown of your head to the sole of your feet. Be healed and restored in Jesus' name.

It's not sin to seek physicians but divine healing is above all things! If you haven't received Christ as your personal LORD and Savior, repent, invite Him in and be transformed. King Asa failed to lift up his eyes to the holy hills when he was diseased in his feet. Bible records, his disease was exceedingly great! The maker of heaven and earth is bigger and greater! *"I will lift up mine eyes unto the hills, from whence cometh my help. My help cometh from the LORD, which made heaven and earth" [Ps.121:1-2;KJV]*.

PRAYER FOCUS

Thank You LORD for Your healing touch! It is written, *"The LORD will sustain, refresh, and strengthen him on his bed of languishing; all his bed You [O LORD] will turn, change, and transform in his illness." [Ps.41:3;Amp.]* in Jesus' name.

June 19

Moved With Godly Fear
Bible Reading: [Heb.11:7; Gen.6:13-22]

"By faith Noah, being divinely warned of things not yet seen, moved with godly fear, prepared an ark for the saving of his household, by which he condemned the world and became heir of the righteousness which is according to faith." [Vs:7;KJV]

Dear friend, the Christian life begins and ends with faith. Christ who calls us into a faith walk is the author and finisher of our faith *[Heb.12:2]*. Faith is to be sure of what we hope for and certain of what we do not see. Many things are going wrong in our world because people are not moved with godly fear. Everywhere in the world, there is divine handwriting on the wall *[Dan.5:5]*. Sometimes we read and don't understand, and sometimes we understand but choose to walk according to the stubbornness of our heart. Perhaps because of the lack of faith, many are not sure that God will perform His WORD. Whatever the case, a man moved with godly fear will respond differently to every divine warning. Only the reality of God's holiness will bring us into godly fear.

God doesn't want anyone to be fearful because He does not give us the spirit of fear *[2 Tim.1:7]*. You can't have godly fear without a living relationship with God through Christ. Godly fear is an essential part of God's salvation plan. All the heroes of faith in the Bible were moved with godly fear and walked in obedience. Godly fear caused Joseph not to make Mary a public example when he realized that she was pregnant *[Matt.1:18-21]*. An angel spoke to him in a dream. Godly fear caused Noah to save his household. Many people are suffering today because they failed to move in godly fear when divinely warned. Likewise nations, churches and families. The people of Nineveh believed God and proclaimed a fast when divinely warned by prophet Jonah *[Jonah 3:5]*. Beloved, Christ will come again. Do you believe it? It is written, *"But of the times and the seasons, brethren, ye have no need that I write unto you. But ye, are not in darkness, that that day should overtake you as a thief." [1 Thes.5:4,4]*.

PRAYER FOCUS

Dear heavenly Father, it's not Your desire that I should perish. Help me to work out my salvation with godly fear and watchfulness daily in Jesus' name.

June 20

Excelling In The Grace Of Giving
Bible Reading: [2 Sam.24:18-25]

"And the King said unto Araunah, Nay; but I will surely buy it of thee at a price: neither will I offer burnt offerings unto the LORD my God of that which doth cost me nothing So David bought the threshing floor and the oxen for fifty shekels of silver. And David built there an altar unto the LORD, and offered burnt offerings and peace offerings. So the LORD was entreated for the land, and the plague was stayed from Israel." [Vs:24-25]

Some people still think that God deserves crumbs. This is evident in their attitude toward giving. To excel in something, means to do extremely well. God takes pleasure whenever His children honor Him with their substance. This is not because He lacks anything. It is written, *"The silver is mine, and the gold is mine, saith the lord of Host." [Hag.2:8].* Every time we offer to God a costly offering, we are raising an altar of remembrance to Him.

From our text, King David had sinned against God. Despite his wrongdoing, God called Him a man after his heart — who shall fulfill all His will *[Acts 13:32]* A meaningful and costly giving is one that starts first with a man's life at the altar of sacrifice, before offering his substance to the LORD. The nation of Israel was spared because of David's repentant heart and thanksgiving offering to God. Apostle Paul commending the Macedonian church says; *"And this they did, not as we hoped, but first gave their own selves to the LORD, and unto us by the will of God."[2 Cor.8:5].* God is calling you to offer yourself wholly and holy to Him today.

PRAYER FOCUS

Dear heavenly Father, I seek to honor You with my life and substance. LORD, bestow upon me the grace of giving in Jesus' name.

June 21

Be Anxious For Nothing
Bible Reading: [Philipp.4:1-13]

"Be careful for nothing; but in everything by prayer and supplication with thanksgiving let your requests be made known unto God. And the peace of God, which passeth all understanding, shall keep your hearts and minds through Christ Jesus." [Vs: 6-7]

Beloved in the LORD, do you worry about everyday life? Whenever we come to the understanding that our heavenly Father loves and cares about our needs, there is no reason to worry. All our worries do not add a single moment to our life. Even birds in the air who don't plant or harvest or store food in barns, are being fed by God *[Matt.6:25-30]*. Our Joy as believers in Christ is not dependent on circumstances. Even in the midst of challenges, believers have every reason to rejoice.

It's important to mention that contentment is an attitude of mind one develops by focusing on that which is above this material world. We must learn to be content in poverty and in wealth. Scripture says, "Not that I speak in respect of want: for I have learned, in whatsoever state I am, therewith to be content." *[Vs:11]*. We enjoy God's peace whenever we trust Him. The worries of this life shouldn't dominate our thoughts. Worries on the job, business, in our homes, at school. We can live an anxiety free thought by trusting God's provision. Therefore, let's seek first the kingdom of God and His righteousness *[Matt.6:33]*.

PRAYER FOCUS

Dear heavenly Father, Thank You for Your love and care for me. LORD, teach me each passing day to be content in every circumstance in Jesus' name.

June 22

Convenient Time
Not Always The Right Time
Bible Reading: [Acts 24:22-27]

"And after certain days, when Felix came with his wife Drusilla, which was a Jewess, he sent for Paul, and heart him concerning the faith in Christ. And as he reasoned of righteousness, temperance, and judgement to come, Felix trembled, and answered, Go thy way for this time; when I have a convenient season, I will call for thee." [Vs:24-2]

Having witnessed to many about Christ over the years, I have come to realize that what men often consider as convenient time, is time to stay in the comfort zone of earthly pleasures and sin. While it is said, today if ye will hear his voice, harden not your hearts, as in the provocation *[Heb.3:15]*. A convenient time is time suitable for one's purpose or needs. God does not work according to man's convenience. He does all things according to the counsel of His will. It is written, "To everything there is a season, and a time to every purpose under the heaven"*[Eccl.3:1]*.

Our convenient time may not be God's right time! Whenever the voice of God is loud and clear, allowing procrastination to set in means a deliberate attempt to reject God's grace *[2 Cor.6:2]*. Procrastination is the thief of time and leaves room for complacency. Choosing to do things your way and time, because you are self-satisfied with your situation. Governor Felix trembled when he got the right message but failed to repent at the right time. The gospel is God's power to change lives. This is the season to set priorities right!

PRAYER FOCUS

Dear heavenly Father, You make all things beautiful in Your time. Grant that my heart will tremble and be responsive to Your word at all times in Jesus' name.

June 23

The Shortest Way
Not Always The Best Way
Bible Reading: [Exodus 13:17-22]

"And it came to pass, when Pharaoh had let the people go, that God led them not through the way of the land of the Philistines, although that was near; for God said, Lest peradventure the people repent when they see war, and they return to Egypt: But God led the people about, through the way of the wilderness of the Red sea:.." [Vs:17-18]

Beloved in the LORD, we are living in a fast-paced world. The desire to see things happening very quickly is obvious in every sector of society, and even in the Body of Christ. The words patience, wait, endurance or longsuffering seem outdated. It is important to note that God is more interested about His purpose being accomplished than how soon we get to our expected end.

Often the challenge in the Body of Christ is that many have not learned how to follow the LORD's leading. Remember that we are shortsighted but God sees beyond and understands far better than we do. It is written, *"For as many as are led by the Spirit of God, they are the sons of God" [Rom.8:14;KJV].*

God's thoughts toward us are thoughts of good. He knows that blessing us with a job, husband, wife, or riches at this moment in time will separate us from His love. He knew if the Israelites had gone directly to Palestine, they would have encountered the warlike Philistines and as a result, suffer great loss of life, or would have returned to Egypt. *"There is a way which seemeth right unto a man, but the end thereof are the ways of death." [Prov.14:12;KJV].* God wouldn't always work in the way that seems best to us. However, His ultimate goal is to see His purpose accomplished and the very best He has for us established. No matter the distance and length of time, He works all things for our advantage!

PRAYER FOCUS

Dear heavenly Father, thank You for Your great power, mercy and love. Forgive me for having leaned on the wisdom of men. Work in me both to will and to act in order to fulfill Your good purpose in Jesus' name!

June 24

Grace In The Wilderness
Bible Reading: [Ezra 9:1-9]

"And now for a little space grace hath been shown from the LORD our God, to leave us a remnant to escape, and to give us a nail in his holy place, that our God may lighten our eyes, and give us a little reviving in our bondage. For we were bondmen; yet our God hath not forsaken us in our bondage, but hath extended mercy unto us in the sight of the kings of Persia, to give us a revival,.." [Vs:8-9;KJV]

Whenever we remember what the LORD has done for us, our hearts ought to be full of gratitude. Sometimes, it's unfortunate that we allow the pagan practices of our environment to influence our commitment to God. Like the Israelites, we are taken into captivity whenever we fail to acknowledge God's unfailing love and make the needed correction in order to walk on the highway of holiness. Regardless of what brings us into captivity or bondage of any kind, God is committed to forgive and extend His mercies. God's grace is powerful enough to cause a remnant to escape captivity. A remnant shall find grace in the wilderness *[Jer.31:2]*

God desires to have a remnant with His identity. A people with a secure hold in His holy place. I pray that God will enlighten your eyes today and give you revival in any form of captivity in Jesus' name. Even before kings, God would give His remnant unusual favor because of His tender mercies. He releases His grace for a purpose. Therefore, do not take God's grace for granted today.

PRAYER FOCUS

Dear heavenly Father, everything I have accomplished is because of Your grace. I pray that You will extend Your mercies to me in the sight of great men [kings and authorities], in order to bring about Your purpose for my life in Jesus' name.

June 25

The Barrier Breaker
Bible Reading: [1 Thes.2:13-20]

"Wherefore we would have come unto you, even I Paul, once and again; but Satan hindered us. For what is our hope, or joy, or crown of rejoicing? Are not even ye in the presence of our LORD Jesus Christ at his coming? [Vs: 18-19;KJV]

Beloved in the LORD, God wants each one of us not to be ignorant of the schemes of Satan and cohorts. I know many in the world, and even some believers in Christ are still harboring false belief about unseen forces. The moment a person declares his position and makes Jesus his personal LORD and Savior, he becomes the first target of the devil.

Beloved, let's not live in illusion! We face a powerful army whose ultimate goal is to hinder the Church of God. He comes to steal, kill and destroy *[Jn 10:10;1 Pet.5:8]*. The trick of the enemy is to turn us away from Christ and back to sin. It is written, *"For we wrestle not against flesh and blood, but against principalities, against powers, against the rulers of the darkness of this world, against spiritual wickedness in high places." [Eph.6:12;2 Cor.4:4;KJV]*.

God has not called us in Christ that we might be Satan/demon conscious. He has called us according to His purpose and grace *[2 Tim.1:9]*. However, He wants us to be aware or knowledgeable about the enemy's devices or tactics. Scripture says, *"Finally, my brethren, be strong in the LORD, and in the power of his might." [Eph.6:10;KJV]*. Christ defeated Satan and cohorts on the Cross, and destroyed all their works *[Col.2:15;1 Jn.3:8]*. The goal of every believer is to enjoy the gains of the Cross, enforce the will of God in every community and to proclaim the Lordship of Christ. Through Christ every believer is victorious. Whatever is born of God overcomes the world *[1 John.5:4]*. All we need to do is to submit ourselves to God's authority, resist the devil, and he will flee from us *[Jam.4:7;Lk 10:19;Matt.16:18]*,

PRAYER FOCUS

Dear heavenly Father, thank You for having given me authority in Christ over Satan and cohorts. I submit myself to Your Lordship and command every enemy to flee from me. In Jesus' name. I decree and declare any hindering force or barrier on my path broken and destroyed by fire.

June 26

When You Are Tuned Into The Right Prayer Frequency
Bible Reading: [2 Kings 20:1-11]

"Hezekiah turned his face to the wall and prayed to the LORD, saying, I beseech thee, O LORD, remember now how I have walked before thee in truth and with a perfect heart, and have done that which is good in thy sight." [Vs:2-3;KJV]

Often we fail to realize how much can be achieved by praying to God instead of complaining about our situation. It's important to note that the event to Hezekiah's death was changed by a divine response to a man's prayer. God is determined to further His purposes on earth and change natural patterns if he can find a man or woman of prayer *[Josh.10:11-13]*

How could you have reacted being in Hezekiah's situation? For the most part, many of us would yield given that the word came from God. However, the prayer and faith, of a man who walked before God in faithfulness, truth and with a whole heart, made all the difference. And Hezekiah said unto Isaiah, *"What shall be the sign that the LORD will heal me, and that I shall go up into the house of the LORD the third day?"* And Isaiah the prophet cried unto the LORD: and he brought the shadow ten degrees backward, by which it had gone down in the dial of Ahaz" *[Vs:11].*

When all you can present to God amid difficult times is your commitment and faithfulness, even nature will respond. Prayer moves the hand of Him who moves the world!

PRAYER FOCUS

Dear heavenly Father, You do miracles so great and no purpose of Yours can be defeated. LORD, I pray for a manifestation of Your power in my situation.

June 27

The Snare Of Another Gospel
Bible Reading: [Gal.1:1-10]

"I marvel that ye are so soon removed from him that called you into the grace of Christ unto another gospel: which is not another; but there be some that trouble you, and would pervert the gospel of Christ." [Vs:6-7]

Beloved in the LORD, which gospel have you chosen to believe? In the free society in which we live, people have right to their religious opinions. Does it mean their ideas are right? A different gospel undermines and dilutes the word of truth. It is written, *"For the time will come when they will not endure sound doctrine; but after their own lusts shall they heap to themselves teachers, having itching ears;" [2 Tim.4:3;KJV]*. Another gospel only perverts and sways many from the truth. Many are on the wrong track today because they have been deceived or have chosen to believe a different gospel. They are zealous but not according to knowledge *[Rom.10:2]*

What then is another gospel? Any gospel that does not consider salvation as a free gift of God through believing in Jesus Christ *[Eph.2:8-9]*. Any gospel that does not declare the Cross as the ultimate source of freedom and victory over sin and death *[1 Cor.5:56-57]*. Any gospel that says all religions are equal, and the right way to God *[1 Tim.2:5-6]*. Any religion that offers salvation by rituals, laws and works. Any gospel that does not exalt Christ as LORD and Savior.

Dear friend, eternal life is the greatest gift of God, and it is only through Christ. Jesus saith unto him, *I am the way, the truth, and the life: no man cometh unto the Father, but by me."[John.14:6]*. But God forbid that I should glory, save in the cross of our LORD Jesus Christ, by whom the world is crucified unto me, and I unto the world." *[Gal.6:14]*. Beloved, are you saved by grace? Is Christ your mediator? Ponder over these words and may the God of peace be with you!

PRAYER FOCUS

Dear heavenly Father, I'm grateful that Your grace has found me. I choose not to believe a false gospel. Today, I declare my love for You and reaffirm my commitment to sound doctrine. Father, let the power of the Cross be evident in my life now and forever! in Jesus' name.

June 28

Snare Of A Double Standard Christian Life
Bible Reading: [Gal.2:11-21]

"For before that certain came from James, he did eat with the Gentiles: but when they were come, he withdrew and separated himself, fearing them which were of the circumcision" [Vs: 12].

Beloved in Christ, why do you desire to live a double Christian life? You seek to do the will of God while trying to satisfy the demands of this evil and perverse world. Scripture says, *"And be not conformed to this world: but be ye transformed by the renewing of your mind,." [Rom.12:2].* One of the reasons why many believers have chosen to have two behavior image patterns is the fear of man. The desire to please men has caused many to compromise their conviction of the Gospel. Remember how Apostle Peter did eat with the Gentiles before some believers came from James but withdrew and separated himself, fearing them which were of the circumcision. *"Fear of man will prove to be a snare, but whoever trusts in the LORD is kept safe" [Prov.29:25;Gal.5:6].*

Our LORD is grieved by lukewarm hearts that just can't seem to choose who they're really for - Jesus or Sin *[Rev.3:19].* The only cure for a double life is a repentant surrender. A believer must purposed in his or her heart to live right with God *[Dan.1:8].* Apostle Paul says this to servants of Christ, "For do I now persuade men, or God? Or do I seek to please men? For if I yet pleased men, I should not be the servant of Christ." *[Gal.1:10].* Dear friend, what is your position today?

Now choose life, so that you and your descendants may live. *[Deut.30:19]*

PRAYER FOCUS

Dear heavenly Father, I desire not to frustrate Your grace by living a double Christian life. LORD, help me each passing day and each step of the way to live up to the truth of the Gospel in Jesus' name.

June 29

The Battle Is The LORD'S
Bible Reading: [2 Chr.20:1-22]

"And they rose early in the morning, and went forth into the wilderness of Tekoa: and as they went forth, Jehoshaphat stood and said, Hear me, O Judah, and ye inhabitants of Jerusalem; Believe in the LORD your God, so shall ye be established; Believe in his prophets, so shall ye prosper." [2 Chr.20:20]

Each passing day we battle temptation, the cares of life, peer pressure and the schemes of Satan and cohorts. Oftentimes, because we do not know what to do, we either compromise our convictions or yield to the enemy. It is written, *"My people are destroyed for lack of knowledge:.."* [Hosea 4:6]. However, King Jehoshaphat not knowing what to do, reaffirmed his loyalty to God in order to deal with the impending threat of the enemy.

When we earnestly ask God for help in our daily struggles, He shows up and enables us to triumph. Believe in the LORD your God, so shall you be established". Our total dependence on God moves Him to command victory for us *[Psalm 44:4]*. We shouldn't be moved by what we see but by what we hear from the LORD. Victory is certain when we follow His guidance.

Choose today to believe God's word through His chosen vessel and you shall prosper. For the battle is not yours but God's.

PRAYER FOCUS

Dear heavenly Father, I acknowledge the fact that no king is saved by the size of his army; nor is great strength enough to save a warrior. All power belong to You and the battle is Yours. Today, I declare that I'm victorious! in Jesus' name.

June 30

A Glorious Triumph
Bible Reading: [Exod.15:1-12]

"Then sang Moses and the children of Israel this song unto the LORD, and spake, saying, I will sing unto the LORD, for he hath triumphed gloriously: the horse and his rider hath he thrown into the sea."

"Who is like unto thee, O LORD, among the gods? who is like thee, glorious in holiness, fearful in praises, doing wonders?" [Vs: 1&11]

Beloved in the LORD, God has triumphed gloriously. Hallelujah! The good news today is that your faith in God through the dark night has been vindicated. One of the most important things about our God is that every day and everywhere, He is at work. God has both a loving character and power. I pray, all that the enemy intends against you this year be brought to nothing before the mighty power of God in Jesus' name.

Like the Israelites, whenever you are confronted by a mighty enemy, mountain or hardship, remember that God's salvation and rescue power has not changed. *"For I am the LORD, I change not; therefore ye sons of Jacob are not consumed." [Mal.3:6]*

Sometimes only a song of praise would put an enemy to flight. It's written, "Let the high praises of God be in their mouth, and a two-edged sword in their hand to execute vengeance on the nations," *[Ps 149:6-7]*. High praises and the Word of God *[Eph.6:17]* are the great weapons at your disposal. May God beautify you with salvation today in Jesus' name.

PRAYER FOCUS

Dear heavenly Father, Today, I lift up my holy hands to celebrate Your mighty power, for You have triumphed gloriously. Amen.

JULY

"I had fainted, unless I had believed to see the goodness of the LORD in the land of the living. Wait on the LORD: be of good courage, and he shall strengthen thine heart: wait, I say, on the LORD."

[Psalm 27:13; KJV]

Jehovah Rohi - [The LORD Is My Shepherd] - Psalms 23:1

7 = [Completion, Perfection & Rest]

July 1

Questing After Truth
Bible Reading: [Jeremiah 5:1-6]

"I will go to the great men and speak to them, for they have known the way of the LORD, the judgement of their God: But these have altogether broken the yoke and burst the bonds." [Vs: 5]

Beloved in the LORD, how passionate are you for the truth? A heart that quests after truth will never go unrecognized by God. Living in an era and community where many proclaimed, "The LORD lives", Jeremiah searched in vain for a man among the poor and great in society, men who had a godly heart and longed after truth. It's important to note that only a strong desire to know the truth and live the truth will determine the strength and significance of a man's testimony as a disciple of Christ. It is written, *"After removing Saul, he made David their king. God testified concerning him: I have found David son of Jesse, a man after my own heart; he will do everything I want him to do." [Acts 13:22;].* Beloved, are you a man after God's heart?

PRAYER FOCUS

Dear heavenly Father, nothing but the truth is acceptable to You. LORD, I incline my heart unto Your instructions and testimonies in Jesus' name.

"My heart's desire unto God, the chief design of my life ....are that... universal holiness may be prompted in my own and in the hearts and ways of others." (John Piper).

July 2

Staying True To The High Calling
Bible Reading: [Micah 3:1-8]

"But truly I am full of power by the Spirit of the LORD, and of judgment, and of might, to declare unto Jacob his transgression, and to Israel his sin." [Vs:8]

Beloved in the LORD, whenever the leadership of a society leads in wickedness, moral decline is obvious. Sometimes it's heartbreaking when things are falling apart in society but there is nobody with the willingness to take bold risks against unrighteousness. Leaders who are supposed to set standards find themselves wanting, and husbands who are supposed to set standards are morally bankrupted. Beloved, what is your contribution to bring light to your community?

As believers in Christ, we have been called to serve God's purpose. In order stay true to this high calling, we must rise above human inadequacies and communicate truth from God's viewpoint. Just how fearful are we sometimes when our limitations become a snare! Micah realized that he couldn't communicate truth by relying on his own strength. He says, *"But as for me, I am filled with power - with the Spirit of the LORD"* Our bold actions will yield incredible results when we are led by the Holy Spirit. It's written, *"But you shall receive power when the Holy Spirit comes on you; and you will be my witnesses..." [Acts 1:8]*. Someone, somewhere is always ready to be saved.

PRAYER FOCUS

Dear heavenly Father, thank You for endowing me with the ability for special communications. Grant that Your word proclaimed today in the power of the Holy Spirit, will deeply convict hearts and yield abiding fruits in Jesus' name.

July 3

Competent Ministers
Bible Reading: [2 Cor.3:1-6]

"Not that we are sufficient of ourselves to think anything as ourselves; but our sufficiency is of God; Who has made us able ministers of the new testament; not of the letter, but of the Spirit: for the letter killeth, but the Spirit giveth life." [Vs: 5-6]

Each passing day as we live the Christian life, one thing must appeal to us in a very personal way: our sufficiency is of Christ. This alone is the power giving continuance of life. Whenever a person thinks that he is sufficient in himself; fear and failure are obvious. Therefore, our total confidence in Christ should be based on the fact that being effective is not dependent on our personal abilities, but in the power of God working through us to accomplish our destiny.

The great apostle Paul acknowledges that his sufficient and confidence as a preacher is based on his commissioning by God through Christ. It is written, *"But by the grace of God I am what I am, and his grace toward me was not in vain; but I labor more abundantly than they all, yet not I, but the grace of God which was with me." [1 Cor.15:10]*. It is important to note that the grace to live a victorious Christian life and to serve God's purpose is only available to those who are converted to faith in Christ by genuine repentance. Only the Spirit of Christ gives life!

Because no man is competent on his own strength, let's humble ourselves today to God and allow the enabling power of the Holy Spirit to help us function effectively for God's glory!

PRAYER FOCUS

Dear heavenly Father, in You, I am fit, worthy and sufficient. LORD, I trust in Your power to function as an effective witness of Christ in Jesus' name.

July 4

Breaking Free From Bad Habits
Bible Reading: [Heb.12:1-11]

"Wherefore seeing we also are compassed about with so great a cloud of witnesses, let us lay aside every weight, and the sin which doth so easily beset us, and let us run with patience the race that is set before us," [Vs: 1]

A bad habit is a negative behavior pattern. As believers in Christ, we cannot allow these habits to hinder us from running the race that is set before us. Some bad practices that the people of the world may consider a way of life are sources of distraction and entanglement.

It's important to note that, in your effort to get rid of some bad habits, people may laugh at you. Do you truly desire freedom? It is written, *"....If ye continue in my word, then are ye my disciples indeed; And ye shall know the truth, and the truth shall make you free." [John 8:31-32]*

Desiring to gain freedom from bad habits means deciding to walk in the realm of joy, beauty and absolute liberty. One must be determined and trust God for help. Remember that, *"for the joy that was set before him endured the cross, despising shame,.." [Vs:2].* Jesus Christ who had no bad habit, took all our bad habits and nailed them to the Cross! Hallelujah!

PRAYER FOCUS

Today I subject bad habits in my life to the authority of Jesus Christ. Today, I proclaim my victory and liberty over bad habits in Jesus' name.

July 5

Rejoicing In the God of my Salvation
Bible Reading: [Hab.3:17-19]

"Although the fig tree shall not blossom, neither shall fruit be in the vines; the labor of the olive shall fail, and the fields shall yield no meat; the flock shall be cut off from the fold, and there shall be no herd in the stalls: Yet I will joy in the God of my salvation." [Vs:17-18;KJV]

Often we allow our environments to determine our spirit. As believers in Christ, we cannot see all that God is doing or will do. Standing firm in the LORD regardless of the situation implies we are confident that God will act at the right time and do the right thing. Come what may, God is worthy of all our trust and praises. Scriptures say, *"It is God who arms me with strength, and makes my way perfect." [Ps.18:32].*

Because God is the true source of strength and an invincible army, every believer must be confident in his or her walk with God. True believers in Christ must triumph because God does two things: *He makes their feet like hinds' feet: this implies that one can't afford to stand still in the midst of terror, but walk through it confidently and victoriously [Ps 91:5].* He makes my feet to walk upon their high places.

This implies, even in times of trouble, hardships and persecution, one shall make progress. He will swiftly ascend to the mountaintops and gracefully gliding over them. The full realization of God's mighty is faith that rolls every mountain.

PRAYER FOCUS

Dear heavenly Father, You are my strength and invincible army. I'm confident that in You, I'm too powerful to be defeated. I command all evil opposing forces or powers to bow to Your lordship in Jesus' name.

July 6

Working Toward Enduring Relationships
Bible Reading: [Luke 22]

"And the LORD said, Simon, Simon, behold, Satan hath desired to have you, that he may sift you as wheat: But I have prayed for thee, that thy faith fail not: and when thou art converted, strengthen thy brethren."
[Luke 22:31-32;KJV].

Beloved in LORD, have ever pondered over what might happen to you if you are out of the power and keeping of the Almighty God? Satan is the accuser of the people of God. Scripture says, " *let Satan should take advantage of us: for we are not ignorant of his devices." [2 Cor.2:11].* The goal of Satan is to hinder us from reaching our full potential and deter us from our destiny. The most reassuring fact is that God always leads us in triumphal procession in Christ. There is no reason to be alarmed as a believer in Christ. If God is for you, who can be against you?

PRAYER FOCUS

Dear heavenly Father, thank You for having raised me up with Christ and seated me with him in the heavenly places *[Eph. 2:6].*

July 7

Success In The Light Of God's Favor
Bible Reading: [Psalm 44:1-8]

"For they got not the land in possession by their own sword, neither did their own arm save them: but thy right hand, and thine arm, and the light of thy countenance, because thou hadst a favor unto them. In God we boast all the day long, and praise thy name forever. Selah." [Vs: 3&8;KJV]

Beloved in the LORD, in whom or in what do you put your trust? The Psalmist wrote, "Some trust in Chariots, and some in horses: but we will remember the name of the LORD our God. They are brought down and fallen: but we are risen, and stand upright *[Psalm 20:7-8;KJV]*. Whenever we face life's realities with the arm of flesh, triumph is farfetched! The arm of flesh has never prevailed against evil opposing forces. Like the Israelites, God wants us to come to full realization to the fact that with intellectual giftedness or military might, the strength of man will only amount to nothing without the light of the His favor.

Reaching our promised land will be a dream come true when our obedience to God and submission to His authority is all we can do. Scriptures record that it is God who works in us to will and to act in order to fulfill His good purpose *[Phil.2:13]*. To be triumphant in Christ is not the product of one's strength but the outcome of God working through us and with us. God who worked in the past with His people has not changed by the power of His name. Only in His name can we make our boast. Each time you feel like the task is too hard or the enemy is great, remember the mighty acts of God and praise His name *[2 Chr.20:21-22]*.

PRAYER FOCUS

Dear heavenly Father, I have heard of Your mighty works in the past. LORD, in the light of Your favor, renew them in my days, grant me good success in Jesus' name.

July 8

Uncommon Opportunities
Bible Reading: [1 Sam.10:1-16]

"Then the Spirit of the LORD will come upon you, and you will prophesy with them and be turned into another man. And let it be, when these signs come to you, that you do as the occasion demands; for God is with you." [Vs:6-7]

The world is full of opportunities that each one of us can access if we desire and are determined. However, there are some opportunities that are appointed or ordained for a season. Such may come once in a lifetime. Many people have missed it because they were not discerning or understood the times *[1 Chr.12:32]*. One can only be privileged to such an opportunity if he or she is at the center of God's will; being at the right place, at the right time. It is written, *"The steps of a good man are ordered by the LORD: and he delighteth in his ways." [Psalm 37:23]*

Like Saul, I know somebody is about to step into a season of uncommon opportunity. It is important to note that Saul never knew what plans the LORD had for his life. He step out in obedience to his father's command to search for missing donkeys not knowing that God had a far-reaching agenda for him. You can image how many have missed such because they failed to recognize the time of God's visitation. No matter the distractions of the enemy, I decree and declare that you will not miss your uncommon opportunity this year in Jesus' name. It's written, *"So it was, when he had turned his back to go from Samuel, that God gave him another heart; and all those signs came to pass that day." [Vs:9]*. May God's presence empower you to fulfill His commands and may every word of God spoken about your life come to pass in Jesus' name.

PRAYER FOCUS

Dear heavenly Father, thank You for the great opportunities You've ordained for me than I can image. LORD, I am fully convinced that everything will come to pass in my life this year according to Your word in Jesus' name.

July 9

The Power & Significance Of Silence
Bible Reading: [Amos 5:13-15]

"Therefore the prudent keep silent at that time, for it is an evil time. Seek good and not evil, that you may live; so the LORD God of hosts will be with you, as you have spoken." [Vs: 13-14]

In the secular world and body of Christ, knowing when to speak and when to keep silent is of utmost importance. Remember what the Scripture says, *"For by thy words thou shalt be justified, and by thy words thou shalt be condemned." [Matt.12:37].* There are countless examples of people who have been implicated because of their words. Beloved, when do you think it's appropriate for you to speak? It is written, *"To everything there is a season, and a time to every purpose under the heaven: ..a time to keep silence, and a time to speak"[Eccl.3:17;KJV].*

Considering the nature of the society we live in today, a corrupt system where false accusations, bribery and deceit has become a way of life, Words can easily be misunderstood. As we immerse ourselves in scriptures, I pray that the LORD will grant us wisdom and discernment. At times when men are pushed to the walls, he who patiently keeps silent is the one who has decided to wait on God's vengeance. It is important to note that every idle word that men speak, they will give an account for it on the day of judgment *[Matt.12:36].* May the LORD grant that we will understand the times and know when to speak.

PRAYER FOCUS

Dear heavenly Father, It's Your desire to lead me daily in triumphal procession in Christ. LORD, grant that I will exercise self-control and choose my words wisely in Jesus' name.

July 10

God's Design
-Bigger- Than Our Limited Perspective
Bible Reading: [Jer.29:10-14]

"For I know the thoughts that I think toward you, saith the LORD, thoughts of peace, and not of evil, to give you an expected end." [Vs: 11]

The giver of life has given us another beautiful month. It's written, *"You saw me before I was born. Every day of my life was recorded in your book. Every moment was laid out before a single day had passed "[Ps 139:16].* It's worth mentioning that nothing this year will take God by surprise. Seeing life from God's viewpoint is necessary. God wants us to see the bigger picture of His design for this year. He is committed to give those who submit to His authority an expected end *[Prov.23:18].*

Beloved, no matter what comes your way, you have to move ahead. Your life can't be grinded to a halt by circumstances because you are in Christ triumphal procession. Like the captive Israelites in Babylon in the days of Jeremiah, there is a new beginning with a strong sense of purpose in God's great design for your life. As you commit yourself to the revealed word of God, rest assured that it's a year designed for you to win big and be fully established in your faith and life.

PRAYER FOCUS

Dear heavenly Father, thank You for a new day and the privilege to be a part of Your great plan. LORD, I'm fully persuaded that I will triumph gloriously, because Your presence and power is with me in Jesus' name.

July 11

Praying With Purpose
Bible Reading: [Luke 6:12-16]

"And it came to pass in those days, that he went out into a mountain to pray, and continued all night in prayer to God. And when it was day, he called unto him his disciples: and of them he chose twelve, who also he named apostles." [Vs:12-13]

The greatest challenge facing the world and the body of Christ is the fact that many important decisions are not made in the place of prayer. When did you last take time off to pray about important matters concerning your life? Jesus' prayer all might was for a specific purpose. He is our role model and a worthy example to follow. Jesus prayed before important events and decisions such as choosing the twelve.

Nowadays, some of us have been deceived into thinking that there is no need of prayer. It is true that we are living in a fast-paced world, but that shouldn't be a license for prayerlessness. Many are suffering today because they rushed into decisions and conclusions without seeking God's guidance in prayer. Jesus for once didn't make such an error. Be it trivial or tough situations, adequate time is needed as a believer to seek God's will for guidance. Your intuition or intellectual prowess is not enough!

Although wise in his military dealings, Joshua and the leaders of Israel were deceived by the Gibeonites. Scriptures record *that "So the Israelites examined their food, but they did not consult the LORD" [Josh. 9:14, NLT].* Pray with purpose this today. Seek guidance and godly counsel and you will triumph in every situation in Jesus' name.

PRAYER FOCUS

Dear heavenly Father, I acknowledge my inadequacy without You. I commit myself to seek You for guidance in every matter this day in Jesus' name.

July 12

The Power Of Divine Insurance
Bible Reading: [Psalm 27:1-6]

"For in the time of trouble he shall hide me in His pavilion: in the secret of his tabernacle shall he hide me; he shall set me upon a rock." [Vs:5;kjv]

Everyone especially those living in the Western world need insurance of some kind: health, property or life insurance. Nobody on earth is immune to trouble, whether believers in Christ or unbelievers. However, the assurance of faith in Christ is the confidence that every true disciple of Christ possesses. This assurance is a strong feeling of confidence about what the LORD has done, is doing, and will do. It is written, *"Being confident of this very thing, that he which hath begun a good work in you will perform it until the day of Jesus Christ." [Philipp.1:6; kjv]*

Assurance of salvation is what gives divine insurance to every believer in Christ. Basically, insurance is a thing providing protection against a possible eventuality [Heb.7:25]. Life is full of eventualities and we must be prepared for all possible outcomes. "The greatest insurance on earth is to be connected with God. The stock market may crash, wars may rage, tragedies may occur, famines, and material crisis may ravage society. But when you are in tune with God, you will not be defeated because He wills His best for His Children." [T.L. Osborn]. Adherence to God's standard of righteousness by faith in Christ is an excellent insurance. "For wisdom is a defense even as money is a defense, but the excellency of knowledge is that wisdom shields and preserves the life of him who has it." [Prov.7:12; amplied]. The fear of the LORD is the beginning of wisdom.

PRAYER FOCUS

Dear heavenly Father, You are a covenant keeping God. I'm confident in Your keeping power today. In Jesus' name

July 13

The Counsel Of The Wicked Shall Not Prosper
Bible Reading: Selected Passages

"Woe to those who devise iniquity, and work out evil on their beds! At morning light the practice it, because it is in the power of their hand." [Mic.2:1]

"Who is he who speaks and it comes to pass, when the LORD has not commanded it? [Lam.3:37]

"Take counsel together, but it will come to nothing; speak the word, but it will not stand, for God is with us." [Isa.8:10]

I'm fully persuaded that the counsel of the LORD concerning you and loved ones shall stand. Nothing can escape God's knowledge or has the power to counter his designs. Are you living right with God? Remember that all things work together for good to them that love God, to them who are called according to his purpose [Rom.8:28]

Men who devise mischief and give wicked counsel always think they have the power and influence to perform it. Because we are confident in whom we have believed [Jesus Christ], let's say, "Now I know that the LORD is greater than all gods: for in the thing wherein they dealt proudly He was above them" [Exod.18:11, KJV]. Hallelujah!

PRAYER FOCUS

Today, I decree and declare: Let the counsel of the wicked against my life/family fail and their purposes be defeated in Jesus' name!

July 14

Living Beyond The Limits
Bible Reading: [1 Chr.4:9-10]

"And Jabez called on the God of Israel, saying, Oh that thou wouldest bless me indeed, and enlarge my coast, and that thine hand might be with me, and that thou wouldest keep me from evil, that it may not grieve me! And God granted him that which he requested." [Vs: 10]

Beloved, have you ever felt like there is an embargo on your destiny? Even your best effort seems fruitless. Much has been tied down to one location and life seems to have come to a standstill! Today I pray that such an embargo placed on your life be lifted by fire, in Jesus' name. What seems to be a limitation to man is not the case with God. God ordained you to move higher in life than where you are presently.

he Bible records that Jabez was more honorable than his brothers but his life was characterized by pain. His mother bore him in a time of great concern and he lived in the midst of unrighteousness. However, Jabez made an earnest request to God in prayer. It is written, *"And this is the confidence that we have in Him, that, if we ask anything according to His will, He heareth us"* [1 John.5:14]. Jabez's passionate prayer changed the outcome of his life. God heard him because of his obedient life in accordance with His will. Beloved, in your unrighteous environment, do you have a genuine walk with God? It is worth mentioning that He wants you to rise today beyond whatever limitation placed on your life by circumstances or the evil one. God has not changed by the power of His name!

PRAYER FOCUS

Dear heavenly Father, I come to You not only with the desire to be relieved of pain, but out of love for You. LORD, I trust in the power of Your Spirit to quicken my life and enlarge my sphere of influence in Jesus' name.

July 15

If God Is For Us
Bible Reading: [Rom.8:31-39]

"What shall we say of this things? If God be for us, who can be against us? He that spared not his own Son, but delivered him up for us all, how shall he not with him also freely give us all things? [Vs: 31-31]

There is no greater joy than to know that God is with us *[Matt.1:23]*. If he is with us, then he cannot be against us. "When we understand how far Jesus had to come to get us, then we can appreciate the extent to which God had to go to save us" (Roger Dickson). God will not withhold anything we need to live for him. His divine power has given us everything we need to live and serve his purpose *[2 Pet.1:3]*. This is the blessed assurance that true believers in Christ receive from their relationship with God. Because he is for us, there is no condemnation for those who belong to Jesus Christ.

PRAYER FOCUS

Dear heavenly Father, thank You for Your redeeming grace that is reaching many and the wonderful gift of Salvation through Jesus Christ our LORD. Amen.

July 16

Growing Through The Test
Bible Reading: [2 Chr. 32:27-31]

"However, regarding the ambassadors of the princes of Babylon, whom they sent to him to inquire about the wonder that was done in the land, God withdrew from him, in order to test him, that he might know all that was in his heart [Vs:31]

Sometimes in life, God would allow us go through the test in order to reveal to us the true nature of our heart. Beloved in the LORD, what's your heart attitude like when you become rich, successful in academics, business, sports et cetera. The Psalmist made a request to God: *"Search me, O God, and know my heart: try me, and know my thoughts: And see if there be any wicked way in me,.."* [Ps 139:23-24].

After King Hezekiah received healing, he developed excessive pride. When envoys came from Babylon, instead of expressing gratitude to God and testifying of His goodness, he was eager to talk about his accomplishments. How too often we are carried away by our self-worth and accomplishments? Scripture says, *"God withdrew from him, in order to test him, that He might know all that was in his heart"[Vs:31]*. It is important to note that God usually test us for our strengthening and purification. God desires that every test will develop our character and prepare us for the next assignment. As we learn through such an experience, we develop the right heart attitude to serve His purpose better.

PRAYER FOCUS

Dear heavenly Father, You resist the proud and give grace to the humble. Grant that the purpose for which You allow me go through every test will be accomplished in Jesus' name.

July 17

Partakers Of Christ
Bible Reading: [Hebrews 3:1-15]

"For we are made partakers of Christ, if we hold the beginning of our confidence steadfast unto the end;" [Vs: 14]

Nowadays there is a strong desire in the hearts of men to participate in something : be it good or bad. Oftentimes our hearts do turn away from God when we refuse to believe in him. A partaker is one who has or takes part or shares along with others. No one can be a child of God and the same time live outside the fellowship of God's people. It is written, *"Those things, which ye have both learned, and received, and heard and seen in me, do: and the God of peace shall be with you" [Phillipp.4:9].*

We are part of God's family if we keep our encouragement. Our confidence and hope demonstrate that our faith is real. Only those who remain faithful to the calling of the gospel will join with Christ in the marriage supper in heaven *[Rev.19:9].* Beloved, are you a partaker with Christ? Focusing on Jesus is key to persevering in the *faith "Today, if you will hear His voice, do not harden your hearts..." [Vs:15]*

PRAYER FOCUS

Dear heavenly Father, thank You for making me heir of God and co-heirs with Christ. May Your grace abound and the gift of righteousness reign in my life to the end in Jesus' name.

July 18

Dangers of Replacing Righteousness With Rituals
Bible Reading: [Matt.15:1-20]

"Then the scribes and Pharisees who were from Jerusalem came to Jesus, saying, "why do Your disciples transgress the tradition of the elders? For they do not wash their hands when they eat bread." He answered and said to them, "why do you also transgress the commandment of God because of your tradition?" [Vs: 1-3;NKJV]

Beloved in the LORD, God wants us to be sincere in our worship of Him. Multitudes in the world are being deceived by believing that they are worshiping God acceptably. Are you willing to follow the traditions of men or be led by the Spirit God? Ceremonial purity is only an outward performance but God desires true inner purity. A ritual is a religious service which involves a series of actions performed in a fixed order. It's worth mentioning that Scriptures do not encourage stereotypes. It's written, *"For as many as are led by the Spirit of God, they are the sons of God." [Rom.8:14;KJV]*.

- *The danger of ritualistic behavior is threefold: It promotes outward purity instead of inward beauty*
- *It makes men to love human praises more than the praise of God.*
- *It makes the Word of God of no effect.*

Many Christians have become religious folks and Churches powerless because of the traditions of men. Seek God's righteousness today. It's not by observing the law or performing some rituals. It's the gift of God that comes by faith in Christ *"For by grace are ye saved through faith; and not of yourselves: it is the gift of God: not of works, lest any man should boast." [Eph.2:8-9]*. True repentance is the way and producing fruits worthy of repentance *[Lk.3:8]*. Is the only evidence. Let Jesus be the center of your life TODAY!

PRAYER FOCUS

Dear heavenly Father, help me not to disobey You in my zeal to preserve the traditions of men. LORD, I seek to do Your will and be led by the Holy Spirit in Jesus' name.

July 19

Don't Know How, But He Did It
Bible Reading: [Psalm 126:1-6]

"When the LORD turned again the captivity of Zion, we were like them that dream. Then was our mouth filled with laughter, and our tongue with singing: then said they among the heathen, The LORD hath done great things for them" [Vs:1-2]

Have you ever been through any form of some of captivity? There is good news for you: the LORD is able to bring good out of very difficult circumstances. Captivity means the condition of being imprisoned or confined. Oftentimes the one held captive is rendered powerless and may be tempted to question God's ability to rescue. The Israelites could not believe that God would work in their lives in order to allow them return to their land. It's important to note that God's ability is beyond human comprehension. *"But thus saith the LORD, even the captives of the mighty shall be taken away, and the prey of the terrible shall be delivered: for I will contend with him that contendeth with thee, and I will save thy children" [Isa.49:25].*

When God sent an angel to rescue Peter from prison, he went out following Him and did not know that it was true. But he thought he was seeing a vision *[Acts 12:1-12]*. With the guards of four squads of four soldiers each to make it impossible for him to escape, God was in Charge, and nothing is too hard for Him *[Jer.32:17]*. God is still at work. No situation is beyond the reach of His grace and power. I decree and declare that your dreams shall come true. In Jesus' name.

PRAYER FOCUS

Dear heavenly Father, I know You have greater plans for my life. I trust that Your supernatural power will cause a turnaround in my condition this season in Jesus' name.

July 20

The Power Of Intercession To Bring Manifestation
Bible Reading: [1 Kings 18:41-46]

Then Elijah said to Ahab, Go up, eat and drink; for there is the sound of abundance of rain." [Vs: 41]

Beloved in the LORD, there's a lot at stake in the world. Recently, the Spirit of God started prompting my heart that there is serious need for intercession. Many believers do not realize that it is not enough to simply receive a word from God and then wait to see it come to pass. There must be intercession to bring to reality the promises of God. Every prophetic word needs the power of intercession to come to fruition. We lose grounds to the enemy when we fail to intercede as individuals, as a family, Church, Community or nation. God is committed to change situations on the face of the earth but can He find a man standing in the gap? *[Ezek.22:30]*. You don't need to be given the title "prayer warrior" or "intercessor" before you participate in Intercessory prayer. Intercession is prayer that pleads with God for your needs and most importantly for the needs of others. The one who engages in intercession must take hold of God's will and refuse to let go until it comes to pass.

Remember, in the days of prophet Elijah, Israel was in such a difficult situation. Under Ahab and Jezebel, Israel began worshiping Baal, a Canaanite fertility god of storm and rain. This caused God to send a drought(famine) upon Israel *[1 Kings.17:1]*. Scriptures record this about Elijah, *"Elijah was a human being, even as we are. He prayed earnestly that it would not rain, and it did not rain on the land for three half years. Again he prayed, and the heavens gave rain, and the earth produced its crops." [Jam.5:17-18]*. A call for drought was a direct attack against those who were deceived that Baal controls the weather. God in whom we believe, controls the events of the earth. He is sovereign over the kingdoms of men. God wants us to believe that whatever He wants us to do, He will provide what we need to carry it through. Prayer moves the hand of Him who moves the world.

PRAYER FOCUS

Dear heavenly Father, You are sovereign over the works of creation. I know You can do all things. TODAY, I commit myself to the service of intercession in Jesus' name. *"...The effectual fervent prayer of a righteous man availeth much" [Jam.5:16]*.

July 21

Power Of The Implanted Word
Bible Reading: [James 1: 19-27]

"Therefore lay aside all filthiness and overflow of wickedness, and receive with meekness the implanted Word, which is able to save your souls. But be doers of the Word, and not hearers only, deceiving yourselves. " [Vs: 21-22]

Beloved in the LORD, we know from Scriptures that faith comes by hearing, and hearing by the Word of God *[Rom.10:17]*. For the most part, the people in our communities have heard a portion of Scriptures. But do all have faith? It is likely for people to keep hearing the good news proclaimed, but it is of no value to them because they are not ready to share the faith of those who obeyed *[Heb.4:2]*. Oftentimes the junk stuff we allow to fill our hearts doesn't give room for the Word of truth to be established in our lives. That's why Scripture says, *"lay aside all filthiness and overflow of wickedness."* Even the Word some have received, the Bible says, *"the worries of this life, the deceitfulness of wealth and the desires for other things come in and choke the word, making it unfruitful" [Mk 4:19]*

"If the Word of God does not rank with your most cherished possessions, you need to do a reality check on your life (John Piper). Everyone who truly desires the Word must rid himself/herself of all filthiness and overflow of wickedness in their lives and receive the implanted Word. The Word of God does not indwell (live in us) unless we behave what we know.

We do not receive the Word to be informed but to be transformed. The Word can profit us by saving our souls if we receive it with the right attitude (meekness). This implies that we must be teachable or be ready to submit to it. Dear friend, are you saved? Where will you spend eternity: Heaven or Hell? The Word of God is implanted only in the hearts of those who conduct their lives according to God's will.

PRAYER FOCUS

Dear heavenly Father, may Your word dwell in richly in all wisdom and spiritual understanding in Jesus' name.

July 22

Putting Up A Tough Fight
Bible Reading: [Jer.12:1-5]

"If you have run with the footmen and they have wearied you, then how can you contend with horses? And if in the land of peace, In which you trusted, they wearied you, then how will you do in the floodplain of the Jordan?" [Vs:5]

Beloved in the LORD, I have witnessed teams that put up a good fight but in the end they were beaten. Then Christian life is an uphill climb! It's a pilgrim's journey marked by difficult or strong resistance. Life was very tough for Jeremiah despite his love for and obedience to God. Often God will not promise us relief but grace in adversity.

In putting up a tough fight, you become brave against somebody or something that seems stronger than you. As believers in Christ, we must be thankful to God for every giant on the way. It's worth noting that the greater the giant or assignment, the greater the assistance from God. God cannot dispatch assistance for an assignment that you are not prepared for. God will only promise you the land but will not possess it for you. He will endow and equip you with all it takes to have good success. As we live each passing day, one thing is so reassuring - He leads us in triumph in Christ. It's written, *"Now thanks be to God who always leads us in triumph in Christ,." [2 Cor.2:14]*.

Beloved, today I strongly believe that God is positioning you according to a higher priority than your preference. May God grant that you will see beyond the eyes of men. His grace is sufficient and in Christ victory is certain! Everyone born of God overcomes the world *[1 Jn.5:4] "I can do all things through Christ which strengthens me" [Philipp.4:13]*.

PRAYER FOCUS

Dear heavenly Father, You give power to the weak and to those who have no might You increase their strength. Thank You for positioning me according to Your higher priority than my preference in Jesus' name.

July 23

Attaining Unto Wise Counsel
Bible Reading: Prov.1:1-7

"A wise man will hear, and increase learning; and a man of understanding shall attain unto wise counsels:" [Vs:5]

The world has seen an increase in knowledge overtime. Scripture says, *"..even to the time of the end: knowledge shall be increased" [Dan.12:4]*. There is no doubt about it, but we've got more problems and less solutions. Wise counsel is a treasure. It is a special ability of advice that enables men to avoid some of the poor decisions and mistakes others have made. Only a man of understanding will attain unto wise counsel.

To attain wise counsel implies one has to desire and reach out for it. It's important to note that there is a spiritual gift of counsel *[Isa.11:2]*. However, one can also gain wise counsel. For this to happen, you must discover the source of it, value it, and reap the benefits of it. It is written, *"..the proconsul, Sergius Paulus, an intelligent man. This man called for Barnabas and Saul and sought to hear the word of God. Then the proconsul believed, when he saw what had been done, being astonished at the teaching of the LORD." [Acts.13:7&12]*.

It's worth noting that he was an intelligent man but he sought after wise counsel. Like Sergius Paulus, many of us, especially the government leaders we consider intelligent are deceived by sorcerers and cult masters. Friend, where will you spend eternity? Heaven or hell? It's written,,*"There is a way which seemeth right unto a man, but the end thereof are the ways of death"* [Prov.14:12].

Attain unto wise counsel today and live the best life God has destined for you.

PRAYER FOCUS

Dear heavenly Father, You are the source of wise counsel. LORD, grant that I will set my priorities right by attaining unto wise counsel and possessing a teachable spirit in Jesus' name. *"Where no counsel is, the people fall: but in the multitude of counsellors there is safety"[Prov.11:14]*

July 24

The Secret Of The LORD
Bible Reading: [Ps 25:14 & Deut.29:29]

"The secret of the LORD is with them that fear him; and he will shew them his covenant." [Ps 25:14]

"The secret things belong unto the LORD our God: but those things which are revealed belong unto us and to our children forever, that we may do all the words of this law." [Deut.29:29]

For the most part, when you tell somebody that you have a secret for him/her, all ears will be itchy to hear. What more about the secret of the LORD? A secret is a confidential matter, something that is kept or meant to be kept unknown or unseen by others. Knowing the secrets of the LORD is one of the covenant benefits of a true child of God. God is willing to reveal his secret concerning you, your family and nation. How important is God's secret to you?

It is written, *"And the LORD said, shall I hide from Abraham that thing which I do; seeing that Abraham shall surely become a great and mighty nation, and all the nations of the earth shall be blessed in him?" [Gen.18:17-18].* God revealed his secret to Abraham for two reasons: Abraham was a depository of the truth. Divine truths will not only be deposited in him, he will live by them. Abraham thought his children the ways of God (godliness), in order that the promises of God might be fulfilled.

There are so many things that God has not yet revealed to us. However, the things revealed in Scriptures belong to men, so that they may know and do the will of God. You've certainly been praying and asking God to reveal something to you. Sometimes God will not speak because he knows our hearts, that we will not do his command. Are you ready to do his will TODAY?

PRAYER FOCUS

Dear heavenly Father, You offer intimacy to those who fear You and hold You in highest honor. LORD, I commit myself to honor You, and to do Your will as You reveal Your secrets to me in Jesus' name!

July 25

Blessed To Be A Blessing
Bible Reading: [Zach.8:1-13]

"And it shall come to pass that just as you were a curse among the nations, O house of Judah and house of Israel, so I will save you, and you shall be a blessing. Do not fear, let your hands be strong. "Thus says the LORD of hosts: 'In those days ten men from every language of the nations shall grasp the sleeve of a Jewish man, saying, "Let's go with you, for we have heard that God is with you." [Vs: 13&23]

When we walk in obedience to the Word of God and do his biddings, his blessings begin to flow in our lives. God expects us to act with integrity and justice. He promises to give those who fear him rich rewards. It's written, *"The blessing of the LORD, maketh rich, and he addeth no sorrow with it [Prov.10:22].* The blessings of the LORD bring health, wealth, peace, joy etc. If a man gains wealth through bribery and corrupt, it's short-lived and adds sorrow.

Divine blessing is the portion of all who have a covenant relationship with Jesus. Are you blessed? There is a clarion call to be a blessing to others [neighbors, family, friends] and especially those in the household of faith. *"Therefore, as we have opportunity, let us do good to all men, especially to those who are of the household of the faith." [Gal.6:10].*

As believers, we were brought forth by the grace of God *[Eph.2:8].* Our joyous character should be a source of motivation for others to worship God. Scripture says, "ten men from every language of nations will take hold of the garment of him who is a Jew, saying, *"we will go with you, for we have heard that God is with you." [Vs:23].* If God is truly with you, you ought to be an aroma of Christ that attracts men *[2 Cor.2:15].* Remember, "But he is a Jew who is one inwardly; and circumcision is that of the heart, in the Spirit, not in the letter; whose praise is not from men but from God." *[Rom.2:29]*

PRAYER FOCUS

Dear heavenly Father, I'm grateful to You for having ordained me a blessing to the world. Grant that my fountain will never stop flowing and help to discern those who are truly in need in Jesus' name.

July 26

Impossible For God To Lie
Bible Reading: [Heb.6:13-20]

"So God has given both his promise and his oath. These two things are unchangeable because it is impossible for God to lie. Therefore, we who have fled to him for refuge can have great confidence as we hold to the hope that lies before us." [Vs: 18;nlt]

Beloved in the LORD, in our human relationships and in society, we believe the oath, vows and covenants we make. We consider them binding. If from human standpoint these give us assurance that something is true, therefore an oath from God or covenant with Christ should inspire a great confidence in us! Have you been trusting God for something concerning His promises? Friend, I would like you to understand today that God's character is absolutely reliable. It is written, *"God is not a man, so he does not lie………. Has he ever spoken and failed to act? Has he ever spoken promised and not carried it through?"* [Num.23:19]

Every Christian ought to have a peace of mind because the things in scriptures that are yet to be fulfilled in our lives are based on the unchangeable promises of God. Often, what I have realized with many believers is they are not willing to endure. *"And so, after he had patiently endured, he obtained the promise."[Heb.6:15].* May God grant you the grace to endure until his word come true in Jesus' name!

PRAYER FOCUS

Dear heavenly Father, You are unchangeable and Your promises are final in Christ. I'm fully persuaded that Your counsel for my life and family shall stand, and You will do all Your pleasure in Jesus' name.

July 27

O God, Strengthen My Hands
Bible Reading: [Nehemiah 6:1-9]
"Great Determination for a Great Cause"

Every great cause goes with a great commitment and a great cause attracts great enemies. You don't need a prophet to inform you about that when charting a worthy cause. People may misuse God's name by saying they know God's will when they have other motives(Vs-7). While others look for a cause to live for, get a worthy cause to die for!

When opposition builds up against you or God's work, it is tempting to pray, "God get me out of this situation." The ploy of the enemy is to intimidate, maneuver, feed incorrect information, generate false rumors and distract attention from your real aim or target. *"If thou faint in the day of adversity, thy strength is small." (Prov.24:10;Isa.40:28-29)*. Apostle Paul says, "But none of these things moved me; nor do I count my life dear to myself, so that I may finish my race with joy, and the ministry which I received from the Lord Jesus, to testify to the gospel of the grace of God." (Acts 20:24)

Nehemiah prayed for strength and continued the work with even greater determination.

"Whatever your hand finds to do, do it with all your might." (Eccl.9:10;Col.3:23)

By trusting God to accomplish your task and by overlooking unjustified insults, you undermine the ploy of the enemy. It is God's desire that you complete your task or mission.

"For the eyes of the LORD range throughout the earth to strengthen those whose hearts are fully committed to Him... " (2 Chr.16:9)

PRAYER FOCUS

Dear heavenly Father, may You empower me to fulfill my purpose and strengthen my hands to do your work in Jesus' name.

July 28

Impossible For God To Lie
Bible Reading: [Heb.6:13-20]

"So God has given both his promise and his oath. These two things are unchangeable because it is impossible for God to lie. Therefore, we who have fled to him for refuge can have great confidence as we hold to the hope that lies before us." [Vs: 18, NLT]

Beloved in the LORD, in our human relationships and in society, we believe the oath, vows and covenants we make. We consider them binding. If from human standpoint these give us assurance that something is true, therefore an oath from God or covenant with Christ should inspire a great confidence in us!

Have you been trusting God for something concerning his promises? Friend, I would like you to understand today that God's character is absolutely reliable. It is written, *"God is not a man, so he does not lie………. Has he ever spoken and failed to act? Has he ever spoken promised and not carried it through?" [Num.23:19]*

Every Christian ought to have a peace of mind because the things in scriptures that are yet to be fulfilled in our lives are based on the unchangeable promises of God. What I have realized with many believers is the fact that they are not willing to endure. *"And so, after he had patiently endured, he obtained the promise." [Heb.6:15]*. May God grant you the grace to endure until his word come true in Jesus' name!

PRAYER FOCUS

Dear heavenly Father, You are unchangeable and Your promises are final in Christ. I'm fully persuaded that Your counsel shall stand, and You will do all Your pleasure in Jesus' name.

July 29

Bless The LORD, O My Soul
Bible Reading: [Psalm 103]

*"But the mercy of the LORD is from everlasting to everlasting on those who fear Him, and His righteousness to children's children." Bless the LORD, all His works, in all places of His dominion.
Bless the LORD, O my soul! [Vs:17&22]*

How often do you spend time to offer praise for the LORD's goodness? It's easy to complain about life but there is plenty for which to praise God and exalt His redemptive work. Counting our blessings gives us a valid reason to be thankful to God and the strength to overcome the challenges of life. One can truly obey God by being faithful and loyal to Him.

Let's add warmth and significance to worship by seizing the opportunity for personal praise and testimony. Celebrate the LORD's kindness, compassion, perfection, provision and forgiveness TODAY!

PRAYER FOCUS

Dear heavenly Father, Your love and forgiveness are infinite and complete. Your redemptive work reaches to all people. Thank You for pouring out grace and mercy upon me in Jesus' name.

July 30

Let Christ Be Fully Formed In You
Bible Reading: [Gal.4:12-19]

*"But it is good to be zealously affected always in a good thing, and not only when I am present with you.
My little children, of whom I travail in birth again until Christ be formed in you." [Vs:18-19]*

Beloved in the LORD, we are living at a time when people are tossed to and fro by any wind of doctrine. Many are zealous but not according to knowledge *[Rom.10:2]*. Some are deceived by the zeal and charisma of false teachers. It's important to note that zeal is no guarantee of truth or that one has believed the truth. They Galatian believers had fallen from grace and had to be renewed in Christ again.

For one to become a disciple i.e. being established in the faith, it involves labor pains on the part of the disciple maker or spiritual father. This intense care for those to whom we are spiritual parents involves; preaching, teaching, counseling, prayers and encouragement for regular fellowship. It is written, *"Epaphras, who is one of you, a servant of Christ, saluteth you, always laboring fervently for you in prayers, that ye may stand perfect and complete in all the will of God." [Col.4:12].*

Like Paul, sometimes we go through the frustration of bringing people into sonship again after a great backsliding. We shouldn't feel that our mission is finished until Christ is fully developed in their lives. It is written, *"Let us not become weary in doing good, for at the proper time we will reap a harvest if we do not give up." [Gal.6:9]*

PRAYER FOCUS

Dear heavenly Father, it's not Your desire that anyone should perish, but everyone should come to repentance. LORD, grant that I will count it all joy to see men saved and labor until Christ is fully formed in them in Jesus' name.

July 31

Ministering To The LORD With Your Substance
Bible Reading: [Luke 8:1-3]

"And certain women, which had been healed of evil spirits and infirmities, Mary called Magdalene, out of whom went seven devils, and Joanna the wife of Chuza Herod's steward, and Susanna, and many others, which ministered unto Him of their substance." [Vs:2-3]

Beloved in the LORD, have you ever considered why the ministry of our LORD Jesus Christ was very successful on earth? One of the reasons is because devoted men ministered to Him. Another season of opportunity has come! It's worth mentioning that the Christian life is not all about receiving from the LORD. There is a clarion call to minister to the LORD with your substance.

Every believer in Christ should count it all joy to minister to the LORD with their substance. When Christ was born wise men from the east came and ministered to him in worship, honoring him with their substance. Like Mary and others in the early Church who ministered to Jesus in person, the LORD has servants all over the world serving his purposes *[1 Cor.9:11]*. Christmas season is a time to celebrate Jesus and to minister to someone with your substance. The blessings of ministering to the LORD with your substance are obvious:

- *By doing so, you are honoring him [Prov.3:9]*
- *You are accessing the presence of great men [Mk 16:9;Prov.18:16].*
- *You are placing yourself in the right disposition to receive from Him.* "But my God shall supply all your need according to his riches in glory by Christ Jesus." *[Philipp.4:19].*

As the LORD speaks to you, obey Him by ministering to someone with your substance this season.

PRAYER FOCUS

Dear heavenly Father, I thank You for the gift of Your Son Jesus Christ to the world. Today I commit myself to honor You with my substance in Jesus' name.

AUGUST

"But unto you that fear my name shall the Sun of righteousness arise with healing in his wings; and ye shall go forth, and grow up as calves of the stall. And ye shall tread down the wicked; for they shall be ashes under the soles of your feet in the day that I shall do this, saith the LORD of hosts."

[Mal.4.2-3; KJV]

Jehovah Tsidkenu [The LORD Our Righteousness] Jeremiah.23:6, 33:16

8 = [New life, New Covenant, New Beginnings]

August 1

Your Giants Are Your Stepping-Stones
"One Step At A Time"
Bible Reading: [Deut.7:12-26]

"The LORD your God will drive out those nations before you, little by little. You will not be allowed to eliminate them all at once, or the wild animals will multiply around you." [Vs:22]

A stepping-stone is something that helps someone advance or achieve something. Sometimes it's very hard for the human mind to understand how God works. For the most part, each one of us would like instant results. Not so with God, He chooses sometimes to work in stages. He takes delight to teach us one lesson at a time, thus letting us go through the process. He does so not because He is not able to do things all at once, but in order to work His far-reaching purpose for our good.

Why one step at a time?

That we may acquire war or battle experience: We must not forget that part of our identity in Christ is that of a soldier. *"He did this to teach warfare to generations of Israelites who had no experience in battle." [Judges 3:2; 2 Tim.2:3-4; Exod.13:17]*

To prove the genuineness of our faith: *"But he knows the way that I take; when he has tested me, I will come forth as gold." [Job.23:10; Jam.1:3; 1 Pet.1:7]*

For our protection and enthronement: Not all giants are meant to kill us. Sometimes God allows giants in your life or path in order to protect you, take away pride, guide you and put you in a position of influence. Start seeing your giants also as a blessing and stepping-stone to greatness. *[2 Cor.12:7;Ps 119:71;1 Sam.18:7]*

PRAYER FOCUS

Dear heavenly Father, thank You for working a far-reaching purpose for me than my mind can understand. LORD, I'm confident that You will perfect that which concerns me in Jesus' name *[Ps 138:8; Gen.50:20]*.

August 2

Trusting God
In The Final Minute For Provision
Bible Reading: [Gen.22:7-14]

Beloved in the LORD, the year is far spent. Like little Isaac some of us are still asking the Father, "Behold the fire and the wood, but where is the lamb for a burnt offering?" Oftentimes man's greatest problem is being anxious to know how and when God will make provision. What catches God's attention is the faith we demonstrate when our human eyes can't see what we so desire. Remember, *"Now faith is being sure of what we hope for and certain of what we do not see." [Heb.11:1;NIV]*. While time is a factor to us, that is not the case with God *[2 Pet.3:8]*. For the most part, when we feel that time is running out, we become impatient with God's timing.

Being faced with a difficult decision, King Saul's impatience caused him to disobey God by not honoring the timing of Prophet Samuel *[1 Sam.13:7-11]*. Regardless of your present circumstance(s), trusting that God would provide in the final minute is more important than anything else. Sometimes in life, delays only test our patience and obedience to God's unfailing promises. God knows what we need and when His provision will make all the difference in our life so that no man will share His glory. It's written, *"For the LORD God is a sun and shield: the LORD will give grace and glory: no good thing will he withhold from them that walk uprightly. O LORD of hosts, blessed is the man that trusted in thee." [Psalm 84:11-12;KJV]*

PRAYER FOCUS

Dear heavenly Father, You are still Jehovah-Jireh, my provider. I'm confident that You will meet my need even at the very last minute. Thank You for Your faithfulness. In Jesus' name. *[Philipp.4:19]*. Now to our God and Father be glory forever and ever. Amen.

August 3

The Power Of The Life-giving Spirit
Bible Reading: [Rom.8:1-6]
"Freedom from sin and power
to do God's will"

"There is therefore now no condemnation to them which are in Christ Jesus, who walk not after the flesh, but after the Spirit. For the law of the Spirit of life in Christ Jesus hath made me free from the law of sin and death." [Vs:1-2]

Going by the law of gravity, anything that goes up must come down. However, not so with the law of aerodynamics in science that explains how an airplane is able to fly. By the sinful nature that man inherited from Adam, he finds himself trapped by a law that goes against his desire. Paul says, *"For the good that I will to do, I do not do; but the evil I will not to do, that I practice" [Rom.7:19]*.

Anything a man does with the flesh only serves the law of sin (sinful nature). Thank God for Jesus who without sin, identified himself with sinful people in order to redeem them *[Eph.1:7]**. What a joy to experience the power of the Holy Spirit that frees every believer from the power of sin that leads to death! *"This I say then, walk in the Spirit, and ye shall not fulfil the lust of the flesh." [Gal.5:16]*. Walking in the Spirit therefore implies that one has decided to be directed by the Spirit-inspired Word in response to the grace of God.

PRAYER FOCUS

"I am crucified with Christ: nevertheless I live; yet not I, but Christ liveth in me: and the life which I now live in the flesh I live by the faith of the Son of God, who loved me, and gave himself for me" [Gal.2:20]. Therefore, I will not frustrate the grace of God in Jesus' name.

August 4

The LORD Is My Defense Attorney and Judge

And the LORD said to Satan, "I, the LORD, reject your accusations, Satan. Yes, the LORD, who has chosen Jerusalem, rebukes you. This man is like a burning stick that has been snatched from the fire." [Vs:2]

Satan is and will always be the accuser of the brethren *[Rev.12:10]*. The accuser of the brethren is cast down to the earth. He accuses them before God day and night. Satan's role is either performed by him or human vessels he uses. The source of accusations or conspiracies brought against us is obvious? These accusations may be true or unfounded but one thing is certain, *"...We have an advocate with the Father—Jesus Christ, the Righteous One." [1 Jn.2:1]*. An advocate is one who pleads another's cause or who helps another by defending him.

God our defense attorney will stand by us especially at critical moments when an offense brought against us is true and everyone seems not ready to identify with us. Oftentimes it is fortunate for us that Satan and associates don't understand the breadth of God's mercy and forgiveness toward those who believe in Him. It is written, *"For he hath made him to be sin for us, who knew no sin; that we might be made the righteousness of God in him" [2 Cor.5:21]*.

Regardless of the guilt and pollution of our sin that might have caused us great harm like the case of Jeshua the high priest, our restoration depends on obedience to God. By reason of the blood of Jesus, today you are acquitted and discharged.

PRAYER FOCUS

Dear heavenly Father, Your grace has found me. By reason of the blood of Jesus, I decree and declare any argument or written ordinance against me neutralized and my case dismissed in Jesus' name *[Heb.12:24;Col.2:14]*.

August 5

The Power & Effects Of Soul Ties
Bible Reading: [Jer.17:9-10]

"The heart is deceitful above all things, and desperately wicked; who can know it? I, the LORD, search the heart, I test the mind, even to give every man according to his ways, according to the fruit of his doings."

A soul tie is like a linkage in the soul realm between two people. It links their souls together, which can bring forth both beneficial results or negative results.

The Positive Effect of Soul Tie

In a godly marriage, God links the two people together and the Bible tells us that they become one flesh. As a result of them becoming one flesh, it binds them together and they will cleave onto one another in a unique way. The purpose of this cleaving is to build a very healthy, strong and close relationship between a man and a woman. It is written, *"And said, For this reason a man shall leave his father and mother and be joined to his wife, and the two shall become one flesh." [Matt.19:5;KJV].* Soul ties can also be found in close strong or close friendships. They are not just limited to marriage, as we can see with David and Jonathan [1 Sam.18:1].

The Negative Effect Of Soul Tie: Ungodly soul ties—

Soul ties can also be used for the devil's advantage. Soul ties formed from sex outside of marriage causes a person to become defiled: *"And when Shechem the son of Hamor the Hivite, prince of the country, saw her(Dinah), he took her and lay with her, and violated her. His soul was strongly attracted to Dinah the daughter of Jacob, and he loved the young woman and spoke kindly to the young woman." [Gen.34:2-3;Ezek.23:17].* This is why it is so common for a person to still have 'feelings' towards an ex-lover that they have no right to be attracted to in that way.

Even 20 years after, a person may still think of their first lover...even if he or she is across the country and has their own family, all because of soul tie!

Demonic spirits can also take advantage of ungodly soul ties, and use them to transfer spirits between one person to another.[Source: ministeringdeliverance.com].

"Do you not know that when he who unites himself with a prostitute, is one with her in body? For it is said, "The two will become one flesh." [1 Cor.6:16;NIV]. Beloved in the LORD, do you have issues with ungodly soul ties? *"And you shall know the truth, and the truth shall make you free." [John.8:32]*

Acknowledge ungodly soul ties.

Confess and denounce it [Prov.28:13] in Jesus' name.

August 6

The Battle Is The LORD's
Bible Reading: [1 Sam.17:45, 50]
Supreme Advantage In The One True God

Then David said to the Philistine, "You come to me with a sword, with a spear, and with a javelin. But I come to you in the name of the LORD of hosts, the God of the armies of Israel, whom you have defied.
So David prevailed over the Philistine with a sling and with a stone, and struck the Philistine and killed him.
There was no sword in the hand of David."[Vs:45]

Having threats from an enemy is commonplace in the world in which we live. Throughout the reign of king Saul, there was an ongoing threat from the Philistines. Like David, each one of us must be determined to silence any giant that threatens our destiny. The secret of victory in any battle against the enemy is not the size of earthly weapons we may possess but the wisdom of God. It is written, *"Wisdom brings strength, and knowledge gives power. Battles are won by listening to advice and making a lot of plans." [Prov.24:5-6]*

In every battle we engage an enemy, God becomes a Game Changer when we understand that the weapons of our warfare are not carnal (earthly), but mighty through Him. It is important to note that though we walk in the flesh, spiritual battles are not battles against flesh and blood *[2 Cor.10:3-5]*. You can change the dynamics of your battle today by total trust in the name of the One who won the battle at the Cross. "And having disarmed the powers and authorities, he made a public spectacle of them, triumphing over them by the cross [Col.2:15]. Just like David prevailed over giant Goliath and Dagon the chief god of the Philistines, I decree and declare that the devil and his associates will be routed before you this season in Jesus' name.

"..the battle is not yours but God's." *[2 Chr.20:15]*

PRAYER FOCUS

Dear heavenly Father, some trust in chariots and some in horses but I trust in the name of the LORD.

August 7

Thanksgiving Begins With Prayer & Praise

"Mattaniah the son of Micah, the son of Zabdi, the son of Asaph, the leader who began the thanksgiving with prayer;..." [Neh.11:17;]

"Come and hear, all ye that fear God, and I will declare what he hath done for my soul. I cried unto him with my mouth, and he was extolled with my tongue. If I regard iniquity in my heart, the LORD will not hear me: But verily God hath heard me; he hath attended to the voice of my prayer. Blessed be God, which hath not turned away my prayer, nor his mercy from me." *[Psalm 66:16-20]*

Thanksgiving is more than a holiday. It is more than just getting together with family and friends to eat and drink. Thanksgiving is built right into the heart of praise and worship. It is an expression of gratitude, especially to God. *"Whoso offereth praise glorified me:.." [Psalm 50:23]*

PRAYER FOCUS

Dear heavenly Father, thank You for all that You have done for me in Jesus' name.

August 8

The Waymaker
Bible Reading: [Isa.43:16-21]

"Thus saith the LORD, which maketh a way in the sea, and a path in the mighty waters; Remember ye not the former things, neither consider the things of old. Behold, I will do a new thing; now it shall spring forth; shall ye not know it? I will even make a way in the wilderness, and rivers in the desert." [Vs:16,18,19]

Traveling the world over by land, sea and air, I have oftentimes been astonished or greatly impressed at what the little wisdom that God has given civil engineers to design and maintain roads, bridges, dams, and similar structures can do. However, every year, some of these structures collapse and ways are blocked. Beloved in the LORD, God is the way maker. He knows the way and understands the future better than we do. It is written, *"Only I can tell you the future before it even happens. Everything I plan will come to pass, for I do whatever I wish." (Isa.46:10;nlt)*. Past miracles are nothing compared to what God will do for us today or tomorrow.

The God who parted the Red sea and then closed it upon the army of Pharaoh is alive! He sees beyond and knows which way is best for us. It is written, *"And it came to pass, when Pharaoh had let the people go, that God led them not through the way of the land of the Philistines, although that was near; for God said, lest peradventure the people repent when they see war, and they return to Egypt." [Exo.13:17]*. If it's man to decide, he will always choose the way that is nearest to his destination. Many believers have gone back to Egypt (the world) because they chose shortcuts or the wrong way. Remember that, *"There is a way that seems right to a man, but its end is the way to death." (Prov.14:12)*. Are you on the right way?

God wants each one of us to absolutely depend upon His leading and walk in total obedience. He may be leading us through an uneasy or unfamiliar path, but there is good news for us. Even so, He does to them that are blind. *"I will lead the blind by ways they have not known, along unfamiliar paths I will guide them; I will turn the darkness into light before them and make the rough places smooth. These are the things I will do; I will not forsake them." [Isa.42:1]*. God wants us today to look forward in faith to the spectacular thing that He is about to do rather than dwelling on the past. When we allow God to make a way for us, He takes all the unknowns into consideration. He is the way maker and cannot be compared to a civil engineer!

PRAYER FOCUS

Dear heavenly Father, You are the way maker. I'm fully persuaded that You will make a way for me this season. Therefore, I totally commitment myself and depend on You as my pathfinder in Jesus' name.

August 9

Unyielding Perseverance
Bible Reading: [Col.1:9-18]

"May you be strengthened with all power, according to His glorious might, for all endurance and patience with joy, giving thanks to the Father, who has qualified us to share in the inheritance of the saints in light"
[Vs:11-12].

God's earnest desire for us is that we should endure to the end. *"But the one who perseveres (endures) to the end will be saved." (Matt.24:13)*. Perseverance or longsuffering means: steadfastness in doing something despite difficulty or delay in achieving success. We become unyielding when we choose not to compromise our conviction in the middle of difficult circumstances. God never promised His disciples an easy life. As a matter of fact, the Christian life is not a comfortable life, but it is a fulfilling one. It is written, *"For you have been given not only the privilege of trusting in Christ but also the privilege of suffering for Him." (Phil.1:29, NLT)*. It's obvious that nobody would like to consider suffering as a privilege. However, in suffering, if we faithfully represent Christ, our message and example will affect us and others for good. It is important to note that suffering for our faith doesn't necessarily mean that we have done something wrong.

Every true disciple of Christ must be of a disposition that allows God to penetrate or influence their lives with His will. Only God is able to produce patience and longsuffering with joy in us. This can only happen in the life of one who has humbled himself under His control *(1 Pet.5:6)*. The more we trust in ourselves, the less God can work in our lives according to the counsel of His will for His good pleasure. It is written, *"So the Apostles departed from the presence of the council, rejoicing that they were counted worthy to suffer shame for His name." (Acts.5:41)*. Hallelujah!

PRAYER FOCUS

Dear heavenly Father, I acknowledge You as the only wise God and the author of patience and perseverance. I trust that You will strengthen me with Your power and grace, as I surrender my attitude and behavior to You TODAY in Jesus' name.

August 10

Open Doors Attract Adversaries
Bible Reading: [1 Cor.16:5-12]

"But I will tarry in Ephesus until Pentecost. For a great and effective door has opened to me, and there are many adversaries." (Vs:8-9)

An open door is a great opportunity that presents itself to us. However, just because an opportunity presents itself or looks appealing does not necessarily mean that we should walk in it or it is from God. Beloved in the LORD, when an opportunity presents itself and you are fully persuaded that it's from God, what do you do about it? Oftentimes we get so excited and try to figure out what to do with it. Inasmuch as open doors bring blessings, they also attract enemies. It is written, *"Lest Satan should get an advantage of us: for we are not ignorant of his devices."(2 Cor.2:11)*. The goal of the devil is to steal every blessing God is bringing our way. If we are united in truth and love as couples or members in the body of Christ, it will be practically impossible for the devil and associates to close our door of opportunities.

It is worth mentioning that while we celebrate what God has done for us, we should trust that He will protect it. We should also ask God for wisdom to maximize such opportunities. It's unfortunate for some people that God opens a door today, and the devil closes it the next day because of their lack of knowledge. However, there is good news for every disciple of Christ today. It is written, *"I know your works. See, I have set before you an open door, and no one can shut it; for you have little strength, have kept My word, and have not denied My name."(Rev.3:8)*. When we keep God's word and hold unto the name of Jesus, we'll give our adversary no place. Remember, *"At the name of Jesus every knee should bow, of those in heaven, and of those on earth, and of those under the earth." (Philipp.2:10)*.

God doesn't open us doors so that we satisfy our fleshly desires and become proud. He does so to enrich us, so that we may be a blessing to others especially those in the household of faith. *"As we have therefore opportunity, let us do good unto all men, especially unto them who are of the household of faith." (Gal.6:10)*. When we understand and do the will of God fully, Satan and cohorts will constantly be on the retreat. May God grant that you will know how to discern if an opportunity is really an open door from Him TODAY!

PRAYER FOCUS

Dear heavenly Father, I thank You for doors You have opened for me since the beginning of the year. I decree and declare a shut-off of the devil's access to my life. I confess that the blessing of the LORD makes me rich and adds no sorrow in Jesus' name.

August 11

Don't Miss Out On Divine Rhythm
Bible Reading: [1 Sam.3:1-13]

"And the LORD called Samuel again the third time. So he arose and went to Eli, and said, "Here I am, for you did call me." Then Eli perceived that the LORD had called the boy. Therefore Eli said to Samuel, "Go, lie down; and it shall be, if He calls you, that you, that you must say, Speak, LORD, for Your servant hears." So Samuel went and lay down in his place." (Vs:8-9, NKJV)

Whenever God wants to do something, there is a divine sound. He's just signaling us about His next move. Unfortunately, many people are missing out on God's rhythm. Rhythm is a strong, regular, repeated pattern of movement or sound. The goal of the devil is to cause us to miss out on what God is about to do. Many sons and daughters of the Kingdom are dancing out of rhythm and cannot clap to the beat. Our goal should be; being in tune with God, listening so that if He has something specific for us to say or do, we can hear and act.

Listening and responding plays a vital role in our relationship with God. The boy Samuel was young. He had personal knowledge of the LORD, but lacked a direct personal experience of Him. Like Samuel, God has spoken directly and audibly to us at various times in different ways and places. Sometimes we miss out on God's rhythm because we are too busy. Sometimes because we are inexperienced, dull or refuse to listen. Some of us are so familiar with the sound of human voices that we cannot discern the sound of God. Then the LORD called yet again, "Samuel!" So Samuel arose and went to Eli, and said, Here I am, for you called me." He answered, "I did not call, my son; lie down again." (Vs:6).

Beloved in the LORD, what have you allowed to get in the way of your communication with God? If you have no personal relationship with God through genuine repentance, it will be practically impossible for you to understand divine rhythm. It is written, *"But the natural man receiveth not the things of the Spirit of God: for they are foolishness unto him: neither can he know them, because they are spiritually discerned." (1 Cor.2:14).* Meditating on God's word daily and spending time in prayer will help us not to miss out on divine rhythm. The more we grow in our relationship with God, the easier it is to know and understand when He is talking to us.

PRAYER FOCUS

Dear heavenly Father, It is Your desire that I should not miss out on divine rhythm. LORD, awaken my ears to be sensitive to divine sound, enlighten my heart to understand Your will and enable me to tune in with You and act accordingly at all times in Jesus' name.

August 12

Our God Is Greater
Bible Reading: [1 Sam.5:1-12]

"When the Philistines took the ark of God, they brought it into the house of Dagon and set it by Dagon. And when the people of Ashdod arose early in the morning, there was Dagon, fallen on its face to the earth before the ark of the LORD.," [Vs: 2-3]

There is no other God whose presence and power can be compared to Jehovah El Shaddai, the Almighty God *[Isa.44:6]*. Beloved, are you connected to the source of greater power? Just like the ark of God was a symbol of God's presence with the Israelites in ancient times, we have God's presence in us and with us, if Christ lives in us. The ark of God in itself was no talisman, but represented the LORD's holy presence. A talisman is an object that is thought to have magic powers and to bring good luck. Beloved, such an object (idol) does not help and will never bring blessing and protection to anyone. Only the blessing of the living God, makes rich and adds no sorry with it *[Prov.10:22]*.

How can we be thankful to God for revealing Himself to us as the source of greater power! Remember, *"That at that time ye were without Christ, being aliens from the commonwealth of Israel, and strangers from the covenants of promise, having no hope, without God in the world: But now in Christ Jesus ye who sometimes were far off are made nigh by the blood of Christ." (Eph.2:12-13)*. Hallelujah! It's unfortunate that many people are still acting in ignorance today like the Philistines. Many are not willing to respond to the Gospel truth until they have experienced affliction. It is written, *"In the past God overlooked such ignorance, but now he commands all people everywhere to repent." (Acts 17:30)*.

What makes God greater is the fact that He is capable of defending Himself and all those who pledge their allegiance to His Lordship. If Dagon one of the Philistines' gods could not defend himself, how would he defend those who put their trust in him? Dear friend, put your trust in the one true God today. It is written, *"Ye are of God, little Children, and have overcome them: because greater is He that is in you, than He that is in the world" (1Jn.4:4,* Jn.10:29*)*.

PRAYER FOCUS

Dear heavenly Father, I acknowledge the fact that Your supremacy over idols or created things cannot be argued about or compete for. Today, let every idol or power of the enemy before me be destroyed by the fire of the Holy Spirit in Jesus' name.

August 13

Staying On Target
Bible Reading: [Prov.30:24-31]

"There be four things that are little on earth, but they are exceedingly wise: The locust have no King, yet they go forth all of them by ranks." [Vs:24,27]

Nowadays it is not common to find people who stay on target and are consistent in what they do or profess. Staying on target means to be focused or to be on track when there are distractions or the possibility of suffering persecution. Beloved in the LORD, have you deviated from your dream, vision or purpose in life? This portion of Scripture takes us to small and insignificant creatures of God's creation to learn wisdom. The gift to learn starts with humility and the control of one's mouth. It is written, *"The law (word) of the LORD is perfect, converting (restoring) the soul: the testimony of the LORD is sure, making wise the simple." (Ps.19:7).* This little creatures are exceedingly wise, stately in their walk and things go well with them. They are able to survive and do accomplish great things in comparison to their size.

Today, I would like us to find out from Scriptures what makes these creatures so exceptional.

Preparedness: It means a state of readiness. How prepared are you for what you are about to do? How prepared are you for winter, for evangelism, for your exams, for battle, to set up your business etc.? God wants us to be prepared and be constantly vigilant. *"Preach the word; be prepared in season and out of season;.."* (2 Tim.4:2)

Fearlessness: Fear has paralyzed many people and caused them to compromise their conviction or deviate from their mission. Those who are bold as a lion act without fear or favor *(Prov.28:1)*. They step out doing the right thing, and fight a good fight of faith. The LORD told Joshua, *"Have not I commanded thee? Be strong and of a good courage; be not afraid, neither be thou dismayed: for the LORD thy God is with thee whithersoever thou goest." (Josh.1:9)*

Possessing great speed: As a matter of fact, sometimes we need to slow down in life. However, because the King's business requires urgency (1 Sam.21:8), we should possess the ability to achieve efficiently whatever one has to do, in time or on time. *"And the LORD answered me, and said, write the vision, and make it plain upon tables, that he may run that readeth it."* (Hab.2:2; Heb.12:1).

Possessing the ability to traverse great cliffs (barrier) without breaking ranks: Each one of us likes to have a breakthrough in life, but oftentimes, we are not willing to face and break barriers in life. Speak boldly to that mountain before you today. *"Who art thou, O great mountain? Before Zerubbabel thou shalt become a plain:..," Not by might, nor by power, but by my spirit, saith the LORD of host.* (Zech.4:6 -7). "They will run like mighty men. They will climb the wall like men of war, and everyone will march in line. And they will not break *their ranks." (Joel 2:7,ikjv).* In order to stay on target, there must be cooperation and order especially when working as a team.

PRAYER FOCUS

Dear heavenly Father, it is Your desire that I should be resourceful and powerful. LORD, enable me to be stately in my walk and empower me with magnificent abilities to accomplish great things for Your glory in Jesus' name. *[Da.11:32]*

August 14

You are Chosen
"The Honor of Divine Election"
Bible Reading: [Psalm 65:1-13]

"Blessed is the man You choose, and cause to approach You, that he may dwell in Your courts. We shall be satisfied with the goodness of Your house, Of Your holy temple." (Vs: 4)

This is the day that the LORD has made; we will rejoice and be glad in it. Beloved, just imagine that on checking your mailbox, you find an invitation letter to attend an event at the Presidency of your nation. I can't describe how you will feel, but for the most part, everyone will be excited and double check it real quick. If we can be that excited having received such from a mere human being, what more God? Divine election is the act of picking out! One is picked out of a multitude. It is written, *"For many are called, but few are chosen." (Matt.22:14)*. It is important to note that those who have been chosen by the LORD are blessed. They have been chosen according to the foreknowledge of God the Father, through the sanctifying work of the Spirit, to be obedient to Christ *[1 Pet.1:2]*

Have you accepted the invitation of the LORD? God desires that each one of us should experience His holy presence. It is written, *"Thou wilt shew me the path of life: in thy presence is fullness of joy; at thy right hand there are pleasures for evermore." [Psalm 16:11]*. Access to God's holy presence has been made possible to all believers everywhere and at any time because of Christ's death on the Cross *[Heb.10:19-23]*. What an honor and privilege! The Psalmist says, *we shall be satisfied with the goodness of Your house, of Your holy temple."* Beloved, where else do you want to seek satisfaction in this life? *O taste and see that the LORD is good: blessed is the man that trusted in him." [Ps 34:8]*. Hallelujah!

PRAYER FOCUS

Dear heavenly Father, One thing have I desired of the LORD, that will I seek after; that I may dwell in the house of the LORD all the days of my life, to behold the beauty of the LORD, and to enquire in His temple. *[Ps.27:4]*

August 15

Partakers Of His Divine Nature
Bible Reading: [2 Pet.1:1-11]

"Grace and peace be multiplied to you in the knowledge of God and of Jesus our LORD, as His divine power has given to us all things that pertain to life and godliness, through the knowledge of Him who called us by glory and virtue." [Vs:2-3)]

It is a wonderful privilege to be a partaker of the divine nature. A partaker is one who takes part in or experiences something along with others. God's divine nature is so awesome that the human mind cannot fully understand or comprehend God. His divine nature is perfect. This nature is unconditional and unmerited love. It is the source of righteousness in the world. Every disciple of Christ has the honor to share God's qualities. We are not chosen by God for salvation on the basis of what we do, but our enthusiasm or passion to grow in Christian virtue confirms that we have been truly chosen by God.

Remember, *"For by grace are ye saved through faith; and that not of yourselves: it is the gift of God:" [Eph.2:8]*. This salvation does not come by works, but our faith in Christ must result in good works. We have received his nature by coming to know Him personally as LORD and Savior. *"But as many as received him, to them gave He power to become the sons of God, even to them that believe on His name" [John 1:12]*. His divine nature enables us to live the Christian life.

God by His divine nature empowers us with His moral goodness. Nevertheless, the responsibility to learn and grow daily is ours, it is not optional. We must go through the process, giving all diligence and obey Him who guides us by His Spirit. *"For it is God which worketh in you both to will and to do of his good pleasure." (Philipp.2:13)*. God does not only intend that we share His divine nature, but that we share His great and precious promises. *"For all the promises of God in him are yea, and in him Amen, unto the glory of God by us." [2 Cor.1:20]*. This enables us to enjoy His divine nature and escape the world's corruption caused by human desires. As we grow in obedience to the will of God, we grow to understand better the nature of God. *"For ye are all children of God by faith in Christ Jesus. And if ye be Christ's, then are ye Abraham's seed, and heirs according to the promise." [Gal.3:26,29]*

PRAYER FOCUS

Dear heavenly Father, thank You for extending grace to us through Jesus Christ for sins for which atonement could not have been possible by keeping the law and by our good works in Jesus' name.

August 16

Right Words & Wisdom No Man Can Resist
Bible Reading: [Luke 21:7-19]

"For I will give you words and wisdom that none of your adversaries will be able to resist or contradict."
[Luke 21:15]

Often we've seen a divide in families as some members follow Jesus and others reject Him. Encountering persecution in our walk with God should never be considered a strange thing. It is written, *"Yea, and all that will live godly in Christ Jesus shall suffer persecution." (2 Tim.3:12)*. Persecution comes in diverse ways, from different cultures and places. The most interesting thing is that the Church will thrive (prosper) despite intense persecution. I have experienced and at the same time witnessed others go through difficult times because of their decision to follow Jesus Christ. The apostles of old rejoiced in tribulations *(Rom.5:3)* because it helped them know Christ better. Paul expressed his earnest desire in this Scripture, *"That I may know him, and the power of his resurrection, and the fellowship of his sufferings, being made conformable unto his death." (Philipp.3:10)*.

The greatest assurance each one of us should have today is that, nothing can separate us from the love of Christ. If God is for us, who can ever be against us? *(Rom.8:35-37)*. We should be confident in the One who has called us: *"For this reason I also suffer these things, but I am not ashamed; for I know whom I have believed and I am convinced that He is able to guard what I have entrusted to Him until that day." (2 Tim.1:12;NASV)*. God is still in control and no matter what setbacks or problems we face, we can trust fully in Him. Amid perilous times, difficult circumstances, in prison, in a law court, God will give us words and wisdom that none of our adversaries will be able to resist or contradict. This Gospel of the Kingdom is unstoppable! It is written, *"And because I preach this Good News, I am suffering and have been chained like a criminal. But the word of God cannot be chained." (2 Tim.2:9,nlt)*. Hallelujah!

PRAYER FOCUS

Dear heavenly Father, I confess that I am of God, and I have overcome all my enemies because greater is He that is in me, than he that is in the world.

"For whatsoever is born of God overcometh the world: and this is the victory that overcometh the world, even our faith." (1 Jn.5:4)

August 17

Obedience
- Gateway To Divine Abundance
Bible Reading: [Isaiah 1:10-20]

"If you are willing and obedient,
You shall eat the good of the land" [Vs:19]

For anyone to have a genuine walk with God, he or she must learn the act of obedience. The word obedience literally means compliance with an order, request, or law or submission to another's authority. Just like children are taught to show their parents obedience, every true disciple of Christ must do same to his or her heavenly Father. In other words, walking in obedience before God is not optional! In this portion of Scripture, God gave the Israelites the promise of temporal blessings as the reward of true repentance. The prophet spoke to a people who were unjust and selfish. His goal was to help them recognize the moral government of God. It is written, *"Let every soul be subject unto the higher powers. For there is no power but of God: the powers that be are ordained of God."* (Rom.13:1). Obedience means submission to another's authority. You cannot have an open heaven over your life when you walk in disobedience. You can't experience a release of God's grace and power when you are not complying with divine order. To comply means to act in accordance with a wish or command.

Many believers in Christ can't punish every act of disobedience because their obedience is not complete. *"And we will be ready to punish every act of disobedience, once your obedience is complete."* (2 Cor.10:6). Genuine conversion or true repentance leads to life, but resisting God's will and turning away from Him results in death. We seek justice and live right with God when we uphold to His standards of fairness. *"Then the LORD appeared to Isaac and said: "do not go down to Egypt; live in the land of which I shall tell you."* Isaac obeyed the LORD's command. "Then Isaac sowed in the land, and reaped in the same year a hundredfold; and the LORD blessed him. The man began to prosper, and continued prospering until he became very prosperous;"* (Gen.26:2,12,13). Hallelujah! Abraham, Isaac and all the heroes of faith walked in obedience; lived by faith and prospered. I decree and declare that the seed and spirit of disobedience to God's word will not find a place in your life in Jesus' name!

PRAYER FOCUS

Dear heavenly Father, Your word says, to obey is better than sacrifice *[1 Sam.15:22]*. LORD, I yield myself to You and make a commitment today to walk with You in obedience in Jesus' name.

The blessing of the LORD, it maketh rich, and he addeth no sorrow with it [Prov.10:22;KJV].

August 18

When Nothing Seems To Make Sense
Bible Reading: [Habakkuk 3:17-19]

When everything that was normal and predictable collapses, when global economic downturn takes a heavy toll on the housing markets, when crop yield dwindles, when your health seems to fail, when the job market seems uncertain and troubles seem more than you can bear, remember that God is alive and in control of the world and its events.

"For I am the LORD, I do not change; Therefore you are not consumed, O sons of Jacob." (Mal.3:6).

Many people have allowed their feelings to be controlled by the events around them. They see their limitations in contrast to God's unlimited power and influence over their circumstances. It's worth noting that your security is not based on temporal blessings but on the LORD Himself. "Behold the proud, his soul is not upright in him; but the just shall live by his faith." (Hab.2:4)

Take your eyes off your difficulties TODAY and look to God. Trust in God's power and providence. Worship Him and do His bidding regardless of your present circumstances. "I will lift up mine eyes unto the hills, from whence cometh my help. My help cometh from the LORD, which made heaven and earth *(Ps 121:1,2)*

PRAYER FOCUS

Dear heavenly Father, I have made You too small in my eyes; O LORD forgive me, heal my heart and show Yourself strong on my behalf. LORD, grant that I may live in the strength of Your Spirit and be confident in Your ultimate power in Jesus' name.

August 19

Don't Be Unbelieving, But Believing!
Bible Reading: [John 20:24-31]

"The other disciples therefore said to Thomas, "We have seen the LORD." So he said to them, "Unless I see in His hands the print of the nails, and put my finger into the print of the nails, and put my hand into His side, I will not believe."

"Jesus said to him, "Thomas, because you have seen Me, you have believed. Blessed are those who have not seen and yet have believed." [Vs:25,29]

It is obvious that sometimes in life, in order to maintain the status quo in unbelief we tend to downplay the testimonies of others about Jesus or the works of God. The Bible and the testimony of believers are all the proof we need. Dear friend, do want to see God's angels ascending and descending or the skies turning red in appearance in order to believe that Jesus Christ resurrected and will come again? It is written, *"But without faith it is impossible to please him: for he that cometh to God must believe that he is, and that he is a rewarder of them that diligently seek him." (Heb.11:6;KJV).* With the testimony of the apostles, God expects belief on the part of anyone who is honest and objective in his or her search for truth.

Today, God is calling each one of us to be a part of the generation of Christians who, through the testimonies of others, would believe without seeing. You can't mask your unbelief in order to justify your unwillingness to surrender your totality to Christ. The LORD is challenging us like Thomas, to believe in His resurrection and the Spirit of Him that raise Christ from the dead! *"And if Christ be not risen, then is our preaching vain, and your faith is also vain." (1 Cor.15:14).* Remember, *"But if the Spirit of him that raised up Jesus from the dead dwell in you, he that raised up Christ from the dead shall also quicken your mortal bodies by his Spirit that dwelleth in you." (Rom.8:11).* Jesus is LORD because He is in control of everything. At the same time, He is God in his being and essence. Let's walk by faith and not by sight TODAY!

PRAYER FOCUS

Dear heavenly Father, I believe that Jesus is the Christ [Anointed one]. I'm fully persuaded that the testimony of Jesus is true and that all the promises God concerning me shall be fulfilled in Jesus' name.

August 20

Renewing Your Spiritual Vitality
Bible Reading: [Heb.12:12-17]

"Therefore strengthen the hands which hang down, and the feeble knees, and make straight paths for your feet, so that what is lame may not be dislocated, but rather be healed. Pursue peace with all people, and holiness, without which no one will see the LORD:" [Vs:12-14]

Spiritual vitality is the quality of possessing a living faith. Nowadays the Church is full of lukewarm, nonchalant and mundane believers. Beloved, what is causing you not to be serious with the things of God? It seems you need someone to plead with you to read your Bible, meditate, pray, give to support God's work, attend fellowship and even share the love of Christ with the lost through evangelism. It is written, *"woe to them that are at ease in Zion, and trust in the mountain of Samaria, which are named chief of the nations, to whom the house of Israel come!" (Amos 6:1).* Is your faith a living faith? A sincere and living Christian doesn't need someone to coax or persuade him/her in order to fulfill all righteousness.

Many believers have grown cold in their love for spiritual things. Some Churches have a reputation of being alive but are dead (Rev.3:1). It is written, *"And it shall come to pass in the last days, that the mountain of the LORD's house shall be established in the top of the mountains, and shall be exalted above the hills; and all nations shall flow unto it." (Isa.2:2).* Is that true about your Church? Are people being added daily or weekly as they are saved?

Knowing that many believers live like the world, dress like the world, walk like the world, behave like the world and talk like the world; can the world be attracted to the Church? LORD, have mercy upon us!

It is time to strengthen the hands which hang down, and the feeble knees. Complaining that you don't have time is just being ungrateful to God. It means God is an option and you are choosing to remain in your comfort zone! "Remember therefore from whence thou art fallen, and repent, and do the first works; or else I will come unto thee quickly, and will remove thy candlestick out of his place, except thou repent." (Rev.2:5). You don't only need to be sorry, you need to repent, change and set your priorities right! Only those who are living a holy life have confident hope of seeing the LORD. *"Seek ye the LORD while he may be found, call ye upon him while he is near: let the wicked forsake his way, and the unrighteous man his thoughts: and let him return unto the LORD, and he will have mercy upon him; and to our God, for he will abundantly pardon" (Isa.55:6-7).*

PRAYER FOCUS

Dear heavenly Father, I acknowledge that I am lukewarm, emotionally and spiritually exhausted. Have mercy upon me, quicken and strengthen my weak hands and feeble knees by the power of Your Holy Spirit in Jesus' name.

August 21

Striving For A Crown
Bible Reading: [1 Cor.9:24-27]

"But I discipline my body and bring it to subjection, lest, when I have preached to others, I myself should become disqualified." [Vs:27]

Before any athlete wins an Olympic goal medal, he is required to exercise discipline and train diligently. While the rest of the world watch the race of life from the grandstand, as believers, our race is toward a heavenly reward. Each one of us must trust in the grace of God and be confident that He will give us the reward if we steer a steady course until the end. There two important questions I would like you to ponder over today:

What are you giving up in order to faithfully run the race?

What investment are you making to equip yourself for the race?

While many are lax about prayer, Bible study and fellowship, winning this eternal race requires purpose and your progress depends on it.

It is written, *"Brethren, I count not myself to have apprehended: but this one thing I do, forgetting those things which are behind, and reaching forth unto those things which are before,"* (Philipp.3:13)Every disciple must not allow the lusts of the flesh to deviate him from the race or exercise less commitment and discipline. To avoid losing the eternal prize, Paul underwent rigorous discipline and self-denial so that he wouldn't be led away from Christ into a life of sin. He concluded, *"Lest, when I have preached to others, I myself should become disqualified."*

PRAYER FOCUS

Dear heavenly Father, I am confident that You've reserved an eternal crown for me. LORD, grant me the grace to exercise self-discipline and train myself in godliness in Jesus' name.

August 22

Engaging The World To Transform It
Bible Reading: [1 Cor.9:19-23]

"To the weak I became as weak, that I might win the weak. I have become all things to all men, that I might by all means save some. Now this I do for the gospel's sake, that I may be partaker of it with you." [Vs:22-23]

As a matter of fact, a believer in Christ should not conform anymore to the patterns of this world. Although we live in the world, we are not of the world. We are no longer ruled by sin, nor are we bound by the principles of the world. As we grow mature in Christ, our interest in the things of the world diminishes. However, we must engage the world in order to transform it. We can't transform the world if we live like, behave like or look like the world. We can't effectively transform the world if we are not willing to allow the Word and the power of the Holy Spirit transforms us by the renewing of our mind.

To engage something means to participate or become involve in. A disciple of Jesus Christ should engage the world with one goal in mind, to 'Save Some'. *"For the Son of man came to seek and to save that which was lost." (Luke 19:10).* We must always look for a common ground with those who come our way and tell them about Christ. It is important to note that, it's not God's will that any man should perish but that all should come to repentance *(2 Pet.3:9).* In order to engage the world, one must be willing to give up his own customs in order to relate with others, sacrifice his rights in order to get the job done of evangelizing the world and making disciples. People need to be saved from the judgement of God in the lake of fire *(Rev.20:10).* It is written, *"And on some, have compassion, making a distinction; but others save with fear, pulling them out of the fire, hating even the garment defiled by the flesh."* (Jude 22-23)

The gospel is the power of God for salvation to everyone who believes *(Rom.1:16).* It's worth noting that unbelievers, no matter how successful they seem to be by worldly standards, are lost and in need of salvation. Where has God positioned you? Engage the world, be sensitive to their needs and concerns. Jesus is the answer for the world TODAY!.

PRAYER FOCUS

Dear heavenly Father, You desire all people to be saved and come to the knowledge of the truth *(1 Tim.2:4).* LORD, help me to conduct myself in a manner worthy of the gospel in Jesus' name.

August 23

Leading A Rich & Fruitful Life
Bible Reading: [Jeremiah 17:5 -13]

"Blessed is the man who trust in the LORD, and whose hope is the LORD. For he shall be like a tree planted by the waters, which spreads out its roots by the river, and will not fear when heat comes; but its leaf will be green, and will not be anxious in the year of drought, nor will cease from yielding fruit." [Vs:7-8]

Trust is the disposition of the heart that results in obedience. It's obvious that when we switch our trust from the LORD to human capabilities we become like shrubs in the desert because of need for water. God tests and examines our hearts daily in order to determine what we love the most. There are many paths before us today. The path we choose will determine our future.

- Trust in man and human alliances.
- Trust in horses and chariots.
- Trust in unrighteous materialism etc.

Whenever we turn our backs on God, we become barren, deceitful and treacherous. But he who trust in the LORD can be confident that when times of crisis come, because of his deep faithfulness, he will drink from the riches of His care for him. The more we trust in God, delight in His presence, the more Fruitful we become. *"Those who are planted in the house of the LORD shall flourish in the courts our God." (Ps 92:13)*

PRAYER FOCUS

Dear heavenly Father, It's Your desire that I should be effective and productive in my knowledge of Jesus Christ. LORD, heal my heart of the lust for material things and mold me into a productive vessel in Jesus' name.

August 24

Living In Vital Union With Christ
Bible Reading: [Col.2:1-10]

"As you therefore have received Christ Jesus the LORD, so walk in Him, rooted and built up in Him and established in the faith, as you have been taught, abounding in it with thanksgiving." [Vs:6-7]

Those who have received Christ are brand-new people on the inside. In this glorious union, we were circumcised with a circumcision not performed by human hands. Christ performed this spiritual circumcision by the cutting away of our sinful nature. Thus it is written, *"Therefore if any man be in Christ, he is a new creature: old things are passed away; behold, all things are become new." (2 Cor.5:17;KJV).* This union implies we now have a new life under a new Master. Our union with Christ is so important because God desired before time began to form for Himself a people that may proclaim His praise *(1 Pet.2:9).*

How can this glorious union be kept alive by the believe in Christ?

- By walking in Him: "Show me thy ways, O LORD; teach me thy paths." (Ps.25:4). "This I say then, walk in the Spirit, and ye shall not fulfil the lust of the flesh." (Gal.5:16;KJV).

- Being rooted in Him: Meditate daily and believe God's word at all times no matter what your circumstance (Josh.1:8)

- Built up in Him: The word of God's grace is able to build a believer in Christ and give him an inheritance among all those who are sanctified (Acts 20:32)

- Established in the faith: Each one of us must be established in the faith. We must continue to believe the truth and stand firmly in it. This doesn't come overnight! The believer must take an active responsibility for this to happen. "So then faith comes by hearing, and hearing by the word of God." (Rom.10:17;KJV)

- Abounding with thanksgiving: Knowing that ingratitude is sin, every believer must abound with thanksgiving. "In everything give thanks: for this is the will of God in Christ Jesus concerning you." (1 Thes.5:18)

PRAYER FOCUS

Dear heavenly Father, You have made me complete in Christ. I recognize the presence and power of Your Spirit in me. LORD, enable me to live the Christian life with zeal and eagerness as I submit my will to You in Jesus' name.

August 25

Testifying To Others About Christ
- A Mark Of Discipleship
Bible Reading: [John 4:27-42]

"Come, see a Man who told me all things that I ever did. Could this be the Christ? Then they went out of the city and came to him. And many of the Samaritans of that city believed in Him because of the word of the woman who testified, "He told me all that I ever did." And many more believed because of His own word." [Vs: 29,39,41]

Over the years many have come to know Christ personally through the testimonies of others. You don't need a glamorous or attractive testimony in order to testify about what the LORD has done for you. Do you excuse yourself from witnessing on the grounds that your friends or loved ones are not ready to believe? There are people all around your neighborhood or city ready to hear God's word. *Behold, I say to you, lift up your eyes and look at the fields, for they are already white for harvest! (Vs:35)*

One day I asked a lady if she has made Jesus Christ her personal friend. It was such a simple approach to evangelism. She told me that the Holy Spirit started convicting her heart on this matter three minutes before I met her. She went further to tell me the story of her life and I finally led her to Christ. Hallelujah! It is written, *"To the law and to the testimony: if they speak not according to this word, it is because there is no light in them." (Isa.8:20)*. Only the word of God is a solid foundation upon which men can base their beliefs. The Holy Spirit is at work to convict men of sin but God needs someone to witness to them about Christ. *"How then shall they call on him whom they have not believed? and how shall they believe in him of whom they have not heard? and how shall they hear without a preacher? (Rom.10:14)*. You can trust God to guide you to someone in need of the Savior TODAY!

PRAYER FOCUS

Dear heavenly Father, for this purpose You saved me to be a witness for Christ. Grant that my testimony will convict hearts and convert souls in Jesus' name.

August 26

God Knows The Real You
Bible Reading: [John 1:43-51]

"Jesus saw Nathanael coming toward Him, and said of him, "Behold, an Israelite indeed, in whom is no deceit!" Nathanael said to Him, "How do you know me?" Jesus answered and said to him, "Before Philip called you, when you were under the fig tree, I saw you." [Vs:47-48]

The real you is not who you are in the eyes of men, but who you are in the sight of God. It is written, *"For your ways are in full view of the LORD, and he examines all your paths." (Prov.5:21;NIV).* Even friends who have lived with you for many years may claim to know you, but not the real you. We often make wrong judgement about people because we do not know them the way God does. A prejudiced mind will not see any good thing in another person or community. Nazareth was not considered famous enough to be the hometown of a great leader.

Nathanael said to Him, "How do You know me?" Jesus captured Nathanael's attention and worship. He did so by revealing his true character and by supernaturally knowing his previous actions. Nathanael had an honest personality and took a remarkable step of faith. I know some of us are uncomfortable if our true personality is revealed to us. However, if one is determined and sincere to approach God like the Psalmist, he will say, *"Search me, O God, and know my heart: try me, and know my thoughts: and see if there be any wicked way in me, and lead me in the way everlasting" [Ps 139:23-24].*

PRAYER FORCUS

Dear heavenly Father, I come to You today with a receptive heart to embrace Your fullness and be transformed into a man of complete integrity in Jesus' name.

August 27

Snare Of The Cult Of Personality
Bible Reading: [Acts 10:1-33]

"As Peter was coming in, Cornelius met him and fell down at his feet and worshiped him. But Peter lifted him up, saying, "Stand up; I myself am also a man." [Vs:25-26].

The cult of personality means expressing great devotion to a person, idea, object, movement, or work (Merriam Webster). The cult of personality is also called Idolatry. Nowadays the cult of personality is commonplace in the world and the body of Christ. Man worship is taking center stage on many platforms in the world. Some of us claim to worship Christ but in reality, we are worshipping man. I am not saying that we shouldn't respect or give honor to whom it is due. Any spirit that accepts worship is of the devil and any man that accepts worship is an idolater.

A fellow human being did not die for you on the cross but Christ did. *"He was delivered over to death for our sins and was raised to life for our justification." (Rom.4:25).* A fellow human being is not the mediator between God and man but Christ is. *"For there is one God and one mediator between God and mankind, the man Christ Jesus (1 Tim.2:5).* The Bible restricts worship to God alone *(1 Cor.10:14).* Instead of accepting worship, Peter pointed Cornelius to Christ. Is Christ the center of your life, family, ministry, Church or denomination? Regardless of your great ability or gifts, let Christ be the center of it all. Though Peter was a Christ-sent Apostle, he would not allow anyone to bow down to him.

PRAYER FOCUS

Dear heavenly Father, have mercy upon me for occasions I have shared Your glory instead of pointing men to Christ. LORD, enable me to serve You with great humility and give You preeminence in all things in Jesus' name.

August 28

Angels On Assignment
Bible Reading: [Daniel 6:10-27]

Then Daniel said to the King, "O king, live forever! "My God sent His angel and shut the lions' mouths, so that they have not hurt me, because I was found innocent before Him; and also, O king, I have done no wrong before you." [Vs:21-22]

Beloved, it is just so amazing how God would defend his faithful servants and His own reputation by His mighty power. Oftentimes we tremble when a decree contrary to God's law is made by a wicked person in authority *(Prov.29:2)*.Today God wants each one of us to know that He overrides human decisions and turns human counsels into foolishness. God is above all authorities, *"...For there is no power but of God: the powers that be are ordained (established) of God" (Rom.13:1)*.

God never leaves us alone, He intervenes with the aid of angels in the challenges we face. *"Therefore, angels are only servants - spirits sent to care for people who will inherit salvation." (Heb.1:14)*. Angels are God's messengers with unique assignment to serve, encourage, reveal God's will, protect His anointed ones and execute His judgements. In their distress, the Israelites cried to God. *"When we cried to the LORD, He heard our voice, and sent an angel and brought us out of Egypt. Here we are in Kadesh, a town on the edge of your territory" (Num.20:16)*.

Beloved in the LORD, I decree and declare that God will bring you to your safe haven today in Jesus' name. Regardless of where you are, angels on assignment have no limits. The assignment of angels is of utmost importance in God's overall plan for humanity. Are you facing a seemingly tough battle like Daniel? It is written, *"For he shall give his angels charge over you, to keep you in all your ways"* (Ps.91:11). So Daniel was taken up out of the den, and no injury whatever was found on him, because he believed in his God. Hallelujah!

PRAYER FOCUS

Dear heavenly Father, thank You for angelic assistance. LORD, may Your angels guide and protect me today in Jesus' name.

August 29

God's Great Goodness
Bible Reading: [Isaiah 63:7-14]

"I will mention the loving kindness of the LORD and the praises of the LORD, according to all that the LORD has bestowed on us, and the great goodness toward the house of Israel, which He has bestowed on them according to His mercies, according to the multitude of His loving kindness" [Vs:7]

From one generation to the next, God's care for His people demonstrates His compassion, provision and protection. Today is another beautiful day to take a moment and reflect on the loving kindness of the LORD, according to all that He has bestowed on us. *"....He gives to all life, breath, and all things" (Acts 17:25).*

For His compassion: "It is of the LORD's mercies that we are not consumed, because his compassions fail not. They are new every morning: great is thy faithfulness." (Lam.3:22-23)

For His provision: "Behold the fowls of the air: for they sow not, neither do they reap, nor gather into barns; yet your heavenly Father feedeth them. Are ye not much better than they?" (Matt.6:26)

For His Protection: "He that dwelleth in the secret place of the most High shall abide under the shadow of the Almighty. I will say of the LORD, He is my refuge and my fortress: my God; in Him will I trust" (Psalm 91:1-2).

For His grace: "And God is able to make all grace abound toward you; that ye, always having all sufficiency in all things, may abound to every good work" (2 Cor.9:8).

God demonstrates His great kindness towards us in order to show the world that He is the only God and that we are His children redeemed by the blood of Jesus (1 Pet.2:9). Therefore, He expects us to honor our relationship with Him and not grieve His Holy Spirit by willfully thwarting His leading by disobedience or rebellion. God told Jeremiah *"The LORD hath appeared of old unto me, saying, Yea, I have loved thee with an everlasting love: therefore with loving kindness have I drawn thee" (Jer.31:3).*

PRAYER FOCUS

Dear heavenly Father, how can I thank You enough for Your loving kindness! LORD, You establish peace for us; all that we have accomplished You have done for us. [Isa.26:12]

August 30

The Little Foxes That Ruin The Vineyards
Bible Reading: [Song Of Solomon 2:1-17]

"Catch for us the foxes, the little foxes that ruin the vineyards, our vineyards that are in bloom"(Vs:15)

Relationship is the way in which two or more people are connected. There are a wide range of relationships to consider: marriage, professional, social and above all else, our relationship with the LORD. A genuine relationship is kept alive by a true commitment to one another. Little things have the tendency to breakdown a love relationship between two people. These little foxes represent potential problems that could damage a relationship. A person will be in debt if the foxes' hole-digging ruins the grapevines. Little sins, like little foxes tear up and ruin a Christian's testimony and that of the Church. Some of these little foxes in a Christian's life are falsehood (lying), anger, pretense lack of forgiveness, cheating, manipulation etc.

One's life cannot effectively grow and bear fruit with the presence of little foxes. Therefore, every true disciple of Christ must be determined to remove all threats and obstacles to relationships. By so doing, one is shows great interest in maintaining the value of his or her vineyard. *"I am the true vine, and My Father is the vinedresser. Every branch in Me that does not bear fruit He takes away, and every branch that bears fruit He prunes, that it may bear more fruit"* (John 15:1-2)/

PRAYER FOCUS

Dear heavenly Father, often I have allowed little foxes to destroy my testimony. LORD, may You have mercy upon me and convict my heart of little sins that undermine all I do and all I believe concerning Your Word and the testimony of Christ in Jesus' name.

August 31

Seizing Every Opportunity To Preach Christ
Bible Reading: Philippians 1:12-21

"But I want you to know, brethren, that the things which happened to me have actually turned out for the furtherance of the gospel, and most of the brethren in the LORD, having become confident by my chains, are much more bold to speak the Word without fear" (Vs:12,14)

Beloved in the LORD, do you know that your present situation is an opportunity for the preaching of the gospel? It's worth mentioning that how we act in situations will reflect what we believe. How do you react when you fail your exams, when Satan works in the lives of evil men to destroy your business or attack your marriage, when you lose your job, or when you are going through some health challenges? It is important to note that misfortunes in life are not the work of God. However, God uses these circumstances to accomplish His purposes (Rom 8:28). The Psalmist says, *"It is good for me that I have been afflicted; that I might learn thy statutes"* (Psalm 119:71). While many in Paul's situation would become bitter and compromise their conviction and faith in Christ, he saw his imprisonment as an opportunity to preach the gospel in Rome. God wanted him there in order to proclaim the good news before the highest Court in the world at the time. It is written, But the following night the LORD stood by Paul and said, *"Be of good cheer, Paul; for as you have testified for Me in Jerusalem, so you must also bear witness at Rome"* (Acts 23:11).

In an intimidating environment in which the disciples had to live, Paul was confident in preaching the gospel. His boldness even in prison was a source of encouragement to many of the local disciples. Not only were they being encouraged, his imprisonment also led to the conversion of the Roman palace guards and some of Caesar's household. *"For I am not ashamed of the gospel of Christ: for it is the power of God unto salvation to every that believeth; to the Jews first, and also to the Greek"* (Rom.1:16; Phil.4:22). We become a source of encouragement to others if we speak boldly for Christ and live faithfully for Him in an intimidating environment. Regardless of the motives some preach Christ, preach Christ out of love today and rejoice that the good news is spreading and prevailing. *"So shall my word be that goeth forth out of my mouth: it shall not return unto me void, but it shall accomplish that which I please, and it shall prosper in the thing whereto I sent it"* (Isa.55:11).

PRAYER FOCUS

Dear heavenly Father, it's not Your will that any should perish, but that all should come to repentance (2 Pet.3:9). LORD, grant that I may possess a selfless attitude and preach Christ without fear or favor in Jesus' name.

SEPTEMBER

"For surely there is an end; and thine expectation shall not be cut off."
[Proverbs 23:18; KJV]

For I know the thoughts that I think toward you, saith the LORD, thoughts of peace, and not of evil, to give you an expected end."
[Jeremiah 29.11;KJV]

****

*Jehovah Elohim - **[LORD God, Creator]** - Gen.2:4*

*9 = **[The finality Of Faith or Divine Completeness]** - Gal.5:22-23*

September 1

A Useful Member Of God's Team
Bible Reading: [1 Cor.3:1-10]

"I planted, Apollos watered, but God gave the increase. So then neither he who plants is anything, nor he who waters, but God who gives the increase." [Vs:6-7]

Success in any divine mission is an outcome of collective efforts. There is no such thing as the man who single-handedly brought revival. Regardless of where God has positioned us; either one of those who provide support services or one of those on the front lines, everyone is important. Each one of us should be thankful to God for the privilege to serve and be accountable to God for the way we serve Christ. To think that one is more important than others because his or her position is glamorous or more visible, such is a carnal way of thinking and expresses spiritual immaturity and insensitivity. Mature disciples are those who are in tune with God's desires. Such are determined deep within their hearts to do things God's way in order to bring Him the glory.

It's important to note that God's work involves many different individuals with a variety of gifts and abilities. A true Church of God is not built on human personality but on Christ. He is our base and our reason for being. Everything must be done according to His pattern. We can only become effective as members in God's team when we set aside our desires to receive glory for what we do. As a matter of fact, each faithful disciple will receive a reward according to his own labor. This reward is not based on the merit of one member's ability over the other. Those who labor in their particular areas of ministry will be rewarded because of faithfulness in Christian service.]

"But in a great house there are not only vessels of gold and silver, but also of wood and earth; and some to honor, and some to dishonour. If a man therefore purge himself from these, he shall be a vessel unto honor, sanctified, and meet for the master's use, and prepared unto every good work." [2 Tim.2:20-21]

PRAYER FOCUS

Dear heavenly Father, Your standard is Church that is built on the foundation of Christ. LORD, grant that my life and thinking will reflect maturity in Christ and the transforming perspective of the Holy Spirit in Jesus' name.

September 2

He Must Increase, But I Must Decrease
Bible Reading: [John 3:22-36]

"He who has the bride is the bridegroom; but the friend of the bridegroom, who stands and hears him, rejoices greatly because of the bridegroom's voice. Therefore this joy of mine is fulfilled. He must increase, but I must decrease. He who comes from above is above all; he who is of the earth is earthly and speaks of the earth. He who comes from heaven is above all." [Vs: 29-31]

From a human viewpoint, very few people on earth will rejoice when another person's marriage, ministry, business, project etc. is gaining more attention or popularity while theirs is decreasing. To John, witnessing the people going to Jesus was a time of rejoicing and not a time of Jealousy. If someone must increase because what he does is of God and brings glory to God alone, one's heart ought to rejoice. Because John knew who Jesus was, he did not give room for competition.

He knew he was only a messenger sent to prepare the way for the Messiah after which his ministry would come to an end. Beloved in the LORD, a disciple of Christ does not compete in the work of God. God has given to each one of us a measure of faith. *"For as we have many members in one body, but all the members do not have the same function. Having then gifts differing according to the grace that is given to us, let us use them:."* (Rom.12:3,4,6).

In the secular world and in the body of Christ, a wrong heart attitude toward sin will entertain envy and competition leading to strive. Therefore, it is necessary for each one of us to know our assignment and its boundary or limit. If He who comes from above is above all, therefore, *"Whatever you do, work at it with all your heart, as working for the LORD, not for human masters." (Col.3:23).* Oftentimes the strive in the body of Christ is because we work in order to gain the praise of men and share God's glory *(Jn 12:43).* Like the disciples of John the Baptist, nowadays our loyalty to our Bishop or Man of God is such that if he is not the one in charge, no other servant of God can be profitable for the Master's use. If your emphasis is more on the success of your ministry, career and marriage than on God's kingdom, watch out against the cult of personality!

Christ must be the center of it all. If Christ is not the center, then it is man's work! Our true mission is to influence people to follow Christ, not us. Jesus must increase, but I must decrease. He is over all because He is the creator of all that exists. All things must be done to the praise and honor of His name. Every true follower of Christ must shift his or her allegiance to Jesus Christ TODAY!

PRAYER FOCUS

Dear heavenly Father, You resist the proud but give grace to the humble. LORD, enable me to serve Your purpose with great humility in Jesus' name.

"Keep thy heart with all diligence; for out of it are the issues of life." (Prov.4:23)

September 3

Exhausted Yet Keeping Up The Pursuit
Bible Reading: [Judges 8:1-21]

"When Gideon came to the Jordan, he and the three hundred men who were with him crossed over, exhausted but still in pursuit. Then he said to the men of Succoth, "Please give loaves of bread to the people who follow me, for they are exhausted, and I am pursuing Zebah and Zalmunna, kings of Midian." (Vs:4-5)

We live in busy times and ours is a fast-paced world. Before the dust clears at the end of each day and life settles down, we realize just how exhausted or tired we've become. Some may not take pleasure in their pursuit because it is a routine activity that gets boring at times.

Occasionally, discouragement sets in because we do not get the necessary support or motivation we need from others. At the breaking of each day, we all engage in different pursuits, whether good or bad. A pursuit is an activity that you spend time and energy doing. It's an attempt to achieve something. In the context of Gideon, a pursuit is the act of following or searching for someone or something, in order to catch or attack the person or thing. In life, there are short term and long term pursuits. No matter the duration of the pursuit or our individual capacities, as humans get exhausted at times. Even strong young lions sometimes grow weak and hungry *(Ps 34:10)*.

Have you ever been so exhausted or burnt out in life? Are you in a pursuit at the moment that seems to take all your time and energy? Has it become a nightmare? Are you feeling discouraged because you don't know how far it gets or when you will come to the finish line? Beloved, it's important to remember that the joy of the LORD is your strength *(Neh.8:10)*. As a disciple of Christ, if you would like to enjoy life's pursuits: professional/career, ministry (Christian service) and academic, seek God and have a clear or strong sense of purpose. Our pursuits as believers in Christ have to be guided: a pursuit that brings absolute glory to God, and a pursuit that enables us maintain a priority relationship with Him than any other thing on earth. If your pursuit is of God, no matter the duration or its humanly impossible nature, one thing is certain, *"For surely there is a future hope; and your expectation shall not be cut off." (Prov.23:18)*. Gideon with 300 chosen men were able to conquer an army of 15,000 men. Hallelujah!

PRAYER FOCUS

Dear heavenly Father, I confess that it is not of him that willeth, nor of him that runneth, but of God that sheweth mercy (Rom.9:16). LORD, I receive strength from You and the spirit of determination to keep up with pursuits in life that will bring You glory in Jesus' name.

September 4

Seeds of Encouragement
In The Soil Of Adversity
Bible Reading: [1 Samuel 30:1-19]

"So David and his men came to the city, and behold, it was burned with fire; and their wives, and their sons, and their daughters, were taken captives. Then David and the people that were with him lifted up their voice and wept, until they had no power to weep. And David was greatly distressed; for the people spake of stoning him, because the soul of all the people was grieved, every man for his sons and for his daughter: but David encouraged himself in the LORD his God." (Vs: 3,4,6)

Adversity is a state or instance of serious or continued difficulty. Unfavorable circumstances will always come but how we react is what matters. While gone from Ziklag, the Amalekites took advantage of the opportunity to capture and burn Ziklag. They captured David's two wives. How frustrating! It is worth noting that the sin of Saul in not destroying the Amalekites resulted in this tragedy. Beloved in the LORD, do you find yourself in a similar situation at the moment?

Remember what the Scripture says, *"We are hard pressed on every side, but not crushed; perplexed, but not in despair; persecuted, but not abandoned; struck down, but not destroyed. We always carry around in our body the death of Jesus, so that the life of Jesus may also be revealed in our body." (2 Cor.4:8-10)*.

Even in the soil of adversity, seeds of encouragement and comfort can be found. David found strength in the LORD and started looking for a solution instead of blaming or criticizing others as we often do. He asked God for direction. In your adverse circumstance, have you asked God for direction? The LORD has promised to exchange valley of trouble and disgrace for a door of hope *(Hos.2:15; Ps.50:15)*. Our relationship with God counts in times of adversity. It is written, *"If thou faint in the day of adversity, thy strength is small." (Prov.24:10)*.

True disciples of Christ must have a strong dependence on God in order that they might find comfort in Him. It's just so amazing how God would take advantage of adversity to work out everything for our good, even that which the enemy meant for evil *(Rom.8:28)*. The helpless young man, a servant to an Amalekite abandoned on the way was used by God to direct David. So David recovered all that the Amalekites had carried away. Hallelujah! *"For everything that was written in the past was written to teach us, so that through the endurance taught in the Scriptures and the encouragement they provide we might have hope." (Rom.15:4)*

PRAYER FOCUS

Dear heavenly Father, in this I am confident: *"Even though I walk through the darkest valley, I will fear no evil, for You are with me; Your rod and Your staff, they comfort me" (Ps 23:4)* in Jesus' name.

September 5

Bought At A Price
Bible Reading: [1 Cor.6:12-20]

"For you were bought at a price; therefore glorify God in your body and in your spirit, which are God's." [Vs:20]

When one becomes a disciple of Christ, he does not belong to himself. He is free to be all that he can be for God. And he said to them all, *"if any man will come after me, let him deny himself, and take up his cross daily, and follow Me."* (Luke 9:23). The attitude that one has the right to do whatever he or she wants with his body is not a godly virtue. A true disciple of Christ must lead a disciplined lifestyle. Because one has been bought with a high price by the blood of Jesus Christ, every part of his life has been claimed by Christ for the Father's glory! His body becomes a holy sanctuary and the divine presence.

The life of a true disciple of Christ must reflect the faith he/she professes. It is written, *" Let us hold fast the profession of our faith without wavering; (for he is faithful that promised;)"* (Heb.10:23). Those who live in sin have no share in the kingdom of God (Ga.5:19-21). Sexual immorality must not be a way of life, even if it is acceptable and popular in our society. If one lives in sin, it's an indication that his heart has not been transformed and mind not renewed by the Holy Spirit. It is important to note that redemption does not come so easily, for no one can ever pay enough *(Ps 49:8)*. Since we have been bought with such a great price as believers in Christ, we should live in thanksgiving to God for giving His Son for our redemption. *"All this is for your benefit, so that the grace that is reaching more and more people may cause thanksgiving to overflow to the glory of God"* (2 Cor.4:15).

PRAYER FOCUS

Dear heavenly Father, I give the totality of my life to You. LORD, work in me both to will and to do of Your good pleasure in Jesus' name.

MY CONFESSION

"I am crucified with Christ: nevertheless I live; yet not I, but Christ liveth in me: and the life which I now live in the flesh I live by faith of the Son of God, who loved me, and gave himself for me." [Gal.2:20]

September 6

Power Of The Voice & The Word
Bible Reading: [Isaiah 40:1-11]

"I am The Voice of one crying in the wilderness: "Prepare the way of the LORD; Make straight in the desert a highway for our God." Every valley shall be exalted and every mountain and hill brought low; the crooked places shall be made straight and the rough places smooth;...The grass withers, the flower fades, but the Word of our God stands forever." (Vs:3,4,8)

As each day unfolds, we hear voices. Today, I pray that you will have the ability to hear a distinct voice, the voice of God that proclaims grace to the people. It is important to note that the voice came from the desert while the Israelites were in captivity in Assyria and Babylonia. Desert or wilderness is a picture of life's trials and sufferings. You might find yourself in an undignified place today but the good news is that the glory of the LORD that the voice revealed is here!

Beloved, even in the wilderness, may you shall find grace! *(Jer.31:2)*. John is spoken of as the voice of the one crying in the wilderness *(Jn 1:23)* while Christ is the Word *(Jn 1:14)*. The Voice is only a revelation of the Word that brings salvation. It is written, *"Therefore He (Word) is also able to save to the uttermost those who come to God through Him, since He always lives to make intercession for them." (Heb.7:25)*. The revealing of the glory of God means your salvation or complete deliverance today from whatever crisis you may be going through.

The Word of God is eternal and unfailing. God's plans as well as the written word will succeed. Everything will pass away but the Word of our God will stand firm forever. I pray that the purpose for which God's Word is released upon your life be accomplished today in Jesus' name.

Let every mountain before you become a level plain, every crooked place be made straight, every rough surface be made smooth in Jesus' name. *"So shall my word be that goeth forth out of my mouth: it shall not return unto me void, but it shall accomplish that which I please, and it shall prosper in the thing whereto I sent it" (Isa.55:11)*.

PRAYER FOCUS

Dear heavenly Father, *forever O LORD, thy word is settled in heaven (Ps 119:89)*. LORD, the best of man's ability and wisdom are not worthy to be compared to Your matchless Word in Jesus' name.

September 7

"Inward Change - Outward action"
The Power Of Restitution
Bible Reading: [Luke 19:1-10]

*Then Zacchaeus stood and said to the LORD,
"Look, LORD, I give half of my goods to the poor; and if I have taken anything
from anyone by false accusation,
I restore fourfold." And Jesus said to him,
"Today salvation has come to this house,
because he also is a son of Abraham" [Vs:8-9]*

Restitution seems to be a lost act in the Body of Christ today. It is a Biblical concept in both the Old and New Testaments. True repentance is an inward transformation that is expressed by a corresponding outward action as led by the Spirit. *"For as many as are led by the Spirit of God, these are sons of God." (Rom.8:14).* Restitution is an act of returning something that has been lost or stolen to its proper owner. While it is Biblical for someone to pay for damages or loss of property, it's not compulsory for a Christian owner to demand Restitution. However, if you are convicted by the Spirit to return an ill-gotten item after your conversion, it is necessary to ask God for wisdom how to go about it. Zacchaeus was a rich Jew who served the Roman government as a tax collector. As a matter of fact, tax collectors were the most unpopular people in Israel because of their dishonest deal or transaction.

As a child of Abraham by descent, Zacchaeus demonstrated his faith in Christ like Abraham. Being man of power and wealth in his society, he humbled himself by showing his genuine spiritual interest in Jesus. *"But he giveth more grace. Wherefore he saith: God resisteth the proud, but giveth grace unto the humble." (James 4:6).* Jesus being omniscient, saw a true son of Abraham in Zacchaeus. We are not saved by works but whenever we humble ourselves to do what is right and pleasing to God, His grace will locate us. Humility attracts God's grace. *"Today, salvation has come to this house".* True faith is expressed by a changed behavior and action. "If I have taken anything from anyone by false accusation, I restore fourfold." Beloved, does your life need strengthening out? No matter your background or how you've lived in the past, by responding to God's love, you will receive forgiveness and be made new! *"But God commendeth his love toward us, in that, while we were yet sinners, Christ died for us" (Rom.5:8).*

PRAYER FOCUS

Dear heavenly Father, It's my desire to live right with You and my fellow brother and sister. I ask for wisdom and grace to be honest in my dealings with others each passing day in Jesus' name.

September 8

Embracing A Community Lifestyle That Is Considerate Of Others
Bible Reading: [Luke 3:7-15]

"The crowds asked, "What should we do?" John replied, "If you have two shirts, give one to the poor. If you have food, share it with those who are hungry." (Vs:10-11).

What Shall We Do?

Communal living is all about a gathering of people or families sharing a common life and responsibilities: sharing substances, interest, values and beliefs. This is opposed to individualistic way of living whereby a person thinks more about himself or immediate relations. He shows independence and individuality in his behavior or actions. The Christian Life-style is communal. "Now all who believed were together, and had all things in common, and sold their possessions and goods, and divided them among all, as anyone had need" *(Acts.2:44-45)*.

God has called every true disciple to right living. Everyone who came to John asked the same question; what should we do? John's call for fruit worthy of repentance was that people should accept the life of participating in the lives of others. As disciples, we must be considerate to others by doing what is good. It is obvious that selfish people will find it difficult accepting these conditions of discipleship. Three key aspects plaguing our societies today are addressed: Sharing what we have with those who are in need.

We should not leave our responsibility to which we have been assigned. Therefore, we should do our job well and with fairness (just & fair). We should be satisfied with our earnings. *"But godliness with contentment is great gain." (1 Tim.6:6).* Make a difference in your world today by being responsible and bearing the fruit of repentance. Let honesty, fairness and contentment be your watchwords TODAY!

PRAYER FOCUS

Dear heavenly Father, You desire to pour Your mercy on those who are considerate of others. LORD, thank You for abundant grace and strength available for me to live a changed life in Jesus' name.

September 9

Going The Shepherd's Way
Bible Reading: [Psalm 23:1-6]

"My sheep hear my voice, and I know them, and they follow me: And I give unto them eternal life; and they shall never perish, neither shall any man pluck them out of my hand" [John 10:27-28].

The shepherd leads the sheep for his own benefit. Rebelling against the shepherd's leading means rebelling against one's own best interest. A true disciple of Christ is one that is completely dependent on Christ for provision, guidance, protection and comfort. Discipleship qualities are expressed in the fact that we obediently follow the one who leads us in the right place and in the right way. It's written, *"I am the good shepherd: the good shepherd giveth his life for the sheep" (John 10:11).*

"In the morning the Shepherd leads the flock from the fold, marching at its head to the spot where they are to be pastured. He watches over them all day, taking care that none of the sheep goes astray, and if any for a time eludes his watch and wanders away from the rest, he seeks such diligently until he is found and brought back. The shepherd guides them either to some running stream or to wells dug in the wilderness. At sunset he brings the flock home to the fold, counting them as they passed under the rod at the door to assure himself that none is missing.

Often he guards the flock through the dark hours from the attack of wild beasts, or the deceitful attempts of the prowling thief." (Excerpt - M.G Easton).

"For the LORD is a sun and shield: the LORD will give grace and glory: no good thing will he withhold from them that walk uprightly." (Ps 84:11)

PRAYER FOCUS

In You Father do I put my trust. I am confident in Your leadership as the great Shepherd of the flock. In You I'm renewed and refreshed daily in Jesus' name.

September 10

Substance For Divine Multiplication
Bible Reading: [John 6:1-13]

"Then Jesus lifted up His eyes, and seeing a great multitude coming toward Him, He said to Philip, 'Where shall we buy bread, that these may eat? But this He said to test him, for He Himself knew what He would do." [Vs:5-6]

So Elisha said to her, "What shall I do for you? Tell me, what do you have in the house?" And she said, "Your maidservant has nothing in the house but a jar of oil." [2 Kings 4:2]

Often we complain about what we don't have but fail to recognize the little we have. At times we limit God in our lives by our perspective of what is or what is not humanly possible. While it is true that God can create something out of nothing *(Heb.11:3)*, He takes pleasure to multiply the effectiveness of the little we offer Him beyond our wildest expectations. He will use whatever and whoever avails himself to advance the work of His Kingdom. The young man gave the five barley loaves and two small fish. It made all the difference! Hallelujah!

As a matter of fact, if we offer Him nothing, He will have nothing to use. God always prefer to work with and through people; our time, ability and resources are great assets (valuable thing) for the Master's use. God's provision is far larger than our faith and the substance we offer *(Acts 17:25)*. He is able to do exceeding abundantly above all that we ask or think, according to the power that works in us (Eph.3:20). God is still doing the miraculous. Trust Him with your substance TODAY for multiplication!

PRAYER FOCUS

Dear heavenly Father, You demonstrate Your tenderness and care daily for those who are faithful to You. LORD, I purpose in my heart not to limit Your blessings because of the lack of faith and unwillingness to honor You with my substance in Jesus' name.

September 11

Power Of Resolve and Conviction In Christian Service
Bible Reading: [Joshua 24:14-25]

"And if it seems evil to you to serve the LORD, choose for yourselves this day whom you will serve, whether the gods which your fathers served that were on the other side of the River, or the gods of the Amorites, in whose land you dwell. But as for me and my house, we will serve the LORD." [Vs:15]

Nowadays many people give in to Christian service as though they are serving human masters. In most parts of the world, the desire of many to serve the LORD has decreased over time. To some, they have to be paid, and if not, they will quit. Others are caught up with the pleasures of life and quest for financial and material possessions. It's is necessary for each one of us to decide what and to whom we have committed our lives to. Resolve is a firm determination to do something or to decide firmly on a course of action. Beloved in the LORD, what is your course of action that brings glory to God? While resolve is to make a definite and serious decision to do something, conviction is a fixed or firm belief. The conviction of a true disciple of Christ is derived from his or her commitment to Scriptures the sole authority. *"Serve willingly, as if you were serving the LORD and not merely people." (Eph. 6:7).* It's important to note that the way we live shows others the strength of our commitment to serving God.

Joshua trusted in God enough to honor Him as holy in the sight of the Israelites. Having recognized that it was God who rescued and preserved them, the people responded clearly, reflecting their determination to follow Joshua's lead in following the LORD. They followed Joshua not because he was their leader but due to the fact that he followed the LORD wholeheartedly, with undivided interest. *"But as for me and my house, we will serve the LORD."* . Friend, what is your resolve in serving the LORD? How strong is your conviction for God's Word and His precious promises? God will not work against your free will but the right to choose doing what pleases Him and to walk in obedience shows how responsible you are as a disciple of Christ.

PRAYER FOCUS

Dear heavenly Father, You have proven Your trustworthiness to me time and again. Today I reaffirm my choice to follow and serve Your purpose in Jesus' name.

September 12

The Power Of Focus
Bible Reading: [Matthew 14:22-32]

"And Peter answered Him and said, "LORD, if it is You, command me to come to You on the water." So He said, "Come." And when Peter had come down out of the boat, he walked on the water to go to Jesus. But when he saw that the wind was boisterous, he was afraid; and beginning to sink he cried out, saying, "LORD, save me!" And immediately Jesus stretch out His hand and caught him." [Vs:28-31].

Many people are sinking in life because of their focus on the waves of difficult situations surrounding them. One of the reasons that even the very elects of God are tossed to and fro, carried about with every wind of doctrine *(Eph.4:14)*, and by the trickery of men is due to the lack of focus on the Word of God. *Focus* is to have direct attention toward something or someone. The choice to focus on whatsoever or whomsoever is yours! One thing that must be very clear to everyone is that there are changing times, seasons, attitudes and personalities.

Focusing on anything on earth is short lived *(Matt.24:35)*. If you desire to create an impact of eternal value, then your focus must be on Christ, the Rock of Ages, the Unchanging Changer, the Author and Finisher of our faith. As long as Peter kept his eyes on Jesus, his faith in the power of the LORD enabled him to walk on the water. The power of focus gives us the stability (emotional & physical) we need to sail through turbulent moment in life.

"Let your eyes look directly forward, and your gaze be straight before you." (Prov.4:25). "I have set the LORD always before me: because He is at my right hand, I shall not be moved." (Ps 16:8)

PRAYER FOCUS

LORD Jesus, I acknowledge that You are the manifestation of the great "I Am". LORD, help me each passing day to maintain a strong focus on You and the power of Your Word in Jesus' name.

September 13

Enjoying A Walking Relationship With God
Bible Reading: [Genesis 5:19-24]

"After he begot Methuselah, Enoch walked with God three hundred years, and had sons and daughters. And Enoch walked with God; and he was not, for God took him." [Vs:24]

God takes pleasure with establishing us in an intimate, daily friendship with Him. Enoch walked with God three hundred years. Friend, how long have you walked with God that you have grown cold in love for Him or considering quitting? *(Gen.3:8)* You can only get the best from God in a walking relationship with Him. *"By faith Enoch was taken away so that he did not see death, and was not found, because God had taken him; for before he was taken he had this testimony, that he pleased God" (Heb.11:5).* Be a hero of faith and a walking partner with God TODAY!

PRAYER FOCUS

LORD, the desire of my heart is to enjoy an everyday walk of unbroken communion with You in Jesus' name.

September 14

Despising Days Of Small Beginnings?
Bible Reading: [Zachariah 4:1-10]

"For who has despised the day of small things? For these seven rejoice to see the plumb line in the hand of Zerubbabel. They are the eyes of the LORD, which scan to and fro throughout the whole earth." (Vs:10)

Generally speaking, people wouldn't like to identify with a project at the initial stage while others will only join when they start seeing a glimpse of success. Is God leading you to start a project: Church planting, setting up a new business, constructing a house, moving to a new location or city etc.? We cannot deny the fact that all these come with some challenges most of the time.

Discouragement only sets in when we start viewing or thinking about the project outside God's will. God's work in our live is often not recognized until after we have struggled through trials. But faith in God and the presence of His empowering Spirit will enable us to overcome seemingly impossible obstacles.

Zerubbabel was given the responsibility of rebuilding the temple in Jerusalem. The people lived in their paneled houses while the LORD's temple was in ruins. As a matter of fact, many of the older Jews were disheartened when they realized the new temple will not match the size and splendor of Solomon's temple. Also, the returned exiles were weak, poor and threatened by their enemies. The words of the LORD to Zerubbabel was reassuring that the accomplishment of such a great task is not by human strength but by His Spirit. *"Yet now be strong, Zerubbabel, says the LORD; and be strong, Joshua, son of Jehozadak, the high priest; and be strong, all you people of the land, says the LORD, and work; for I am with you, says the LORD" (Haggai 2:4).*

It is worth noting that it is only through the Spirit of God that anything of lasting value is accomplished. As you perform your duty, you should be determined not to trust in your own strength or abilities. Just begin where you are and be faithful in small task or opportunities. All you need is God on your side. He is more concerned about what is right and not what is impressively beautiful or magnificent. Move on for the joy of the LORD is your strength TODAY!

PRAYER FOCUS

Dear heavenly Father, that I have accomplished this far, You have done for me. I'm confident that though my beginning be small or insignificant, my latter end will greatly increase [Job.8:7] in Jesus' name. Amen.

September 15

Solitary Place Experience
Bible Reading: [Mark 1:35-45]
"For This Purpose I Have Come Forth"

Now in the morning, having risen a long while before daylight, He went out and departed to a solitary place; and there He prayed. And Simon and those who were with Him searched for Him. When they found Him, they said to Him, "Everyone is looking for You." But He said to them, "Let us go into the next town, that I may preach there also, because for this purpose I have come forth." [Vs:35-38]

For every spiritual task, prayer is inevitable . There can be no effective Christian service, transformation and lasting impact without a prayer force. Prayer is the vital link between us and God. Our LORD Jesus cultivated the attitude of going to solitary places to pray. Does prayer really matter to you? If one has not learned the discipline of breaking away from others to talk with God, he can't be an effective tool in the Master's hand. The Church needs fire in the pulpit.

The challenge with the Church of God today is that it has allowed the distractions and cares of this life to rob us of our prayer life. *"And this is the confidence that we have in Him, that, if we ask anything according to His will, He heareth us" (1 John 5:14:Rev.5:8).* It is important to note that Jesus Christ did nothing outside the will of His Father. Despite his busy ministry, he sought time to pray. Prayer equipped him to preach, teach, heal, and cast out demons. *"And so it was, when Jesus had ended these sayings, that the people were astonished at His teaching, for He taught them as one having authority and not as the scribes" (Matt.7:28-29).*

After spending time with the Father in the school of prayer, He had a clear purpose and direction for each day's mission. Remember that he did not only need direction but power that comes from being in the place of prayer. All the carnal services and manipulation in the Body of Christ is the outcome of a prayerless lifestyle. All the confusion in the Body of Christ today is the result of men who never spent quality time with God and had to step out without a clear vision and definite purpose. *"For this purpose I have come forth."* What is the purpose for doing what you have engaged yourself to do? Will it bring glory to God? Is there any urgency in doing it? "Let's go into the next towns, that I may preach there also." Souls are heading to hell! Ask the Holy Spirit for direction and take the gospel to the next person, town, city and nation. *The Ethiopian eunuch said to Philip, "How can I, unless someone guides me?" And he asked Philip to come up and sit with him (Acts 8:31).* Somebody is waiting for you to guide him or her into God's truth and the right way (John 14:6).

PRAYER FOCUS

Dear heavenly Father, without You I can do nothing. LORD, more than ever before, I am determined to spend quality time in the School of prayer and serve Your purpose in my generation in Jesus' name.

September 16

The Watchful Disciple
Bible Reading: [Luke 21:34-38]

"But take heed to yourselves, lest your hearts be weighed down with carousing, drunkenness, and cares of this life, and that Day come on you unexpectedly. Watch therefore, and pray always that you may be counted worthy to escape all these things that will come to pass, and to stand before the Son of Man." [Vs:34, 36]

Beloved in the LORD, do you doubt the fact that Christ will come again? The world is full of distractions and the LORD warns us to be careful about a lot of things. A true disciple of Christ is always to be alert and ready for Christ's return. To take heed means to be cautious with or pay attention to someone or something. The starting point is for the believer to guard his heart with the help of the LORD. *"Keep thy heart with all diligence; for out of it are the issues of life" (Prov.4:23;KJV).* Another version says, "Guard your heart above all else, for it determines the course of your life" (NLT). In other words, if you don't guard your heart, the course of your life will be determined by the cares (worries) of this life, deceitfulness of riches and the desires for other things. Our heart constitutes our feelings of love and desires and it dictates to a great extent how we live because we always find time to do what we enjoy. *"For all that is in the world, the lust of the flesh and the lust of the eyes and the boastful pride of life, is not from the Father, but is of the world" [1 John 2:16].*

A disciple should be more concerned about how much of his life the Holy Spirit has, submitting himself daily to His leading and draw constantly on His power. As believers, we ought to work faithfully at the tasks God has entrusted to our care and not to let our minds and spirit be dulled by careless living and foolish pursuit of pleasures. *"Watch therefore, and pray always that you may be counted worthy to escape all these things that will come to pass, and to stand before the Son of Man." [Vs:36]*

PRAYER FOCUS

Dear heavenly Father, It's my heart's desire to be spiritually ready for the coming of the LORD. I'm determined to be watchful, careful and to walk circumspectly in Jesus' name.

September 17

Being With God On The Mountain
Bible Reading: [Exod.34:29-35]

"Now it was so, when Moses came down from Mount Sinai (and the two tablets of the Testimony were in Moses' hand when he came down from the mountain), that Moses did not know that the skin of his face shone while he talked with Him. So when Aaron and all the Children of Israel saw Moses, behold, the skin of his face shone, and they were afraid to come near him." [Vs: 29-30]

Spending time alone with God far outweighs anything that the human mind can fathom and that a man's heart can desire. Because of time spent with God on the mountain, the countenance of Moses glowed. We may not all have the same experience but the truth is that, spending sufficient time with God in prayer, Bible reading and meditation should have such an effect on one's life that people will know one has been with God. The Israelites knew Moses had been with God and likewise the members of the Sanhedrin realized that Peter and John had been with Jesus *(Acts 4:13)*.

Often we spend sufficient time with God only when we have pressing needs. What about personal fellowship with God in the place of prayer and the Word?

Spending quality time with God is a life changing experience. If under the Old Covenant Moses had such an experience, what more under the New Covenant? As true believers in Christ, we have unveiled ourselves from the Old Testament law and we are able to perceive the glory of Jesus, as we grow daily in the grace and knowledge of Him. Our lives are being transformed into the image of Jesus by our obedience to His will.

PRAYER FOCUS

Dear heavenly Father, thank You for the privilege to experience greater glory under the New Covenant - through Your life giving Spirit in Jesus' name.

September 18

Setting Your Priorities Right
"One thing is needed"
Bible Reading: [Luke 10:38-42]

And Jesus answered and said to her, "Martha, Martha, you are worried and troubled about many things. But one thing is needed…" [Vs-41,42]

We are living in a world full of competing interests. People are worried and distracted by many things. The care of this life is taking a toll on many and the devil is gaining access in many homes. When's the last time you skipped a meal or chores to get to know Jesus a little better and to listen to what He has to say to you? Jeremiah spent time on the word: *"Thy words were found, and I did eat them; thy word was unto me the joy and rejoicing of mine heart: for I am called by thy name, O God of hosts." (Jer.15:16)*

"They devoted themselves to the Apostles' teaching and to fellowship, to the breaking of bread and to prayer." (Acts 2:42)

Students and followers do sit at the feet of their teachers. That is the hallmark of true discipleship. At the time Jesus was present in the house, Martha's priorities were wrong. She was doing a needed and good work. However, the situation demanded a change in her priorities considering the fact that the end of Jesus' ministry was drawing near.

Mary had chosen that good part: It is good to care for the physical needs of the hour. However, the spiritual needs of man are always more important. Many in the body of Christ use the service of physical needs as an excuse to neglect the spiritual food that is more important. Mary's priorities were determined by what was most important at the time. What about your priorities TODAY?

PRAYER FOCUS

This is the day that the LORD has made; I will rejoice and be glad in it. Father, I purpose in my heart to set my priorities right today in Jesus' name.

September 19

When Truth Fails In Society
Bible Reading: [Jeremiah 5:1-31]

"Therefore I said, "Surely these are poor. They are foolish; for they do not know the way of the LORD, the judgment of their God. I will go to the great men and speak to them, for they have known the way of the LORD, The judgement." [4-5]

Nothing but the truth is acceptable to God. However, sometimes truth may be scarce and society becomes dysfunctional i.e. not operating normally or properly in the fear of God. Many societies and nations in the world have come to a crossroad because no righteous person lives there. A righteous person is one that lives according to God's laws and deals with other people accordingly. Such an honest person is dependable, truthful and faithful to God. Nothing closes the door of God's acceptance more than hypocrisy, lying or pretense.

Jeremiah like Abraham, faced a similar situation in his days. And Abraham came near and said, "Would You also destroy the righteous with the wicked? " Suppose there were fifty righteous within the city; would You also destroy the place and not spare it for the fifty righteous that were in it? (Vs:23-24). Like in the days of old, God is challenging us today to find one honest and truthful person in the entire city. Remember that God is willing to spare any city if one righteous person can be found to stand in the gap on behalf of the land. *"Do I take pleasure in the death of the wicked (sinners)? Declares the Sovereign LORD. Rather, am I not pleased when they turn from their ways and live?" (Eze 18:23; 2 Pet.3:9).*

God holds anyone responsible if he leads people astray by his example. The absence of true followers at any level (uneducated to great men) of society in Jerusalem was a great challenge. Even leaders who were expected by the LORD to teach and guide the people had fallen! *"For the time is come that judgment must begin at the house of God: and if it first begin at us, what shall the end be of them that obey not the gospel of God? (1 Pet.4:17).* Just how significant is your testimony in your city or nation TODAY?

PRAYER FOCUS

Dear heavenly Father, I yield myself to You as an instrument that You might work out Your purpose for my community and nation. LORD, grant me the grace to set an example for the believers in speech, in conduct, in love, in faith, and in purity - in Jesus' name.

September 20

The Healing Of Wayward Hearts
Bible Reading: [Jeremiah 3:18-23]

"Return, you backsliding children, and I will heal your backslidings." [Jer.3:22]

A wayward heart is one that turns away from what is right or proper. Every believer has the responsibility with the help of the Holy Spirit to check their heart attitude towards sin. What would be the attitude of your heart if you adopt a lifestyle that does not please God? Truth means that the inner attitudes and thoughts of our hearts match the words we speak and what we do. We often forfeit the best God has for our lives when we choose to walk after the foolish desires of our own hearts. God wanted the Israelites to acknowledge Him as their Father, He wanted to offer them a beautiful land and the finest possession in the world. It's important to note that God is committed to providing us with the best if we are ready to cooperate with Him. *"If you are willing and obedient, you shall eat the good of the land." [Isa.1:19]*

It brings pain to God's heart to watch His people compromise their convictions and walk after the foolishness of their hearts. The first generation of the Israelites had to suffer the pain of captivity and never saw their land again. However, their children and grandchildren confessed, repented of their sins and were restored. They were released by the Medo-Persians and allowed to return to Palestine. The advantage of believing God's Word is that we don't have to learn by hard or painful experience the destructive results of sin. Are you a backslider? *"The backslider in heart shall be filled with his own ways: and a good man shall be satisfied from himself" (Prov.14:14).* Consider how far you have fallen! Repent and do the things you did at first [Rev.2:5]: prayer, evangelism, meditation, Bible study, giving of tithe and offering, devotion to public reading of Scriptures, to preaching, to teaching and fellowship.

PRAYER FOCUS

Dear heavenly Father, today I acknowledge my backsliding. LORD, heal my heart and make it ever true. Bless me with an obedient heart as I renew my love and commitment to You in Jesus' name.

September 21

Standing Before God In The Breach
Bible Reading: [Psalm 106:19-31]

"Therefore He said that He would destroy them, had not Moses His chosen one stood before Him in the breach (gap), to turn away His wrath, lest He destroy them." [Vs:23]

The best gift you can offer a loved one or your nation today is to stand in the gap to avert (turn away) the wrath of God or the onslaught of the enemy. Ancient cities had walls for defense and protection from potential aggressors. Whenever a wall was breached, an enemy could then attack the inhabitants of a city through the breach (Eccl.10:8). At Horeb, the Israelites sought to manifest the glory of God in a golden calf idol. Like the Israelites, whenever we turn our thinking to worship something that man has created after his own imagination, we are practicing the sin of idolatry. It could only take Moses, standing in the gap through intercession to avert the wrath of God. Just imagine families, whole communities, and nations that have been destroyed by the devil because there was no one to stand in the breach!

"And I sought for a man among them, that should make up the hedge, and stand in the gap before me for the land, that I should not destroy it: but I found none." (Eze 22:30). By standing in the gap you will spare somebody from destruction TODAY!

PRAYER FOCUS

Dear heavenly Father, You are plenteous in mercy and rich in love. By reason of the blood of Jesus Christ, I stand in gap on behalf of loved ones and my nation to resist the devil's onslaught and avert judgment in Jesus' name.

September 22

Having A Good Testimony Of The Truth
Bible Reading: [3 John 1-14]

"Beloved do not imitate what is evil, but what is good. He who does good is of God, but he who does evil has not seen God. Demetrius has a good testimony from all and from the truth itself. And we also bear witness, and you know that our testimony is true." (Vs:11-12)

Your testimony as a believer in the LORD Jesus Christ is evidence or proof of a genuine walk and relationship with Him. This walk defines how you conduct yourself in a manner worthy of the gospel of Christ *(Phil.1:27)* , standing fast in one spirit, with one mind, making great effort, with others contending earnestly for the faith of the gospel *(Jude 3)*. It's obvious that in the world in which we live, many love human praise more than praise from God. While the testimony from men about a believer is good, God wants us to focus our minds on the testimony from the truth itself. In other words, if truth speaks, let it speak on your behalf.

A believer should have a good reputation concerning the truth that is in him *(John 15:4)*. This truth is not to believe in a set of rules that conform to correct doctrine but behaving after the nature of truth Jesus revealed to us *"For the law was given by Moses, but grace and truth came by Jesus Christ." (John 1:17)*. Walking in truth means to walk in love that was manifested on the Cross. Walking in love means to care for our brother as Jesus cared for our sins on the Cross. May God help all His saints today in Jesus' name!

PRAYER FOCUS

Dear heavenly Father, Your testimony is sure, making wise the simple. LORD, I ask for the grace to live out the truth in every aspect of my life in Jesus' name. Amen.

"But whoso looketh into the perfect law of liberty, and continueth therein, he being not a forgetful hearer, but a doer of the work, this man shall be blessed in his deed." [James 1:25]

September 23

The Quality Of Your Fruits
"Chosen To Bear Fruit"
Bible Reading: [Isaiah 5:1-7]

"Now let me sing to my Well-beloved a song of my Beloved regarding His vineyard: My Well-beloved has a vineyard on a very fruitful hill. He dug it up and cleared out its stones, and planted it with the choicest vine. He built a tower in its midst, and also made a winepress in it; so He expected it to bring forth good grapes, but it brought forth wild grapes, but it brought forth wild grapes." (Vs:1-2]

The act of bearing fruit is one of the most important lessons every disciple of Christ should learn. Beloved in the LORD, imagine a father expecting his son to bear good fruits, he offers his son a very fruitful hill but all he can get in return is a small, sour and hard grape that is useless for producing wine. Like Israel, oftentimes we find ourselves in a privileged position with all the advantages to produce much and high quality fruits as disciples of Christ but we fail to meet God's expectations. Everything was done for Israel in order that faithfulness be produced and God's name be glorified. One can't claim to be a disciple of Christ without bearing fruit.

"Herein is my Father glorified, that ye bear much fruit; so shall ye be my disciples" [John 15:8].

Does God expect men today to bear fruits? The answer is YES!

Fruit of repentance: "Bring forth therefore fruits meet for repentance:" (Matt.3:8). A man can profess to be a Christian but there is no fruit of repentance. Repentance is not only to be sorry for sin, but to turn from sin and live a changed life. "By their fruit you will recognize them.," [Matt.7:16]

Fruit of the Spirit (righteousness): The nature and character of God (Gal.22:23). Love-joy-peace-forbearance-kindness-goodness-faithfulness-gentleness and self-control. Is this evident in your life. Growth in Christlikeness in character is the key to discipleship.

Fruit of ministry: Are you productive in your knowledge of Christ. What about the talents/gifts God has blessed or endowed you with? Remember, we are saved to serve. Paul writing to the brethren at Corinth, "Even if others think I am not an apostle, I certainly am to you. You yourselves are proof that I am the LORD's apostle." (1 Cor.9:2). No one can bear quality fruit if he chooses to live by his own values rather than God's. We become fruitless when we leave God out of our lives by allowing sin to come in. There can be no shift to righteousness or fruitfulness when we are satisfied with where or the way we are today! [John.15:16]

PRAYER FOCUS

Dear heavenly Father, I confess that without you I can do nothing. LORD, I ask for a glorious transformation of my spiritual life from laxity/laziness/luke-warmness to fruitful vitality in Jesus' name.

September 24

Showing An Attitude Of Expectation
Bible Reading: [Habakkuk 2:1-4]

"I will stand my watch and set myself on the rampart (watchtower), and watch to see what He will say to me, and what I will answer when I am corrected." [Vs:1]

Expectation is a strong belief that something will happen or be the case. As believers in Christ, sometimes we have high expectations but we are not well positioned to receive a message from the LORD. This is not a year for you to miss out on what God is doing or what He has in store for you. God works out His plans in His perfect timing. An attitude of expectation is needed daily to appropriate what the LORD has for our lives. Oftentimes we run to God, establish a case before Him but fail to position ourselves. The prophet positioned himself in a place of prayer on a watchtower in order to wait for God's reply. It is written, *"That ye be not slothful(lazy), but followers of them who through faith and patience inherit the promises."* [Heb.6:1]. Your situation or circumstance shouldn't be a cause for alarm. It shouldn't be a reason to be worried, frightened, or concerned about. *"But the just (righteous) shall live by their faith and trust in God."*

In the days of Habakkuk, evil and injustice seemed to have the upper hand in the world. He felt there was some justification for his complaint concerning the suffering of the righteous at the hand of the unrighteous, who seemed to prosper in all they do. He was surprised that God would use a nation more wicked than Judah to punish Judah. Like Habakkuk, we too often feel angry and discouraged when we see what is going on. Often, those who commit evil think God is slow and will not bring judgment *"Because the sentence against an evil deed is not executed speedily, therefore the hearts of the sons of men among them are given fully to do evil"* [Eccl.8:11]. Regardless of how we feel or think, evil is never beyond God's control. God uses whatever unusual instrument He chooses to bring correction or punishment. It is not in the power of man to decide what God should do but to wait patiently upon him. *"For surely there is an end; and your expectation shall not be cut off"* [Prov.23:18]. Wait and watch for God's response. The vision is for an appointed time. It will sure come to pass.

PRAYER FOCUS

Dear heavenly Father, even through difficult times, I am fully convinced that You will bring out the best for my life. LORD, I trust that You will direct everything things according to Your purpose concerning me in Jesus' name.

September 25

Training For Reigning
Bible Reading: [Hebrews 3:1-14]

"For we are made partakers of Christ, if we hold the beginning of our confidence steadfast unto the end" (Heb.3:14).

"But he that shall endure unto the end, the same shall be saved" (Matt.24:13).

From Scripture, it is obvious that at the end of the age the world will be experiencing the deepest darkness and the greatest glory of the LORD at the same time *[Isa.60:1-3;1 Jn 5:19]*. *"No great Christians were ever revealed until they were confronted with great darkness. Great darkness is coming but glory is also coming" (Rick Joyner).* The world will never see God's great light through us if we live a compromising life. Training to reign implies we must develop a deep love for the truth. For this to be possible, we must sink our roots into the Word of God, know what and whom we have believed, and be determined that even at the cost of our lives, we will not compromise that which He has entrusted to our care. *"For this reason I also suffer these things, but I am not ashamed; for I know whom I have believed and I am convinced that He is able to guard what I have entrusted to Him until that day" [2 Tim.1:12].*

Throughout church history, persecution has only served to increase and strengthen the Church. Likewise it is the darkness that helps to make the light manifest. *"In Him was life, and the life was the light of men. And the light shinneth in darkness; and the darkness comprehended it not" (John 1:5). "For whatsoever is born of God overcometh the world: and this is the victory that overcometh the world, even our faith" [1 Jn.5:4].* Every believer must train in righteousness in order to reign. As Christians, must seize every opportunity to grow in God's ways as well as His truth. Those who persevere in faith have assurance that they are indeed part of God's family.

PRAYER FOCUS

Father, without You I can do nothing. LORD, help me to remain faithful to the calling of the gospel and to keep an obedient heart daily in words and deeds in Jesus' name.

September 26

Confidence That Is Rewarding
Bible Reading: [Heb.10:32-39]

"Therefore do not cast away your confidence, which has great reward. For you have need of endurance, so that after you have done the will of God, you may receive the promise:" [Vs:35-36]

Confidence is the feeling or belief that one can have faith in or rely on someone or something. Faith involves confidence and certainty. We can build our confidence today by believing in God's character and promise: He is who he says and will do what He says. Scriptures encourage us not to abandon our faith in the face of adversity or persecution but to make our faith real by enduring what we are going through. It is important to note that suffering is normal for a person who identifies with Christ and his community. *"If thou faint in the days of adversity, thy strength is small" [Prov.24:10; Phil.1:29]*. We can rest assured in the fact that because of what He has done in the past, He will do greater things in the future.

We cast away our confidence when we become comfortable or lazy in our Christian responsibilities to grow in the knowledge of Christ. Sometimes we become dull of hearing, lazy in our commitment, and indifferent concerning all that God has done for us through the Cross. As disciples of Christ, we must be diligent to remember that we are called by God to follow His word and not to conform to man-made religious inventions or the standards of the world.

PRAYER FOCUS

Heavenly Father, I look up to You with confidence and trust that You will enable me to remain faithful in the face of adversity or persecution today in Jesus' name.

September 27

Each One - Teach One
Bible Reading: [2 Tim.2:1-13]

"You therefore, my son, be strong in the grace that is in Christ Jesus. And the things that you have heard from me among many witnesses, commit these to faithful men who will be able to teach others also." [Vs:1-2]

God's grace is in Christ. This grace is unmerited favor that a person enjoys when he surrenders his life to Christ. Our strength in the realm of grace is motivated by the fact that one is saved by grace *"But by the grace of God I am what I am, and His grace toward me was not in vain; but I labored more abundantly than they all, yet not I, but the grace of God which was with me" (1 Cor.15:10; Eph.2:8-9)*. Because we are saved by grace, we should live by *grace [Col.2:6]*. This implies every disciple has to trust completely in Christ and His power, and not trying to live for Christ in his own strength.

Each one teaches one. It is the responsibility of every disciple to instruct faithful men in order to carry on with our spiritual heritage and lineage. This lineage of teaching will continue until Christ comes. Therefore, those who break this lineage of instructions have failed in their spiritual responsibilities as Christians. One is able to teach the truth only when he knows the truth. As we read the Bible, each one should ask the LORD to show him His timeless truths and how it ought to be applied in one's life. May God give us understanding of His word TODAY!

PRAYER FOCUS

Heavenly Father, thank You for Your grace which is sufficient for me. LORD, I ask for an open and receptive heart for Your word. Grant me the ability to teach the next person You truth in Jesus' name.

September 28

Lord Open my Mind
Bible Reading: [Luke 24:36-49]

"And He opened their understanding, that they might comprehend the Scriptures." [Vs:45]

The LORD does not take pleasure seeing any of His precious ones being ignorant of the mysteries of the Kingdom of God. Remember that the secret of the LORD is with them that fear Him; and He will shew them His covenant *[Psalm 25:14]*. Like the disciples of old, sometimes we get so excited that our emotions and thinking fail to catch up with the realities of God's presence. God does unusual things at times that the human mind cannot comprehend. But if we carefully study the Scriptures with the help of His Spirit, we will come to full understanding.

Jesus had to prove to them that He was actually there in His resurrected body. Something that was written in the Scriptures and told them before His death on the Cross *[Matt.16:21]*. Beloved, do you need the LORD to prove to you that He will come again? May the LORD open your eyes to understand the Scriptures. The role of the Holy Spirit is so significant. *"But the Comforter, which is the Holy Ghost, whom the Father will send in my name, he shall teach you all things, and bring all things to your remembrance, whatsoever I have said unto you" John 14:16]*. If your conversion to Christ is genuine, then the anointing of the Holy Spirit you have received will teach you all things as you read, meditate and study the Word of God *[1 John 2:27]*.

PRAYER FOCUS

Heavenly Father, I pray that the Holy Spirit will open my mind to understand the Scriptures and enable me to put Your word into practice in Jesus' name.

September 29

Judgment Belongs To God
Bible Reading: [Luke 9:51-56]

"And when His disciples James and John saw this, they said, LORD, do You want us to command fire to come down from heaven and consume them, just as Elijah did? But He turned and rebuke them, and said, "You do not know what manner of spirit you are of." [Vs:54,55]

In many cities the LORD went to, people received the good news with joy. The disciples had been with Jesus for about three years, constantly enjoying an environment of fellowship. Finally, the time came when they had to experience rejection. Beloved, what would be your attitude if you experience rejection as a witness of Christ? Some disciples of Christ rarely go out to witness to the lost for fear that they may be rejected or ridiculed. I remembered sharing the gospel with someone more than a decade ago, who rejected it and was determined joining another religion. I prayed a short prayer for him and left. Interestingly, after two years, I made him serving the LORD as a disciple in a Bible believing Church in that city.

You do not know what manner of spirit you are of. James and John did not understand that their spirit of retaliation was actually the spirit of the world. Inasmuch as people accept the gospel, we must bear in mind that some may reject it. Because of a wrong attitude, Jesus' disciples wanted to retaliate by calling down fire from heaven on the people. The LORD wants us to learn rejection without desiring to retaliate. There is a set time for judgment *[Heb.9:27]*, and vengeance therefore must be left to God. Like our LORD, we are sent to seek and save the lost *[Lk 19:10]*.

It is the LORD's heartbeat. When God gives us a course of action, we must be determined to go there no matter what awaits us. Has God sent you? Be focus with determination to do what He has assigned you and He will honor His word *[Isa.55:11]*. Let's walk in obedience and leave judgment in God's hands.

PRAYER FOCUS

Heavenly Father, I'm fully convinced You desire that all men be saved. LORD, I pray for the right attitude towards those who reject me as an ambassador of Christ. I ask that You will enable me to exercise self-control and be passionate for soul winning in Jesus' name.

September 30

One Thing You Lack "Total Commitment"
Bible Reading: [Luke 18:18-23]

And he said, "All these things I have kept from my youth." So when Jesus heard these things, He said to him, "You still lack one thing. Sell all that you have and distribute to the poor, and you will have treasure in heaven; and come, follow Me." [Vs:21,22]

Sometimes we boast of the things we have done as a means to justify ourselves before God. Like the Pharisees, the rich young ruler was trusting in his performance of law-keeping. Are you still boasting about your good works as a way to justify yourself before God? You cannot be a true disciple of Christ without placing total trust in God in all aspects of life and belief. You must not come to Jesus with your own self-righteousness as the Pharisee. *"But we are all as an unclean thing, and our righteousness are as filthy rags" (Isa.64:6).* No matter how good and kind you are, no matter the works of charity you do, no matter how much people speak well of you and acclaim you, no matter the extent to which you keep the commandments, if you don't come to Christ on His terms and conditions, you cannot be saved. No one can, by his own achievements be saved. *"For by grace are ye saved through faith; and that not of yourselves: it is the gift of God: Not of works, lest any man should boast" (Eph.2:8-9).*

Self-righteousness must be discarded for total dependence on God for direction. We must like the young ruler discard everything would hinder total commitment to Christ. You can't define discipleship based on the level of commitment you are willing to give. Lukewarm Christians convince themselves that God is pleased with their lukewarm discipleship. *"And he said to them all, If any man will come after me, let him deny himself, and take up his cross daily, and follow me" [Luke 9:23].* The young ruler's riches had made him comfortable and gave him power and prestige. *"Sell all that you have and distribute to the poor -and come, follow Me."* We are more secure if we follow Jesus without compromise than we are with all our wealth, power and prestige. Get rid of anything that has become more important than God. Surrender your all to Him TODAY!

PRAYER FOCUS

Heavenly Father, You take no pleasure in half-hearted and lukewarm Christians. Today I commit and dedicate myself to You in Jesus' name.

OCTOBER

Hast thou not known? Hast thou not heard, that the everlasting God, the LORD, the Creator of the ends of the earth, fainted not, neither is weary? There is no searching of his understanding.

He giveth power to the faint; and to them that have no might he increaseth strength. Even the youths shall faint and be weary, and the young men shall utterly fall: But they that wait upon the LORD shall renew their strength; they shall mount up with wings as eagles, they shall run, and not be weary; and they shall walk, and not faint."

[Isaiah 40:28-31;KJV]

****

Jehovah Nissi - **[The LORD my Banner]** *- Exod.17:15*

10 = **[Completion or Entirety]**

October 1

Sleeping At The Wrong Time
Bible Reading: [Acts.20:1-12]

"And there sat in a window a certain young man named Eutychus, being fallen into a deep sleep: and as Paul was long preaching, he sunk down with sleep, and fell down from the third loft and was taken up dead." [Vs:9]

Sleep is one of the best things the LORD has given man. He knows that we all need this precious resting time. Your busy schedule cannot downplay the seriousness of lack of sleep. However, sleeping at the wrong time has a bearing on the success of a person. Just image a student sleeping all night daily when exams are fast approaching; a student sleeping while lectures are going on; just imagine a businessman sleeping all day when markets are open and business partners are waiting; just imaging a medical doctor sleeping during night service while patients are languishing in pain; just imagine a driver of a passenger bus sleeping on the highway; just imagine a soldier on guard sleeping while an enemy is advancing. It is written, *"but while men slept, his enemy came and sowed tares among the wheat and went his way"* (Matt.13:25).

Meditate on what these Scripture say, *"Indeed, he who watches over Israel will neither slumber nor sleep"* (Psalm 121:4). *"I must work the works of him that sent me, while it is day: the night cometh, when no man can work"* (John 9:4). God does not sleep nor slumber. He is conscious about His task to watch over His people. Eutychus fell asleep while Paul was preaching. This act of indiscipline almost cost him his life. Thanks to God for His mercy!

PRAYER FOCUS

Heavenly Father, help me to be disciplined with the use of my time, and to sleep when it is appropriate in Jesus' name.

October 2

Understanding Night Seasons
Bible Reading: [Psalm 30:1-12]

"...... Weeping may endure for a night, but joy cometh in the morning." [Vs:5]

Night seasons are seasons when everything around us seems to be crumbling or falling apart. When it seems no one cares about our wellbeing. When it seems our future is hopeless. When everyone seems to have abandoned or forsaken us. It is important to note that night seasons happen to everyone, whether believers in Christ or unbelievers.

It is written, *"And he went a little further, and fell on his face, and prayed, saying, O my Father, if it be possible, let this cup pass from me: nevertheless not as I will, but as thou wilt." [Matt.26:39]*. The Psalmist says: *"I am weary with my groaning; all night I make my bed swim. I drench couch with my tears. My eye wastes away because of grief; it grows old because of my enemies" [Psalm 6:6, 7]*.

The Apostle Paul says: *"At my first answer no man stood with me, but all men forsook me: I pray God that it may not be laid to their charge." [2 Tim.4:16]*. Sometimes at night seasons, we are hard pressed on every side *"We are hard pressed on every side, but not crushed; perplexed, but not in despair; persecuted, but not abandoned; struck down, but not destroyed." [2 Cor.4:8]*

Night season is a time to reflect on God's amazing grace, His love, His goodness/kindness, His compassion, His mercy and redemptive power. It's a time to reflect on God's promises. God works His purposes in our lives even during night seasons *"And we know that all things work together for good to them that love God, to them who are the called according to His purpose" [Rom.8:28]*.

PRAYER FOCUS

LORD, help me through night seasons not to compromise my conviction. I put my trust in Your power, grace and unfailing love in Jesus' name.

October 3

Stubborn Faith
Bible Reading: [Dan 6:1-28]

"Now when Daniel knew that the writing was signed, he went home. And in his upper room, with his windows open toward Jerusalem, he knelt down on his knees three times that day, and prayed and gave thanks before his God, as was his custom since early days. Then these men assembled and found Daniel praying and making supplication before his God. And they went before the king, and spoke concerning the king's decree:.." [Vs: 10-12]

Sometimes as believers in Christ, we find ourselves in certain situations that we must exercise stubborn faith. Stubborn faith implies one is having or is determined not to change his attitude or position on something (strong conviction), in spite of good reasons to do so. In a political environment where favoritism gave one the opportunity for advancement, the wicked presidents and princes developed a scheme by which they might rid the kingdom of righteous Daniel. Daniel stood alone, although he knew about the law against praying to anyone except the king.

Some of us have already stopped praying because we have received some threats from strange places especially from neighbors or colleagues with the occult. Some of us had long stopped evangelizing our community because of the nasty experiences we encountered last time. While we try to live at peace with everyone as believers, sometimes conflict with the world, ungodly laws and its authorities cannot be avoided. There are some laws that can be obeyed regardless of the culture in which one lives and some that must not be obeyed by believers. It is always premature to bow to the pressure of ungodly laws/unbelievers because God has power they know nothing about. God has the power to defend His faithful servants and His own reputation.

PRAYER FOCUS

Heavenly Father, I choose today to obey You rather than man. LORD, give me wisdom and grace to do Your will in Jesus' name.

October 4

Perfect Love Casts Out Fear
Bible Reading: [1 John 4:17-21]

"There is no fear in love; but perfect love casteth out fear: because fear hath torment. He that feareth is not made perfect in love." [Vs:18]

We mature daily as our relationship with God grows. We can only have confidence in facing the day of judgement as our love grows more mature and complete in God's love. Many people are afraid of the day of judgement because of a guilty conscience. The day of judgement will be terrifying for those who don't know God. *"And as Paul reasoned of righteousness, temperance, and judgement to come, Felix trembled, and answered, Go thy way for this time; when I have a convenient season, I will call for thee." [Acts 24:25].*

Beloved, are you still waiting for a convenient time to put things right with God?. But God demonstrates His own love toward us, in that while we were still sinners, Christ died for us *[Rom.5:8].* God first loved us in our raw state. Because of His unfailing love, let fear has no place in our lives.

PRAYER FOCUS

Dear heavenly Father, I thank You for Your immeasurable love for me. LORD, I focus on You and trust that Your love bestowed on me will quiet my fears in Jesus' name.

October 5

Stay At Your Post
Bible Reading: [Neh.6:1-9]

So I sent messengers to them, saying, "I am doing a great work, so that I cannot come down. Why should the work cease while I leave it and go down to you?" [Vs:3]

One of the greatest challenges nowadays is for men to stay at their post. The main goal of Satan and his associates is to intimidate, discourage, distract you from your assignment and possibly stop you from working. He will be persistent in organizing an occasion for destruction. Our enemies were trying to make us afraid, saying, *"Their hands will be weakened in the work, and it will not be done"* [Vs:9]

The expression to stay at your post means to do what you should do and not run away from your responsibility. Are you at your post - doing what you are supposed to do, when and where you are supposed to do it? In His defense Jesus said to them, *"My Father is always at his work to this very day, and I too am working"* [John 5:17].

One of the reasons why many can't stay at their post is because they haven't made their assignment or work a priority project. *"I am doing a great work, so that I cannot come down."* Apostle wrote to Timothy, *Stay at your post reading Scripture, giving counsel, and teaching* [1 Tim.4:13-16;MSG]. Paul, a man who stayed at his post now gives his spiritual son what it takes to do same. Everyone called according to God's purpose and grace must show tremendous determination and character to remain steadfast in his or her responsibility. When opposition builds up against you or God's work, depend absolutely on God and victory will be yours.

PRAYER FOCUS

Now therefore, O God, strengthen my hands that I may take my work to completion in Jesus' name.

October 6

Obedience Through The Process
Bible Reading: *[Job.23:10]*

*"But He knows the way that I take;
When He has tested me, I shall come forth as gold."*

It is quite exciting knowing that God has wonderful plans for our lives. However, this can't come to fruition if we don't go through a divine process. God allows us go through a process in order to refine us so that godly character may be fully formed in us. In refining a metal, the raw metal is heated with fire until it melts. The impurities are separated from it and rise to the surface. They are removed leaving a pure metal. That's same with God's refining and purifying process. God is a refiner's fire and takes pleasure seeing us through the process [Mal.3:3]. You can never become a vessel of honor for the Master's use if you haven't been through the process [2 Tim.2:21]. Why many people find it difficult to go through the process is because it always begins with you leaving the familiar ways. I have come to realize that in life, everyone would like to stay in their comfort zone. In the Christian life, that is not the case. Jesus gives us the standard for true discipleship, *"And he said to them all, If any man will come after me, let him deny himself, and take up his cross daily, and follow me."* [Luke 9:23]

The process takes the form of hardships, afflictions, shame, failures, trials etc. It's important to note that the process is designed to cause us to trust God in everything. The fact that you are in the process does not mean that God is not with you. About Joseph, it is written, *"He sent a man before them — Joseph - who was sold as a slave. They hurt his feet with fetters, He was laid in irons, until the time that his word came to pass, the word of the LORD tested him"* [Psalm 105:17-19]. Joseph went through the process and God was with him. *"And the LORD was with Joseph, and he was a prosperous man; and he was in the house of his master the Egyptian"* [Gen.39:2]. As believers, we must stay obedient through the process because it will work out for our good (Rom.8:28). *"Rejoice in hope; patient in tribulation; continuing instant in prayer"* [Rom.12:12].

PRAYER FOCUS

Heavenly Father, I am fully persuaded that Your plans for me are not to harm me but to give me hope and a future. LORD, lead me in Your truth and teach me. Grant me the grace to go through the through the process in Jesus' name.

October 7

The Joy Of lifting Up The Plight Of Men
Bible Reading: [Gen.14:1-24]

"Now when Abram heard that his brother was taken captive, he armed his three hundred and eighteen trained servants who were born in his own house, and went in pursuit as far as Dan....So he brought all the goods, and also brought back his brother Lot and his goods, as well as the women and the people." [Vs: 14,16]

I can hear someone saying, "No one cares about my plight." A plight - is a dangerous, difficult, or otherwise unfortunate/unfavorable situation. Millions of people in the world find themselves in one unfortunate situation or the other. As a captive to Chedorlaomer, Lot faced torture, slavery and possibly death threats. Abraham didn't hesitate to lift up the plight of his nephew when he learned that he was a prisoner. Many in the Body of Christ are nonchalant, indifferent or lack empathy toward the plight of men. They are not moved by people's difficult situations. Peter and John were moved by the plight of the lame man at the gate of the temple. *"Then Peter said, silver and gold have I none; but such as I have given I thee: In the name of Jesus Christ of Nazareth rise up and walk" [Acts.3:6].*

Let's look at the mission statement of our LORD Jesus Christ: *"The Spirit of the LORD is upon me, because he hath anointed me to preach the gospel to the poor; He hath sent me to heal the brokenhearted, To preach deliverance to the captives, and recovering of sight to the blind, to set at liberty them that are bruised, to preach the acceptable year of the LORD" [Lk 4:18-19] "How God anointed Jesus of Nazareth with the Holy Ghost and with power: who went about doing good, and healing all that were oppressed of the devil; for God was with him" [Acts.10:38].*

Like Abraham and our LORD Jesus Christ, you can start from somewhere. Investing five minutes daily to intercede for somebody in a difficult situation(oppressed, depressed, brokenhearted or entangled by the cord of sin: addiction, alcoholism, prostitution etc.). Fasting once a month to cry out to God for mercy and mighty deliverance for a nation at crossroad or at war. Donating goods to the poor, needy, orphans, refugees etc. Donating financially to a worthy cause or charity. It is written, *"Is not this the fast that I have chosen? To loose the bands of wickedness, to undo the heavy burdens, and to let the oppressed go free, and that ye break every yoke?" [Isa.58:6; Jam.1:27]*

PRAYER FOCUS

Heavenly Father, You are the creator of heaven and earth, and the God of all flesh. LORD, there is nothing too hard for You. Oh, that You will stretch out Your mighty hand and cause a turnaround in the life of a loved one for whom Christ died in Jesus' name.

October 8

Doing Nothing Against The Truth But For The Truth
Bible Reading: [2 Cor.13:1-10]

"Now I pray to God that you do no evil, not that we should appear approved, but that you should do what is honorable, though we may seem disqualified. For we can do nothing against the truth, but for the truth" [Vs: 8]

Anyone under the influence of the Spirit of God seeks to do nothing against the great system of truth. Truth must be focused on integrity of life and conversation, opposed to hypocrisy, or scandalous living. In other words, we must own, defend, and practice truth. Any attempt to fight against the truth, is a planned act to fail. It is written, *"Yea, truth faileth; and he that departeth from evil maketh himself a prey: and the LORD saw it, and it displeased him that there was no judgment" (Isa.59:15).* Truth is failing in many marriages, homes, relationships, ministries, churches, businesses, organizations and governments. Do you wonder why things aren't working in many circles today as they ought to? It's because truth is failing. Sin fills the vacuum left when God's truth no longer fills our lives. *"Thy word (truth) have I hid in mine heart, that I might not sin against thee" [Psalm 119:11].*

The Pharisees hated the truth and sought to kill the truth. *"And the Pharisees went forth, and straightway took counsel with the Herodians against him, how they might destroy him"* [Mark 3:6]. *Jesus saith unto him, I am the way, the truth, and the life [John 14:6].* Truth shall prevail, no matter how long it may take. The goal of every believer is not to be sin conscious but to grow in grace, and increase in holiness. "We have far more need to pray that we may not do evil, than that we may not suffer evil" (Matthew Henry). Every disciple must be willing and be determined to do what is right. Exercising discipline of wayward disciples in the Church of God is for the purpose of preaching and defending the truth of the gospel. If truth is lacking from the pulpit, what shall the world do? It is written, *"Sanctify them through thy truth: thy word is truth [John 17:17].*

PRAYER FOCUS

Dear heavenly Father, You are the God of truth. I submit myself to You and embrace the truth of the Gospel in its totality. LORD, enable me to continue in truth, live in it, walk in it, proclaim it, and worship You in Spirit and in truth in Jesus' name.

October 9

Inseparable Twin Pillars In Daily Life
"The Power Of The Word & Prayer"

"But we will give ourselves continually to prayer, and to the ministry of the word." [Acts 6:4]

If you desire to enjoy your everyday life, you must create a special place for the word of God in your life. The length of time you allocate for the word daily tells us how important the word of God is to you. It is written, *"Your words were found, and I ate them, and your words became to me a joy and the delight of my heart; for I have been called by Your name, O LORD God of hosts." [Jer.15:16]*. You can't devote yourself to prayer when you have not yet devoted yourself to the LORD. You can't devote yourself to the LORD when you have not yet devoted yourself to the word. *"How then shall they call on Him in whom they have not believed? How shall the believed in Him of whom they have not heard? .....So then faith comes by hearing, and hearing by the word" [Rom.10:14&17]*. The word of God is life to those who find it and health to all their flesh *[Prov.4:22]*. For the word of God is quick, and powerful, and sharper than any two-edged sword, piercing even to the dividing asunder of soul and spirit, and of the joints and marrow, and is a discerner of the thoughts and intents of the heart *[Heb.4:12]*

If prayer is mere communication with God, everyone would like to indulge in it. However, many don't know what it takes for prayers to be answered. *"Ye ask, and receive not, because ye ask amiss, that ye may consume it upon your lusts" (James 4:3)*. *"And this is the confidence that we have in Him, that, if we ask anything according to His will, He heareth us: And if we know that He hears us, whatsoever we ask, we know that we have the petitions that we desired of Him" [1 John 5:14-15]*. The place of prayer transcend or goes beyond mere communication with God. In the place of prayer, we must learn how to fellowship with God. Fellowshipping with God in prayer brings heaven's joy to the heart of man. Fellowship comes from the Greek word 'Koinonia' which means communion with God. *"these I will bring to my holy mountain and give them joy in my house of prayer...." [Isa.56:7]*.

There is tremendous power in the place of prayer. The place of prayer is the epicenter of global impact and transformation *"......, The effectual fervent prayer of a righteous man availeth much" [James 5:16]*.

PRAYER FOCUS

Dear heavenly Father, Your presence is indispensable. LORD, I renew my devotion to the place of prayer and the word TODAY! Use me as a vessel of honor to demonstrate Your power to the world in Jesus' name.

"I fear the prayer of John Knox more than all the assembled armies of Europe." Mary, Queen of Scots. Quote, *"LORD, give me Scotland or I die! [John Knox]*

October 10

Thousand Instructors In Christ But One Father
Bible Reading: [1 Cor.4:14-21]

"For though ye have ten thousand instructors in Christ, yet have ye not many fathers: for in Christ Jesus I have begotten you through the gospel." [Vs:15]

Every true father has the responsibility to instruct his children in the way they should go. Like earthly fathers, so do spiritual fathers. A true father affirm his genuine concern for the well-being of his children. Any child who cannot differentiate between the voice of his father and that of other parent is confused. Likewise a sheep that can't differentiate between a hireling (a person who works for reward) and a good shepherd. Jesus said, *"My sheep listen to my voice; I know them, and they follow me" [John 10:27]*. The Corinthian church had a challenge because the arrogance of some, had caused contentions among them. As a result of countless tutors pulling them to and fro with every wind of teaching, Paul, as a Christ-sent apostle had the obligation to correct matters in a manner by which only a Christ-sent apostle could. Because he started the Corinthian Church, he could be trusted to have its best interests at heart. *"Therefore, I urge you, be imitators of me" (Vs:16)*. Paul wanted them to mimic his life-style. He had modeled a life style after Christ and was confident to tell others to follow his examples.

What about you? *"But you, Timothy, certainly know what I teach, and how I live, and what my purpose in life is. You know my faith, my patience, my love, and my endurance" [2 Tim.3:10]*. Some people talk about faith, they may know all the right words to say, but their lives don't reflect God's power. There is a clear distinction between knowing the right words and living them out. Beloved, let your life show that God's power is really working in you.

PRAYER FOCUS

Heavenly Father, the gift of a spiritual father is a blessing from you. LORD, I acknowledge spiritual authority and pray that I will be aware of Your presence at all times in Jesus' name.

October 11

God Shows No Partiality
Bible Reading: [Acts.10:34-43]

Then Peter opened his mouth and said: "In truth I perceive that God shows no partiality. But in every nation whoever fears Him and works righteousness is accepted by Him." [Vs:34-35]

Partiality is unfair bias in favor of one person or thing. In every nation the longing souls are restless for God. It is the responsibility of everyone to get their minds properly renewed according to the knowledge and revelation that is in the Word. Oftentimes the people of the world show special considerations but it is not so with God. *"Who shows no partiality to princes nor regards the rich above the poor, for they all are the work of His hands" [Job.34:19].* Most of the early believers were Jews, and to them it was a serious offense even to think of associating with Gentiles. That has not changed much in this present world. God accepts everybody from race, tribe, class, color, language and culture. The good news of Christ is for everyone! *"All that the Father giveth me shall come to Me; and him that cometh to me I will in no wise cast out" [John 6:37].* Any person who will reverently obey and fear God is accepted.

Like Peter who struggled later with partiality, many believers in Christ especially those in the western world are playing this hypocrisy. *"When Cephas came to Antioch, I opposed him to his face, because he stood condemned. For certain men came from James, he used to eat with the Gentiles. But when they arrived, he began to draw back and separate himself from the Gentiles because he was afraid of those who belonged to the circumcision group. The other Jews joined him in his hypocrisy, so that by their hypocrisy even Barnabas was led astray"(Gal.2:11-14).* Salvation is by grace through faith in Christ. It's the favor of God. Peter knew the right thing to do but he was driven by fear of what his Jewish believers would think of him. We shouldn't compromise the truth of God's word for any reason whatsoever. Changing our convictions of the word to please men is the worst thing to do. If you are persuaded that someone is doing harm to himself/herself or the Church of God, then open rebuke is better than secret love *[Prov.27:5]*. Are you committed to show someone the right way to Christ TODAY?

PRAYER FOCUS

Dear heavenly Father, I put my trust in the sufficiency of Christ to live the Christian life without showing partiality. LORD, may Your love fill my heart and compel me in Jesus' name.

October 12

When Men Choose To Ignore Wise Or Godly Counsel
Bible Reading: [Acts 27:9-24]

"Now when much time had been spent, and sailing was now dangerous because the Fast was already over, Paul advised them, saying, "Men, I perceive that this voyage will end with disaster and much loss, not only of the cargo and ship, but also our lives." Nevertheless the centurion was more persuaded by the helmsman (ship captain) and owner of the ship than by the things spoken by Paul." [Vs:9-11]

Often life presents us with challenges and decisions that are not easy to handle or make on our own. *"Where no counsel is, the people fall: but in the multitude of counselors there is safety" [Prov.11:14].* Wise counsel is a gift of advice that enables an individual to avoid poor decisions and mistakes. Wise counsel helps us to halt or break any bad cycle of severe consequences from poor decisions. *"The fear of the LORD is the beginning of wisdom, and knowledge of the Holy One is understanding" [Prov.9:10].*

Godly counsel can only be received by those who maintain an attitude of humility. Some of us may find it difficult to receive godly counsel because it is coming from people we are richer, more educated, older and more experienced than them. Sometimes when godly counsel is against our wishes or desires, we despise it. Paul had realized what would happen if they went on. He gave a warning to the ship's officers, but they and the Roman officer were unlikely to listen to an imprisoned Jewish rabbi with no experience as a seaman. *"No one had eaten for a long time. Finally, Paul called the crew together and said, "Men, you should have listened to me in the first place and not left Crete. You would have avoided all these damage and loss" (Vs:21).* Beloved, If you had listen to godly counsel, you would have avoided a failed relationship, a broken marriage, bankruptcy, accident, demotion, political scandals, ministry/spiritual crises etc.

Make up your mind to listen keenly to a godly person, (not just a religious folk) who will help you assess a perilous situation, pray with you, seek guidance, decide on action, and lead you in solving difficult problems. Paul says, *"For there stood by me this night an angel of the God whom I belong and serve. Therefore, take heart, men, for I believe God that it will be just as it was told me" [Vs:23,25].* Wise counsel is all you need today, don't despise it!

PRAYER FOCUS

Heavenly Father, Your Word [godly counsel] is a beacon of light. Bless me with a teachable spirit to learn, a humble heart to receive and grace to live by it in Jesus' name.

October 13

Recognizing The Boundaries Of Your Divine Assignment
Bible Reading: [Eph.3:1-13]

"For this reason I Paul, the prisoner of Christ Jesus for you Gentiles— if indeed you have heard of the stewardship of the grace of God that is given to me for you; how that by revelation He made known to me the mystery, as I wrote before in few words." [Eph.3:1-3]

God does not operate by trial and error. He created each and every one for a unique purpose. Everyone called according to God's purpose is a solution to something. God has endowed us with talents/gifts and there is a location where He wants us. You can only impact your world through your assignment. *The starting point is to surrender your life to Christ and be obedient to His voice [Jn.10:27].* Your success lies in finding your place in God's big plan. It's most important to note that God is meticulous in the way He does things. He is very careful and precise. God geographically assigns people (unique place) and specifically assigns them (unique work). You are not designed to do just anything but specific things well.

Paul knew his assignment and observed his boundaries. Then he said to me, *"Depart, for I will send you far from here to the Gentiles" [Acts.22:21].* Likewise Jesus Christ — He answered, *"I was sent only to the lost sheep of Israel" [Matt.15:24].* The greatest challenge/confusion in the Body of Christ is that many don't know their assignment and location. As a result, Christian service is done haphazardly.

God chose Paul and gave him a revelation of his assignment — to share the gospel with the Gentiles. He gave him the power to do it so that the Gentiles should now be included in God's family. *"For I neither received it from man, nor was I taught it, but I received it through the revelation of Jesus Christ" [Gal.1:12].* You can't do much more than your capacity or the grace God has given you. *"But to each one of us grace has been given as Christ apportioned it i.e. according to the measure of Christ's gift" [Eph.4:7].* When you operate in your measure of grace and where God has assigned you, you are bound to be successful. When man gives you a revelation that is not from God, the same man will dictate what you should do and where you should go. It's impossible to reach your best if you operate outside God's purpose and grace.

Obedience to your divine assignment will attract divine assistances: favor, finances, helpers and angelic hosts. Make your divine assignment your top-most priority TODAY!

PRAYER FOCUS

Heavenly Father, here I am to do Your will. LORD, I ask that You will reveal Your detailed plan to me every step of the way and give me the ability to share the good news in Jesus' name.

October 14

Leaving A Heritage Of Obedience To God
Bible Reading: [2 Kings 10:18-30]

"Then Jehu and Johonadab the son of Rechab went into the temple of Baal, and said to the worshipers of Baal, "Search and see that no servants of the LORD are here with you, but only the worshipers of Baal." Thus Jehu destroyed Baal from Israel." [Vs:23,28]

Heritage can refer to practices or characteristics that are passed down through the years, from one generation to the next. Beloved, the kind of heritage you leave behind when you are gone will determine what your children will follow. *".... Also their children and their children's Children have continued doing as their fathers did, even to this day" [2 Kgs 17:41].* If parents are serving Baal, it's most likely that their children will continue in their footsteps. If parents are dedicated to improving their community and excellence in public service — so will their children. If parents had great compassion or empathy for the poor/orphans/needy, If parents are dropouts from school, If parents are drug addicts, If parents are giving into prostitution, If parents are drunkards, If parents are men of faith in God - most likely will be their children. *"The heritage a parent leaves may be positive or negative, or a mixture of both, just as the estate a parent leaves may include assets and liabilities" [Source unknown]*

Abraham is one among many in the Scriptures who left a heritage of obedience to God. *"He redeemed us in order that the blessing given to Abraham might come to the Gentiles through Christ Jesus, so that by faith we might receive the promise of the Spirit" [Gal.3:14].* Another example of a man who left a rich godly heritage was Johonadab the son of Rechab. For 2000 years, his descendants obeyed a special vow to abstain from wine *[Jer.35]*. They remained steadfast in their commitment while others were breaking covenant with God. God used them as an example of a people who will not compromise their conviction, by sending Jeremiah to tempt them with wine in order to demonstrate their commitment and dedication to God. God knew they will keep their vow. The Rechabites were true example and presented a great testimony of a people determine to keep their lives pure by living apart from the pressures and temptations of society. You can make a positive difference in your world TODAY!

PRAYER FOCUS

Dear heavenly Father, I am convinced that what a person sows, that he will also reap *[Gal.6:7]*. LORD, I'm determined to leave a heritage of obedience to You for my posterity to follow — enable me by Your power in Jesus' name.

October 15

Snare Of Mixing Faith With Selfish Ambitions
Bible Reading: [Acts 8:4-25]

"And when Simon saw that through the laying on of the apostles' hands the Holy Ghost was given, he offered them money, saying, "Give me this power also, that anyone on whom I lay my hands may receive the Holy Spirit. But Peter said to him, "Your money perish with you, because you thought that the gift of God could be purchased with money!"
[Vs:18-20]

Many times in history people have mixed faith with personal ambitions. In the world in which we live, everything seems to have a price. Because of bribery, corruption and materialism, many (politicians, businessmen, Christian leaders etc.) like Simon have brought the same mindset into the Church of God and using faith to their own selfish ends and not for the sake of Christ.

Scripture says such a heart is not right with God - it is filled with selfish ambition. Peter knew the motives of Simon and condemned it. Simon who had astonished the people of Samaria by the practice of sorcery before, wanted to regain his position of power and greatness among the people. His bitterness had poisoned his mind *(Heb.12:15)*. *"Every way of a man is right in his own eyes: but the LORD weighs the heart." (Prov.21:2)*. God wants us to thoroughly examine our hearts and motives today!

The gifts and calling of God cannot be purchased with money. No amount of money can buy salvation, forgiveness of sin or the anointing of the Holy Spirit. These can only come by repentance and faith in Christ. What is commonplace in the Christendom today is that many are selling the gift/grace of God and many are offering money to buy/pay for their deliverance, healing, breakthrough etc. It is very important to note that it is not a problem to bless a vessel that God is using in cash or in kind. However, if money is demanded as a condition for breakthrough prayers, then it is not right! Peter said to him, *"Your money perish with you, because you thought that the gift of God could be purchased with money"[Vs:20]*

"Heal the sick, cleanse the lepers, raise the dead, cast out devils: freely ye have received, freely give" [Matt.10:8].

PRAYER FOCUS

Dear heavenly Father, I acknowledge the fact that it is by grace I have been saved, through faith. I surrender my heart to You to conform myself to the submissive nature of a true disciple of Christ in Jesus' name. Amen

October 16

Being Zealous For The Right Thing, With The Right Motive
Bible Reading: [Psalm 69:7-13]

"I have become a stranger to my brothers and an alien to my mother's children; because zeal for Your house has eaten me up, and the reproaches of those who reproach You have fallen on me." [Vs:8-9]

Zeal is great energy or enthusiasm in pursuit of a cause or an objective. Everyone has a zeal for something. Some it will be a zeal for money, Some zeal for pleasure, some zeal for chasing after men or women, some zeal for acquiring material things, some zeal for work and some zeal for the LORD. It is dangerous to have zeal without knowledge *[Prov.19:2; Hosea 4:6]*. Jesus Christ demonstrated great zeal when he threw the money changers out of the temple (Matt.21:12). *"And His disciples remembered that it was written, 'the zeal of thine house hath eaten me up'" [John.2:17].*

Zeal also means, diligently striving to do the good works that Christ has given us to do *(2 Tim.1:9; Eph.2:10)*. Zeal is the fuel of our passion. Despite all the calamities that were inflicted on David, the zeal of God consumed him. Every day presents numerous opportunities for us to put our zeal for God in action. Why are people no more zealous for Christ? The answer is simple; there are many competing interests with God's love in our lives today than ever! In the world in which we live, those who would commit themselves totally to the LORD will likely be ridiculed by those who are comfortable with indifference (lukewarmness). Even David who denied himself normal comforts to seek God in prayer, was ridiculed by the wicked.

If zeal for God truly consumes us, we will act upon every opportunity that is presented. *"Know now that there shall fall unto the earth nothing of the word of the LORD, which the LORD spake concerning the house of Ahab: for the LORD hath done that which he spake by his servant Elijah. And Jehu said to Jehonadab, come with me, and see my zeal for the LORD. So they made him ride in his chariot" [2 kings 10:10,16]*. The zeal of Jehu at the time was a holy anger to ensure that the descendants of Ahab will not continue to promote the evil of Ahab and Jezebel in Israel *[1 Kings 18:16-19]*. Jehonadab also demonstrated his zeal by separating himself and his family from the materialistic, idol-worshiping culture at the time.

PRAYER FOCUS

Dear heavenly Father, It's Your desire that I should have zeal with knowledge and be committed to every good work. Help me live out my calling with great zeal and passion in Jesus' name. *"Never be lacking in zeal but keep your spiritual fervor, serving the LORD" [Rom.12:11; Gal.4:18].*

October 17

The Proven Authority Over Natural Forces
Bible Reading: [Matt.8:23-27]

"And He said unto them, why are ye fearful, O ye of little faith? Then He arose, and rebuked the winds and the sea; and there was a great calm" [Vs:26]

Often physical forces like storms threaten the very existence of humanity. These storms come in different forms. Though there was an impending great storm, Jesus fell asleep on a cushion. As storms that were common on the sea of Galilee, so are the storms of life. We face some storms in life unexpectedly. However, if we know who God is, we will understand that He controls both the storms of nature and the storms of the troubled heart *"...But the people that do know their God shall be strong, and do exploits." [Dan.11:32;1 John 5:4]*

As experienced fishermen, the disciples lacked faith in Jesus, despite the many opportunities they had to experience his power and authority. It is important to note that the storms of life do challenge us to entrust our lives to Jesus for protection and deliverance. That is what true discipleship is all about. Active faith that depends on the Master, the Author and Finisher of our faith *[Heb.12:2]*. Those who walk by faith will, like the Messiah, experience opposition (i.e. cost of discipleship). However, faith is the moving cause of all actions and faith moves mountains!

Teacher, do You not care that we are perishing? The good news is that Jesus is concerned with every storm we face in life. The fact that He may be silent does not mean he is not working behind the scene. He knows the strength of every storm that comes our way and knows he has power over the elements of nature. He has control over events in the supernatural realm and the realm of man *[Col.1:16]*. The moment we come to the understanding that Jesus is the Creator of all that exists, then we will realize that nothing is outside his power to control. Only in his presence will there be great emotional calm in our lives *[Phil.4:7]*. *"But the men marveled, saying, what manner of man is this, that even the winds and the sea obey Him!" [Vs:27]*.

PRAYER FOCUS

Dear heavenly Father, I'm fully persuaded that Jesus is God and Creator of everything that exists *[Jn.1:3]*. In the name of Jesus Christ, I rebuke the wind and command any satanic storm ranging against my life/family/Church to be still.

"....when the enemy shall come in like a flood, the Spirit of the LORD shall lift up a standard." [Isa.59:19]

October 18

The Power Of Empathy
Bible Reading: [Mark 6:30-44]
"The key that unlocks the door to our kindness and compassion."

> *"And Jesus, when He came out saw a great multitude and was moved with compassion for them, because they were like sheep not having a shepherd. So He began to teach them many things —— But He answered and said to His disciples, "You give them something to eat." And they said to Him, " Shall we go and buy two hundred denarii worth of bread and give them something to eat?" [Vs:34,37]*

Empathy is the ability to understand and share the feelings of another. Compassion and sympathy all have to do with having passion (feeling) for another person because of his or her suffering. Empathy is the feeling of actually participating in the suffering of another. *"Rejoice with those who rejoice; mourn with those who mourn" [Rom.12:15]*. Often we miss opportunities to relieve others' pain, most likely because we are not aware of others' needs or we are not practicing empathy. When it was getting late, the disciples asked the LORD to send the crowd away but Jesus said, *"You feed them."* Remember that they were a nation of people who had not been spiritually led for years and thus sought someone to give them guidance.

While His disciples wondered how they could feed the multitude, they failed to understand that the power and faith in Christ they had to cast out demons could enable them effect divine provision. It is important to note that the LORD will never ask you to do what you can't, without his power. *"....for without Me you can do nothing." [John 15:5]*. Oftentimes our response to matters of life only takes into consideration what we are capable of doing — not considering Jesus' power. What an error! Jesus said, *"You are in error because you do not know the Scriptures or the power of God." [Matt.22:29]*

God takes pleasure in manifesting His glory in us and through us but our lack of understanding sometimes is a hindering factor. Let's begin to see what is possible with God as we empathize with others. When facing a seemingly impossible task, do what you can and ask God to do the rest. He makes the impossible happen. With five loaves and two fish, five thousand people ate, were filled and took up twelve baskets full of fragment (leftovers) and of fish. Having lived a human life, our LORD can and does empathize with all of our weaknesses. *"For we have not an high priest which cannot be touched with the feelings of our infirmities; but was in all points tempted like as we are, yet without sin." [Heb.4:15]*. Jesus was truly the Son of God who had the power over creation [Jn 1:1,2].

PRAYER FOCUS

Dear heavenly Father, You know how we are formed and You remember that we are dust. LORD, help me to be sensitive to the need and plight of others in Jesus' name.

October 19

Why Sit We Here Until We Die
Bible Reading: [2 Kings 7:1-20]

"Now there were four men with leprosy at the entrance of the city gate. They said to each other, "why stay here until we die? If we say, 'We'll go into the city' - the famine is there, and we will die. And if we stay here, we will die. So let's go over to the camp of the Arameans and surrender. If they spare us, we live; if they kill us, then we die." [Vs:3-4]

Like the inhabitants of Samaria, sometimes we are so preoccupied with our problems such that we cannot even think outside the box. As a matter of fact, there was a serious problem in the land: famine that led to extreme scarcity of food, prices of food and other commodities spiking, as a result, people could not afford the very basic necessities of life. Negative circumstances will always come but instead of us overwhelmed or crushed by them, developing an attitude of expectancy is very important. Have you come to a crossroad in life and you think your situation is beyond God's ability to rescue? Beloved, that only demonstrates a lack of faith. *"God is able to do exceedingly abundantly above all that we ask or think according to His mighty power at work in us [Eph.3:20;Isa.30:21].*

Hopes were gone for the inhabitants of Samaria and even the officers at the gate doubted the prophetic word from Elisha that food will be sold for normal price the following day. Remember that whenever there is seemingly impossible situation: health crises, marital and academic challenges, financial meltdown/bankruptcy, food scarcity etc., and our doubts are the strongest, God can open the floodgates of heaven. *Why sitting here until we die?* The four lepers who sad at the gate of Samaria were determined to face the reality of their desperate situation: the famine in the land and the presence of the Syrian army at the border. *A step of faith is enough to change the status quo! [Matt.17:20].* Whenever we make up our minds to rise up in faith, our situation or enemies will see the finger of God *[Exod.8:19]* or hear a miraculous noise caused by God. He is committed to honoring the faith of His Children in conformity with His word.

PRAYER FOCUS

Dear heavenly Father, I am fully persuaded that You have not changed by the power of Your name.*[Heb.13:8]*. I look up You for another mighty demonstration of Your power and provision in Jesus' name.

October 20

Be It Unto Me According To Thy Word
Bible Reading: [Luke 1:26-38]

*"For with God nothing will be impossible.
And Mary said, Behold the handmaid of the LORD;
be it unto me according to thy word.
And the angel departed from her."* [Luke 1:37-38, KJV]

When all is outside the control and power of man, God is able. Talking about virgin birth is seemingly impossible to the human mind especially to medical practitioners who know how babies are born. You may be going through humanly impossible circumstances at the moment and wonder if there will be light at the end of the tunnel. Sorrow seems to weigh you down and dims your hope. Remember the words of the prophet, *"Ah LORD God! behold, thou hast made the heaven and the earth by thy great power and stretched out arm, and there is nothing too hard for thee:"* [Jer.32:17]. I strongly believe that God is going to cause a turnaround to your situation this season. He speaks from a turnaround perspective, so do not close down any avenue of God's provision in your ordeal or disappointment.

It is worth noting that Mary did not earn the right to be chosen for this unique work of God to bring the Redeemer into the world. With many young women of her time with the same spiritual qualities, she found favor with God. Think about her situation: accepting what the angel told her could lead to much pain, her peers would ridicule her, her fiancé could come close to leaving her *[Matt.1:19]*. Nevertheless, she had a strong conviction of what the angel said. God is able to do beyond what we can imagine. She said to the angel, *"how can this be, since I do not know a man?"* The Holy Spirit's power will make a difference! All you need to do is to submit to God's will. He can work out His plan through you if you don't limit His choices. Is there a word or promise in the Scriptures about your situation? It is written, *"Forever, O LORD, thy word is settled in heaven. Thy faithfulness is unto all generations:..."* [Psalm 119:89-90].

PRAYER FOCUS

Dear heavenly Father, I know that You can do all things; no purpose of Yours can be thwarted. Be it unto me according to Your word in Jesus' name *[Job.42:2]*.

October 21

To Whom Much Is Given, Much Is Required
Bible Reading: [Luke 12:41-48]

"And the LORD said, "Who then is that faithful and wise steward, whom his master will make ruler over his household, to give them their portion of food in due season? Blessed is that servant whom his master will find so doing when he comes." [Vs:42-43]

True disciples of Christ are required to exercise faithfulness and wisdom with the truth that has been revealed to them. God will not hold any true disciple of His responsible for gifts He has not given him. It is expected of those who have been blessed with talents, wealth, finance, knowledge, time, and the like to use these well to glorify God and benefit others. The second coming of Christ is certain but when He shall come, will He find you doing what He assigned you to do? Faithfulness requires that we manage those things which God has entrusted to our care wisely and unselfishly. We are held responsible to know our Master's will. *"He has shown you, O man, what is good; And what does the LORD requires of you —but to do justly, to love mercy, and to walk humbly with your God" [Micah 6:8].*

Beloved, ignorance is no excuse. Those who are ignorant of the will of God will be lost. They will face punishment because they have no remedy for the sin that separated them from God. Remember that the law of sin and death cannot deliver anyone from the bondage of sin *[Rom.8:1-2]*. *"Truly, these times of ignorance God overlooked, but now commands all men everywhere to repent, because He has appointed a day on which He will judge the world in righteousness by the Man whom He has ordained,.." [Acts.17:30-31].* Salvation therefore is only in Christ *[Acts.4:12;Eph.2:8]*. We must be ready for His coming. Those who are in Christ have been granted the abundant grace of God, the Word of God, and the gifts of the Holy Spirit *[Rom.12:6-8]*. *"As each one has received a gift, minister it to one another, as good stewards of the manifold grace of God." [1 Pet.4:10].* Be a watchful and faithful steward of the manifold grace of God TODAY!

PRAYER FOCUS

LORD, I commit myself to use the resources, talents/gifts, given me to serve humanity in Jesus' name.

"I thank Christ Jesus our LORD, who has given me strength, that He considered me trustworthy, appointing me to His service" [1 Tim.1:12].

October 22

Let's Rise Up And Build
Bible Reading: [Nehemiah 2:11-20]

"And I told them of the hand of my God which had been good upon me, and also the King's words that he had spoken to me. So the said, "Let us rise up and build." Then they set their hands to this good work. [Vs:18]

The statement 'let's rise up and do something' is to assume a standing position after lying, sitting, stagnating or delaying. Has God put burden in your heart for a given task? Are you trying to cope with your situation or you truly want to make a difference? As a matter of fact, fear has stopped or paralyzed many from rising up. I would like you to know that if God has called you to a task, He will help you to accomplish it. When we fail to pray, difficult decisions don't fall into proper perspectives and as a result, appropriate actions don't follow. Acknowledging the fact that the hand of God is upon one's life is the first step for a successful mission. *"Except the LORD build the house, they labor in vain that build it:..."* [Psalm 127:1;KJV]. By wisdom a house is built, and through understanding it is established [Prov.24:3]. Without God's strength, our efforts will be in vain. Commit thy works unto the LORD, and thy thoughts shall be established [Prov.16:3]. When God's purposes are at work, don't fail to trust Him for success. *"Then said the LORD unto me, thou has well seen: for I will hasten my word to perform it."* [Jer.1:12].

Preparation, planning and survey are key elements to achieving a great task. Why rush into a project without firsthand information and a realistic strategy? Some who are too spiritual and zealous may think that faith is the key! Of course, faith is important but zeal without knowledge will cause us to make mistakes. *"For which of you, intending to build a tower, sitteth not down first, and counted the cost, whether he have sufficient to finish it?* [Luke 14:28]. In Nehemiah's days, city walls were essential. They offered security and were a symbol of strength and peace.

He was burdened because Jerusalem did not look like the city of the great King *[Ps 48:2]*. The damage on the walls of Jerusalem was too extensive and Nehemiah had to make thoughtful considerations and put in place a concrete plan of action.

A clear vision provides solution *[Prov.29:18]*. No true vision exist without resistant from an opponent or an enemy. The enemy will do all to undermine one's credibility. Sometimes when an enemy mocks your work, it is evidence that you are doing the right thing. Your enemy will never cherish your progress. Sometimes we face a lot of resistance because we voice our intentions to our enemies even before the project begins. Like Nehemiah, be confident about this, *"The God of heaven Himself will prosper us: therefore we His servants will arise and build, but you (my enemies) have no heritage or right or memorial in Jerusalem."* [Vs:20]

PRAYER FOCUS

Dear heavenly Father, I am fully persuaded that You are working in me and through me to accomplish the project You have put in my heart *[Phil.2:13]*. LORD, I pledge my resources, time, knowledge, experience and skills where duty calls in Jesus' name.

October 23

Time Has Not Changed Human Attitudes
Bible Reading: [Judges 17:1-13]

"In those days there was no King in Israel; everyone did what was right in his own eyes." "Then Micah said, "Now I know that the LORD will be good to me, since I have a Levite as priest!" [Vs: 6,13]

The attitude that prevailed in the days of Micah is similar to today's prevailing attitude. The Bible says, *"everyone did what was right in his own eyes."* Beloved, are your eyes open to see the double standards in the world and Christendom today? Youths are doing what is right in their own eyes; government officials are doing what is right in their own eyes; religious leaders are doing what is right in their own eyes; women and men are doing what is right in their own eyes.

The truth is that God has not left our conduct and opinions up to us. God has given us standards! Anyone who has not submitted to God will end up doing whatever seems right in his eyes. *"For God is not the author of confusion, but of peace, as in all churches of the saints"* [1 Cor.14:33].

This generation has so much given into idolatry. Idolaters are those who have created a god after their own imagination and religious behavior after their own desires. *"Having a form of godliness, but denying the power thereof: from such turn away."* [2 Tim.3:5]. God will never bless any idolatrous belief and behavior of ours no matter how best we make it attractive.

Often, our good intentions are not good enough! The decline of society's standards does not mean we should conform to it *[Rom.12:2]*. Like in the days of Micah, many have become the hired hand *[John 10:12]*. They are not called and commissioned, but love the filthy lucre in the form of monthly paycheck. The Lord admonishes true shepherds to *Care for the flock that God has entrusted to their care. Watch over it willingly, not grudgingly — not for what you will get out of it, but because you are eager to serve God."* [1 Pet.5:2]. Everyone seems to put his or her own interest first. To know what God expects of us and to have the strength of doing it, we need to draw closer to God in prayer and His word daily.

PRAYER FOCUS

Dear heavenly Father, thank You for the power of the life—giving Spirit of Christ that has freed me from the power of sin and death. LORD, I am fully persuaded that You will perfect your purpose for me today in Jesus' name.

October 24

Our Present Help In Times Of Trouble
Bible Reading: [Psalm 46:1-10]

"God is our refuge and strength, a very present help in trouble. Therefore will not we fear, though the earth be removed, and though the mountains be carried into the midst of the sea;" [Vs:1-2]

Life is full of struggles and troubles. However, some lessons are only learned in the place of trouble. Sometimes, in order for God to get our attention and turn us back to Him, He must take us to the valley of trouble before we can find the door of hope. Webster's dictionary defines trouble as distress, affliction, danger, or annoyance. It goes on to define it as pain, disease or malfunction; the cause of disturbance, to inconvenience or bother. The world has those to whom it looks for protection, and guidance in the time of trouble. Believers have in God their refuge from the storms and distress of life. He is not merely a temporal retreat; he is our eternal refuge and can provide strength in any circumstance. The courage of God's people rests in the fact that God has control over all things. He says,

"Be still, and know that I am God; I will be exalted among the nations, I will be exalted in the earth." (Vs:10). May God be exalted in your situation in Jesus' name.

In the valley of trouble we must walk by faith, not by sight. While we may consider trouble as a threat to our existence, there are some important lessons we can learn during troubled times that will help shape our lives. Trouble enables us to be humble in order to learn the ways of God. *"It was good for me to be afflicted so that I learn your decrees."[Ps.119:71].* Some of us have had to learned the act of intercession because of trouble. Only trouble can effectively change the way we appreciate God's blessings. Sometimes, only trouble can draw out what is in our own heart and show our true mettle to others around us. A lady once received these words from Samuel Rutherford in her trouble, *"Your heart has been pierced open by this affliction to show what is really in your heart."* The must reassuring fact is that God is able to transform every valley of trouble into a door of hope and expectations. *"I will return her vineyards to her and transform the valley of trouble into a gateway of hope...," [Hosea 2:15]*

PRAYER FOCUS

Dear heavenly Father, I'm fully convinced that even in the valley of trouble You are with me. LORD, grant me the grace to face all demanding situations in a spirited and resilient way in Jesus' name.

October 25

Your Circle Of Friends Will Influence Who You Become
Bible Reading: [1 Kings 12:1-20]

"Then King Rehoboam consulted the elders who stood before his father Solomon while he still lived, and he said, "How do you advise me to answer these people?" And they spoke to him, saying, "If you will be a servant to these people today, and serve them, and answer them, and speak good words to them, then they will be your servants forever." But he rejected the advice which the elders had given him, and consulted the young men who had grown up with him, who stood before him." [Vs:6-8]

God does not intend any one of us becomes a mediocre or failure in life. His thoughts toward us are good, to give us hope and future. How then can God work His purpose concerning a man who chooses to surround himself with people whose lifestyle is not consistent with God's standards? *"As iron sharpens iron, so a man sharpens the countenance of his friend"[Prov.27:17]*. There is a mental sharpness that comes from being around good people. The minds of the elders would have helped king Rehoboam see his ideas with new clarity, refine them, and shape them into brilliant insights. For the most part, the negative influence comes when one surrounds himself with people who focus on issues involving their ego. The young men who surrounded the King were those who were spoiled by the lavish living of the king's court, and thus did not want to give up their lifestyle. You may wonder why people don't give up many bad habits or attitudes!

Your life is a sum total of all the decisions you have ever made whether good or bad.

Rehoboam's decision to heed the advice of his younger advisers was disastrous. It led to the secession of the northern tribes, and thus his kingdom was divided. Choose today to be around discussion partners who can challenge you and stimulate your thoughts. Its written, *"Let us consider how to provoke one another to love and good works," [Heb.10:24]*. Two friends who bring their good ideas together can help each other become sharper. They complement one another by correction when each stumbles. *"Finally, brethren, whatsover things are true, whatsoever things are honest, whatsover things are just, whatsoever things are pure, whatsoever things are lovely, whatsoever things are of good report; if there be any virtue, and if there be any praise, think on these things." [Phil.4:8]*. May the God of peace be with you in Jesus' name.

PRAYER FOCUS

LORD, may You bless me with wise counselors and covenant partners that will influence my destiny for Your glory in Jesus' name. *[Prov.15:22; 1 Cor.15:33]*

October 26

Going Yonder To Worship
Bible Reading: [Gen.22:1-19]

"And Abraham said unto his young men, Abide ye here with the ass; and I and the lad will go yonder and worship, and come again to you." [Gen.22:5]

There is no better example of a true worshipper than that revealed in our text. There can be no true worship without obedience and sacrifice. It's obvious that obeying God is often a struggle because it may mean giving up something we truly want or like. Basically, worship is an expression of admiration and adoration. We worship God for who He is. Like Abraham, when we can't reconcile in our mind what God is saying, let's only do what He commands us to do and leave the future to Him.

By going yonder to worship we are not talking about you traveling a long distance to a designated place like Abraham did 50 miles to mount Moriah. Jesus sharing His thoughts with the Samaritan woman said, *"Our fathers worship in this mountain; and ye say, that in Jerusalem is the place where men ought to worship——But the hour cometh, and now is, when the true worshippers shall worship the Father in spirit and in truth: for the Father seeketh such to worship Him." [John.14:20,23]*. Going yonder— we are talking about you sacrificing your own will and surrendering it to God. Remember that the sacrifice that pleases God is a heartbroken of self-will, a heart surrendered to God *[Ps.40:6-8;51:7]*. When God tested Abraham's faith, his immediate and unquestionable obedience was amazing. God is giving us a bigger opportunity today to obey Him and place on the altar of sacrifice what is so precious to our heart. Because worship is a spiritual act, the word of God urges us in view of God's mercy, to offer our bodies as a living sacrifice, holy and pleasing to God *[Rom.13:1]*.

Going yonder to worship means freely willing to offer the best to God against the odds. True worshippers of God know that everything belongs to God and hold nothing back but obediently give Him what He asks *"And they exceeded our expectations: they gave themselves first of all to the LORD and then by the will of God also to us." [2 Cor.8:5]*. A true worshipper does not go to God with the aim that He will provide His need. He goes to God because it's a privilege and honor to be in His presence. God in direct response will provide his need. *"He who did not spare his own Son, but gave him up for us all—how will he not also, along with him, graciously give us all things?" [Rom.8:32]*. When we give to God what He asks, He returns to us far more than we could imagine.

PRAYER FOCUS

Heavenly Father, the silver is Yours and the gold is Yours. LORD, I am freely willing to lay all that I am and all that I have on the altar to worship You.

October 27

Operating In The Strength And Energy Of God
Bible Reading: [1 Pet.4:1-11]

"Do you have the gift of speaking? Then speak as God Himself were speaking through you. Do you have the gift of helping others? Do it with all the strength and energy that God supplies. Then everything you do will bring glory to God through Jesus Christ. All glory and power to Him forever and ever! Amen
[1 Pet.4:11]

Every week most of us face a difficult task. We have constant challenges and obstacles in our path. Each one of us is working his way through life, in the hope of eternal life. But there isn't a good work that we undertake where Christ can't be involved. One thing we must understand is that on our own we can do nothing without God *[John.15:5]*. To operate means to perform a function. If truly we can do nothing on our own, then there is every reason for us to depend on the strength that God provides. Paul says, *"I worked harder than any of them, though it was not I, but the grace of God that is with me."* *[1 Cor.15:10]*. He did worked hard but his effort was in some way not his. *"I work hard and struggle to do this, using the energy that he powerfully provides in me."* *[Col.1:29]*

The goal of every sacrifice or service we render is to bring glory to God. We all are blessed by God with natural abilities(talent) from birth. Though these gifts are not same as the Spirit-given gifts, they should be used in serving others. When we use our abilities the way God leads us, to be of a blessing to others, men will see Christ in us and praise God for the help they have received. God would be glorified because the origin of the gifts would be identified to be from Him. *"For it is God at work in you, both to will and to work for His good pleasure."* *[Phil.2:13]*

PRAYER FOCUS

Dear heavenly Father, all that I am and all that I have is from You. LORD, I confess that I can do nothing with Christ who strengthens me. Amen

October 28

The Quest for Power & Self-importance What a trap!
Bible Reading: [Isaiah 22:15-25]

> *This is what the LORD, the LORD of Heaven's Armies, said to me: "Confront Shebna, the palace administrator, and give him this message: who do you think you are, and what are you doing here, building a beautiful tomb for yourself- a monument high up in the rock?*
> *[Vs: 15-16, NLT]*

The quest for power and self-importance has brought untold sufferings to humanity especially in developing countries. A quest is all about seeking or pursuing something important. Self-importance is an attitude showing that someone has an overly high opinion of his or her own importance. Scripture wants us of self-importance: *"For I say, through the grace given me, to every man that is among you, not to think of himself more highly than he ought to think; but to think as to think soberly, according as God hath dealt to each man a measure of faith" [Rom.12:3]*. As a palace administrator, Shebna held the highest possible position in the royal court. Instead of serving the purpose for which he was employed, he spend time building a beautiful tomb. This lavish burial place was intended to last for centuries.

Beloved, do you see this attitude manifesting in the lives of our leaders today? A leader: government official, chief executive officer (CEO), religious leader or the head of the home (husband) — is like a father to the people when he truly cares for them and addresses their needs. In contrast, Shebna was concerned only about himself (self-centeredness). Thinking only about your own interest and welfare?

PRAYER FOCUS

Dear heavenly Father, the earth is yours and everything in it. Help me to be a faithful steward and deliver me from all unholy desires and the quest for power and Self-importance in Jesus' name.

October 29

God Calls & Uses Unexpected Vessels
Bible Reading: [1 Cor.1:26-31]

"For you see your calling, brethren, that not many wise according to the flesh, not many mighty, not many noble, are called. But God has chosen the foolish things of the world to put to shame the wise, and God has chosen the weak things of the world to put to shame the things which are mighty;" [Vs:26-27]

Vanity keeps telling us that we are intelligent, beautiful, clever, talented, and well cultured, but our main Scripture in 1 Corinthians should pull us back to reality. Some people think God should have surrounded Himself with the elites to give Himself advantage over Satan. That's not the case! Think about Jesus calling His twelve disciples, He did not go after the Scribes and Pharisees but after fishermen. *"Now when they saw the boldness of Peter and John, and perceived that they were uneducated and untrained men, they marveled. And they realized that they had been with Jesus" [Acts.4:13]*. Socially and culturally, most Corinthian Christians were ordinary people, except a few that were wealthy. The reason God chooses despised humble people is to demonstrate His judgment on human pride. *"For by grace you have been saved through faith, and that not of yourself; it is the gift of God, not of works, lest anyone should boast"[Eph.2:8-9]*. God is sovereign over all of our plans and desires. He gives authority and salvation to whomever He wills, even to the lowest of men [Dan.4:17].

It's worth mentioning that no amount of human knowledge can replace or bypass Christ's work on the cross. No person can boast that his achievements helped him or her secure eternal life. *"And this is eternal life, that they might know thee the only true God, and Jesus Christ, whom thou hast sent" [John.17:3]*. Salvation is totally from God and only simple faith can get a person into God's kingdom. When people are united with Christ Jesus, God makes them righteous, holy, free, possessing wisdom and knowledge. This work of Christ is an expression of God's wisdom.

He is the source of and the reason for our personal and living relationship with Christ. *"For whom He foreknew, He also predestined to be conformed to the image of His Son,....Moreover whom He predestined, these He also called; whom He called, these He also justified; and whom He justified, these He also glorified" [Rom.8:29-30]*. Therefore, he who glories, let him glory in the LORD! *"But let him who glories glory in this, that he understands and knows me, that I am the LORD, exercising loving-kindness, judgment, and righteousness in the earth. For in these I delight, says the LORD" [Jer.9:24]*.

PRAYER FOCUS

Dear heavenly Father, even the highly skilled, intellectually gifted and well educated cannot replace or bypass the work of the Cross. Your grace has found me just as I am. I'm humbled by Your love and majesty. Thank You LORD Jesus!

October 30

When The Message Sounds Unpopular!
Bible Reading: [Jeremiah 20:7-18]

"O LORD, You induced me, and I was persuaded; You are stronger than I, and have prevailed. I am in derision daily; everyone mocks me. For when I spoke, I cried out; I shouted, "Violence and plunder!" Because the word of the LORD was made to me a reproach and a derision daily." [Vs:7-8]

Nowadays though the word of God seems common in most part of the world, the message is not popular as one may think especially in the western world. In the days of Jeremiah, the materialistic greed of Judah had led her into apostasy and God was committed to take away all the treasures in which she had trusted. In a materialistic world like ours, how can the message be welcomed when the world's value system focuses on -what one possesses, how much money one can make and who one can impress? If we are not careful, every message that goes out from the mouth of politicians, businessmen, and even some men of God would be to impress the itching hears of the masses. A message sounds unpopular when it is not liked or it is despised.

Although his message became unpopular, he actually spoke the word of God from his heart. He underwent misery because of his divine assignment and was totally forsaken. Nevertheless, in order for God's justice to stand, his people had to be warned. How many believers and preachers would serve God's purpose like Jeremiah today? Are we interested in wealth and fame or the souls of men? Paul says; *"Therefore I testify to you this day that I am innocent of the blood of all men. For I did not shrink from declaring to you the whole counsel(will) of God" [Acts.20:26- 27].* Jeremiah faithfully proclaimed God's word and received nothing in return but persecution and sorrow. *"God's call doesn't register in a vacuum; only a person who is committed to doing God's will can receive a call"* [Thomas Hale].

When the message sounds unpopular - the messenger God calls is one whose heart cries of millions living in darkness — heading to hell fire! *[John 5:29;Rev.21:8]*.They are concerned for the young girls whose parents sell them into sexual slavery to provide for the family, for millions of street children and their hopeless existence, and above all, they are concerned for the glory of God (David Sills). *"For I am not ashamed of the gospel, because it is the power of God that brings salvation to everyone who believes: first to the Jew, then to the Gentile" [Rom.1:16].*

PRAYER FORCUS

Dear heavenly Father, may Your heartbeat for perishing souls be my heartbeat. LORD, let the living message of God's love and redeeming grace becomes fire in my bones in Jesus' name.

October 31

How Are The Mighty Fallen!
Bible Reading: [2 Samuel 1:17-27]

"I am distressed for you, my brother Jonathan; You have been very pleasant to me; Your love to me was wonderful, surpassing the love of women. How the mighty have fallen, and the weapons of war perished!" [Vs:26-27].

What kind of attitude do you put up when you hear that a fellow believer in Christ has fallen?\ Certainly, in the world in which we live many will rejoice; believers and unbelievers alike especially if the person had been so vocal against sin. Here, we see a different scenario. As for Jonathan, David loved him deeply from the heart — his love for Jonathan surpassed the love of women. We would assume that David would have rejoiced over the death of Saul, who had denied him his kingship and who pursued him as a fugitive (escapee) from justice. Saul had caused much trouble for David but when he died, David was not bitter instead he composed a song of lamentation (mourning) for the king and his son. His words expressed the attitude of somebody who had within his heart the forgiveness of God *[Matt.6:12]*. May God heal every wound and bless us with a forgiving heart in Jesus' name.

How are the mighty fallen! Some fall because of pride, female/male, love for money, death in battle, discouragement and disgrace.

Because of Pride: "Pride goeth before destruction, and an haughty spirit before a fall." (Prov.16:18; Jam.4:6); Finance/Greed: "For the love of money is the root of all evil: which while some coveted after, they have erred from the faith, and pieced themselves through with many sorrows." (1 Tim.6:10; 2 King 5:25-27). Sexual Immorality: "One evening David got up from his bed and walked around on the roof of the palace. From the roof he saw a woman bathing. The woman was very beautiful,..." (2 Sam.11; Judges.16).*

Discouragement and Disgrace: giving up one's faith is not the answer to discouragement. *"....but David encouraged himself in the LORD his God." (1 Sam.*

30:1-8). No disgrace is beyond the reach of God's grace! *"My little children, these things I write to you, so that you may not sin. And if anyone sins, we have an Advocate with the Father, Jesus Christ the righteous,..." (1 John.2:1-2). "For though the righteous fall seven times, the rise again,.." (Prov.24:16).* Rise up from where you have fallen, the grace of God is sufficient!!

PRAYER FOCUS

Heavenly Father, It's Your desire that I should be steadfast in the faith *[Rom.12:11]*. LORD, bless me with a forgiving heart and grant me the courage to lay aside anything that hinders me to run the race to the end.

NOVEMBER

"Be careful for nothing; but in everything by prayer and supplication with thanksgiving let your requests be made known unto God. And the peace of God, which passeth all understanding, shall keep your hearts and minds through Christ Jesus."

[Phil.4:6-7;KJV]

****

Jehovah Mekoddishkem - ***[The LORD Who Sanctifies]*** *- Exod.31:13*

11 = ***[Represent Chaos, disorder, and judgment]***

November 1

When The Message Becomes Rare!
Bible Reading: [1 Sam.3:1-21]

"Now the boy Samuel ministered to the LORD before Eli. And the word of the LORD was rare in those days; there was no widespread revelation. Now Samuel did not yet know the LORD, nor was the word of the LORD yet revealed." [Vs: 1&7]

At the present time, one may conclude that the gospel message is commonplace. To say that something is rare, it means it is scarce, not found in large number and consequently of interest or value. Although God had spoken directly and audibly with Moses and Joshua, His word became rare during the three centuries of rule by judges. Even when Eli was the high priest, no prophets were speaking God's messages to Israel. *"After that whole generation had been gathered to their ancestors, another generation grew up who knew neither the LORD nor what he had done for Israel" (Judges 2:10).* Because the word of God was rare in those days, there was no widespread revelation. It is written, *"Where there is no vision, the people perish: but he that keepeth the law, happy is he" [Prov.29:18].*

Beloved, it may be hard for you to accept that the message from the throne room of grace is rare in this generation. We hear the word preached everywhere: in cities, on media and in the country. Many more preachers than ever before. The truth is that many people have become more religious than ever *[Rom.10:2]*. Remember that the sons of Eli grew up in a religious atmosphere but had no true or right relationship with God. They expressed contempt for God through their actions. They either refused to listen to God or allowed greed (materialism) to get in the way of communication with Him. We have learned to sing and dance hallelujah song, but are we true believers? Are we consecrated or set apart for a holy use or purpose? *"Make every effort to live in peace with everyone and to be holy; without holiness no one will see the LORD" (Heb.12:14).*

Nowadays there are millions of church goers but just a few consecrated and committed believers. What's the cause? The message is rare! Most messages today are to excite or entertain congregations. Many congregations have been reduced to mere religious and social grounds. Messages have become motivational in nature and there is a high quest for motivational speakers. Why are people not inspired? Why are people not transformed? Why are there no abiding fruits? Why so many mundane believers? etc. Because the message has become rare! It became rare because men who wait in the place of prayer and the word are rare! *"Did not our heart burn within us while He talked with us on the road, and while He opened the Scripture to us?" [Luke 24:32; Ezra 7:10; 10:9-12].*

Repent and Be transformed TODAY!

PRAYER FOCUS

Dear heavenly Father, I acknowledge the fact that listening and responding is vital in my relationship with You. LORD, I surrender myself totally to You and choose this day to live in Your presence and serve your purpose in Jesus' name.

November 2

Making Christ's Last Command Our First Concern
Bible Reading: [Matt.28:16-20]

And Jesus came and spoke to them, saying, "All authority has been given to Me in heaven and on earth." Go therefore and make disciples of all the nations,.." (Vs:18-19).

"As You sent Me into the world, I also have sent them into the world." [John 17:18]

The command to go and make disciples is not an option. It is a command to all who have made Jesus Christ the LORD and Savior of their lives. The worst thing that can happen in life is to see people going into a Christless eternity without ever hearing that the creator of the world loves them and has a plan for their lives. We are not all evangelists in a formal sense but Christ's mission is for every true believer. We are witnesses of Christ *[Acts 1:8]*. It's an obligation for us to take God's great message of salvation to others so that they can respond to the Good news.

How will your loved ones and neighbors hear it unless someone tells them? *[Rom.10:14-17.*

We must share the Good news because men are lost and heading to a Christless eternity in hell. We must share it in our communities, campuses, villages, towns and cities. The King's business requires urgency. *"He sends out His command to the earth; His word runs very swiftly." (Psalm 147:15).* The LORD Jesus Christ is sending us not just to preach His word, not just to make converts but disciples. The question is, are you a disciple? A disciple is one who repents of sin, trusts in Jesus for salvation, and obeys His teachings.

A true disciple belongs to a community of believers where he fellowships and is taught the word of God. A true disciple is one who has been baptized. Baptism unites a believer with Jesus Christ in his or her death to sin and resurrection to new life. How can you make disciples when you are not one? How can you teach others when you are not taught? How can you baptized new converts when you have not been baptized. Those who are obedient to the great commission are privileged to have Christ authority and presence go with them. *",...and lo, I am with you always, even to the end of the age."*

PRAYER FOCUS

Dear heavenly Father, by this You are glorified, that I bear much fruit; showing myself Your disciple *[John 15:7-8].*

November 3

Looking Beyond The World's Value System
Bible Reading: [Heb.11:23-29]

"By faith Moses, when he became of age, refused to be called the son of Pharaoh's daughter, choosing rather to suffer affliction with the people of God than to enjoy the passing pleasures of sin, esteeming the reproach of Christ greater riches than the treasures in Egypt; for he looked to the reward." [Vs:24-26]

Everyone on earth thinks daily either by the world's value system or by the truth of the word of God. Those who think by the world's value system conform to this world but those who desire to think by the truth of God's word allow themselves to be transformed by the renewing of their minds in order to prove what is that good, acceptable and perfect will of God *[Rom.12:2]*. When Moses was born, his people where slaves in Egypt. That was enough for him to grow up with a slave mentality (servitude). When his life was spared at the command of Egyptian officials to kill all Hebrew baby boys, he was fortunate to grow up in the arena of wealth, popularity and prestige. In his privileged position, it was easier for him to conform to the standards of Egypt the world's superpower at the time. To his credit or achievement, he was gifted, *"Moses was educated in all the wisdom of the Egyptians and was powerful in both speech and action." [Acts.7:22]*

It took faith for Moses to give up his place in Pharaoh's palace. It is written, *"But without faith it is impossible to please Him, for he who comes to God Must Believe that He is, and that He is a rewarder of those who diligently seek Him." [Heb.11:6]*. Faith takes us to the place where we are sure of what we hope for and certain of what we do not yet see. This assurance helps every true believer to see the eternal values of God's Kingdom (Kingdom Benefits). Beloved, the passing pleasures of sin and treasures of world can't be compared to Christ greater riches. Of Christ, it is written, *"....for the joy that was set Him, He endured the cross, despising the shame, and has sat down at the right hand of the throne of God." (Heb.12:5).*

The world's value system focuses on: *"What I can get, what I can achieve, who we can impress, What I can possess, where I live, what I drive, how much education I have, how much money I make, who knows my name, and how successful I am."*

The kingdom mindset focuses on: *"What I can give, who I can love, how God can use me, how significant and accepted I am regardless of what I make, where I live, what I drive, or who knows my name." (Steve Rebus)*

"However, I consider my life worth nothing to me; my only aim is to finish the race and complete the task the LORD Jesus has given me—the task of testifying to the good news of God's grace." [Acts.20:24;Phil.3:8]

PRAYER FOCUS

Dear heavenly Father, nothing in this world can be compared to what You are worth. LORD, grant that my eyes will be opened to and focused on the long-range benefits of Your Kingdom at all times in Jesus' name.

November 4

Divinity Shapes Our Ends
Bible Reading: [Jer.10:23-25]

"O LORD, I know that the way of man is not in himself: it is not in man that walketh to direct His steps." [Vs:23]

A man may choose his path for good or evil, for failure or success but one thing is certain, God has the final say. Therefore, life does not depend on human desire or effort, but on God's mercy. So it is God who decides to show us mercy. We can neither choose it nor work for it *[Rom.9:16]*. We have to accept the fact that our conduct in life depends on something more than our choices. *"The LORD directs the steps of the godly. He delights in every detail of their lives"[Psalm 37:23]*. Our rectitude and strength comes from the LORD. He delights in those who follow His ways and put their trust in Him.

The behavior of a righteous man is ordered by God. This is based on the fact that he has voluntarily submitted to His will. When we surrender to the will of God, He begins to work in us, giving us the desire and the power to do what pleases Him *[Phil.2:13]*. God does not work in us so that we should be happy, but in order to fulfill His purpose. The joy of the LORD then becomes our strength as we do His will. Those who are called according to God's purpose have a new mind-set and a new perspective on life. They look for their security in heaven, not on earth. Remember that all things work together for their good because God is with them.

PRAYER FOCUS

Dear heavenly Father, I'm so grateful for the life and breath You have given me. O LORD, may You mold me into a vessel of honor [special purpose] in Jesus' name.

November 5

Making God's Word Of No Effect By Human Traditions
Bible Reading: [Mark 7:1-23]

"The Pharisees and scribes asked Him, why do Your disciples not walk according to the tradition of the elders, but eat bread with unwashed hands?" He answered and said to them, "Well did Isaiah prophesy of you hypocrites, as it is written: 'This people honors Me with their lips, but their heart is far from Me.' [Vs: 6,7]

Often we allow our human traditions; our little rules and regulations to nullify the power of God's word. To say that the traditional way of doing something is the only way it can be done is to add to the commandments of God. Like the Pharisees, sometimes we use God as an excuse to neglect our family and societal responsibilities. God's word is as important as God Himself.

When we strictly follow religious/traditional practices while allowing our hearts to remain distant from God, we become hypocrites like the Pharisees. The essence of God's word is to refresh our souls and make us wise as we follow Him daily in obedience. *"The law of the LORD is perfect, refreshing the soul. The statutes of the LORD are trustworthy, making wise the simple"* [Psalm 19:7].

It is written, *"For the law was given through Moses, but grace and truth came through Jesus Christ"* [John.1:17]. While the Pharisees defined purity by outward acts and restrictions (law), grace says we become pure on the inside as we allow Christ to renew our minds and transform us into His image. *"...but be transformed by the renewing of your mind. Then you will be able to test and approve what God's will is — His good, pleasing and perfect will"* [Rom.12:2]. While the Pharisees think that giving only to God makes them right with Him, the grace we have received teaches us to love and bless our parents, widows, orphans, the poor and needy. *".....Stand fast therefore in the liberty wherewith Christ hath made us free, and be not entangled again with the yoke of bondage"* [Gal.5:1].

PRAYER FOCUS

Dear heavenly Father, It is for freedom that Christ has set me free. LORD, I look to You for guidance and focus my mind on the things that are true, pure, noble, lovely and of good report in Jesus' name [Phil.4:8-9].

November 6

Looking For The Right Thing at The Wrong Time
Bible Reading: [John 20:1-10]

"Finally the other disciple, who had reached the tomb first, also went inside. He saw and believed. They still did not understand from Scripture that Jesus had to rise from the dead." [Vs:8,9]

The reason you might be suffering or stagnating at this very moment in time is because you are looking for the right opportunity in the wrong place or at the wrong time. It is common sense that if you graduate from a medical school, you don't need to applying for an engineering job simply because the company has advertised an opportunity. In the secular world or the Christendom, you can only get the right opportunity in the right place at a given moment in time.

In the Body of Christ, the greatest challenge most of the time is ignorance of what the word of God says. Some of us are still holding on to former things and traditions while God is moving on. His disciples came looking and were troubled about the empty tomb failing to understand what scriptures say about the resurrection of Christ. *"They will flog Him and kill Him, and on the third day He will rise again. But the disciples did not understand any of these things" [Lk 18:33,34].* I pray that the LORD will open the eyes of your understanding in Jesus' name.

It's not time to look for the living among the dead. It is not time to bow down, but to look up to the risen LORD, seated at the right hand side of the Father. *In their fright the women bowed down with their faces to the ground, but the men said to them, *"why do you look for the living among the dead?"* [Lk.24:5] When Stephen was threatened by the Sanhedrin, he looked up to heaven.

God does everything on earth according to the counsel of His will *[Eph.1:11]*. Get to the Word of God and the place of prayer, and God will connect you with the right business partners, right school, right husband, right wife etc. Stop looking for the right thing in the wrong place or at the wrong time TODAY! The LORD is your guide/ helper.

PRAYER FOCUS

Dear heavenly Father, I seek to understand Your Word and purpose for my life. I am fully persuaded that You are able to guide and connect me with the right destiny partners/opportunities in Jesus' name.

November 7

Snare of Intermarriage
Bible Reading: [Neh.13:22-31]

"Did not Solomon King of Israel sin by these things? Yet among many nations there was no King like him, who was beloved of his God; and God made him King over all Israel, nevertheless pagan women caused even him to sin." [Vs:26]

Nowadays it has become normal for a believer in Christ to talk about marrying a non-believer. Our lighthearted attitude towards sin has made us to serve God without reverence [fear & respect]. To many, God has become an elementary school pupil to follow their command instead of them following God's Command and leading of His Spirit. Some have taken the license of grace to go on sinning. Beloved, grace doesn't give us the liberty to sin but the power to live right with God. Remember that the people had promised not to allow their children to marry heathens or pagans *[Ezra 10:30]*. Unfortunately, in the absence of Nehemiah, the people had been intermarrying, and breaking their solemn covenant with God. Nowadays many believers are intermarrying with the world in many different ways. It is written, *"Be ye not unequally yoked together with unbelievers: for what fellowship hath righteousness with unrighteousness? And what communion hath light with darkness?" [2 Cor.6:14]*

The principle of separation is a life changing principle. If in the presence of other believers you are a believer and in the absence of believers you are an unbeliever — then you are deceiving yourself, not God. *"Therefore, my dear friends, as you have always obeyed — not only in my presence, but now much more in my absence— continue to work out your salvation with fear and trembling" [Phil.2:12]*. Pagan women did cause King Solomon to sin. Friend, what is destroying your relationship with God and causing you to sin? Confession is agreeing with God that our thoughts, words, and actions are wrong and contrary to His will. Repent today and put your life right with God.

PRAYER FOCUS

Dear heavenly Father, I'm sorry for my lighthearted attitude towards sin . LORD, I ask for forgiveness and plead for your mercy in Jesus' name.

"These are the ones I look on with favor: those who are humble and contrite in spirit, and who tremble at my word" [Isa.66:2]

November 8

Settling For Less In Life
Bible Reading: [Number 32:1-23]

"Therefore they said, "If we have found favor in your sight, let this land be given to your servants as a possession. Do not take us over the Jordan." [Vs-5]

"The whole land of Canaan, where you now reside as a foreigner, I will give as an everlasting possession to you and your descendants after you; and I will be their God." [Gen.17:8]

What on earth will cause you to settle for less when God has the best for your life? The Israelites were poised to enter Canaan, thus settling anywhere before Canaan was not God's ideal for them. Canaan was the promised land and not the east side of the Jordan river. I know many of us have a thousand reasons why we are choosing to settle where we want even if it's not the will of God.

Simply because we are blessed where we are doesn't necessarily mean it's God's best for our lives. The manifestation of God's presence and power is strongest at the center of His will. When we settle for less as Christians, we will have a form of Christianity/godliness that is robbed of its power *[1 Tim.3:5]*. We will gradually lose the sense of His presence, lose sight of His standards and set our own standard of righteousness (Rom.10:3).

"Do not ask how far you can go before you are out of the will of God. Ask instead how to find the center of the will of God" (Bill Kiefer).

PRAYER FOCUS

Heavenly Father, I'm am fully persuaded that You have the best for me in this life. LORD, I'm determined today to seek only Your perfect will and to live in the fullness of Your presence in Jesus' name.

November 9

I Say To You——Arise
Bible Reading: [Luke 7:11-17]
"The Command of Faith"

"And when the LORD saw her, He had compassion on her. And He said to her, "Do not weep." Then He came and touched the coffin. And those who carried him stood still. And He said, "Young man, I say to you, arise." [Vs: 13-14]

The widow's only son was her means of support and hope for the future. She had lost her husband, and here her only son was dead. Her future was bleak unless someone came to her aid. We could do nothing to help ourselves but God had compassion on us and sent Jesus to raise us to life with Him *[Eph.2:4-7]*. It worth mentioning that a Jew was rendered unclean by touching a dead body or a coffin *[Lev.21:1]*. Christ has the power to heal diseases and raise the death. With the eyes of faith, I can see Jesus reaching out to you with compassion, replacing your disgrace with grace, your ashes with beauty, your mourning with dancing, spirit of despair with garment of praise/oil of joy, your failure with success, your bankruptcy with encouragement, your disappointment with appointment, your barrenness with fruitfulness in Jesus' name. It is written, *"But if the Spirit of Him who raised Jesus from the dead dwells in you, He who raised Christ from the dead will also give life to your mortal bodies through His Spirit who dwells in you." (Rom.8:11)*

While mountains are used in Scripture to symbolize strength and stability, they are also used to represent great difficulties and seeming impossibilities. Remember that even some mountains of difficulty are meant by God to bless you *[Isa.49:11]*. It takes faith for the power that comes from God to be exercise through us. Oftentimes Satan and cohorts erect roadblocks which become mountains barring our way *[1 Thes.2:18]*. Exercising Christ's authority is sometimes referred as the command of faith. This comes with a right relationship and standing with God — you must be a true believer i.e. born again - not living in sin—*[Acts 19:15]*.

The command of faith is one of many kinds of prayer. *"It is a very deliberate exercise of Christ's own authority and name in a situation where His glory is at stake, where His kingdom is being hindered, or where Christ calls you to demonstrate His power to prove He is the living God" (Wesley L. Duewel).*

November 10

A Revelation Of God's Glory

"And the glory which You gave Me I have given them, that they may be one just as We are one." [John.17:22]. "Then make my joy complete by being likeminded, having the same love, being one in spirit and of one mind." [Phil.2:2]

God's glory is the goal of all things. The word glory comes from the Latin *gloria*, meaning "fame, renown") and is used to describe the manifestation of God's presence. God's glory signifies His beauty, His honor - God's glory is defined based on the context in which it is used. *"The heavens declare the glory of God" [Psalm 19:1].* When used in reference to natural objects "glory" may refer to the brightness of heavenly bodies.

God's glory is revealed in the expression of unity. The glory of God is the beauty of His Spirit - beauty that comes from His character. The Holy Spirit is the Spirit of unity. He unifies our hearts with the Father and fellow believers in the body of Christ. The Church is one because of the oneness that exists between the Father and Son. The community of believers should display the same glory that Jesus displayed from the Father. If the Church lives in the Spirit, reflects God's glory and love, and shows unity sustained by a shared knowledge of God, then its testimony will astonish the world.

PRAYER FOCUS

Father, may You unite us as a powerful witness to the reality of God's love. Let Your glory be seen in us in Jesus' name.

November 11
Treasures In The Hands Of Babes
Bible Reading: [Luke 10:17-24]

In that hour Jesus rejoiced in the Spirit and said, "I thank You, Father, LORD of heaven and earth, that You have hidden these things from the wise and prudent and revealed them to babes. Even so, Father, for so it seemed good in Your sight." (Vs: 21)

The wise and prudent always fall short of divine revelations because of their proud attitudes, claiming to be wise in their own eyes. No one has ever seen God, but the unique One who Himself is God *[Jn.1:18]*. Because of this, Jesus was revealed in order to reveal the Father. The disciples of Old experienced Jesus firsthand. It was a privilege , living in such a time that God had chosen to personally reveal Himself through the Son. They witnessed the arrival of God's promised salvation. However, the wise and prudent at that time found it difficult to understand what God was doing through the Son.

"You have hidden these things from the wise and prudent and revealed them to babes." God uses simple things that a child can understand to shame those who think themselves wise, but are foolish in God's eyes. It is written, *"I will destroy the wisdom of the wise, and bring to nothing the understanding of the prudent." Where is the wise? Where is the scribe (teacher)? Where is the disputer of this age? Has not God made foolish the wisdom of this world? [1 Cor.1:19-20]*. Just because many of life's rewards seem to go to the powerful, intelligent, rich and good-looking, these elites think spiritual truth should be given in like manner. It's not by human effort or ability that we come to Jesus, but through childlike trust.

While the prophets of old made many divine predictions and desired to see what we see and experience in Christ today, many people in the world are taking this great opportunity for granted. *"Of this salvation the prophets have inquired and searched carefully, who prophesied of the grace that would come to you" [1 Pet.1:10]*. Because of technology and the availability of resources, this generation is privileged to know so much about Christ. The question is: how much of Christ is revealed to you personally? Do you have a genuine relationship with Him or you are a mere churchgoer? How much of God is seen through your lifestyle on a daily basis? Is your gentleness evident to all men? In order not to take the unsearchable riches of Christ for granted, let's embrace spiritual truth with a teachable spirit and childlike trust. It is written, *"The secret of the LORD is with them that fear Him; and He will show them His covenant." (Ps 25:14)*

PRAYER FOCUS

Heavenly Father, I have come to know that with privilege comes responsibility. LORD, I surrender myself to the counsel of Your will and ask that You bless me with a teachable spirit, a humble and obedient heart in Jesus' name.

November 12

Faith Tested By Fire
Bible Reading: [1 Pet.1:3-12]

"That the genuineness of your faith, being much more precious than gold that perishes, though it is tested by fire, may be found to praise, honor, and glory at the revelation of Jesus Christ,." [Vs:7]

Beloved in the LORD, how genuine is your faith? Genuine faith is one that has been tested in the furnace of trial. While a trial is the true test of virtue, faith is the assurance of things hoped for *[Heb.11:1]*. We often depend on our own abilities when life seems easy and oftentimes we compromise our conviction when the going gets tough. Depending on God in the face of hardship is the realization of our own powerlessness without Him. Knowing that God knows our calamity reassures us that He is working all things for our case. *"And we know that all things work together for good to them that love God, to them who are called according to His purpose [Rom.8:28].*

Trials were never meant to drown us, but to build us up and deepen our reliance on God. Our trials, struggles, hardships, and persecution refine and strengthen our faith, making us useful to God. *"But he knows where I am going. And when he tests me, I will come out as pure as gold" [Job.23:10]*. God is not ignorant about our path of life. We must accept trials as part of the refining process that burns away impurities in our lives and prepares us to meet Christ. The trying of our faith works patience *[Jam.1:3]* and helps us grow to be the kind of people God wants.

PRAYER FOCUS

Dear heavenly Father, I pray for strength to endure hardship and ask for grace to remain true to the faith in difficult times in Jesus' name.

"Let us therefore, come boldly unto the throne of grace, that we may obtain mercy, and find grace to help in time of need." [Heb.4:16; Isa.43:2]

November 13

Enjoying The Comfort Of Scriptures
Bible Reading: [Rom.15:1-6]

"For whatever things were written before were written for our learning, that we through the comfort of the scriptures might have hope." [Vs: 4]

God has not stopped working with His people. As He worked with His people in time past, so He works today with believers in Christ. It is written, *"My people are destroyed for lack of knowledge" (Hosea 4:6).* Gaining knowledge from the Scripture will affect your attitude toward the present and the future. As Christians, it is important for us to learn from the examples of the prophets who lived in the past in order to understand God's moral values and standards. While the people of the world go after temporal things in order to derive satisfaction and comfort in life, there is greater worth pondering over the promises of God.

Events of old encourage us to have patience concerning the work of God in our lives and others. They give us encouragement by revealing that God is faithful to His promises and work *"For no matter how many promises God has made, they are "Yes" in Christ. And so through Him the "Amen" is spoken by us to the glory of God" [2 Cor.1:20].* When we know more about what God has done in the past, it increases our confidence about what He will do in the future. The Psalmist says, *"Bless the LORD, O my soul, and forget not all His benefits: who forgives all your iniquities, who heals all your diseases, who redeems your life from destruction, who crowns you with loving-kindness and tender mercies, who satisfies your mouth with good things, so that your youth is renewed like the eagle's" [Psalm 103:2-5].* God's will is the best for us and searching the holy Scripture is just the right thing to do in order to enjoy comfort.

PRAYER FOCUS

Oh God of patience and comfort, as I study Your word diligently, may You enable me to walk in fulfillment of Your plan for my life in Jesus' name.

"I would have despaired unless I had believed that I would see the goodness of the LORD in the land of the living." [Ps 27:13;NASV]

November 14

Seeing Beyond The Man
Bible Reading: [Matt.13:53-58]

"Now He did not do many mighty works there because of their unbelief." [Vs: 58]

Unbelief blinds people to the truth and robs them of hope. Unbelief is evident when we turn away from God or walk in disobedience contrary to what His word teaches. Many can't see God's mighty work in their lives because of unbelief. Whenever there is no longing for the truth in the heart of men, God sees no need to confirm the spoken word. Oftentimes, when men become so familiar with God's servants or the manifestation of His power, they show contempt and lack respect. The saying goes, *"Familiarity breeds contempt."* People do not respect someone they know well enough to know his or her faults. *"Is this not the carpenter's son? Is not His mother called Mary? And his sisters, are they not all with us?*

As a preacher, I know how it feels like ministering in my hometown. When people are acquainted with you, they find it difficult to bring themselves to believe the message. At times, because of a prejudiced mind, people would refuse to believe in the miraculous work of God through the hand of His servant. The reception of God's word depends on one's heart.

Where then did this man receive all these things? Remember that God anointed Jesus of Nazareth with the Holy Spirit and with power. He went about doing good and healing all who were oppressed by the devil, for God was with Him" [Acts.10:38]. It is true that your friend used to be your classmate, he used to be your colleague, he used to beg for bread etc. but the grace and anointing of God has made all the difference in ! Has God called a man? *It is written, "And those he predestined, he also called; those he called, he also justified; those he justified, he also glorified" [Rom.8:30].*

If you can't see God's work, perhaps it could be the result of your unbelief. The father instantly cried out, *"I do believe, but help me overcome my unbelief!" [Mk.9:24].* While lack of faith can hinder God's saving activity, Jesus challenged the man to believe in the power of God. See beyond God's chosen servant with the eyes of faith. See his uncommon significance. Faith is required both to understand the gospel message and to experience God's miracles. The LORD is still working TODAY! [John 5:17]

PRAYER FOCUS

Dear heavenly Father, You are mighty to save and deliver. LORD, may you perform a mighty work in my life and community this season in Jesus' name.

November 15

The Pitfall Of Lying Spirits
"Walking in a false spirit"
Bible Reading: [Micah 2:6-11]

"If a man should walk in a false spirit and speak a lie, saying, " I will prophesy to you of wine and drink," Even he would be the prattler (spokesman) of this people [Vs: 11]

If we like only God's comforting messages, we may likely miss what He has for us. The Spirit of truth leads people to the truth. He convince them of those things that are true, and opposes Satan's interest. He points people to the scriptures, resulting in love for God and others, thus exalting Jesus alone as the true Christ! Whenever you see people being exalted, be it in the Body of Christ, know that the cult of personality [man worship] has taken center stage. Whenever an object is worshipped, then idolatry is at work. False prophets are possessed with a lying spirit and/or spirit of divination. Nowadays people are so inclined to the spirit of falsehood because of itchy ears. They want to hear something about their situation regardless of the channel being used. If truth is not elevated, it means the spirit of falsehood is at work *"To the law and to the testimony! If they do not speak according to this word, it is because there is no light in them." [Isa.8:20]*. A true teacher of God speaks the truth regardless of what the listeners want to hear.

False spirits are at work in false prophets, false brethren [Gal.2:4], false teachers [2 Pet.2:1], false apostles [2 Cor.11:13]. Whenever we reject that which is true and right, it means we have decided to go in the wrong direction. *"And the people of Berea were more open-minded than those in Thessalonica, and they listened eagerly to Paul's message. They searched the Scriptures day after day to see if Paul and Silas were teaching the truth." [Acts 17:11]*

PRAYER FOCUS

Dear heavenly Father, grant me the spirit of discernment and help me to overcomer false teachers with the word of truth in Jesus' name.

November 16

Come What May
"Yet I Will Rejoice In The LORD"
Bible Reading: [Hab.3:17-19]

"Though the fig tree may not blossom, Nor fruit be on the vines; Though the labor of the olive may fail, and the fields yield no food; Though the flock may be cut off from the fold, And there be no herd in the stalls - Yet I will rejoice in the LORD" [Vs: 17]

Reaffirming our trust in the LORD is of utmost importance to our daily walk with God and victory in Christ. It gives a good picture of unconditional love. *"Who shall separate us from the love of Christ? Shall tribulation, or distress, or persecution, or famine, or nakedness, or peril, or sword?" [Rom.8:35].* In the face of hostile environment, in times of starvation and loss, amid the storms of life and disturbing international affairs, we must stand firm in the LORD. Even if God does not pours out material blessing on us again, He is still worthy of all the truth and praise we can give. Our faith in God must grow beyond the affairs of this world. It is written, *"Rejoice in the LORD always. And again I say, rejoice!" (Phil.4:4).* The demeanor of the Christian life-style is one of rejoicing. When nothing makes sense, when troubles seem more than we can bear, let's put our trust in God's ability to give strength.

Our faith in God should be our victory and cause of rejoicing. *"For whatever is born of God overcomes the world. And this is the victory that has overcome the world—our faith. Who is he who overcomes the world, but he who believes that Jesus is the Son of God?" [1 John 5:4-5]* Are you born of God? Do you believe that Jesus is the Son of God? *"For with the heart man believeth unto righteousness; and with the mouth confession is made unto salvation"(Rom.10:10).* Remember that our human limitations can't match God's unlimited control over our destiny and circumstances. When we cannot see what God is doing, let's rest assured that He will do what is right.

My Confession

Come what may, nothing shall separate me from the love of Christ.

PRAYER FOCUS

Heavenly Father, I reaffirm my love for You and In this I am confident; that You will give me a surefooted confidence through difficult times and make me walk on my high hills in Jesus' name. Amen

November 17

Understanding The Dynamics Of Effective Prayer Agonizing
Bible Reading: [Col.4:1-13]

"Epaphras, who is one of you, a servant of Christ, saluteth you, always laboring fervently for you in prayers, that ye may stand perfect and complete in all the will of God." [Vs:12]

As we grow in our love for the LORD, we will naturally desire to talk to Him. There are different kinds of prayer, but it takes a pure heart and right heart attitude for our prayers to be answered by God. Our earnest prayers for others in the faith show our deep love and concern for them. Laboring fervently in prayer is a Greek word that is used to describe a woman in labor pains. The word labor also denotes hard work. It means giving oneself to something completely. Scripture talks about labor of love [1 Thes.1:3]. It also teaches us to labor in the word and in teaching [1 Tim.5:17]. The English word "agony" comes from the word "labor". In connection with prayer, several words are used. Travail - referring to childbirth. Travail means to bring forth a measure of life or growth. Travail - is the prayer that brings birth. Many wonderful things have happened on earth because somebody travailed in prayer. With such earnest striving, we should also offer our prayers to God.

Prayer is not a onetime event but a continuous offering of ourselves to God as a channel in response to the promptings of the Holy Spirit. *"Epaphras always laboring fervently for you in prayers."* He gave himself totally to prayers and not only that, his prayer was goal directed *"that ye may stand perfect and complete in all the will of God."* As long as they were not standing perfect in the will of God, he prayed passionately for them. Insofar as grace means God's unmerited favor, God has purposed according to His divine will that something will only happen on the face of the earth if we give ourselves to prayer. Prayer is not only about God, but also about us to be in the right disposition to receive His blessings.

PRAYER FOCUS

Dear heavenly Father, thank You for establishing prayer as a medium of communication and fellowship. LORD, like Epaphras, I give myself totally to prayer and ask that Your Spirit will enable me to pray without ceasing in Jesus' name.

November 18

A Fair-minded Believer
"Attitude In Hearing God's Word"
Bible Reading: [Acts 17:10-13]

"These were more noble than those in Thessalonica, in that they received the Word with all readiness of mind, and searched the scriptures daily, whether those things were so." (Vs-11) "For this cause also thank we God without ceasing, because, when ye received the Word of God which ye heard of us, ye received it not as the Word of men, but as it is in truth, the Word of God, which effectually worketh also in you that believe." [1 Thes.2:13]

True nobility in the sight of God is that one allows God to speak to him through His inspired Word [2 Tim 3:16]. Fair-minded people look at and judge things in a fair and open way. Often, those who do not ask God to speak to them through His Word will be misled either by their emotions, traditions, or false teachings. *"Search from the book of the LORD, and read: not one of these shall fail"* [Isa.34:16].

What made the Bereans a noble people?

- Their willing reception of the Word of God unlike the unbelieving Thessalonian Jews. They were free of prejudice - having a readiness of mind to receive the Word.
- They examined what was heard by comparing it to the Old Testament Scriptures which certainly were Scriptures available in the Synagogues at the time. They could not be easily cheated or tricked by accepting almost anything that was thought them. Believers are admonished to prove all things, and hold fast that which is good [1 Thes.5:21]
- They guarded Paul's safety protected Paul by getting him out of the region [2 Thes.3:2]
- They continued to grow in their faith. They were energetic by searching the Scriptures daily [Acts.2:42]

No matter who the teacher is, we are called to investigate new teachings in comparison with the Bible. Be a fair-minded believer TODAY!

PRAYER FOCUS

Dear heavenly Father, I pray for an unusual desire and readiness of mind to search Scriptures in order to know You better. Bless me LORD with the Spirit of wisdom and revelation in Jesus' name.

November 19

Dealing With Evil Conspirators
Bible Reading: [Ezek.11:1-13]

And He said to me: "Son of man, these are the men who devise iniquity and give wicked counsel in the city." [Vs-2]

A conspiracy is a secret plan by a group to do something unlawful or harmful. It's a combination of men for an evil purpose. Conspirator — is a person who takes part in a conspiracy. Evil is when you join somebody to destroy someone else. No believer in Christ should desire to injure anybody. Evil conspirators will go full length to form an alliance in order to damage or discourage an effort that leads to progress. Evil conspirators are found in families [Gen.37:18], Churches [2 Cor.11:26], schools, communities, cities and governments.

There are many evil and powerful organizations controlling the banking systems, media, educational systems and much of our present day workforce. They control the way our societies are governed and their members infiltrate key sectors of the society. These secret organizations with a global conspiracy have a clear goal: to rule the world and force everyone to worship Satan.

Sometimes evil conspiracies will emanate from a source one would least expect *"Because the LORD revealed their plot to me, I knew it, for at that time he showed me what they were doing" [Jer.11:18-19]*. I sincerely pray that God will reveal to you all that evil conspirators are plotting against your life this year in Jesus' name [Jer.33:3]. *"Behold, they shall surely gather together, but not by me: whosoever shall gather together against thee shall fall for thy sake" [Isa.54:15]*.

PRAYER FOCUS

"Oh God arise, let my enemies be scattered: let them also that hate Him flee before Him." [Psalm 68:1] in Jesus' name!

November 20

Changing The World With A Changeless Message
Bible Reading: [Acts 28:17-31]

"Therefore let it be known to you that the salvation of God has been sent to the Gentiles and they will hear it!" [Vs: 28]

The message that Jesus Christ is Savior and LORD for all who call upon His name is the message that believers in Christ are to take to the world so that many more may hear and believe. Because deep darkness covers the face of the earth, the light of the gospel must shine so that men might see the light. Remember that the god of this world has blinded the minds of men not to receive the light of the glorious gospel of Christ *[2 Cor.4:4]*. Therefore, let's arise at the command of the LORD. *"Arise, shine; For your light has come! And the glory of the LORD is risen upon you. Behold, the darkness shall cover the earth, And deep darkness the people; But the LORD will arise over you, and His glory will be seen upon you. The Gentiles shall come to your light, and Kings to the brightness of your rising" Isa.60:1-3].* God promises to be with His people in the business of spreading the good news of His love and redeeming grace. It is worth mentioning that the message remains the same, but the method changes from one cultural group to another and from one generation to another. Therefore, changing the world entails that we become all things to all people.

God's redemptive plan through Christ includes everyone regardless of tribe or nationality. Since the Jews had been given the opportunity to accept the faith, it was now time for the Gentiles to be offered this salvation. Like Paul, let's have a strong sense of purpose and calling to save men TODAY! *"I am obligated both to Greeks and non-Greeks, both to the wise and the foolish. That is why I am so eager to preach the gospel also to you who are in Rome" [Rom.1:14-15]*

PRAYER FOCUS

Heavenly Father, thank You for entrusting us with the great commission. May Your word accomplish Your desire and purpose for which it is sent out in Jesus' name.

November 21

Truth From The Inside Out
Bible Reading: [Psalm 12:1-8]

"Everyone lies to their neighbor; they flatter with their lips but harbor deception in their hearts. [Vs: 2]. "Behold, You desire truth in the inner parts, and in the hidden part You will make me know wisdom." [Psalm 51:6]

The culture of an ungodly society is defined by hypocrisy and deception. Sincerity and truth have become extremely valuable nowadays because they are rare. Many people have become liars and flatterers in order to advance their ungodly agendas. Scripture tells us, *"And king David wrote in the letter, saying, "Set Uriah in the forefront of the hottest battle, and retreat from him, that he may be struck down and die" [2 Sam.11:15]*. Uriah and many soldiers died as a result of David wicked schemes. We may be tempted to believe that lies are relatively harmless, even useful at times. But God does not overlook lies, flattery and deception. The LORD acted immediately by sending Prophet Nathan to confront David of his evil heart *[12:1]*. David acknowledged his wrongdoing and genuinely repented of his sin. No sin is beyond forgiveness!

When we feel as though sincerity and truth have nearly gone out of existence, we have one hope: the Word of God. *"The words of the LORD are pure words, Like silver tried in a furnace of earth, purified seven times"[Psalm 12:6]*. We can never please God by our outward actions no matter how good, if our inward heart attitude is not right. *You desire truth in the inner parts.* Right conduct is the outcome of a clean heart and spirit. Jesus prayed for His disciples, *"I do not pray that You should take them out of the world, but that You should keep them from the evil one. They are not of the world, just as I am not of the world. Sanctify them by Your truth. Your word is truth" [John.17:15-16]*.

PRAYER FOCUS

Dear heavenly Father, You desire truth in the inner parts. LORD, I ask that You sanctify my heart and renew a right spirit within me in Jesus' name.

November 22

The Power Of Your Testimony Of God's Grace
Bible Reading: [1 Tim.1:12-17]

"And I thank Christ Jesus our LORD who has enabled me, because He counted me faithful, putting me into the ministry, although I was formerly a blasphemer, a persecutor, and an insolent man; but I obtained mercy because I did it ignorantly in unbelief. And the grace of our LORD was exceedingly abundant, with faith and love which are in Christ Jesus." [Vs: 12-14]

All those who have been redeemed by the blood of Jesus Christ, delivered from the power of darkness and conveyed into the kingdom light have a testimony of God's grace. Our past life shouldn't hold us captive, instead our present knowledge of what we did in the past should keep you humble. While mercy is God's goodness as a solution to human misery, grace is the good pleasure of God that offers us benefits or favors which we do not deserve. Man's sin can never be greater than the grace of God. No matter how shameful our past, God also can forgive and use us.

Paul in his zeal acted ignorantly in unbelief. However, Scriptures tell us, *"And the times of this ignorance God winked at (overlooked); but now commandeth all men everywhere to repent" [Acts.17:30].* A man cannot experience the grace of God if he chooses to walk in disobedience. Those who are outside Christ, and unwilling to repentantly come into a covenant relationship with Him are missing the most important lifetime experience "grace". Grace is a gift, but must be received through obedience. Grace will give you a testimony and your testimony will make you an overcomer. *"And they overcame him by the blood of the Lamb, and by the word of their testimony" [Rev.12:11].* Why not testify of God's grace in your life TODAY!

PRAYER FOCUS

Dear heavenly Father, I thank You for Your great mercy extended toward me through Christ in Jesus' name.

November 23

Building On The Right Foundation
Bible Reading: [Matt.7:21-28]

"Therefore whoever hears these sayings of Mine, and does them, I will liken him to a wise man who built his house on the rock: and the rain descended, the floods came, and the winds blew and beat on that house; and it did not fall, for it was founded on the rock."
[Vs:24-25]

Any religious system that is not based on Jesus and His teachings will simply not stand in the end. To build on the rock means to be a hearing and responding disciple, not a false and superficial one. A true disciple must humbly seek the grace of God, being aware that he is not save through observing the Law or by good works *[Eph.2:8-9]*. The rock is the foundation of God's grace. A disciple does not obey the word of God because he wants to earn credits and justify himself before God, but he should obey in response to the love of God. The will of the Father is expressed in Jesus' teachings. Remember that neither charismatic gifts nor public accomplishments in Jesus' name will necessarily bring God's acceptance; the decisive issue is obedience. *".....Behold, to obey is better than sacrifice, and to hearken than the fat of rams"* [1 Sam.15:22].

Many people are building on a false or inferior foundation. The consequences of ignoring the Word of God are great. What about your life's purpose? Are you headed for destruction or eternal life? *"This is eternal life, that they might know thee the only true God, and Jesus Christ, whom thou hast sent"* [Jn.17:3]. Is the Word of God transforming your behavior and attitude?

Therefore beloved in the LORD, consider where, how and what you are building your life, home and career on. There is just no way you can weather the storms of life if practicing obedience is not your solid foundation TODAY!

PRAYER FOCUS

Heavenly Father, only Your Word gives us New Birth and Salvation *[Acts.4:12;17:25]*. I pledge my loyalty to You and commit myself to obeying Your word in Jesus' name.

November 24

Taking The Grace Of God In Vain
Bible reading: [2 Cor.6:1-10]

We then, as workers together with Him also plead with you not to receive the grace of God in vain. For He says: "In an acceptable time I have heard you, and in the day of salvation I have helped you." Behold, now is the accepted time: behold, now is the day of salvation. [Vs:1-2]

To take something in vain means to consider it useless, unprofitable, worthless or fruitless. While mercy is God's goodness to answer human misery and guilt, grace is the undeserved generosity of God toward humanity. If God is going to give you His grace and power, then He will definitely want you to do something with it. It is the responsibility of every believer in Christ to find out what their true divine purpose in the LORD is all about. As Christians, we must fully understand that God has a perfect plan for each person that surrenders to Him. In that plan is all of God's grace and power that a believer will need to fully accomplish all of his divine assignment.

Whenever we hear God's word and do not let it affect our lives in what we say and do, it implies the message has reached us in vain *"For unto us was the gospel preached, as well as unto them: but the word preached did not profit them, not being mixed with faith in them that heard it" [Heb.4:2]*. Is the word of God producing the fruit of righteousness in you? Is the power of God in you being used to glorify God or self?

Whenever we give in to peer pressure and comprise our conviction, we are taking God's grace in vain. Whenever we fail to do our divine assignment after haven't received the power of God, we are taking the grace of God in vain. Paul says, *"But by the grace of God I am what I am, and His grace toward me was not in vain; but I labor more abundantly than they all(apostles), yet not I, but the grace of God which was in me. Therefore, whether it was I or they, so we preach and so you believed"[1 Cor.15:10-11]*. What about you, do you witness about Christ for others to be saved? With the grace we have received, let's work together in a team effort and with God to impact the world for whom Christ died.

PRAYER FOCUS

Heavenly Father, thank You for the marvelous gift of Your kindness. Have mercy upon me for occasions I ignored Your kindness and took Your grace for granted in Jesus' name.

November 25

Enlarging The Place Of Your Tent "Stretching Out!"
Bible Reading: [Isa. 54:1-10]

"Enlarge the place of your tent, and let them stretch out the curtains of your dwellings; do not spare; lengthen your cords, and strengthen your stakes."[Vs-2]

God is not limited by the boundary of your territory or by the world's system. To enlarge your tent means to position yourself in order to accommodate growth. God wants us to unleash the power of our faith as we watch Him demonstrate His limitless power in our lives and situations. Therefore, to enlarge the place of your tent is not just a request but a command. To enlarge also means to grow large, wide, beyond. It means to increase capacity, thinking big, to break out, to make more room. I know that some of us are still limited by our space or how things have turned out over the years. If what you are experiencing in your life right now is below your expectations, then you need to increase your capacity in order to receive more from God.

Your capacity is a measure of what you can receive, hold or absorb. It determines what you are capable of receiving. You desire a big business but you have limited capacity, you desire a thousand member church but you have not developed capacity, you desire a life partner but your capacity is not such that can accommodate another person. Whatever the case, capacity building is very important. Do you spend time in capacity development - by reading books or attending programs that can challenge or stretch you out? God has blessed us with skills, gifts and other potential. It is our responsibility to develop them. Your spiritual capacity refers to your walk with God and daily living in righteousness: reading, studying and meditating on the word of God.

PRAYER FOCUS

Oh LORD, that You will bless me and increase the place of my tent in Jesus' name.

November 26

The Watchful Believer
Bible Reading: [Luke 21:34-38]

"Watch therefore, and pray always that you may be counted worthy to escape all these things that will come to pass, and to stand before the Son of Man." [Vs-36]

To be watchful means to be on the lookout especially for danger or opportunity. Believers are always to be alert and ready for Christ's return. Christ is coming again, and we need to watch and be spiritually fit. *"But of that day and hour no one knows, not even the angels of heaven, but My Father only"* [Matt.24:36]. We shouldn't be like the five foolish virgins who were unprepared. To be a watchful believer means to be on the lookout because the our adversary the devil, as a roaring lion, walks about, seeking whom he may devour.

Many are unable to move at God's command because they have allowed careless living, drinking, smoking, or foolish pursuits of pleasure to control their lives; while others have allowed life's anxieties to overburden them. God demands we should work faithfully at the tasks He has entrusted to us.

You can't be a watchful believer without a strong desire for prayers. Prayer is the key! It is not just mere uttering of words to God, but being in His abiding presence. Scripture advises us to pray that we might be strong enough to escape the coming horrors i.e. the strong feelings of fear and shock of end time events. The ultimate goal of our heavenly Father is that every believer should stand approved before Jesus Christ at His second coming.

PRAYER FOCUS

Heavenly Father, I trust You with my whole life. Help me to be a watchful believer in Jesus' name.

November 27

The Snare Of Spiritual Prostitution
Bible Reading: [1 Chr.5:18-26]

"But these tribes were unfaithful to the God of their ancestors. They worshiped the gods of the nations that God had destroyed. So the God of Israel caused King Pul of Assyria to invade the land and take away the people of Reuben, Gad, and the half-tribe of Manasseh as captives" [1 Chr.5:18-26].

Prostitution means to sell oneself for low purposes, for things of little value. Faith in anything besides God is detestable in God's eyes. God's people are to be faithful to Him; to chase after other gods is to commit spiritual adultery. As true Christians, we are called to love the LORD and give Him the honor of being our only guiding light.

Whenever we want to serve God but our hearts wander; we say that we love Him, but we make Him an option and give priority to other things; we want Him in our lives but not really as LORD, it is a clear sign that the spirit of prostitution is having a hold on us. *"They do not direct their deeds toward turning to God, for the spirit of harlotry(prostitution) is in their midst, and they do not know the LORD"* [Hosea 5:4]. *"A spirit of prostitution leads them astray; they are unfaithful to their God"* [Hosea 4:12].

The Children of Israel, especially their leaders and warriors, had great reputation and showed excellence in their skills and leadership qualities, but failed in the most important aspect of being faithful to God. Their unfaithfulness led them to exile(captivity). Many so called Christians have neglected their true purpose to please God by trying to measure up to society's standards for fame and success.

PRAYER FOCUS

Heavenly Father, I acknowledge my unfaithfulness to You and failure I serve You with a sincere heart and undivided interest. LORD, heal my heart in Jesus' name.

November 28

Seeing Through The Face Of Deception
Bible Reading: [Joshua 9:1-23]

"But they said to Joshua, "We are your servants." And Joshua said to them, Who are you, and where do you come from?" So they said to him: "From a very far country your servants have come, because of the name of the LORD your God: for we have heard of His fame, and all that He did in Egypt" [Vs-8,9]

Deception is the act of making someone believe something that is not true: It's the act of deceiving someone. We are living in an era where many can no longer tell what is true from what's false. *"But evil people and impostors will flourish. The will deceive others and will themselves be deceived" [2 Tim.3:13].* Individuals, families, institutions and even nations are being deceived. Though wise in his military dealings, Joshua was still deceived by the Gibeonites. Before discovering all the facts concerning the origins and intentions of the Gibeonites, the leaders of Israel had made a covenant with them that could not be broken.

Beloved, have you ever entered into a contract or covenant with someone only to discover later that you were deceived? *It is written, "Where no counsel is, the people fall: but in the multitude of counselors there is safe" [Prov.11:14].* Some of us know it all, and see no need to ask husband, wife, parents, colleagues and subordinates for advice.

It is the responsibility of leaders to lead through wise choices. You may be surprised to know that these days, children of God are easily being deceived than unbelievers. Oftentimes, they flow out in compassion without wisdom or discernment. *"And the LORD commended the unjust steward, because he had done wisely; for the children of this world are in their generation wiser than the children of light"[Lk 16:8].* Keep in mind that the leaders had acted in good faith, but were deceived. *"And it happened at the end of three days, after they had made a covenant with them, that they heard that they were their neighbors who dwelt near them" (Vs-16).* Unfortunately, they had acted alone before consulting the LORD [Vs-14]. How we rush into marriage and Career decisions without consulting God! May God have mercy upon us.

PRAYER FOCUS

Dear heavenly Father, forgive me for occasions I have made You too small in my eyes and leaned on the wisdom of men. LORD, deliver me from an form of deception today in Jesus' name.

November 29

The Power Of Spiritual Discernment
Bible Reading: [Acts 16:16-34]

"Jesus answered and said unto them, Because it is given unto you to know the mysteries of the kingdom of heaven, but to them it is not given." [Matt.13:11]

Discernment is the process of making careful distinction in our thinking about the truth. It is the ability to decide between truth and error, right and wrong. It's the ability to see the truth. Discernment is not optional for believers, it is required. Failure to distinguish between truth and error leaves the Christian in a vulnerable situation where he or she is subject to all manner of false teachings and manipulation of demons. *"Jesus answered and said unto them, Ye do err, not knowing the scriptures, nor the power of God" [Matt.22:29]*. Spiritual discernment is not just a God-given awareness of evil, but has to do with the ability to distinguish truth from error.

Spiritual Discernment cannot be attained from secular education but is given by revelation of Jesus Christ to the believer. Many believers live compromising lifestyles because of the inability to distinguish between that which is false and that which is true. And this is largely the result of limited knowledge of the Scriptures *"And that from a child thou hast known the holy Scriptures, which are able to make thee wise unto salvation through faith which is in Christ Jesus" (2 Tim.3:15)*. We receive spiritual discernment by revelation of Jesus Christ and it is developed by the way of training in righteousness. *"But solid food is for the mature, who by constant use have trained themselves to distinguish good from evil" [Heb.5:14]*. This enables the believer to avoid being tossed to and fro by waves, and carried about by every wind of doctrine.

The most important aspect of spiritual discernment is being able to distinguish the voice of the devil from the voice of God *[1 John 4:1]*. The fact that someone speaks the truth does not necessarily mean it is of God.

PRAYER FOCUS

Dear heavenly Father, It is Your desire that I should not be in error and be deceived by false men. LORD, grant me the spirit of discernment in Jesus' name.

November 30

Exercising Self-control
In The Face Of Adversity
Bible Reading: [Matt. 11:1-10]

And when John had heard in prison about the works of Christ, he sent two of his disciples and said to him, "Are You the coming One, or do we look for another? [Vs: 2,3]

God has several short-term and long-term lessons for every one of us. Our troubles don't define us but the way we handle them does. Self-control is the ability to control oneself, in particular one's emotions and desires especially in difficult situations. You may not fully understand people's feelings in trauma and trial, much more with everyday struggles, bills, family challenges, emotional crises, disappointments and illnesses. However, when circumstances or situations begin to work against you, you are having a signal of adversity. Adversity is a difficult or uncomfortable situation. These are setbacks or problems that can happen at any time, they can be big or small. Life can never be void of adversity. You may try to avoid it in life but at some point you have to face it in order to grow and mature. Adversity in life comes in different forms and ways. Whatever the form, Scripture says, *"If you faint in the day of adversity, your strength is small"* [Prov.24:10].

In the face of adversity, If you doubt t God's work in your life, look at the evidence in Scripture and the changes in your life. Self-control in the face of adversity means you have faith enough to believe that God is turning your valley of trouble into a door of hope. In other words, you are not moved in times of adversity. It is written, *"We are hard pressed on every side, but not crushed; perplexed, but not in despair; persecuted, but not abandoned; struck down, but not destroyed. We always carry around in our body the death of Jesus, so that the life of Jesus may also be revealed in our mortal body"* [2 Cor.4:8-10]. In the face of adversity, don't turn away from Christ; turn to him and trust in His finished work on the cross.

PRAYER FOCUS

Heavenly Father, I count it all joy going through any form of adversity. I am fully persuaded that the trying of my faith is working out Your greater purpose for my life in Jesus' name

DECEMBER

"For unto us a child is born, unto us a son is given: and the government shall be upon his shoulder: and his name shall be called Wonderful, Counsellor, The mighty God, The everlasting Father, The Prince of Peace. Of the increase of his government and peace there shall be no end, upon the throne of David, and upon his kingdom, to order it, and to establish it with judgement and with justice from henceforth even forever. The Zeal of the LORD of host will perform this."

[Isaiah 9:6-7;KJV]

"And she shall bring forth a son, and thou shalt call his name JESUS: for he shall save his people from their sins."

[Matt.1:21;KJV]

****

Jehovah Sabaoth **- [The LORD Of Hosts]** *- 1 Sam.1:3*

12 = [God's Government/Divine Arrangement]

December 1

Procrastination - The Thief Of Time!
Bible Reading: [Acts 24:22-27]

"Now as he reasoned about righteousness, self-control, and the judgment to come, Felix was afraid and answered, "Go away for now; when I have a convenient time I will call for you." [Vs 25]

Procrastination is the action of delaying or postponing something. As the proverb goes, "If you put off doing what you ought to do, you will end up not having enough time to do it properly." Have you started preparing for your exams? Oh, that can wait till tomorrow!. Have you started looking for a job? Oh, that can wait until next week.

Have you been baptized since you repented of your sins? Oh, that can wait until next year! Do you tithe your resources to God or honor Him with your substance? Oh, that can wait until I have a good job. When you start living in the realm of convenience, you just become a procrastinator. You do things only when it is easy and convenient for you. You do things only when you want, not when the LORD wants! Many people have missed their season of opportunities because of Procrastination.

Why are you delaying your decision? As for governor Felix, he had to delay his decision hoping that Paul would bribe him. It is worth noting that Paul's conversation with the governor was interesting until they focused on righteousness, self-control, and the judgment to come *[Acts 24:24-26]*. As long as the gospel doesn't touch people's lives too personally, they will welcome your conversation. When it does, some will resist or run. Are you delaying your decision concerning marriage hoping that you will see a perfect wife or husband to be? You may be mistaken! Don't feel discouraged or disappointed when someone runs away after such a powerful witness of the gospel with simplicity and clarity! Remember that the gospel is not effective until it convicts the heart and becomes life-changing.

PRAYER FOCUS

Dear heavenly Father, procrastination is not of God. I rebuke the spirit of procrastination and command its influence against me to cease in Jesus' name.

December 2

Illegitimate Users Of The Name Of Jesus
"Duplicating God's Power"
Bible Reading: [Acts 19:11-20]

"And there were seven sons of one Sceva, a Jew, and chief of the priests, which did so. And the evil spirit answered and said, Jesus I know, and Paul I know; but who are ye? And the man in whom the evil spirit was leaped on them, so that they fled out of that house naked and wounded." [Vs: 14-16]

An Illegitimate user of something is a person that has not been given authorization to use it. He is exercising power illegally, not in accordance with accepted standards or rules. The fact that a person can pronounce the name of Jesus or has become a member of a Christian fellowship doesn't necessarily give him the mandate to use the name of Jesus Christ. The name of Jesus is not a magical formula. Because of the quest for wealth, health, happiness, success in business, career and marriage, many have been deceived and derailed. Seeing the power of God at work by the hands of Paul to drive out demons, the seven sons of Sceva were impressed. This prompted them to do likewise with someone possessed by evil spirits, thinking that the power of God can be tapped by reciting the name of Jesus like a magic charm. The outcome was obvious: *"And the evil spirit answered and said, "Jesus I know, and Paul I know; but who are you?" (VS 15)* It is worth mentioning that every evil spirit will recognize the authority of Jesus, but will not recognize those who pretend to have supernatural authority in His name.

Friend, do you take delight in the name of Jesus? Do you know Him personally or have a true relationship with Him by genuine repentance? The seven sons of the Jewish chief priest called on the name of Jesus without knowing Him in person. God works His power only through those whom He chooses. It is written, *"You are of God, little children, and have overcome them, because He who is in you is greater than he who is in the world" [1 John.4:4].*

PRAYER FOCUS

Heavenly Father, there is no other name under heaven given among men by which we must be saved except the name of Jesus Christ. Today, I invoke the name of Jesus in my family, church and name.

December 3

Snare Of Apathy Toward God's Word
Bible Reading: [Amos 8:1-14]

"Behold, the days are coming," says the LORD, "That I will send a famine on the land, not a famine of bread, nor a thirst for water, but of hearing the words of the LORD. They shall wander from sea to sea, and from north to east; they shall run to and fro, seeking the word of the LORD, but shall not find it [Vs:11-12]

Apathy is a lack of interest, enthusiasm, or concern. What can be said about this generation? It's a generation that has become mundane, so religious but lack interest in spiritual things. A generation that is distracted and caught up with the affairs and pleasures of life. Many still look everywhere for answers to life's problems except in Scripture. Like in the days of prophet Amos, the people's main interest was in enriching themselves, even if that meant cheating.

God sent His servants to speak His word directly to Israel but they commanded the prophets and holy men not to prophesy. They showed disregard and violated God's calling *"But you caused the Nazirites to sin by making them drink wine, and you commanded the prophets, 'shut up!" (Amos 2:12).* No greater loss of opportunity could be experienced by a people who had forgotten the law of God *(Hosea 4:6).* When they rejected true servants of God, the LORD took away His messengers and distant Himself. It is written, *"Draw near to God and He will draw near to you. Cleanse your hands, you sinners; and purify your hearts, you double-minded" [James 4:8].*

Beloved, do you have appetite for God's word? Is making money more important to you than anything else? For the little time you give to God, is your heart in your worship of him? Scripture tells us, *"These people honor me with their lips, but their hearts are far from me" (Matt.15:8).* Oftentimes, we make optional the things that should be our priority. Can we still find passionate and noble men/women like Mary? *"And Martha had her sister called Mary, who also sat at Jesus' feet and heard His word." (Lk.10:39).* It is important for us to know the truth and help others know it before a time comes when they cannot find it. *"Seek the LORD while He may be found; call on Him while He is near" (Isa.55:6).* God is still saying something.

PRAYER FOCUS

Oh Bread of Life, feed me and enlarge my heart to receive more of Your word in Jesus' name.

December 4

God's Spokesman:
Obedience To The Heavenly Vision
Bible Reading: [Amos 7:10-17]

Then Amos answered, and said to Amaziah: "I was no prophet, Nor was I a son of a prophet, But I was a sheep breeder and a tender(grower) of sycamore fruit. Then the LORD took me as I followed the flock, and the LORD said to me, Go, prophesy to My people Israel." [Vs-14,15]

In times of apostasy or falling away, God needs strong men who will stand up and teach His word to those who have turned their backs on the truth. The double standards and worldly lifestyles of many preachers and believers today is not different from that of the people of Israel in the days of Amos. Amos was a simple farmer whom God chose. Without any special preparation, education, or upbringing, Amos obeyed God's call. It is worth mentioning that *God doesn't call the qualified, but qualifies the called [Rom.8:30;Acts 4:13].*

While Amos was called to speak the mind of God to the people, Amaziah the Chief priest in Bethel was more interested in financial gain and position. Amaziah would not speak the truth to King Jeroboam who worshipped at Bethel, nor to the Israelites who were backsliding. That is a true picture of the Body of Christ today. Many servants of God and believers would compromise their conviction for the sake of money or riches. Nowadays, our pulpits and are robbed of the fire of God's holy presences because we are letting our desires for fame, prestige, power, and money to come between us and obeying God.

Regardless of the religiosity of this generation, people have fallen from the standard of God's word [Rom.12:1-2]. In some countries, it's likely that when you stand up for the truth, charges will be brought against you. Amos was considered as an enemy because he spoke out against the king and his advisers, questioning their authority and exposing their sin. Then Amaziah said to Amos: *"Go, you seer! Flee to the land of Judah. There eat bread, and prophesy."[Vs-12].* He said so because he saw his payroll in jeopardy and position threatened.

Beloved, are you standing up for the truth in this perverse and crooked generation? Would you compromise your conviction as a believer in order to keep your job or position? Would you flee in the face of opposition and persecution for speaking the truth? Would you preach just what people like to hear? Obedience is the test of a faithful believer or servant of God.

PRAYER FOCUS

Dear heavenly Father, thank You for having called me according to Your purpose and grace. LORD, I ask for boldness to speak your word without fear or favor in Jesus' name.

December 5

Narrow Gate - The Right Way
Bible Reading: [Luke 13:22-33]

Then one said to Him, "LORD, are there few who are saved?" And He said to them, "Strive to enter through the narrow gate, for many, I say to you, many will seek to enter and will not be able" [Vs: 23-24]

It is very easy to think that everyone who identifies himself with the Christian community or professes Christ is saved! The word 'strive' means to make great effort to achieve or obtain something. We don't strive to obtain salvation because we can't save ourselves. Salvation is the gift of God, but we must strive to live a wholesome Christian life in holiness Scripture tells us to *"Make every effort to live in peace with everyone and to be holy; without holiness no one will see the LORD" [Heb.12:14].* The gate is narrow not because God has made it so, but because of the unwillingness of men to submit to the will of God. They have chosen the way of indifference, luke-warmness, self-righteousness, laziness and hypocrisy. They have decided to establish their own standard of righteousness, and are zealous, but not based on knowledge *"Brethren, my heart's desire and prayer to God for Israel is that they may be saved. For I bear witness that they have a zeal for God, but not according to knowledge.." (Rom.10:1-3)*

"Enter by the narrow gate; for wide is the gate and broad is the way that leads to destruction, and there are many who go in by it" [Matt.7:13]. Because the way is broad and popular, does not make it the right way. Because the way is recognized, legalized by the governments of the world and even some denominations, doesn't make it the way! Because celebrities approve of it, doesn't make it the right way. *"And do not be conformed to this world, but be transformed by the renewing of your mind, that you may prove what is that good and acceptable and perfect will of God" [Rom.12:2].*

True faith in Christ will always lead to a changed life and the transformation of one's mind in its entire attitude toward God

PRAYER FOCUS

Dear heavenly Father, I acknowledge the fact that Jesus is the way, the truth and the life. Today, I pledge my full commitment to You and to enter life through the narrow way against all odds in Jesus' name.

December 6

Saving For The Future
"Hard Work Pays Off"
Bible Reading: [Prov.6:6-17]

"Go to the ant, thou sluggard; consider her ways, and be wise: which having no guide, overseer, or ruler, provideth her meet in summer, and gathereth her food in the harvest." [Vs: 6-8]

At the present time, there are many in society who are lazy in reference to physical labor. Here, an example is given of the diligent ant that worked continuously. With diligence and foresight, the ant prepared for its existence through hard work. The ant is considered as an example because it uses its energy and resources economically. *"A dream doesn't become reality through magic; it takes sweat, determination and hard work" [Colin Powell]*

Lazy people sleep rather than make necessary provisions. They are the opposite of self-motivated and industrious people. *"Then, as I looked and thought about it, I learned this lesson: A little extra sleep, a little more slumber, a little folding of the hands to rest - then poverty will pounce on you like a bandit; scarcity will attack you like an armed robber." [Prov.24:32-34].* Do you work for survival or you continuously depend on others for survival? If the social system of any country or the benevolent of men is robbing you from hard work, then you need to repent and sit up in life!

"For you remember, brethren, our labor and toil; for laboring night and day, that we might not be a burden to any of you, we preached to you the gospel of God."[1 Thes.2:9]. While it is true that the ultimate meaning and fulfillment in life do not come from hard work, the laziness is condemned *[Eccl.2:17-26; 4:5-6].* Lazy people are foolish, their lack of productivity leads to poverty. Diligent people are wise; their activities lead to wealth and life. You can't save for the future if you are not hard working. Hard work is a dignified and important part of creation. *"Seest thou a man diligent in his business? He shall stand before kings; he shall not stand before mean men" [Prov.22:29].*

PRAYER FOCUS

Dear LORD, deliver me from the spirit of laziness and instill the spirit of hard work in me in Jesus' name.

December 7

The Evidence Of Gentleness
Bible Reading: [Phil.4:5-7]

"Let your gentleness be known to all men. The LORD is at hand." [Vs-5]

Gentleness does not mean weakness. Instead, it takes a strong person to be truly gentle. Gentleness implies one is reasonable and charitable, not just to those in the Body Christ, but also to those outside the Body. Gentleness is one of the fruit of the Holy Spirit. If we want the fruit of the Spirit to grow in us, we must join our lives to Christ.

Gentleness involves humility and thankfulness toward God. It's a polite and restrained behavior towards others. Every Christian should have a reputation for being a patient and enduring person toward the faults and weaknesses of others. Christians should bear with one another's differences in opinion. As believers, we have to be considerate in our responses to others even in the face of persecution. We should leave vengeance in God's hands.

It is to our advantage to have a gentle attitude toward God because He is Omniscient and we are not. Therefore, we need not worry about anything because our heavenly Father loves us and cares about our needs. Show evidence of gentleness TODAY.

PRAYER FOCUS

Dear heavenly Father, may you bless me with a meek and gentle spirit in Jesus' name.

December 8

Good And Perfect Gifts
Bible Reading: [James.1:12-18]

"Do not be deceived, my beloved brethren. Every good gift and every perfect gift is from above, and comes down from the Father of lights, with whom there is no variation or shadow of turning." [Vs-16,17]

A gift is a thing given willingly to someone without payment. The gift that the Father gives is good because He is good and His mercy endures forever. His gifts are perfect in that they are complete and full. God does not only give the world light from the sun, moon and stars from which we perceive light, He is also the originator of the Light that came into the world for the salvation of all men. He is the Father of light and in Him there is no darkness. With God, there is no variation nor shadow of turning. He is the same yesterday, today and tomorrow.

"If you then, being evil, know how to give good gifts to your children, how much more will your Father who is in heaven give good things to those who ask Him!" [Matt.7:11]. Beloved child of God, If evil parents know how to give good gifts to their children, there is no reason to limit your faith in God and be afraid to approach Him. Remember, *"He who did not spare His Son, but gave him up for us all—how will he not also, along with him, graciously give us all things? [Rom.8:32]* Our heavenly Father is committed to give us all things. It is worth mentioning that any gift from Him (above) is lasting. It makes rich and adds no sorrow. It is such a blessing and brings wealth and health *[Prov.10:22]*.

Jesus said to His disciples, *Until now you have not asked for anything in my name. Ask and you will receive, and your joy will be complete. [John 16:24]*. Today offers you an opportunity to ask God for something in the name of Jesus Christ. Oftentimes, we ask and do not receive because we ask with wrong motives, that we may spend what we get on pleasures *[James. 4:3]*. What a joyful thing to ask God for a gift TODAY in the name of Jesus Christ!!

PRAYER FOCUS

Dear heavenly Father, You are a covenant keeping God. Today I ask for the gift of (X). Thank You for answering my prayer in Jesus' name *[1 John.5:14]*.

December 9

Acceptable Sacrifices
Bible Reading: [Gen.4: 1-13]

"If you do well, will you not be accepted? And if you do not do well, sin lies at the door, and its desire is for you, but you should rule over it." [Vs-7]

It is worth mentioning that God takes into consideration both our motives and the quality of what we offer Him. True worship requires that we give God preeminence in all things. God desires the best from us, not leftovers. While Abel was able to give God the best animal, Cain's chose to offer something of inferior quality to God. When we don't act according to the will of God in our giving, we will not enjoy the blessings of giving. Abel's offering was accepted by God. Not that firstlings of the flock were superior to the offering of the fields, but his sacrifice was more excellent in that it came from a generous and sincere heart. While Abel did it out of faith, Cain certainly did it out of selfish ambition.

If you do well, will you not be accepted? Beloved in the LORD, are you doing the right thing? Cain's knowledge of his sin assumes his knowledge of what God had originally commanded concerning an offering that is acceptable to Him. It is worth mentioning that, *"The sacrifices of the wicked is an abomination; how much more when he brings it with wicked intent!"[Prov.21:27]*. If you bring an offering to God with a wicked heart or wrong motive, it will be rejected. Whenever we fail to do the right thing, we give room to the enemy to manipulate our lives. God is so concerned about an offering offered to Him in righteousness.

Some of us want God to accept our offerings when we are not will to offer first our lives to Him in righteousness. Apostle Paul praised the Macedonian Churches on the basis that they gave beyond their ability and were freely willing. Scripture says, *"They gave, not only as we had hoped, but they first gave themselves to the LORD, and then to us by the will of God" (2 Cor.8:3,5)*. God values the quality of what we offer Him and upholds His standards. Scriptures say, *"He will sit as a refiner and a purifier of silver; He will purify the sons of Levi, and purge them as gold and silver, that they may offer to the LORD an offering in righteousness" [Mal.3:3]*

PRAYER FOCUS

Heavenly Father, I acknowledge my wrong motive towards giving and ask for Your mercy. I'm determined today to do the right thing by giving the best of my time, talent/gifts and possessions in Jesus' name.

December 10

Your Latter Days Will Be Greater
"The Best Is Yet To Come"
Bible Reading: [Job.42:1-17]

"And the LORD restored Job's losses when he prayed for his friends. Indeed the LORD gave Job twice as much as he had before. Now the LORD blessed the latter days of Job more than his beginning" [Job.42:10,12]

Dear friend, I have come today by the authority of Christ to tell you that your latter will be greater. No matter what you've been through, the best is yet to come. In every situation, you matter! You might have heard about others testifying of God's goodness, but I am fully convinced that the time has come for you to see the glory of God in your life and circumstances. *"I had only heard about You before, but now I have seen You with my own eyes" (Vs-5; John.9:3)*. Your future is not determined by the pre-judgment of any man. Often, men form a judgment on an issue or a person prematurely without having adequate information. At times people judge not knowing or having a clue of what God is doing. They do so not having all the revelation concerning the eternal purpose of God. Remember that *"In Him we were also chosen, having been predestined according to the plan of Him who works out everything in conformity with the purpose of His will" (Eph.1:11)*. God is omniscient, and thus knows all things. Your destiny is determined by the will of God. For He says to Moses, *"I will have mercy on whom I have mercy, and I will have compassion on whom I have compassion" [Rom.9:15]*.

You don't need to question God's sovereignty and justice. God is in Charge and in control. Don't be locked into time, unable to see beyond today! Questioning God's sovereignty only exposes one's foolishness. Remember, *"And we know that all things work together for good to them that love God, to them who are the called according to His purpose" (Rom.8:28)*. True faith is a product of humility. True faith acknowledges that we have made God to small in our eyes, acknowledges our folly and need to repent of wrongdoing, praying for those who have prejudge or hurt us and forgiving those who have accused us wrongly. God is still alive, the God of Elijah has not changed! He is about doing a new thing in your life. Your healing, restoration, victory, are all at the corner! *"For all the promises of God in him are yea, and in him Amen, unto the glory of God by us." [2 Cor.1:20]*. As you make up your mind to dwell in God's presence for the rest of your life, may you be overwhelmed by His holiness and the wonders of His mighty power today!

PRAYER FOCUS

Dear heavenly Father, I am fully persuaded that You can do all things, and no one can stop You. May You have Your way in my life as I humbly put my trust in You in Jesus' name.

December 11

Faith And Works
Bible Reading: [James 2:18]

But someone will say, " You have faith, and I have works." Show me your faith without your works, and I will show you my faith by my works" [Vs18].

True faith involves total commitment and submission to God. We are made right with God through faith and not by obeying the law. While it is true that our good deeds can never earn salvation, true faith always results in a transformed life and acts of kindness. In Rom.3:28, Paul admonishes that salvation is not by works, but by faith in Jesus. James speaks against those who confuse mere intellectual assent with true faith. Intellectual assent is a decision made in our head that lacks the commitment of our heart.

Let's make a clear distinction here:

Works of law: Doing good deeds in order to earn salvation. *Nobody was and is put right with God by works of the law no matter the magnitude and quality! [Gal.2:16] "For by grace you have been saved through faith, and that not of yourselves; it is the gift of God, not of works, lest anyone should boast" [Eph.2:2-8]*

Works of faith: True love for God is an act of obedience to the commandments of God. It's an outflow of God's love and grace in the life of the believer by the Holy Spirit. This faith is expressed through benevolent actions toward one's fellow man. Scripture tells us that *"The religion that is pure and undefiled before God and Father is this: to orphans and widows in their trouble, and to keep oneself unspotted from the world [James 1:27].*

PRAYER FOCUS

Dear heavenly Father, unconditional love moved You to offer Jesus Christ as a precious gift to humanity. May my life be an expression of Your love and true faith in Jesus' name.

December 12

Building Spiritual Momentum
"Christ's love Compels Us"

"And let us consider how to stir up one another to love and good works, not neglecting to meet together, as is the habit of some, but encouraging one another, and all the more as you see the day drawing near." [Heb.10:24-25;ESV]

Our Christian life should be active and growing. Momentum is the quantity of motion of a moving body, measured as a product of its speed. *"Spiritual momentum comes when we take our life that God is transforming, by the power of the gospel and the work of the Holy Spirit, and we get it in motion, we move forward with Jesus" (Greg Faulls)*. If we are slowed down by life's challenges, we can regain momentum by starting anew and then moving forward with speed.

Dwelling in the past can slow us down tremendously. Scripture tells us, *"Do not call to mind the former things, Or ponder things of the past. Behold, I will do something new"[Isa.43:18-19]*. Peer pressure is a killer of spiritual momentum. Sometimes our passion for prayer, zeal for evangelism, enthusiasm for studies, generosity in giving, desire to sacrifice, ambition and determination for hard work are killed by those who are not comfortable with it. They try to slow down our pace of motion. If you want everyone to be comfortable with it or get on board before you move on, you will only end up living your life as a mediocre. You may question why so many intelligent people end up living a mediocre life, while others become inspirational figures?

We are called to achieve different things and our speed ought to be different. Never allow the clock to tick down on your destiny while you are doing nothing. *"Therefore, since we are surrounded by such a great cloud of witnesses, let us throw off everything that hinders and the sin that so easily entangles. And let us run with perseverance the race marked out for us, fixing our eyes on Jesus, the pioneer and perfecter of faith" (Heb.12:1-2)*. While you may think there is no need to build spiritual momentum, Satan and cohorts see a great need and opportunity. *"Therefore rejoice, you heavens and you who dwell in them! But woe to the earth and the sea, because the devil has gone down to you! He is filled with fury, because he knows that his time is short" (Rev.12:12, NIV)*. Yes, his time is short! How about you? Choosing to spend your time in despair/discouragement/disappointment!? When king David was greatly distressed because his men were talking about stoning him; each one was bitter in spirit because of his sons and daughters. **But David found strength in the LORD his God"** [1 Sam.30:6; Isa.40:31]. Building spiritual momentum involves prayer, meditation, and study of God's word and regular fellowship with others in the faith.

PRAYER FOCUS

Oh LORD, grant that I may be fervent in spirit at all times and grow in the knowledge of Your will each passing day in Jesus' name.

December 13

A Rewarding Discipleship
Bible Reading: [Matt.10:37-42]

"And he who does not take his cross and follow after Me is not worthy of me. ....And he who receives a righteous man in the name of a righteous man shall receive a righteous man's reward." [Vs-37,42]

Deciding to follow and serve Jesus is a great mission. When we are willing publicly to identify with Him, to experience opposition, and to be committed to face even suffering and death for His sake, then we are ready to take up our cross and follow Jesus. God accepts the one who acknowledges Him publicly. A true disciple of Christ loves Him above all other things and is willing to follow Him regardless of any physical or social consequences. *"Here is a trustworthy saying: If we died with him, we will also live with him; if we endure, we will also reign with him. If we disown him, he will also disown us; if we are faithless, he remains faithful, for he cannot disown himself"* [2 Tim.2:11-1]

Loving the world and clinging to it may cause us to forfeit the best from Christ. *"Do not love the world or anything in the world. If anyone loves the world, love for the Father is not in them"* (1 John 2:15). Those who receive the disciples into fellowship by accepting their teachings are actually receiving Jesus and His teachings. Receiving Jesus is more than acknowledging his Sonship. It means acting in obedience to His will. Those who receive Jesus shall receive the reward one receives for receiving a prophet or a righteous man *[Mk 9:41]*. A righteous man is one who conforms his behavior according to Scriptures and is approved by God.

PRAYER FOCUS

Dear heavenly Father, I acknowledge that greater love has no man than One to lay down his life for his friends. LORD, today I pay allegiance to You. Making Your priority my priority in Jesus' name.

December 14

Your Promotion Will Attract Enemies
Bible Reading: [2 Sam.5:17-25]

"But when the Philistines heard that they had anointed David king over Israel, all the Philistines came up to seek David; and David heard of it, and went down to the hold." (Vs-17;KJV)

Your success, breakthrough, promotion and enthronement in life will not only attract friends but also enemies. The Philistines were Israel's most powerful enemy. When Israel was divided and David was King of Judah to the south, the enemy didn't border. But when they learned that David was planning to unite all Israel, they tried to stop him. As long as a people, a family, Church and nation are divided, they will not be a threat to the enemy. You are not a threat to the enemy when you are living in sin, barren, poor or stagnating in life. When something positive or great happens, enemies will begin to show up. Apostle Paul says *"For a great door and effectual is opened unto me, and there are many adversaries" [1 Cor.16:9,KJV]*.

We fail many times in life because we do what we want without considering the will of God. We often like to do things our way, ignoring what Scripture says about our situation. Sometimes we take the glory of God for ourselves. What would you do today if promoted or enthroned by God? As for David, he sought for the opportunity to unify the people under God in order to protect the nation.

PRAYER FOCUS

Dear heavenly Father, without You I will amount to nothing before my enemies. I ask that You protect every opportunity and gift I have received from You in Jesus' name.

December 15

To Obey Is Better Than Sacrifice
Bible Reading: [1 Sam.15:10-35]

So Samuel said:

"Has the LORD as great delight in burnt offerings and sacrifices, and to heed than the fat of rams. For rebellion is as the sin of witchcraft, and stubbornness is as iniquity and idolatry. Because you have rejected the Word of the LORD, He also has rejected you from being king." [Vs-22,23]

Beloved, how obedient are you to instructions given by the LORD through His servant or any higher authority? Obedience means to comply with an order, request, or law, or submission to another's authority. One mark of a true disciple of Jesus Christ is the ability to recognize and willingness to submit to spiritual authority. Children must be taught to show their parents obedience and submit to their authority. *"Let every soul be subject unto the higher powers. For there is no power but of God: the powers that be are ordained of God. Whosoever resisteth the power, resisteth the ordinance of God: and they that resist shall receive to themselves damnation" [Rom.13:1-2].* Obedience means the willingness to follow godly instructions. A disciple is a learner and follower. Not willing to follow instruction means resisting instruction.

King Saul was given a simple instruction from God through His servant but he was unable to do exactly what he was told to do. *"Now go and attack Amalek, and utterly destroy all that they have, and do not spare them. But kill both man and woman, infant and nursing child, ox and sheep, camel and donkey" [15:3].* The instruction was a simple one. In the secular world, a successful soldier is one who follows the instructions of the leading commander. We must learn to follow simple instructions at home, in church, in school and at the jobsite. People who don't like to follow instructions can't effectively fit in with society. As a result, they find it difficult to integrate or belong.

King Saul finally attacked the Amalekites but didn't carry out the LORD's instructions to the letter. And Saul said to Samuel, *"But I have obeyed the voice of the LORD, and gone on the mission on which the LORD sent me, and brought back Agag king of Amalek; I have utterly destroyed the Amalekites. But the people took of the plunder, sheep and oxen" (Vs-20).* That is the attitude of some believers in the Body of Christ, who claim to follow instructions but do not do so to the letter or choose to resist God's will. Saul became both rebellious and stubborn and God finally rejected him and took away his kingdom. Saul continued to justify his wrong doing by blaming others *(Vs-15,24).* Following God's instructions directly from His Word or through His servant is not optional. It's a sign of respect for spiritual authority. Scripture tells us, *"And Samuel went no more to see Saul until the day of his death" (Vs-35)*

PRAYER FOCUS Dear heavenly Father, I have come to know the importance of following instructions and submitting to spiritual authority. Today I am determined to follow You wholeheartedly in Jesus' name.

December 16

Perfecting for Every Good Work
Bible Reading: [Heb.13:15-21]

"Now the God of peace, that brought again from the dead our LORD Jesus, that great shepherd of the sheep, through the blood of the everlasting, make you perfect in every good work to do His will" [Vs-20-21]

God works in us to make us the kind of people that would please Him, and He equips us to do the kind of work that would please Him. *"For it is God which worketh in you both to will and to do of His good pleasure." (Phil.2:13)*. Every believer is perfected through the blood of Jesus Christ. When we respond to the sacrificial blood and finished work of Christ on the Cross, we give God the opportunity to work in us. Jesus as a shepherd cares for His sheep. He is the Bishop of our souls and desires that we prosper in all things *[1 Pet.2:25]*.

We need to be equipped for everything we do in life. God uses His Word to transform our lives and prepare us to carry out His unique and perfect plan. He will always give ability, direction and the resources we need to carry out His will *[Exod.35:35]*. When He calls a man, He qualifies and equips him. He will not abandon us to figure things out on our own. God perfects us in every good work so that we may do His will. It is written, *"Epaphras, who is one of you, a servant of Christ, saluteth you, always laboring fervently for you in prayers, that ye may stand perfect and complete in all the will of God." [Col.4:12]*. Oh the joy that we stand perfect and complete in all the will of God TODAY!!

PRAYER FOCUS

"But now, O LORD, thou art our father; we are the clay, and thou our potter; and we all are the work of thy hand." [Isa.64:8]. LORD, work in us to accomplish Your far reaching purpose this year in Jesus' name.

December 17

Dangers Of Luke-warmness

"I know thy works, that thou art neither cold nor hot: I would thou wert cold or hot. So then because thou art lukewarm, and neither cold nor hot, I will spit thee out of my mouth" [Rev.3:15-16]

There is nothing more disgusting than a lukewarm attitude. Some have become ignorant of their true spiritual condition because of their riches. Some have allowed their troubles to overwhelm and overtake them, causing lack of zeal for the things of God. Like the Laodicea Church, many churches today have become indifferent and lazy group of Christians who have lost their zeal for good works, prayer and evangelism. Are you a lukewarm Christian? Do you recognize your spiritual poverty? Luke-warmness means to lack passion for the things of God. Many have formed a religion after their own desires. A religion governed by leisure, and lacks spirituality and commitment to Jesus.

Because Laodicea was a rich city, some believers assumed that the acquisition of material possessions was a sign of divine blessings. When brethren fail to do anything for Christ, idleness sets in. To some believers, the watching of television program, movies and the use of social media have become more valuable than cultivating an intimate relationship with God. Half-hearted and self-sufficient believers settle for less than God's best for their lives. Nothing can be compared with having a vital relationship with Jesus Christ and a true fellowship with other believers. That is why it is said, *"Wake up, sleeper, rise from the dead, and Christ will shine on you" [Eph.5:14]*

PRAYER FOCUS

Oh LORD, Wilt thou not revive us again: that thy people may rejoice in thee? Show us thy mercy, O LORD, and grant us thy salvation [Ps.85:6-7]

"Never be lacking in zeal, but keep spiritual fervor, serving the LORD" [Rom.12:11]

December 18

Dealing With Crossroads In Life
Bible Reading: [2 Chr.20:12]

"O our God, wilt thou not judge? For we have no might against this great company that cometh against us; neither know we what to do: but our eyes are upon thee." [Vs-12]

We live in a very unstable world and very often, we find ourselves at major crossroads where we have to make important choices. Crossroads in life are major junctions that we need to make important decisions about matters that might have far-reaching consequences and a long-lasting effect in our lives. Individuals, families, churches, universities, and even nations experience seasons of crossroad. Sometimes we embark on a journey that is full of obstacles and then faced with decision of whether to turn back or continue on. The following aspects are commonplace with crossroads in life:

- One may choose to take a simpler or shorter path.
- One may make hasty decisions without giving it much thought.
- One may continue to stay stuck in the same situation or position for years.

The question today is, how can I sail through a season of crossroad without having regrets later on? King Jehoshaphat and his people came to a crossroad and knew not what to do. *"And Jehoshaphat feared, and set himself to seek the LORD, and proclaimed a fast throughout all Judah. And Judah gathered themselves together, to ask help of the LORD: even out of all the cities of Judah they came to seek the LORD."* (Vs-3,4). Crossroad in life gives us the opportunity to seek God for help and direction. It's not a time to allow fear to paralyze us or discouragement to overwhelm us. There is no battle so great or situation too hard for God. You might be going through a crossroad right now. This is what the LORD says: *"Stand at the crossroads and look; ask for the ancient paths, ask where the good way is, and walk in it, and you will find rest for your souls..."* (Jer.6:16). At crossroads, it's important to look to God for wisdom through prayer and scripture reading. At crossroads, it's important to seek godly counsel and make the best decision about which direction to take based on inspiration and the guidance of the Holy Spirit. *"Believe in the LORD your God, so shall ye be established; believe his prophets, so shall ye prosper."*

PRAYER FOCUS

Dear heavenly Father, I acknowledge the fact that without Your help at crossroads in life, I will be stuck and confused. I ask for the ability to make clear decisions and be willing to take daring actions as led by the Holy Spirit in Jesus' name.

December 19

Creating A Legacy Of Faith
Bible Reading: [1 Chr. 13:1-14]

"David was afraid of God that day, saying, "How can I bring the ark of God to me?" So David would not move the ark with him into the City of David, but took it aside into the house of Obed-Edom the Gittite. The ark of God remained with the family of Obed-Edom in his house three months. And the LORD blessed the house of Obed-Edom and all that he had." [Vs-12-14]

The ark of God was a symbol of the LORD's presence with His people in the history of Israel. It is also known as the ark of the covenant of the LORD *[Deut.10:8]* and ark of the testimony. The ark served various functions during Israel's history: like a guide to Israel in the wilderness. The ark is spoken of as the throne of God or the divine presence *[1 Sam.4:4]*. It was borne only by the priests and Levites. God struck Uzza when he put his hand to hold the ark, for the oxen carrying it stumbled [Vs-9-10]. Absence of the ark of God meant absence of God's presence with His people. *"So it was that the ark remained in Kirjath Jearim a long time; it was there twenty years. And all the house of Israel Lamented after the LORD" (1 Sam.7:2).* Praise God, the presence of the LORD is in the lives of all those who have genuinely repented of their sins and embraced Christ as Savior and LORD in their lives today.

Just like the ark of God was of utmost importance to King David and Israel, so having the divine presence in our lives daily should be of great importance to every believer in Christ. This only happens when we have a genuine walk in the holiness of God. Blessings come with the presence of God in our lives, homes, Churches, communities and nations. *"The ark of God remained with the family of Obed-Edom in his house three months. And the LORD blessed the house of Obed-Edom and all that he had."* It is worth mentioning three types of blessings here: (1) Material blessing - 1 Chr.13:14 (2) Gatekeeper - activity in the things of God - 1 Chr. 16:36-38 (3) Blessing of his offspring - 1 Chr.26:4-8

Obed-Edom was able to create a legacy of faith. A legacy is the imprint you leave on the future. Parents handing the baton to the next in line. Obed's choice to accept the keeping of the ark in his home, led to blessings for himself and his family. When David finally moved the ark from Obed's home to Jerusalem, Obed-Edom had a desire for the LORD and moved with God. He became a worship leader, a musician, and a doorkeeper for the ark. His desire for a relationship with God established not only a personal relationship, but also for his children and grandchildren. Paul told Timothy, *"when I call to remembrance the genuine faith that is in you, which dwelt first in your grandmother Lois and your mother Eunice, and I am persuaded is in you also" (2 Tim.1:5;NKJV)*

All true believers in Christ have the Holy Spirit in them.

Leave a legacy of faith today

PRAYER FOCUS

Dear heavenly Father, I purpose in my heart to keep myself pure and to leave a legacy of faith in Jesus' name.

December 20

Biblical Stewardship
Bible Reading: [Luke 12:42-46]

"And the LORD said, Who then is that faithful and wise steward, whom his lord shall make ruler over his household, to give them their portion of meat in due season? (Vs-42) "Moreover it is required in stewards that a man be found faithful." (1 Cor.4:2)

The basis of Christian stewardship is that God is the creator of everything and has absolute rights of ownership over all things *[Acts 17:24-25]*. If we fail to accept this fact, nothing else can be said about stewardship in the Biblical context. Stewardship is more than just managing our time, resources and finances. It is our obedient witness to God's sovereignty. To be a faithful steward implies we fully acknowledge the fact that we are not our own but belong to Christ, who gave Himself for us.

Four important aspects of Christian Stewardship to be considered:

Ownership: God owns everything, we are simply caretakers or managers acting on His behalf. Therefore, stewardship is the commitment of one's self and possessions to God's service. *"The earth is the LORD's, and the fullness thereof; the world, and they that dwell therein" (Psalm 24:1)*

Responsibility: For all that God has entrusted to our care. We are responsible for managing His holdings, desires, and purposes.

Accountability: God has entrusted His resources, abilities and opportunities to our care. Someday, it will be required of us to give an account of how we have managed what rightfully belongs to Him.

Reward: All faithful stewards will be rewarded in this life and in the life to come *[Col.3:23-24]*. Every disciple of Christ must exercise the same faithfulness and wisdom with the truth that is revealed to them. The LORD expects us to be faithful to the mission He has given us.

PRAYER FOCUS

Dear heavenly Father, I acknowledge Your sovereignty over creation. LORD, all that I have belongs to You and all that I have accomplished You have done for me in Jesus' name.

December 21

Where Are You Casting Your Net?
Bible Reading: [Mark 1:16 - 20]

"And Jesus said unto them, Come ye after Me, and I will make you to become fishers of men. And straightway they forsook their nets, and followed Him." [Vs-17,18]

Jesus called His disciples to fish for people with the same energy they had used to fish for food. When Christ calls us by His grace, we must not only remember what we are, but we must also consider what He can make us into. In order catch a fish, we must know what equipment to use, the habitat and depth of the water we are fishing in, as well as the kind of bait the fish will go after. The gospel is like a net, lifting people from dark waters into the light of day and transforming their lives. The gospel message has the power to change lives, shine light into darkness, and deliver evil men from hell. *"For I am not ashamed of the gospel of Christ: for it is the power of God unto salvation to everyone that believeth; to the Jew first, and also to the Greek" [Rom.1:16].*

God wants to use us today to fish for people's souls. Every one of us (disciples) must be about the business of catching men and women for Christ. If Christ caught us, we must catch others. It is written, *"The fruit of the righteous is a tree of life; and he that winneth souls is wise" (Prov.11:30). And they that be wise shall shine as the brightness of the firmament; and they that turn many to righteousness as the stars for ever and ever" (Dan.12:3).* Be a soul winner TODAY!

PRAYER FOCUS

Dear heavenly Father, thank You for having called me to be a fisher of men. LORD, I receive Your grace to go fishing and the ability to cast my net in the right place in Jesus' name.

December 22

God Chasers: The Pursuit Of God
Bible Reading: [2 Chr.26:1-5]

"And Uzziah sought God in the days of Zechariah, who had understanding in the visions of God: and as long as he sought the LORD, God made him to prosper." (Vs-5)

"My soul followeth hard after thee: thy right hand upholdeth me." [Ps.63:8]

The basis of any true success in this life is our trust in the LORD. Our faith in God needs to be real, extending to our whole life and activities. God, the One who has called us according to His purpose and grace wants true fellowship, and true fellowship must be two-way. God shouldn't be the only one to initiate fellowship. An earnest pursuit of God releases divine blessings.

Remember that *"The blessings of the LORD, it maketh rich and he added no sorrow with it" (Prov.10:22).* Uzziah prospered as long as he sought God. He had a great longing to be with God. He spent time together with him and enjoyed to be in His presence.

Are you God's friend? (James 2:23)

Do you strongly desire His presence?

"As the deer panteth after the water brooks, so panteth my soul after thee, O God. My soul thirsteth for God, for the living God: when shall I come and appear before God? " (Psalm 42:1-2). God deserves more than our attention; He deserves our affections. He wants us to know Him better and to follow hard after Him. We reap benefits from the LORD when we follow hard after Him more than any human relationship would offer. God wants us to pursue him actively and relentlessly TODAY!

PRAYER FOCUS

Dear heavenly Father, true fellowship is what You desire from me. I'm determined to be a person after Your heart and to do everything You want me to do in Jesus' name

[Acts.13:22].

December 23

A Shelter In The Time Of Trouble
Bible Reading: [Psalm 27:1-14]

"For in the time of trouble He shall hide me in His pavilion: in the secret of His tabernacle shall He hide me; He shall set me up upon a rock." (Vs-5)

Every one of us has been a prisoner of fear at one time or the other. Fear of rejection, fear of what the future holds, fear of being misunderstood, fear of failure, fear of addiction to drugs and alcohol, fear of broken marriage/homes, fear of sickness, pain and even death. Though one may feel totally deserted by everyone, God will still be there. *"God hath not given us the spirit of fear; but of power, and of love, and of a sound mind" (2 Tim.1:7).* Many have made it a goal to run to God only when they experience difficulties in life. As for David, he lived constantly in the presence of the LORD and could handle any challenging situation. The truth is that many of our difficulties could be avoided or managed far more easily by seeking the help of the LORD and His guidance beforehand.

Your experience may be a sad one at this very moment, but remember that with God, all things are possible. *"But Jesus beheld them, and said unto them, with men this is impossible; but with God all things are possible. " (Matt.19:26).* We can conquer fear by trusting in the LORD who brings salvation. We must be confident that in this present life, God will see us through whatever difficulty. Once humbled by the calamities of life, one submits to the directions of God.

Sometimes, it is necessary for one to go to the depths of despair in order to be taken to the heights of adoption and honor. It may take a time of waiting but it is worth it because God often uses times of waiting to refresh, renew, and teach us. God's love and providence is sufficient for all our needs TODAY!

PRAYER FOCUS

Heavenly Father, "this I recall to my mind, therefore I have hope. Through the LORD's mercies we are not consumed, Because His compassions fail not. They are new every morning; great is Your faithfulness. The LORD is my portion, says my soul, "Therefore I hope in Him!" (Lam.3:21-24).

December 24

Religion That Is Acceptable To God
Bible Reading: [James 1:21-27[

"Pure religion and undefiled before God and the Father is this, to visit the fatherless and widows in their affliction, and to keep himself unspotted from the world." (Vs-27)

Orphans and widows had very little means of economic support in the first century (James C. Galvin). Most of them were reduced to beggars, some selling themselves as slaves, or starving, unless a family member was willing to care for them. By caring for these people, the church put God's Word into practice. The responsibility of maintaining the pure and undefiled religion is placed on the shoulders of each individual disciple.

True religion is defined by looking into the perfect law of liberty and put it into practice *[Jam.1:25]*. Any religion that is created after either the selfish lusts of man or traditions of the fathers is a worthless religion. Two important aspects of a religion that is pure and undefiled:

To visit orphans and widows in their affliction

To keep ourselves unstained from the world. The believer who seeks to allow the Word of God direct his life, keeps himself from the things of the world *[Rom.12:1,2; James 4:4]*. Giving with no thought of receiving, shows what it means to truly serve others. Then Christianity is a way of life. Let's be determined to keep ourselves unstained from the world and make God's priorities our priority TODAY!

PRAYER FOCUS

Dear heavenly Father, thank You for teaching me what true religion is all about. Help me to look into the perfect law of liberty with understanding and put it into practice in Jesus' name.

December 25

Being About My Father's Business
Bible Reading: [Luke 2:41-50]

"And He said unto them, How is it that ye sought me? Wist ye not that I must be about my Father's business?" [Lk 2:49;KJV].

This statement was made before the beginning of Jesus' official ministry that began when He was about thirty years old. Although Joseph and Mary knew much about Him, a full understanding of His unique relationship with the Father or His mission was not known to His parents. Jesus was both human and divine. Many are still struggling with the issue of Identity, but at age 12, Jesus was able to understand the heart of God. *"And Jesus increased in wisdom and stature, and in favor with God and man." (Lk 2:52).* When He reached the age of thirty, He did His business in reference to fulfilling the eternal plan of redemption through the cross. He came not for His own business, but for the Father's business. He was purpose driven.

Jesus and His disciples must be about their Father's business. *Did you not know that I must be* about My Father's business? His dealings were obvious:

For I came down from heaven, not to do mine own will, but the will of him that sent me (John 6:38). The Son of Man came to seek and to save the lost (Lk 19:10)

My house shall be called a house of prayer for all nations (Mark 11:17). How God anointed Jesus of Nazareth with the Holy Ghost and power: who went about doing good(Acts 10:38)

For this purpose the Son of God was manifested, that He might destroy the works of the devil (1 John 3:8)

You may know the plan of your earthly father, but do not know the will of God in heaven? Do you know your identity? Do you know God personally as your heavenly Father? What drives you in this life? Beloved, life will be incomplete and meaningless if you do not know God and His plan for humanity. As a boy at 12, Jesus had greater value for the things of the Kingdom *(Matt.6:33).* While others set their hearts on temporal things, His heart was with God and on things above. If we are spiritually regenerated people, adopted into God's family, having the same Father as Christ, then we must put a higher priority on the Father's business TODAY!

PRAYER FOCUS

Dear heavenly Father, It is of utmost importance that I should seek first Your Kingdom and Your righteousness [Matt.6:33]. Have mercy upon me for not setting my priorities right!

December 26

The Power Of Godly Expectations

"For surely there is an end; and thine expectation shall not be cut off." (Prov.23:18)

"They looked unto Him, and were lightened: and their faces were not ashamed. (Ps 34:5)

"I will lift up mine eyes unto the hills, from whence cometh my help. My help cometh from the LORD, which made heaven and earth." (121:1,2)

Expectation: A belief that something will happen because it is likely (Oxford, ALD). Friend, you can only get or experience what you expect. There is tremendous power release by unwavering and godly expectations. Expectations based on human assumptions can sometimes cause trouble. Scriptures encourage us to trust in the LORD and to expect good things from Him *"My soul, wait thou only upon God; for my expectation is from Him" [Ps 62:5]*. We all need to have expectation if we want to see God's promises come to pass.

"Your life follows your expectation - because expectation is a form of faith. While hope may motivate us, expectation is the next step which prepares us for what we believe will happen. Your entire life is ordered around what you expect to receive, either good things or bad things" (Mark & Nicki). Thus, expectation can be realistic or unrealistic.

A believer must always keep in mind that the outcome of a godly life is eternal life. While the outcome of earthly expectations is a feeling of discouragement, godly expectations lead to freedom and hope of eternity with the LORD.

PRAYER FOCUS

Dear heavenly Father, thank You for Your precious promises and the wonderful plans You have for my life (2 Pet.1:4) I decree and declare that my expectations in the LORD and the land of the living will not be cut off in Jesus' name. Amen

December 27

Boasting In The Cross
"Dead to Sin, But Alive to God's Love"

"But God forbid that I should glory, save in the cross of our LORD Jesus Christ, by whom the world is crucified unto me, and I unto the world." (Gal.6:14)

"I am crucified with Christ: nevertheless I live; yet not I, but Christ liveth in me: and the life which I now live in the flesh I live by the faith of the Son of God, who loved me, and gave himself for me." (Gal.2:20)

We are living in a world in which people boast about anything and everything. Some brag about Church attendance, academic prowess, professional accomplishments, religious superiority, husband, wife, children, etc. Paul had so many religious accomplishments to boast about like others, if he wanted to *(Phil 3:5-6)*. He attended the best schools, had all the right connections and was a very zealous person. When he surrendered his life to Christ, he realized that he had nothing to boast about except in the cross.

It's worth mentioning that in the ancient world crucifixion was nothing to boast about. Boasting or bragging especially about one's religious accomplishments is not a good thing. People did that in the days of Paul and many are doing same today, even in the Body of Christ. Scripture says, *"Thus saith the LORD, let not the wise man glory in his wisdom, neither let the mighty man glory in his might, let not the rich man glory in his riches: But let him that glorieth glory in this, that he understandeth and knoweth me, that I am the LORD which exercise lovingkindness judgement, and righteousness, in the earth: for in these things I delight, saith the LORD" [Jer.9:23,24]*

The cross means the death of sin. Christ died on the cross not only to atone for sin, but to completely bring it to an end. The cross is the place where God demonstrated His greatest love. If there is something to brag about, consider the cross. The cross is an expression of the beauty of God's love. *Boasting in the cross is not an exclusive boast (James Boice).* Jesus invites everyone from every tribe, tongue and nation to come to Him, have forgiveness and share the eternal love of God.

PRAYER FOCUS

Father, thank YOU for the finished work of Christ on the cross!

December 28

Committing The Word Of Life To Faithful Men
Bible Reading: [2 Tim 2:1-13]

"Thou therefore, my son, be strong in the grace that is in Christ Jesus. And the things that thou hast heard of me among many witnesses, the same commit thou to faithful men, who shall be able to teach others also." [Vs-1,2]

"How then shall they call on him in whom they have not believed? And how shall they believe in him of whom they have not heard? And how shall they hear without a preacher? [Rom.10:14]

Passing the torch to the next generation is a hallmark of true discipleship. The next generation of disciples is the future of the Church and the nation as well. Remember that *"Righteousness exalteth a nation: but sin is a reproach to any people" [Prov.14:34].* God has always demanded His people to teach the next generation. Coming this far in our walk with the LORD, we have been taught by someone else. It's the responsibility of every disciple to teach those who *come to the faith (2 Tim 2:24). God commanded the Israelites to teach His word to their Children (Ps 78:5).* It's a terrible thing to raise a generation that knows little or nothing about God and His requirements. *"And also all that generation were gathered unto their fathers: and there arose another generation after them, which knew not the LORD, nor yet the works which He had done for Israel" (Judges 2:10)*

The most important criterion of men who will teach others is that they must be faithful to God and His word. Disciples are just as good as the people who teach them (disciple makers). Faithful men so that what they teach will not be neglected by how they live. You can't teach on giving when you are not a giver (tithe, offering, alms etc.), you can't teach about holiness when you are not living a holy life, you can't teach others to do evangelism when you don't, you can't teach others to pray when you don't, you can't teach others to be regular to fellowship when you don't. It only makes you a hypocrite! If the church were to consistently follow Paul's advice, it would expand geometrically as well-taught believers would teach others and commission them, in turn, to teach still others.

As a believer, you don't have to be strong in your own strength but in God's strength. A believer must receive power from God and allow it to flow through him. All true believers exist in the sphere of grace in their union with Christ. *We are saved by grace (Eph.2:8), justified by grace (Rom.5:1,2), live by grace (Col.2:6) and can only serve God by grace (Heb.12:28).* Our strength in the LORD is therefore a result of our realization that our salvation is by of God's grace. Let's impact the world with God's power received by grace TODAY!

PRAYER FOCUS

Dear heavenly Father, thank You for undeserved favor, Your wonderful grace!

LORD, I acknowledge the need to commit Your word unto faithful men in Jesus' name.

December 29

Priorities Of Heavenly Citizens

"But our citizenship is in heaven. And we eagerly await a Savior from there, the LORD Jesus." [Phil.3:20;NIV]

"If ye then be risen with Christ, seek those things which are above, where Christ sitteth on the right hand of God." [Col.3:1]

When we made a personal decision to follow Christ, we were unified with Him. A priority is the main focus of a person, what he invests the great deal of his time in and gives attention to. The priority of an earthly citizen is temporal, concerning the things of this world. A heavenly citizen thinks of things that have eternal value. *"By faith Abraham made his home in the promised land like a stranger in a foreign country; he lived in tents, as did Isaac and Jacob, who were heirs with him of the same promise" (Heb.11:9)*

The new heavenly position of a believer in Christ should affect everything about him: how he lives, walks, communicates and what he wears, etc. His passion for Christ should be to know Him and make Him known.

It is worth mentioning that as a heavenly citizen, your transformed and changed lifestyle must be evident:

- Changed identity; bearing the marks of the LORD Jesus Christ.
- Changed perspective, oriented toward the second advent of Christ.
- Changed destiny; living everyday life to fulfill purpose purposes. *"At one time we too were foolish, disobedient, deceived and enslaved by all kinds of passions and pleasures. We lived in malice and envy, being hated and hating one another." (Titus 3:3).* The life I now live in the flesh I live by the faith of the Son of God *(Gal.2:20)*
- Changed position; *"And God raised us up with Christ and seated us with him in the heavenly realms in Christ Jesus" (Eph.2:6)*
- Changed priorities; As heavenly citizen, set your priorities right and let your privileged position in Christ impact your every action!

PRAYER FOCUS

Dear heavenly Father, thank You for the privileged position I have in Christ. Once I was lost but now I am found. May glory and honor be ascribed to You both now and forever in Jesus' name.

December 30

Unchanging God In Perilous Times
"The LORD My Deliverer"
Bible Reading: [2 Sam.22:1-7]

"I will call on the LORD, who is worth to be praised: so shall I be saved from mine enemies." (Vs-4)

"For I am the LORD, I change not; therefore ye sons of Jacob are not consumed." (Mal.3:6) "But thou art the same, and thy years shall have no end." (Psalm 102:27)

We are living in perilous times. Because of the increase of wickedness, *the love of many have grown cold. But the one who perseveres to the end will be saved (Matt.24:12,13).* In this ever changing world, God is an anchor for the soul. God protects those who show their allegiance to Him through obedience to His will. God is the strength and power of the one who has given himself to the instructions of His Word.

Though confronted with the gravest of dangers, God does not change by the power of His name. Let God's power roll every obstacle or onslaught of the enemy against you. In Jesus' name. Regardless of the threats of your environment or threats of ungodly men, God will surely come to your rescue. Men often change in reference to their obedience to God but God does not change in reference to His promises *(Heb.6:17,18).* "For in the time of trouble He shall hide me in His pavilion: in the secret of His tabernacle shall He hide me; He shall set me up upon a rock" (Psalm 27:5). "He that dwelleth in the secret place of the Most High shall abide under the shadow of the Almighty" [Psalm 91:1]

PRAYER FOCUS

I decree and declare:

Let every scheme or conspiracy of the enemy against me be brought to naught. In Jesus' name *A thousand shall fall at my side, and ten thousand at my right hand; but it shall not come near me in Jesus' name (Psalm 91:7)* "One of you routs a thousand, because the LORD your God fights for you, just as He promised" [Joshua 23:10]

December 31

Hard Work Honors God
Bible Reading: [Prov.31:10-29]

"For even when we were with you, we commanded you this: If anyone will not work, neither shall he eat. For we hear that there are some who walk among you in a disorderly manner, not working at all, but are busybodies. Now those who are such we command and exhort through our LORD Jesus Christ that they work in quietness and eat their own bread." [2 Thes.3:10-12]

It takes hard work to be successful as a businessman, an academics, a husband or wife, a pastor/servant of God, a teacher, a cook, a farmer, a politician, a musician, etc. I acknowledge the fact that God performs miracles but most of the time things on earth don't happen miraculously. For this reason we cannot undermine the value of hard work. Hard work entails a great deal of effort or endurance. *"And the LORD God planted a garden eastward in Eden; and there He put the man whom He had formed." "And the LORD God took the man, and put him into the garden of Eden to dress it and keep it." [Gen.2:8,15].* Man's duty was not only to cultivate the garden but also to preserve and protect it from all intruders. God's original plan was not for man to live by miraculous provisions. He wants us to work in quietness and eat our own bread.

God takes pleasure in people who are industrious. Industrious people are diligent and hard-working. Diligence means to be careful and persistent in your work or effort. *"Seest thou a man diligent in his business? He shall stand before kings; he shall not stand before mean men" [Prov.22:29;KJV].* Friend, are you investing your time, energy, strength, talent/gifts in what God created you for? Nobody on earth was created without a talent. *"Each of you should use whatever gift he has received to serve others, faithfully administering God's grace in its various forms." (1 Pet.4:10).* God made an investment in you when He created you and He expects a return on that investment. God doesn't want us to take advantage of the benevolent attitude of others in order to make ends meet because of laziness. May you distinguish yourself through hard work TODAY!

PRAYER FOCUS

Dear heavenly Father, I thank You for all the abilities You have endowed me with. I'm determined to use what You have given me to benefit others and advance the Your kingdom on earth in Jesus' name.

KEY REFERENCES

NLT Illustrated Study Bible: Tyndale House Publishers. Inc. Comparative Study Bible (1999):
Published by Zondervan

Dickson Teacher's bible: Africa International Missions (Int. King James Version) Life Application Study Bible: (NKJV) - Tyndale House Publishers Inc.

MacArthur Study Bible (NKJV)

Jehovah Titles: The Ryrie Study Bible (NAST):
Moody Press

Reference Guide To Biblical Numerology
by Brian G. Chilton (Jan.13, 2018)